D1297225

OCEAN AND COASTAL MANAGEMENT LAW

IN A NUTSHELL®

FIFTH EDITION

DONNA R. CHRISTIE
Professor Emerita of Law
Florida State University
College of Law

ANASTASIA TELESETSKY
Professor of Law
University of Idaho
College of Law

WEST
ACADEMIC
PUBLISHING

COPYRIGHT © 1994 WEST PUBLISHING CO.
© West, a Thomson business, 1999
© 2007 Thomson/West
© 2015 LEG, Inc. d/b/a West Academic
© 2019 LEG, Inc. d/b/a West Academic
      444 Cedar Street, Suite 700
      St. Paul, MN 55101
      1-877-888-1330

West, West Academic Publishing, and West Academic are trademarks of West Publishing Corporation, used under license.

Printed in the United States of America

ISBN: 978-1-64242-555-0

*Donna Christie
dedicates this book to her boys:
Austin, Aidan and Mark*

*Anastasia Telesetsky
dedicates this book:*

*To my husband Matt and to all those
nameless ocean stewards who
champion ocean protection.*

OUTLINE

TABLE OF CASES

References are to Pages

XXV

OCEAN AND COASTAL MANAGEMENT LAW

IN A NUTSHELL®

FIFTH EDITION

INTRODUCTION

Coastal and ocean management law focuses on a *place* rather than on a generally recognized field of law. Coastal and ocean law comprises aspects of property, land use regulation, water law, natural resources law, constitutional law, federal and state statutory law, and international law in the special context of the coastal and ocean environment. Natural interrelations of land, water, and natural resources are complex and have equally intricate legal consequences that have resulted in ongoing conflicts over public and private rights, boundaries, jurisdictions, and management priorities.

The term "coastal zone" was coined by the Commission on Marine Science, Engineering, and Resources, also known as the Stratton Commission, in its 1969 report, *The Nation and the Sea*. The Commission observed that:

> The coast of the United States is, in many respects, the Nation's most valuable geographic feature. It is at this juncture of the land and sea that the great part of this Nation's trade and industry takes place. The waters off the shore are among the most biologically productive regions of the Nation.

The Commission found, however, that the value of the coastal zone as a vital natural system and as a focal point for trade and recreation was threatened by increasing population concentration and commercial, recreational, and residential development.

The recognition that the coasts are a national resource in need of more effective management led to enactment of the Coastal Zone Management Act of 1972 (CZMA). The CZMA provided federal funding for states to develop and administer coastal programs according to guidelines set out in the Act. Although state participation was voluntary, the incentives provided by the CZMA—federal funding and the promise that federal actions would be consistent with state plans—led to the participation of all U.S. coastal states and territories in the program. The CZMA allowed for a great deal of flexibility and a wide range of approaches for coastal management programs. These programs range from networks of existing state laws to special regulatory regimes created to manage development in the coastal zone. Most of the effort during the first decades, however, was focused on the land side of the coastal zone.

More than thirty years later, domestic and international developments have brought more attention to the coastal zone's "wet side." Ocean fisheries have collapsed; dead zones have proliferated around the world; and global warming is leading to sea level rise and dangerous ocean acidification. Global warming has also led to melting of the Arctic icecap, exposing the potential for exploitation of Arctic's continental shelf and leading to controversies over sovereignty over Arctic resources and access. The *Deepwater Horizon* oil spill led to new questions about our management of ocean resources. The oceans are also seen as the sites and sources of renewable energy production, but as these uses intensify, more user conflicts and additional impacts on the ocean environment will develop.

The United States Commission on Ocean Policy (USCOP), created by the Oceans Act of 2000 to comprehensively review national ocean policy, found that "[o]ur failure to properly manage the human activities that affect the nation's oceans, coasts, and Great Lakes is compromising their ecological integrity, diminishing our ability to fully realize their potential, costing us jobs and revenue, threatening human health, and putting our future at risk." USCOP, Executive Summary, *An Ocean Blueprint for the 21st Century: Final Report of the U.S. Commission on Ocean Policy* (2004). In 2010, President Obama established the United States' first national ocean policy by Executive Order 13547, creating an ethic of stewardship of the oceans and intended:

> . . . to ensure the protection, maintenance, and restoration of the health of ocean, coastal, and Great Lakes ecosystems and resources, enhance the sustainability of ocean and coastal economies, preserve our maritime heritage, support sustainable uses and access, provide for adaptive management to enhance our understanding of and capacity to respond to climate change and ocean acidification, and coordinate with our national security and foreign policy interests.

The failure of Congress to implement this policy by legislative mandate or dedicated funding left the future of U.S. oceans policy vulnerable. On June 19,

2018, President Trump issued Executive Order 13840, which revoked Executive Order 13547 and focused on economic growth and national security, rather than stewardship and sustainability.

Ocean and coastal law and regulation are now at a point where major changes are needed to assure that marine and coastal ecosystems will retain their viability in this century. This book focuses on the special environmental and institutional concerns of the area where land and water meet. The user conflicts, the jurisdictional gaps and overlaps, and the clash of public and private, state and national, and national and international interests all contribute to a legal regime that continues to evolve to attempt to address the challenges of sustainability.

CHAPTER I

PUBLIC AND PRIVATE RIGHTS IN THE COASTAL ZONE

A. OWNERSHIP OF LAND UNDER NAVIGABLE WATERS

An analysis of public and private rights in the coastal zone must begin with a discussion of basic property interests and boundaries between public and private ownership. This discussion necessarily involves a look at the historical evolution of these property interests in the United States.

1. ENGLISH ROOTS OF PUBLIC OWNERSHIP UNDER NAVIGABLE WATERS

Under English common law, the King exercised both ownership and dominion over lands subject to the ebb and flow of the tides, often referred to as lands under navigable waters. In *Shively v. Bowlby*, 152 U.S. 1, 14 S.Ct. 548, 38 L.Ed. 331 (1894), the United States Supreme Court explained that ownership by the sovereign was based on the fact that such lands were incapable of cultivation and private occupation. Because the natural uses of these lands—navigation, commerce, and fishing—were public in nature, title to these lands vested in the King, as sovereign and representative of the nation.

Upon settlement of the colonies, these rights of the King passed to the grantees in the royal charters. After the American Revolution, title and dominion over lands under tidal waters vested in the original states subject to the rights surrendered by the Constitution to the federal government. *Martin v. Waddell's Lessee*, 41 U.S. 367, 10 L.Ed. 997 (1842).

2.   THE EQUAL FOOTING DOCTRINE

As the United States acquired territory by treaty, cession from states, or discovery and settlement, the United States government held title to the lands under tidal or navigable waters for the benefit of the states that would be created from the territory. Under the "equal footing doctrine," as explained in *Pollard v. Hagan*, 44 U.S. 212, 3 How. 212, 11 L.Ed. 565 (1845), states admitted into the Union after adoption of the Constitution are entitled to the same rights as the original states in the tidal waters and in the submerged lands. In *Pollard,* the Supreme Court held that Alabama, a state created from lands ceded to the United States by Georgia, succeeded to all the sovereign rights and jurisdiction formerly possessed by Georgia. In *Shively v. Bowlby*, 152 U.S. 1, 14 S.Ct. 548, 38 L.Ed. 331 (1894), the Supreme Court confirmed that the admission of Alabama on an equal footing with respect to lands under navigable waters was not based merely on the terms of the cession of the territory to the United States by Georgia, but that such rights in navigable waters were "inherent in her character as a sovereign independent State, or indispensable to her equality with her sister States." Id. at 34.

3. INTERPRETATION OF PRE-STATEHOOD GRANTS

Lands under navigable waters acquired by the United States could be conveyed prior to statehood. In *Shively v. Bowlby*, 152 U.S. 1, 14 S.Ct. 548, 38 L.Ed. 331 (1894), the United States had conveyed lands bounded by the Columbia River to private owners while Oregon was a territory. The state of Oregon later sold the adjacent land below the high water mark. A dispute arose over the effect of the previous federal grant on the lands below the high water line. The U.S. Supreme Court indicated that grants of land under navigable waters would be narrowly construed because of the special governmental and trust capacity in which these lands were held. In contrast to the general rule of construction that provides that ambiguities in a grant or deed are construed strictly against the grantor, the Court held that land under navigable waters could only be conveyed by express grant. The Court explained as follows:

> The rule of construction in the case of such a grant from the sovereign is quite different from that which governs private grants. The familiar rule and its chief foundation were felicitously expressed by Sir William Scott: "All grants of the Crown are to be strictly construed against the grantee, contrary to the usual policy of the law in the consideration of grants; and upon this just ground, that the prerogatives and rights and emoluments of the Crown being conferred upon it for great purposes, and for the public use, it

shall not be intended that such prerogatives, rights and emoluments are diminished by any grant, beyond what such grant by necessary and unavoidable construction shall take away." *The Rebeckah*, 1 C. Rob. 227, 230.

Id. at 10. Because there was no explicit language in the grant, the Court held that the federal grant conveyed no title or right in the land below the high water mark.

When territories were acquired by the United States by cession or treaty, property rights acquired by the landowners under the former sovereign depended on the terms of cession or treaty. In general, the United States was obligated to recognize earlier French, Spanish, and Mexican land grants, and courts apply the law of the grantor nation in interpreting a grant. The result is that the determination of choice of law in interpreting grants of coastal property may be extremely complex. See, e.g., *Miller v. Letzerich*, 49 S.W.2d 404, 408 (Tex. 1932) (explaining that "the validity and legal effect of contracts and of grants of land made before the adoption of the common law must be determined according to the civil law in effect at the time of the grants"). French and Spanish civil law of the period, however, also recognized that the sovereign owned the lands under navigable waters.

B.   THE BOUNDARY BETWEEN PUBLIC
AND PRIVATE LANDS

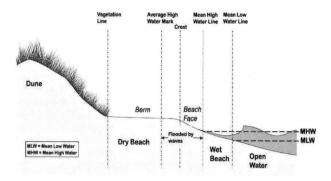

Source: James G. Titus, Rolling Easements Primer 16,
Climate Ready Estuaries Web site, U.S. Environmental
Protection Agency (June 2011).

1.   THE MEAN HIGH TIDE LINE

The simplicity of the principle that the state owns
lands beneath navigable waters while the upland is
subject to private ownership begins to break down
immediately when one considers that the line
between the water and coastal uplands is in constant
flux. With some exceptions, there are two high tides
and two low tides daily. The daily high and low tides
do not have the same reach. The reach of the tides
also varies with the time of the month and the time
of the year. The major force affecting tides is the
moon, and during the monthly phases of full moon
and new moon, higher tides, called spring tides,
occur. During the first and third quarter phases of
the moon, lower tides, or neap tides, occur. The moon

goes through other long-term periodic changes, such as variation in its cycle, declination, and distance from earth. The moon completes a cycle of all its variations in approximately 18.6 years. Tides are also affected by weather with many areas experiencing higher tides in winter when the winds affect the reach of the water. On most beaches, the line of vegetation is an indicator of the highest reach of the ocean water. See Frank E. Maloney & Richard C. Ausness, *The Use and Legal Significance of the Mean High Water Line in Coastal Boundary Mapping,* 53 N.C.L. Rev. 185, 195–198 (1974).

In *Borax Consolidated, Ltd. v. City of Los Angeles,* 296 U.S. 10, 56 S.Ct. 23, 80 L.Ed. 9 (1935), the U.S. Supreme Court was required to determine the boundary between an 1881 federal grant of land on Merman Island and the "tidelands and submerged lands" adjacent to the island in Los Angeles Harbor conveyed by the state of California to the city in 1911. Applying federal law to interpret the extent of the federal grant, the Court held that tidelands controlled by the state extend to the high water mark. The Court reviewed the meaning of ordinary high water in civil and common law and rejected both the civil law's definition of the highest reach of the waves in winter and the English common law rule of the average of the medium tides between the spring and neap tides. In order to include all lands that are normally covered by tides, the Supreme Court concluded that the boundary must be the mean of *all* the high tides. The definition was borrowed from the United States Coast and Geodetic Survey that had noted that the average should be taken over a "considerable period of time" and that the periodic variation in tides had a period of 18.6 years.

2. STATE VARIATIONS ON THE HIGH TIDE BOUNDARY

Although *Borax* sets out the federal rule, most states have also adopted the mean high tide line and the *Borax* definition of the mean high tide as the boundary between public and private property as the rule of state law. There are variations, however. For example, Texas law defines the boundary as the mean of the higher of the two daily high tides if the ownership originates from a Spanish or Mexican grant, but if title is traced to a post-statehood grant, the boundary is the mean of all the high tides, the common law rule. *Luttes v. State*, 324 S. W. 2d 167 (Texas 1958). Louisiana, a civil law state, recognizes public ownership to the reach of the highest tide in winter. Louisiana Civil Code, Art. 451. Hawaii's Supreme Court defines the shore boundary as the " 'ma ke kai' . . . along the upper reaches of the wash of waves, usually evidenced by the edge of vegetation or by the line of debris left by the wash of waves." *In re Ashford*, 440 P.2d 76 (Hawaii 1968). Maine, Massachusetts, Delaware, Pennsylvania, and Virginia recognize the mean low tide as the public/private boundary. Until relatively recently, New Hampshire had also been widely considered a "low tide state." In 1994, however, the New Hampshire Supreme Court issued an advisory opinion indicating that the state, as early as 1889, had rejected the 1647 Massachusetts colonial ordinance establishing a low tide line boundary. *Opinion of the Justices*, 139 N.H.

82, 649 A.2d 604 (1994). Subsequent legislation attempting to assert public rights to "the furthest landward limit reached by the highest tidal flow" was found, however, to be an unconstitutional taking of private property. *Purdie v. Attorney General*, 143 N.H. 661, 732 A.2d 442 (1999).

3. INDETERMINACY OF THE TIDE LINE

Even when the definition of the boundary is certain, physically determining the mean high water line may be difficult. The tidal range is the *vertical* height the water moves, not the distance on the ground between the low and high tide lines, commonly known as the "reach" of the tide. It is not a physical mark made on the ground by the waters. The tide line is the intersection of the tidal plane with the land. See *Borax Consolidated v. Los Angeles,* 296 U.S. 10, 22 (1935). The amount of land covered by the high tide, therefore, varies depending on the coastal topography. In some areas, particularly along the coast of the Gulf of Mexico, the slope of the land is so slight that minor discrepancies in tidal calculations can affect hundreds of acres of land. Dynamic sandy beaches also create a problem in fixing a high tide boundary line, because the profile of the beach is in such constant flux that the intersection of the beach with the tidal plane can change radically from day to day. See Donna Christie, *Of Beaches, Boundaries, and SOBs*, 25 J. Land Use & Envtl. L. 19, 24–25 (2009).

C. AMBULATORY BOUNDARIES

Shorelines are rarely stable and are subject to constant, gradual change from natural processes and human activities. Storms and flooding may drastically change the character of the coast in a very short time. Most states consider the legal boundary, as well as the physical water boundary, ambulatory. A littoral owner may gain or lose land affected by the processes of accretion, erosion, avulsion, or reliction.

1. ACCRETION AND EROSION

Accretion is the process by which upland is created by the gradual depositing of sand or sediment along the shore by the waters. The material that is deposited is known as alluvion or accretions. The accumulation of alluvion must be gradual and imperceptible. In general, when the water boundary moves seaward by the process of accretion, the property boundary also moves. In *St. Clair County v. Lovingston*, 90 U.S. 46, 23 L.Ed. 59 (1874), the Supreme Court identified three reasons for the rule of accretion: First, the Court noted the maxim *de minimis non curat lex.* (The law does not care for small things.) The point here is not that the total accretions over a period of time must be small, but that the amount of land accreted at any moment is so small as to be imperceptible. Second, the rule preserves the landowner's right of access to the water. In *Hughes v. Washington*, 389 U.S. 290, 88 S.Ct. 438, 19 L.Ed.2d 530 (1967), the U.S. Supreme Court noted that "[a]ny other rule would leave riparian owners continually in danger of losing the access to water which is often the most valuable feature of their property." The final reason for the accretion rule is that the owner bearing the burden of potential losses of property in contiguity to water should also receive any benefits from accretion.

The cause of the accretion may be relevant in determining whether the boundary changes. A well-established exception to the accretion rule is that a riparian or littoral owner does not gain title to accreted property that is the result of acts of that owner. Courts have found that to permit acquisition of such accreted land would be tantamount to allowing the owner to appropriate state property.

Whether the accretion is natural or caused by human activities, often called "artificial" accretion, may be relevant even in circumstances where the upland owner is not directly involved. The U.S. Supreme Court, in *St. Clair County v. Lovingston,* id., established the federal rule that whether accreted land is the result of natural or artificial causes (not attributable to the upland owner) is irrelevant to the boundary determination. Some states, most notably California, have taken the position that artificial accretion, whether caused by the littoral owner or unrelated parties, cannot result in extension of the upland boundary, reasoning that the accretions are merely manmade deposits on state public trust lands. The California Supreme Court later mitigated the harshness of this rule by holding that accretions are deemed artificial only if directly caused by human activities in the immediate vicinity of the accreted land. *California v. Superior Court of Sacramento County*, 44 Cal.Rptr.2d 399, 900 P.2d 648 (1995).

Erosion is the gradual wearing away of land by water. Erosion, like accretion, results in movement of the property boundary.

2. AVULSION

Avulsion is any sudden and perceptible change in the shoreline by action of the water. Because the change occurs quickly and the original boundary is still considered identifiable, the boundary does not change. The state of Texas does not, however, recognize the doctrine of avulsion in regard to its hurricane-riddled coastal shorelines. Noting that the result of applying the general rule of avulsion to fluctuating coastlines "would be unworkable, leaving ownership boundaries to mere guesswork," the Texas Supreme Court reaffirmed that "[t]he division between public and private ownership remains at the mean high tide line in the wake of naturally occurring changes, even when boundaries seem to change suddenly." *Severance v. Patterson*, 345 S.W.3d 18, 32–34 (Tex. 2009).

In other states, the difficulty in establishing the boundary is addressed by creating a rebuttable presumption of accretion or erosion that must be overcome by the party claiming an avulsive change. See 78 Am.Jur.2d Waters § 329 (2010) (stating that "in the absence of evidence to the contrary, the law will presume accretion rather than avulsion. . . .").

3.   SUBSIDENCE AND SEA LEVEL RISE

Stresses on today's environment have also produced two other phenomena that can affect boundaries. First, withdrawal of large amounts of petroleum and water from coastal areas, particularly in Texas and Louisiana, has caused the land to sink or subside allowing encroachment of water. Second, global warming is causing sea level rise that is currently detectable in many areas.

a. Subsidence

Although such gradual changes would seem to be of the type that justifies boundary relocation, Texas courts have recognized a limited right of reclamation of subsided land. In *Coastal Industrial Water Authority v. York*, 532 S.W.2d 949 (Tex. 1976), the Texas Supreme Court distinguished subsidence from erosion. Unlike erosion, subsidence does not involve the removal of land from its location and is not an ordinary hazard of riparian ownership. Unless the public is already using the site for navigation, the owner has a right to protect or reclaim the land, "rather than to watch helplessly as his boundary retreats." But see, *TH Investments, Inc. v. Kirby Inland Marine, L.P.*, 218 S.W.3d 173, 186–90 (Tex. App. 2007) (limiting *York* because tide waters did not cover the property, and the case involved only subsidence without any erosion).

b. Distinguishing Sea Level Rise?

Professor Joseph Sax has noted that sea level rise also differs from the circumstances giving rise to the traditional common law rules:

> The rate and magnitude of the rising sea levels are physically quite different from the historical experience out of which the common law rules grew. The rising sea level is neither gradual like traditional accretion, erosion, or reliction; nor is it sudden and violent like traditional avulsion. We are facing a historically distinct situation that is not a good factual fit with the "background" rules.

See Joseph L. Sax, *Some Unorthodox Thoughts About Rising Sea Levels, Beach Erosion, and Property Rights*, 11 Vt. J. Envtl. L. 641, 645 (2010). He has proposed that resolution requires "a balance between the littoral owner's claimed property rights and the state's property rights as the owner of the land seaward of the MHTL." Id. at 646. He proposed application of a balancing approach to accommodate "the fact that both owners have a legitimate interest and are innocent victims of a phenomenon beyond their control." Id.

c. Fixing Ambulatory Boundaries

The uncertainties caused by ambulatory boundaries have led some states to attempt to fix water boundaries at a certain date. Because federal common law recognizes ambulatory boundaries, the law chosen to interpret a grant may be critical to determination of the boundary.

(1) Hawaii

Hawaii's law had recognized the right to accretions and, consequently, an ambulatory boundary, but required upland owners to register such claims and prove by a preponderance of the evidence that the accretion is natural and permanent (in existence at least twenty years). In 2003, the Hawaii State Legislature passed Act 73 providing that owners of oceanfront lands could no longer register or quiet title to accreted lands unless the accretion restored previously eroded land. Act 73 also provided that lands accreted after the date of the Act would be "[p]ublic lands" or "state land." The Intermediate Court of Appeals of Hawaii held that Act 73's permanent fixing of the boundary divested a littoral owner's rights to any existing accretions to oceanfront property that were unregistered or unrecorded as of the effective date of Act 73. The court did find, however, that property owners "have no vested right to future accretions that may never materialize and, therefore, Act 73 did not effectuate a taking of future accretions without just compensation." See *Maunalua Bay Beach Ohana 28 v. State*, 122 Haw. 34, 222 P.3d 441 (2009).

(2) The Saga of Hughes, Bonelli and Corvallis Sand & Gravel

The supreme court of the State of Washington interpreted the 1889 state constitution as fixing coastal boundaries as of the date of statehood. In *Hughes v. Washington*, 389 U.S. 290, 88 S.Ct. 438, 19 L.Ed.2d 530 (1967), the Hughes' oceanfront land had been transferred to a private owner by the federal government prior to statehood. Hughes' ownership of accretions to the land depended upon whether state or federal law governed. The U.S. Supreme Court held that federal law must govern a federal grant of lands bordering tidelands. The Court reasoned that coastal boundaries are too closely related to the vital interest of the United States in its international boundaries to be governed by state law.

Hughes was followed in *Bonelli Cattle Co. v. Arizona*, 414 U.S. 313, 94 S.Ct. 517, 38 L.Ed.2d 526 (1973), in applying federal law to determine an ambulatory boundary issue involving the navigable Colorado River. However, in *Oregon ex rel. State Land Board v. Corvallis Sand & Gravel Co.*, 429 U.S. 363, 97 S.Ct. 582, 50 L.Ed.2d 550 (1977), the Court overruled *Bonelli,* holding that state law applies to the question of whether state title to a riverbed follows the course of a navigable river as it moves. The Court explained that although the equal footing doctrine dictates that federal law applies for purposes of determining the boundaries of a navigable riverbed upon a state's admission to the Union, state property law thereafter controls boundaries.

In *California ex rel. State Lands Commission v. United States*, 457 U.S. 273, 102 S.Ct. 2432, 73 L.Ed.2d 1 (1982), the Supreme Court considered whether *Corvallis Sand & Gravel* overruled *Hughes* as well as *Bonelli*. The United States owned property on the north side of the entrance to Humboldt Bay continuously since California's statehood. Because of jetties built at the mouth of the bay by the United States, 184 acres of land accreted on the north shore. California argued that the reasoning in *Corvallis* also required that state law, in this case the state law concerning artificial accretions, must be applied to tidelands boundaries. The Supreme Court disagreed, noting that *Bonelli* had not expressly relied on *Hughes* and that the *Corvallis* opinion recognized that federal law would continue to apply if "there were present some other principle of federal law requiring state law to be displaced." The Court reiterated the finding in *Hughes* that oceanfront property is "sufficiently different . . . so as to justify a 'federal common law' rule of riparian proprietorship." Id. at 283. The Court also distinguished the case from both *Corvallis* and *Hughes* by observing that the case involved land in which the United States had never terminated its interest, and not merely the interpretation of a federal grant to a private landowner. An alternative statutory holding was based on section 5(a) of the Submerged Lands Act of 1953, 43 U.S.C.A. § 1313(a), which expressly withheld from the grant to the states all accretions to lands reserved by the United States. The concurring justices found that the Submerged Lands Act was controlling and that the discussion of *Hughes* was consequently dicta. The "continuing vitality" of *Hughes* may, therefore, still be in question.

d. Boundaries and Beach Restoration

Fixing the boundary between private and public ownership is also a normal part of the procedure for beach restoration projects. The process usually involves pumping massive amounts of sand barged from off-site onto eroded beaches to extend them at least 100 yards seaward. Recent projects usually also involve dune restoration to improve the life of the project and provide additional protection to upland property. In general, the government will survey and establish the mean high water line boundary prior to filling the state lands seaward of that boundary. Most state laws addressing beach restoration provide for that boundary to remain fixed after the project. In *City of Long Branch v. Jui Yung Liu*, 203 N.J. 464, 4 A.3d 542 (N.J. 2010), the New Jersey Supreme Court applied both the public trust doctrine and the principle of avulsion in finding no taking of the Lius' property by a beach restoration project.

> [T]he doctrine of avulsion itself is founded on principles of equity. The beach replenishment program [which the court determined constituted an avulsion] erected a buffer protecting the Lius' property, and therefore the Lius were a direct beneficiary of the replenishment program. ... In the end, however, under the public trust doctrine, the people of New Jersey are the beneficiaries. Because the old mean high water mark remains the boundary line between private and public property, there was no true loss of land to the Lius or gain to the State.

Id. at 486. In *Stop the Beach Renourishment, Inc. v. Fla. Dep't of Envtl. Prot.*, 560 U.S. 702 (2010), the U.S. Supreme Court unanimously held that the state supreme court's upholding of a beach restoration statute fixing the boundary did not constitute a judicial taking of the upland property owner's vested right to accretions. In *New Jersey v. New York*, 523 U.S. 767, 784 (1998), the U.S. Supreme Court recognized analogous activity, artificial land-filling increasing the area of Ellis Island, as an avulsive event under federal law, leaving the boundary in place.

D.   THE SIGNIFICANCE OF PUBLIC OWNERSHIP

1.   THE PUBLIC TRUST DOCTRINE IN ROMAN AND ENGLISH LAW

Tidelands and lands below navigable waters are owned by the state in a special capacity—in the public trust. The public trust doctrine can be traced to Roman law. The Institutes of Justinian provided that "[b]y the law of nature these things are common to mankind—the air, running water, the sea, and consequently the shores of the sea." Justinian Code 530 AD. The air, sea, shore, and water, as *res communes,* were not subject to private ownership. The doctrine seemed to disappear during the Middle Ages, but reemerged in Tudor England, apparently as a basis for the Crown to control tidelands and navigable waterways. Under English common law, public trust or sovereignty lands were not *res communes.* Title, *jus privatum,* was held by the King as sovereign, while dominion over the lands, *jus publicum,* was vested in the Crown as a trust for the benefit of the public. The public trust doctrine was adopted in the United States as part of the English common law.

The classic rationale for the public trust doctrine was elaborated by the Supreme Court in *Shively v. Bowlby*, 152 U.S. 1, 14 S.Ct. 548, 38 L.Ed. 331 (1894):

> Lands under tide waters are incapable of cultivation or improvement in the manner of lands above high water mark. They are of great value to the public for the purposes of commerce, navigation and fishery. Their improvement by individuals, when permitted, is incidental or subordinate to the public use and right. Therefore the title and the control of them are vested in the sovereign for the benefit of the whole people.

Id. at 57.

2.   SUBSTANTIVE SCOPE OF THE MODERN PUBLIC TRUST DOCTRINE

Modern jurisprudence has not limited the purposes of the trust to the traditional public uses of commerce, navigation, and fishing. The doctrine has evolved to reflect the public's contemporary interests in navigable waters and tidelands. See generally, Joseph L. Sax, *The Public Trust Doctrine in Natural Resources Law: Effective Judicial Intervention,* 68 Mich. L. Rev. 471 (1970).

a. Modern Uses of Public Trust Waters

Most states recognize recreational use as part of the public trust. State courts have also identified environmental and ecological protection and preservation of scenic beauty as within the trust. See, e.g., *Marks v. Whitney*, 98 Cal.Rptr. 790, 491 P.2d 374 (1971) (One of the most important public uses of tidelands is preservation of land in its natural state for open space, habitat, scientific study, and its favorable effect on scenery and climate.); *Kootenai Envtl. Alliance, Inc. v. Panhandle Yacht Club, Inc.*, 671 P.2d 1085, 1095 (Idaho 1983) (The public trust doctrine protects "navigation, fish and wildlife habitat, aquatic life, recreation, [and] aesthetic beauty."); *State v. Trudeau*, 408 N.W.2d 337, 343 (Wisc. 1987) ("The rights Wisconsin's citizens enjoy with respect to bodies of water held in trust by the state include the enjoyment of natural scenic beauty. . . ."). The California Coastal Act of 1976 (Pub. Resources Code, § 30251 provides that: "The scenic and visual qualities of coastal areas shall be considered and protected as a resource of public importance. Permitted development shall be sited and designed to protect views to and along the ocean and scenic coastal areas, to minimize the alteration of natural land forms, to be visually compatible with the character of surrounding areas, and where feasible, to restore and enhance visual quality in visually degraded areas. . . ." Cf. *Schneider v. California Coastal Comm'n*, 140 Cal. App. 4th 1339 (2006) (holding that the Commission had no authority to impose development conditions to protect views of the coastline from offshore, ocean-based vantage points).

The public trust doctrine has also been proposed as an important common law tool for governments in development of strategies to respond to climate change and sea level rise. See, e.g., Tim Eichenberg, et al., *Climate Change and the Public Trust Doctrine: Using an Ancient Doctrine to Adapt to Rising Sea Levels in San Francisco Bay*, 3 Golden Gate U. Envtl. L.J. 243 (2010); Margaret E. Peloso & Margaret R. Caldwell), *Dynamic Property Rights: The Public Trust Doctrine and Takings in a Changing Climate*, 30 Stan. Envtl. L.J. 51 (2011).

b. Enforcing the Public Trust Doctrine

The public trust doctrine has never prioritized uses, but by broadening the substantive scope of the doctrine, states have created more opportunities for public trust values, e.g., navigation and environmental protection, to come into conflict with each other. In *Weden v. San Juan County*, 135 Wash.2d 678, 958 P.2d 273 (1998), the Washington Supreme Court was required to address the controversial issue of regulating personal water craft (PWC). In determining that a county ordinance prohibiting navigation and recreational use by PWCs is consistent with the state's public trust doctrine, the court found that "it would be an odd use of the public trust doctrine to sanction an activity that actually harms and damages the waters and wildlife of this state." See also *Renard v. San Diego Unified Port Dist.*, 328 Fed. Appx. 575 (2009) (holding that boaters do not have a constitutional right to unregulated long-term anchorage in public navigable waters); and *Samson v. City of Bainbridge Island,* 149 Wn. App. 33, 202 P.3d 334 (Wash. Ct. App. 2009), *cert. denied,* 166 Wash. 2d 1036, 218 P.3d 921 (2009) (holding that a local government ban on private recreational docks to protect scenic vistas did not violate the public trust doctrine by restricting access to the water by waterfront owners).

Because the public trust doctrine itself establishes no priorities among protected uses, state legislatures, agencies and local governments generally must balance or prioritize competing interests based on the appropriateness of the use to the particular area of the coast or ocean. See generally, Donna R. Christie, *Marine Reserves, the Public Trust Doctrine and Intergenerational Equity,* 19 J. Land Use & Envtl L. 427 (2004).

A violation of the public trust doctrine by a private individual would generally be considered a public nuisance and, therefore, not subject to abatement by members of the public. Some states have, however, specifically recognized citizens' rights to sue a private party to prevent or abate a violation of the public trust doctrine. See, e.g., *Gillen v. City of Neenah,* 580 N.W.2d 628, 636 (Wi. 1998) (finding that the "public trust doctrine establishes standing for the state, or any person suing in the name of the state for the purpose of vindicating the public trust, to assert a cause of action recognized by the existing law of Wisconsin"); *Marks v. Whitney,* 491 P.2d 374, 381–83 (Cal. S.Ct. 1971) (private party standing to raise public trust issues in quiet title actions to tidelands); *Paepcke v. Public Bldg. Comm'n*, 263 N.E.2d 11, 18 (1970) (stating that "[i]f the 'public trust' doctrine is to have any meaning or vitality at all, the members of the public, at least taxpayers who are the beneficiaries of that trust, must have the right and standing to enforce it"). See also, Richard J. Lazarus, *Changing Conceptions of Property and Sovereignty in Natural Resources: Questioning the Public Trust Doctrine*, 71 Iowa L. Rev. 631, 646 (1986).

3. THE GEOGRAPHIC SCOPE OF THE PUBLIC TRUST DOCTRINE

a. The Public Trust and "Navigable Waters"

Public trust lands have generally been described as lands beneath navigable waters. However, the term "navigable" has no plain meaning in law and can only be defined in its statutory or common law context. In England, navigable waters were apparently those affected by the ebb and flow of the tide. See *Phillips Petroleum Co. v. Miss.*, 484 U.S. 469, 477–478 (1988). In an early case, *The Propeller Genesee Chief*, 53 U.S. 443, 12 How. 443, 13 L.Ed. 1058 (1851), the U.S. Supreme Court extended admiralty jurisdiction beyond tide waters to all waters of "navigable character." In *The Daniel Ball*, 77 U.S. 557, 19 L.Ed. 999 (1870), the Supreme Court explained that virtually all waters in England that are in fact navigable are tidally influenced. The Court distinguished the circumstances of the United States which contains mighty inland rivers and large lakes which bear commerce. In determining that a "different test" must be applied to determine the navigability of rivers in the United States, the Court held that:

> [t]hose rivers must be regarded as public navigable rivers in law which are navigable in fact. And they are navigable in fact when they are used or are susceptible of being used, in their ordinary condition, as highways for commerce, over which trade and travel are or may be conducted in the customary modes of trade and travel on water.

Id. at 565. Although *The Daniel Ball* involved a question of the scope of the federal Commerce Clause, this definition of navigability has also come to be known as the "federal title test" and has been adopted by many states as the definition of navigability for purposes of the state title to submerged lands.

Navigability in fact, as defined in *The Daniel Ball,* is not directly determined by merely establishing the depth or width of a water body, nor does it require proof of actual use. See *Utah v. United States,* 283 U.S. 64, 82 (1931) ("[W]here conditions of exploration and settlement explain the infrequency or limited nature of such use, the susceptibility to use as a highway of commerce may still be satisfactorily proved."). The definition has an element of local custom. Even narrow streams may have been plied by fur traders in canoes, and shallow streams may have been susceptible to commerce by barges with a shallow draft. At the time of statehood, the relevant point of time for establishing navigability for state title purposes, these types of vessels represented in many instances the "customary modes of trade and travel on water." See *The Montello*, 87 U.S. 430, 440–441 (20 Wall.) (1874).

b. Modern Recreational Use and Navigable Waters

Modern recreational use of waters has occasionally been viewed as evidence of navigability. For example, New York's legislature has found the common law standard for navigability based on commercial use to be anachronistic and inconsistent with state policy to develop state waters for beneficial uses, including recreation. New York courts have found use by canoeists relevant to the issue of commercial navigability. E.g., *Adirondack League Club v. Sierra Club,* 92 N.Y.2d 591, 706 N.E.2d 1192 (N.Y. 1998). The Mississippi Supreme Court specifically recognized that navigability in fact and customary modes of travel are terms with a "dynamic quality." Therefore, waters of modest size and capacity that are currently capable of use by fishermen and recreational boaters are navigable in fact. The court noted that reliance on *The Daniel Ball's* commercial navigability test is misplaced and confusing when the scope of federal Commerce Clause jurisdiction is not the issue. *Ryals v. Pigott,* 580 So.2d 1140 (Miss. 1990). The North Carolina Supreme Court has also found that if a water is navigable for purposes of pleasure boating, it is navigable at law even if the water has never been used for trade or commerce. *Gwathmey v. North Carolina,* 342 N.C. 287, 464 S.E.2d 674 (1995).

Navigability in fact for title purposes must be established for the water body at the time of statehood on a case-by-case basis. The U.S. Supreme Court recently clarified in *PPL Montana, LLC v. Montana*, 565 U.S. 576, 132 S.Ct. 1215 (2012), that reliance on present day recreational use has limited application in determination of state title. The Court held that the "Montana Supreme Court . . . erred as a matter of law in its reliance upon the evidence of present-day, primarily recreational use of the Madison River." Id. at 601. While the court could consider such evidence, it was limited to "that which shows the river could sustain the kinds of commercial use that, as a realistic matter, might have occurred at the time of statehood. Navigability must be assessed as of the time of statehood, and it concerns the river's usefulness for 'trade and travel,' rather than for other purposes. . . ." Id. Evidence of present day recreational use is relevant only to the extent that it "may bear upon susceptibility of commercial use at the time of statehood" and "informs the historical determination [of] whether the river segment was susceptible of use for commercial navigation at the time of statehood." The Montana Supreme Court's reliance upon present-day, recreational use, "at least without further inquiry," was held to be "wrong as a matter of law." Id. at 1233–1234. See also *North Carolina v. Alcoa Power Generating, Inc.*, 853 F.3d 140 (4th Cir. 2017)(finding that the constitutional nature of state ownership of navigable waters and the Equal Footing Doctrine required that "navigability for title" is a federal question for the 13 original states as well as later admitted states and federal jurisdiction is appropriate.) *PPL Montana* calls cases such as *Ryals* and *Gwathmey* into question, at least for purposes of determining title to waterbeds.

c. Waters Subject to the Ebb and Flow of the Tide

For over a century it was a matter of debate as to whether such cases as *The Propeller Genesee Chief* and *The Daniel Ball* rejected or merely supplemented, the English ebb and flow of the tide test for defining the scope of navigable waters for state title purposes. ("The doctrine of the common law as to the navigability of waters has no application in this country. Here the ebb and flow of the tide do not constitute the usual test, as in England, or any test at all of the navigability of waters." *The Daniel Ball* at 563). The U.S. Supreme Court addressed this issue directly in *Phillips Petroleum Co. v. Mississippi*, 484 U.S. 469, 108 S.Ct. 791, 98 L.Ed.2d 877 (1988). The case involved the ownership of submerged land several miles north of the Mississippi Gulf coast. The waters over these lands were not navigable in fact, but were influenced by the tides. The Mississippi Supreme Court had found that all lands subject to the tides up to the present day high tide line are navigable *in law* and are owned by the state. The U.S. Supreme Court agreed that cases extending the definition of navigability to all waters that are navigable in fact did not withdraw application of admiralty jurisdiction and the public trust doctrine from waters subject to the ebb and flow of the tide. As a matter of *federal* law, title to lands under all waters that are navigable in law passed to the state upon entry to the Union. The Court noted that once title passed to the state, state law controlled the subsequent disposition of public trust lands. The Supreme Court found that Mississippi law had consistently held that public trust lands include tidally affected lands and upheld Mississippi's claim to submerged lands under tidewaters although the waters were not navigable in fact.

d. State Law Development of the Public Trust Doctrine

Because federal law had played its role once title had transferred to the states, public trust law has not developed uniformly among the states. As noted earlier, the substantive and geographic scope of the public trust may differ among states: Public trust uses are rarely limited to the original triad of commerce, navigation and fishing; several states have acknowledged ownership by the riparian owner to the low tide line; and some states also limit the test for navigability to either the navigability in fact test or the ebb and flow of the tide test. See Frank E. Maloney & Richard C. Ausness, *The Use and Legal Significance of the Mean High Water Line in Coastal Boundary Mapping,* 53 N.C.L. Rev. 185 (1974).

States have generally considered the geographic scope of the public trust doctrine co-terminus with state-owned lands under navigable waters. In *PPL Montana,* supra, the U.S. Supreme Court suggested that states have "misapprehend[ed]" the nature of the public trust doctrine and seemed to reject any claim to constitutional underpinnings for the doctrine. The Court reiterated that the scope of the public trust doctrine is based on ancient Roman civil law, English common law, and state law and is *not* dependent on ownership of the lands under navigable waters, which is a matter of federal constitutional law and the equal-footing doctrine. But see, Gerald Torres & Bellinger, Nathan, The Public Trust: The Law's DNA, 4 Wake Forest J. L. Pol'y 281 (2014).

> . . . While equal-footing cases have noted that the State takes title to the navigable waters and their beds in trust for the public, the contours of that public trust do not depend upon the Constitution. Under accepted principles of federalism, the States retain residual power to determine the scope of the public trust over waters within their borders, while federal law determines riverbed title under the equal-footing doctrine. Id. at 603–604.

Divorcing the public trust doctrine from the ownership of "lands under navigable waters" superficially seems to create opportunities for states to broaden the scope of both the nature and geographic scope of the public trust. Extension of the doctrine to waters over lands not actually owned by the state would, however, seem to change the state's posture from owner to regulator and make the state susceptible to 5th amendment takings claims, discussed infra. The state's public trust authority over waters it defines as navigable today, however, may be considered quite independent of title to underlying lands. See, Richard C. Ausness, *The*

*Supreme Court and the PPL Montana Case:
Examining the Relationship Between Navigability
and State Ownership of Submerged Lands*, 31 Va.
Envtl. L.J. 168, 222, 225 (2013)(arguing that "[w]hile
at first blush the *PPL Montana* decision appears to
represent a defeat for environmental interests, in
reality it may be viewed as an acknowledgement that
concepts like the public trust doctrine are better
suited to protect water resources, fish and wildlife,
recreation, and water quality than navigability or
state ownership of submerged lands").

4. DIVESTMENT OF PUBLIC TRUST LANDS

Public trust lands, held by states in this special
governmental capacity, can be alienated, but the
trust imposes certain limitations.

a. Illinois Central Railroad Co. v. Illinois

The leading case explaining these limitations,
Illinois Central Railroad Co. v. Illinois, 146 U.S. 387,
13 S.Ct. 110, 36 L.Ed. 1018 (1892), involved the
validity of an 1869 grant by the Illinois legislature of
virtually all the submerged lands in the harbor of
Chicago to Illinois Central Railroad. Four years later
the statute was repealed, and Illinois filed suit to
establish ownership of the harbor. The U.S. Supreme
Court described the nature of the state's obligation in
the following excerpt:

> The trust devolving upon the State for the
> public, and which can only be discharged by the
> management and control of property in which
> the public has an interest, cannot be

relinquished by a transfer of the property. The control of the State for the purposes of the trust can never be lost, except as to such parcels as are used in promoting the interests of the public therein, nor can be disposed of without any substantial impairment of the public interest in the lands and waters remaining. . . . A grant of all the lands under the navigable waters of a State has never been adjudged to be within the legislative power; and any attempted grant of the kind would be held, if not absolutely void on its face, as subject to revocation. . . .

. . . The ownership of the navigable waters of the harbor and of the lands under them is a subject of public concern to the whole people of the State. The trust with which they are held, therefore, is governmental and cannot be alienated, except in those instances mentioned of parcels used in the improvement of the interest thus held, or when parcels can be disposed of without detriment to the public interest in the lands and waters remaining.

Id. at 454–455. The Court found that the attempted transfer of the submerged lands of Chicago Harbor was an abdication of the public trust and was voidable or void.

The Eleventh Circuit used a similar rationale in *Marine One, Inc. v. Manatee County*, 898 F.2d 1490 (11th Cir. 1990), to find that a permit holder had no protectable property interest in a permit to build a marina. The court found that a permit to build on state-owned submerged lands is a mere license which may be revoked without compensation if the use interferes with the interests of the public under the public trust doctrine.

The Supreme Court seemed to retreat somewhat from the *Illinois Central* holding in *Appleby v. City of New York*, 271 U.S. 364, 46 S.Ct. 569, 70 L.Ed. 992 (1926). Where the City of New York had transferred several blocks of land under the navigable waters of the Hudson River for purposes of filling for waterfront improvements, the Court held that the city did not have unrestricted power to control navigation and wharfage in the waters over the lots. Although Appleby had not subsequently filled the entire area, the city had expressly conveyed the *jus publicum* as well as the *jus privatum* in the lands and had not required that the lands actually be filled. The Court distinguished the right of the public to continue to ply the waters over the lots from the city's power to dredge the lots or appropriate for profit the use of the waters for moorings for adjoining piers— uses which largely excluded the owners' use of the land and waters.

Clearly, states have alienated and continue to alienate submerged trust lands. In general, however, the courts will not construe conveyances to incorporate public trust lands unless *expressly* included. See *Shively v. Bowlby*, 152 U.S. 1, 14 S.Ct. 548, 38 L.Ed. 331 (1894). In addition, even in the case of express conveyances by the state, some courts will find that the waters are still impressed with the *jus publicum,* unless the transfer expressly conveys the title free of public trust rights. See, e.g., *Gwathmey v. North Carolina*, 342 N.C. 287, 464 S.E.2d 674 (1995).

b. Transfers Within the Public Trust

Many transfers of public trust lands have related to the improvement of commerce and navigation by building docks, wharves, navigation channels, or other harbor improvements and are generally characterized as within trust purposes. Courts have also upheld transfers of trust lands for uses less directly related to the public's trust interests in navigable waters. In *City of Madison v. State*, 1 Wis.2d 252, 83 N.W.2d 674 (1957), the Wisconsin Supreme Court found that the transfer by the state of a portion of the submerged lands of Lake Monona to be filled to build a public auditorium was consistent with the public's use of the land for recreation and did not impair the former uses of the lake. The California Supreme Court found in *Boone v. Kingsbury*, 206 Cal. 148, 273 P. 797 (1928), that leasing ocean tidelands and submerged lands to oil prospectors furthered the public trust by promoting commerce. *Morse v. Oregon Division of State Lands,* 285 Or. 197, 590 P.2d 709 (1979), found that extension of an airport runway into state-owned estuary tidelands could be justified under the public trust doctrine. The Illinois Supreme Court held in *People v. Chicago Park District*, 360 N.E.2d 773 (Ill. S.Ct. 1976), however, that "to preserve meaning and vitality in the public trust doctrine," the public interest served by the grant of state submerged land must not be "only incidental and remote." Id. at 781. The Third Circuit Court of Appeals in *West Indian*

Co. v. Government of the Virgin Islands, 844 F.2d 1007 (3d Cir. 1988), analyzed and succinctly summarized the standard reviewing courts have applied to transfers of trust lands as follows:

> The courts carefully scrutinize any conveyance of submerged lands to determine if it is in complete congruence with the fiduciary obligations owed to the public by the sovereign. If the conveyance represents a deliberate and reasonable decision of the sovereign that the transaction of which the conveyance is a part affirmatively promotes the public interest in submerged lands, the courts have deferred to the sovereign's decision.

Id. at 1019. See also, e.g., *Caminiti v. Boyle*, 107 Wash.2d 662, 732 P.2d 989 (1987).

c. Adverse Possession of Public Trust Lands

Most states have not allowed individuals to acquire state lands through adverse possession. Although many state statutes on adverse possession do not specifically exclude public trust lands, courts have generally been unwilling to apply the adverse possession doctrine to such lands. See, e.g., *Gatt v Hurlburt*, 131 Or 554, 284 P 172 (1930); *O'Neill v. State Highway Dep't*, 50 N.J. 307, 235 A.2d 1 (1967); *Coastal States Gas Producing Co. v. State Mineral Bd.*, 199 So.2d 554 (La.App. 1967). See generally, 55 A.L.R.2d 554, § 16. Tidelands (The general rule that title by adverse possession or prescription cannot be acquired as against the state has been applied in a number of cases involving tidelands). Some courts have, however, applied the doctrine of equitable estoppel to validate claims to public trust lands. Courts have often found the application of equitable or legal estoppel to be justified when the parties have relied upon an invalid state conveyance of public trust lands, developed the land, and paid taxes for an extended period. Because such lands have usually been filled and used privately for many years, quieting title in private parties has been found not to interfere with public uses of navigable waters or the exercise of governmental powers. See, e.g., *Trustees of the Internal Improvement Fund v. Lobean,* 127 So.2d 98 (Fla. 1961); *Greater Providence Chamber of Commerce v. State*, 657 A.2d 1038 (R.I. 1995).

d. The Public Trust Doctrine and Marketable Title Acts

Marketable title acts, passed to simplify land transactions, may also affect state title to public trust lands. These acts extinguish claims that are not part of the recorded chain of title for a requisite number of years, giving the owner a marketable title subject only to interests specifically exempted in the statute. Public trust lands have not always been specifically exempted in the statutes, but it is not clear that application of marketable title acts to these lands would meet the trust obligations of state governments. The Florida Supreme Court, in *Coastal Petroleum Co. v. American Cyanamid Co.*, 492 So.2d 339 (Fla. S.Ct. 1986), did not address the issue of whether the government had the power to make such a disposition of public trust lands, finding instead no legislative intent to apply the marketable title law to trust lands without "some indication that [the legislature] recognized the epochal nature of such revocation [of the public trust doctrine]." The court held that the legislature would not be found to have overturned "well-established law" and to have "casually dispose[d] of irreplaceable public assets" without specific reference to public trust lands . . ."). Id. at 345. But see, North Carolina v. Alcoa Power Generating, Inc., 853 F.3d 140, 155 (4th Cir. 2017) (holding that not applying the MTA to lands acquired by the state by virtue of its sovereignty or to public trust lands "run[s] directly counter to the purposes of the MTA and to all norms of real property law. It is therefore not surprising that the North Carolina Supreme Court, in applying the MTA in a dispute over a State Commission's ownership of real property, implicitly assumed that the MTA applies to the State.").

If a marketable title act *is* found to be applicable to public trust lands in a particular state, an additional issue will arise: Can the record title owner exclude public use of navigable waters over those lands? In other words, does the act vest only bare title, *jus privatum*, or does the act also extinguish the *jus publicum?*

The statute of limitations of the federal Quiet Title Act of 1972 (QTA), 28 U.S.C.A. § 2409a, has been interpreted to foreclose state claims to public trust lands that are also claimed by the federal government. In *Block v. North Dakota ex rel. Board of University & School Lands*, 461 U.S. 273, 103 S.Ct. 1811, 75 L.Ed.2d 840 (1983), North Dakota attempted to use the act's waiver of the federal government's sovereign immunity to make a claim to an allegedly navigable river in which the United States had been issuing riverbed oil and gas leases to private entities. Although the U.S. Supreme Court held that the case was barred by the QTA's statute of limitations, the Court also found that the act did not effectuate a transfer of title if the state actually had title to the land. Obviously sympathetic to the state's claims, the Supreme Court intimated that the state should continue to press the claim until the United States was induced to file a quiet title action and settle the issue on the merits. Upon Congress' amendment of the QTA in 1986 to exempt states from the statute of limitations, North Dakota again brought suit, but failed to establish that the waters of the Little Missouri River were navigable at the time of statehood. *North Dakota ex rel. Bd. of Univ. & School Lands v. United States*, 972 F.2d 235 (8th Cir. 1992).

5. IS THERE A FEDERAL PUBLIC TRUST DOCTRINE?

The Supreme Court has referred in numerous cases to the both a federal trust in submerged lands held for the states while territories and the public trust doctrine of individual states. In *Shively v. Bowlby*, 152 U.S. 1, 49 (1894), two years after *Illinois Central*, the Court described the trust obligation of federal government in regard to the states as holding title and dominion over tidelands and waters "for the benefit of the whole people, and . . . 'in trust for the future states." The Court acknowledged, however, the authority of Congress "to make grants to perform international obligations, or to effect the improvement of such lands for the promotion and convenience of commerce with foreign nations and among the several states, or to carry out other public purposes appropriate to the objects for which the United States hold the territory." Id. at 48.

When the Court in *Shively* described the nature of the trust for future states, it was clear that the federal trust is based on much the same common law public trust principles adopted from England.

The congress of the United States, in disposing of the public lands, has constantly acted upon the theory that those lands, whether in the interior or on the coast, above high-water mark, may be taken up by actual occupants, in order to encourage the settlement of the country, but that the navigable waters and the soils under them, whether within or above the ebb and flow of the tide, shall be and remain public highways; and, being chiefly valuable for the public purposes of commerce, navigation, and fishery, and for the improvements necessary to secure and promote those purposes, shall not be granted away during the period of territorial government, but, unless in case of some international duty or public exigency, shall be held by the United States in trust for the future states . . . . [I]n short, [such lands] shall not be disposed of piecemeal to individuals, as private property, but shall be held as a whole for the purpose of being ultimately administered and

dealt with for the public benefit by the state . . . .
Shively, id. at 49–50.

The Oregon District Court directly addressed the question of the existence of a federal public trust doctrine recently in *Juliana v. United States*, 217 F. Supp. 3d 1224 (D. Or. 2016), motion to certify appeal denied, No. 6:15-CV-01517-TC, 2017 WL 2483705 (D. Or. June 8, 2017), which is asserting a "right to a climate system capable of sustaining human life as a fundamental right." On the question of a federal public trust doctrine, the court noted that the D.C. federal district court held that federal public trust claims were foreclosed by *PPL Montana*'s statement that "the public trust doctrine remains a matter of state law." *Alec L. v. Jackson*, 863 F.Supp.2d 11, 15 (D.D.C. 2012). In an unpublished memorandum decision, the D.C. Circuit affirmed, holding that "[t]he Supreme Court in *PPL Montana* . . . directly and categorically rejected any federal constitutional foundation for that doctrine, without qualification or reservation." *Alec L. ex rel. Loorz v. McCarthy*, 561 Fed.Appx. 7, 8 (D.C. Cir. 2014). But the Oregon court also noted that two federal courts have concluded the public trust doctrine applies to the federal government. See *United States v. 1.58 Acres of Land Situated in the City of Boston, Suffolk Cnty., Mass.*, 523 F.Supp. 120, 124 (D. Mass. 1981); *City of Alameda v. Todd Shipyards Corp.*, 635 F.Supp. 1447, 1450 (N.D. Cal. 1986). In those cases, the courts held that state public trust lands acquired by the federal government by eminent domain were not subject to public trust obligations under state law, but the lands were subject to a federal public trust. Agreeing with the *Alameda* and *1.58 Acres of Land* courts, the Oregon court stated that there is "no reason why the public trust doctrine, which came to this country through the Roman and English roots of our civil law system, would apply to the states but not to the federal government." *Juliana*, at 1259.

To what resources does a federal public trust apply? The *Juliana* court noted that the federal government "holds public assets—at a minimum, the territorial seas—in trust for the people." *Juliana*, at1258–59. Is the EEZ federal public trust resource? Air? For consideration of the rationales for and the consequences of recognizing a federal public trust doctrine, see Gerald Torres & Nathan Bellinger, The Public Trust: The Law's DNA, 4 Wake Forest J. L. Pol'y 281 (2014); see also Michael Blumm & Lynn Shaffer, The Federal Public Trust Doctrine: Misinterpreting Justice Kennedy and Illinois Central Railroad, 45 Envt'l Law 399 (2015).

E. RIGHTS OF RIPARIAN OR LITTORAL OWNERS

1. THE SCOPE OF RIPARIAN OR LITTORAL RIGHTS

Riparian land borders running waters; littoral land borders a lake or ocean. The term "riparian" is commonly used in both circumstances, however, and the rights associated with ownership of both types of land seem to be mostly the same today. "Riparian" will generally be used here, unless the context is particular to littoral land. But see, Alyson C.

Flournoy, Beach Law Cleanup: How Sea-Level Rise Has Eroded the Ambulatory Boundaries Legal Framework, 42 Vermont L. Rev. 89 (2017)(raising questions about whether the riparian and littoral common law principle can continue to be treated as the same in light of sea level rise).

a. General Principles of Riparian Rights

As members of the public, riparian owners have all the rights of the public in navigable waters. In addition, riparian owners have common law rights attributable to their ownership of lands contiguous to navigable waters. In general, common law riparian rights include a right of access to reach the water, the right to accretions, a qualified right to wharf out, the right to make commercial use of water access, the right to make reasonable use of the water, and the right of navigation in common with the public. Riparian rights have been characterized as vested property interests. See, e.g., *Walton County v. Stop Beach Renourishment, Inc.*, 998 So.2d 1102 (Fla. S.Ct. 2008); *In re Protest of Mason*, 78 N.C.App. 16, 337 S.E.2d 99 (1985); *Bach v. Sarich*, 74 Wash.2d 575 445 P.2d 648 (Wash. S.Ct. 1968).

b. Right of Access

The right of access includes a number of different aspects and forms the theoretical basis for most of the other riparian rights. Beachfront owners have an exclusive right of access over their property to reach the water. (The public has no right to cross private land to reach navigable waters.) The right to exploit the riparian's access commercially is also clearly derivative of the exclusive right of access.

c. Right to an Unobstructed View

The right to an unobstructed view, recognized in some states, can be considered a recognition of the riparian's right of visual access to the water—a right to a viewscape not generally recognized as a property interest. See, e.g., *DBL, Inc. v. Carson*, 262 Ga. App. 252, 255, 585 S.E. 2d 87, 91 (2003) (docks obstructing view).

Recent litigation related to this issue does not technically depend on a riparian right to a view, but has involved beach restoration projects that obstructed ocean views. In these cases, dunes were constructed to protect the upland property and extend the project life of the restored beach. In condemnation proceedings related to the easement acquired for the dune, property owners claimed that they were entitled to severance damages to compensate for the remaining property's loss of value due to loss of the view. In *Borough of Harvey Cedars v. Karan*, 214 N.J. 384 (2013), the New Jersey Supreme Court overturned a $375,000 jury award and held that in such an eminent domain "partial taking," just compensation must take into account not only the reduction in fair market value attributable to the loss of view, but also the "quantifiable benefits arising from the storm-protection project." Florida's legislature addressed the issue by amending its beach restoration legislation to provide:

In any action alleging a taking of all or part of a property or property right as a result of a beach restoration project, in determining whether such taking has occurred or the value of any damage alleged with respect to the owner's remaining upland property adjoining the beach restoration project, the enhancement, if any, in value of the owner's remaining adjoining property of the upland property owner by reason of the beach restoration project shall be considered. If a taking is judicially determined to have occurred as a result of a beach restoration project, the enhancement in value to the owner's remaining adjoining property by reason of the beach restoration project shall be offset against the value of the property or property right alleged to have been taken. If the enhancement in value shall exceed the value of the damage, if any, to the remaining adjoining property, there shall be no recovery over against the property owner for such excess.

Fla. Stat. § 161.141. Severance damages should not be equated with recognition of a right to a view. Florida has, however, specifically found a compensable taking of the riparian right of view when a bridge obstructed the view of a homeowner to the navigable waterbody. *Lee County, Florida v. Kiesel*, 705 So.2d 1013 (Ct. of Appeals, 1st Dis. 1998). The right to a view for oceanfront property is unique. Views of landscapes and other waterscapes that add value to property have never been protected as property interests.

d. Right to Accretions

The right to accretions may also be considered an aspect of access. If accreted land does not belong to the upland owner, the newly accreted land would cut off the upland owner from the sea. If the land no longer borders the water, it is by definition, not riparian or littoral. The right of access, along with other exclusive riparian rights, could be lost. But cf., *Stop the Beach Renourishment* (2010) (statutorily protecting the upland owner's right of access after beach restoration); and *Maunalua Bay Beach Ohana 28* (2009) (requiring upland owners to register claims to accretions and prove by a preponderance of the evidence that the accretion is natural and permanent"), supra.

(1) Interference with the Right to Accretion

The riparian's right to accretion and alluvion, the material deposited, may also arise in a different context. Longshore currents, or littoral drift, constantly carry sand from beaches, but they also deposit new sand on beaches. Depending on whether more sand is carried away or deposited, the beach erodes or expands. Groins, jetties, or other structures intended to stabilize shorelines and navigation channels interrupt the longshore currents, causing deposition of suspended sand and resulting in "starvation" of downdrift beaches. In cases where the downdrift beaches are some distance away from the structures and multiple factors may contribute to the erosion, verifying causation presents a problem in establishing liability for the downdrift property damage. See, e.g., *Applegate v. United States*, 1996 WL 208458 (Fed. Cl. 1996). Where causation can be established, finding a theory upon which to base liability has been the major obstacle.

Many courts have rejected the "common enemy rule," which shields an owner from liability for diversions of surface water that cause accumulation of water on neighboring lands, as a defense in such cases. In *Lummis v. Lilly*, 385 Mass. 41, 429 N.E.2d 1146 (1982), a contiguous landowner constructed a groin that caused the beach to narrow on Lummis' downdrift property. The Massachusetts Supreme Court declined to invoke the common enemy rule and applied instead riparian law that allows each riparian reasonable use of the common waters. Reasonable use may result in diminution, obstruction, or change in natural water and sediment flow, but must consider the common rights of other riparian owners. The court found that the same rule should be applicable to littoral owners. The standard of reasonableness will also be applicable to cases that use a nuisance theory of liability. See Wendy B. Davis, *Reasonable Use Has Become the Common Enemy: An Overview of the Standards Applied to Diffused Surface Water and the Resulting Depletion of Aquifers*, 9 Alb. L. Envtl. Outlook J. 1, at 9 (2004).

A right to alluvion provides a more direct basis for liability for downdrift erosion in an emerging concept called "sand rights." The argument is that the littoral owner has a vested property interest in the sand that would be naturally transported to the shore. In California, where this sand rights doctrine was conceived, the protection of the sand transport system is viewed as an extension of the public trust doctrine. See Michael A. Corfield, Comment, *Sand Rights: Using California's Public Trust Doctrine to Protect Against Coastal Erosion,* 24 San Diego L. Rev. 727 (1987).

(2) Interference with Accretions as a Taking of Property by the Government

If coastal erosion is caused by a government project, affected property owners have made claims that the government has unconstitutionally "taken" property without compensation. In *Applegate v. United States*, 1996 WL 208458 (Fed. Cl. 1996), more than 200 property owners south of the Canaveral Harbor Project sought compensation for loss of their property above the mean high-water mark due to erosion and flooding caused by the building and maintenance of the port and navigation channels. The court did not recognize a right to the continued flow of sand, but instead analogized the situation to dam flooding cases. The Federal Claims Court found that it is well "settled that flooding and attendant erosion of private property by the Government amount to a taking." Although the court recognized the basis for the plaintiffs' takings claims, issues involving proof of loss and causation created hurdles to recovery or compensation by property owners in the case. See also *Banks v. United States*, 78 Fed. Cl. 603 (2007) (where the Army Corps of Engineers conceded liability for erosion caused by jetties and was liable for the part of the erosion above the high

water mark that it caused to plaintiffs' properties
and failed to mitigate).

e. Access to the Navigable Channel

The littoral owner's right of access is generally
recognized to include the ability to reach the
navigable part of the adjacent waters. The littoral
owner does not have, however, a right of free
navigation superior to the rights of the public in
general. An often-litigated scenario involves the
obstruction of a riparian owner's navigation of
adjacent waters by the construction of a low bridge or
causeway or by the plugging of canal because of
pollution problems. The overwhelming majority of
cases have found that once the riparian has been
afforded the ability to access navigable waters, the
riparian's special rights go no further. Interference
with the public's general right of navigation is not an
actionable injury to a riparian. See, e.g., *Miller v.
Mayor of New York*, 109 U.S. 385, 3 S.Ct. 228, 27
L.Ed. 971 (1883); *Gilman v. City of Philadelphia*, 70
U.S. 713, 18 L.Ed. 96 (1865); *Becker v. Litty*, 318 Md.
76, 566 A.2d 1101 (1989); *Colberg, Inc. v. State*, 67
Cal.2d 408, 62 Cal.Rptr. 401, 432 P.2d 3 (1967);
Thiesen v. Gulf, F. & A. Ry. Co., 75 Fla. 28, 78 So. 491
(1917); *Carmazi v. Board of County Comm'rs*, 108
So.2d 318 (Fla. App. 1959). The few cases finding a
cause of action in the riparian involved a statutory
right or application of the principle that a riparian
may suffer special injury, different from the public,
when navigation is obstructed. See *Ritter v. Standal*,
98 Idaho 446, 566 P.2d 769 (1977) (Idaho statute
made obstruction of a navigable estuary a public

nuisance); *Webb v. Giddens*, 82 So.2d 743 (Fla. 1955)
(boat rental business cut off from navigable portion
of lake by causeway); *Game & Fresh Water Fish
Comm'n v. Lake Islands, Ltd.*, 407 So.2d 189 (Fla.
1981) (prohibition on airboats denied island property
owners access to the island).

f. The Qualified Right to Wharf out

The qualified right to wharf out is related to the
right to reach the navigable part of the water. This
right has also been interpreted to include the right to
fill in or dredge shallow areas to provide access to
deeper   waters.   Historically,   states   encouraged
erection of wharves, piers, and docking facilities to
stimulate commerce and navigation by enacting so-
called "riparian acts." Some states have even granted
private ownership of submerged lands when the
riparian made such improvements. See, e.g., *Jackson
v. Revere Sugar Refinery*, 247 Mass. 483, 142 N.E.
909 (1924). However, several states that originally
granted private ownership of submerged lands when
the riparian made such improvements have since
amended their laws or overruled these decisions. See
*City of W. Palm Beach v. Board of Trustees of the
Internal Improvement Trust Fund*, 714 So.2d 1060
(Fla. Dist. Ct. App. 4th Dist. 1998); *Clement v. Burns*,
43 N.H. 609 (1862). Today, the right to wharf out is
strictly limited, if it can be said to exist at all.
Virtually all states regulate the construction of
wharfs, docks, and piers through pollution control or
dredge and fill legislation and through zoning and
other police power regulation at the local level. See
e.g., *Dep't of Ecology v. City of Spokane Valley*, 167

Wash.App. 952, 275 P.3d 367 (2012) (holding that the "owner-noncommercial use" exemption of the Shoreline Management Act was inapplicable to a real estate developer because the planned docks would not be built for the applicant's private use); *Samson v. City of Bainbridge Island*, 218 P.3d 921 (Wash. 2009) (upholding a local government ban on private recreational docks by waterfront property owners to protect scenic vistas).

States may also require permission to use or occupy state lands below the highwater line. In navigable waters, structures require a permit from the U.S. Army Corps of Engineers. At this point, the so-called right to wharf out may be better described in most states as merely creating a license or priority for a riparian owner to construct an adjacent dock.

The right of the riparian to wharf out inherently conflicts with public use of the foreshore and the obstructed navigable waters. In the absence of an exclusive lease or specific legislation, the riparian cannot exclude the public from waters around or under a pier. See *Capune v. Robbins*, 273 N.C. 581, 160 S.E.2d 881 (1968) (swimmer attempting a trip from Coney Island to Florida on a paddleboard could not be prohibited from passing under defendant's pier). Most jurisdictions require piers and other coastal structures to be built in a manner that does not obstruct (or mitigates obstruction of) passage by the public along the foreshore. See, e.g., *Barnes v. Midland R.R. Terminal Co.*, 218 N.Y. 91, 112 N.E. 926 (1916); *Caminiti v. Boyle,* 107 Wash.2d 662, 732 P.2d 989 (1987); cf. *Va. Marine Res. Comm'n v.*

Chincoteague Inn, 61 Va. App. 371 (2013) (holding that although a portion of the floating platform to accommodate overflow seating from the Inn's restaurant was temporarily moored over state-owned bottomlands, it was not encroaching over the bottomlands such that it violated the rights of the people of the Commonwealth to use the bottomlands).

Wharves or docks that unreasonably interfere with navigation may be a public nuisance. A private nuisance may arise where docks or piers cut off the access of other riparians to navigable waters. There is no single formula for equitably apportioning a "line of navigability" between or among riparians in all situations. Courts have tried extension of the land boundary lines, lines perpendicular to the shore, and in the case of lands abutting a cove, drawing a line across the mouth of the cove and extending boundaries to that line in a way to create areas roughly in ratio to the riparians' water frontage. Each case is a fact specific, equitable determination that, as much as possible, preserves the owners' access to a navigable channel and unobstructed view. See, e.g., *Langley v. Meredith*, 237 Va. 55, 376 S.E.2d 519 (1989) (apportioning areas for wharfs for adjacent owners by applying a ratio of the water frontages to the line of navigability); *Hayes v. Bowman*, 91 So.2d 795 (Fla. 1957); *Dorrah v. McCarthy*, 265 Ga. 750, 462 S.E.2d 708 (1995).

2. LIMITS ON RIPARIAN RIGHTS— THE NAVIGATION SERVITUDE

a. The Nature of the Navigation Servitude

The navigation servitude, because of its link to navigable waters and the protection of navigation, is often confused with the public trust doctrine. The navigation servitude, however, is a paramount federal servitude on navigable waters based on the commerce power rather than on ownership or trust responsibilities. One commentator asserts a link, however, arguing that the American navigation servitude results from a mistaken interpretation of the English public trust doctrine by U.S. courts. See William B. Stoebuck, *Condemnation of Riparian Rights: A Species of Taking Without Touching,* 30 La. L. Rev. 394, 436–37 (1970).

The navigation servitude allows removal of any impediment to navigation without compensation to an owner and in some cases severely limits traditional riparian uses. See, e.g., *Palm Beach Isles Assocs. v. United States,* 58 Fed. Cl. 657 (2003); *United States v. 30.54 Acres of Land,* 90 F.3d 790 (3d Cir. 1996); *Donnell v. United States,* 834 F.Supp. 19 (D.Me. 1993); *Lewis Blue Point Oyster Cultivation Co. v. Briggs,* 229 U.S. 82, 33 S.Ct. 679, 57 L.Ed. 1083 (1913). In addition, many of the values associated with riparian ownership are not compensable if riparian property is condemned in conjunction with an exercise of Congress' power over navigation, even if the benefit to navigation is incidental. See *Oklahoma v. Guy F. Atkinson Co.,* 313 U.S. 508, 61

S.Ct. 1050, 85 L.Ed. 1487 (D.C. Okl. 1941); *United States v. Twin City Power Co.*, 350 U.S. 222, 76 S.Ct. 259, 100 L.Ed. 240 (1956). The navigation servitude has often been criticized as being at odds with the Fifth Amendment. See generally, Eva H. Morreale, *Federal Power in Western Waters: The Navigation Power and the Rule of No Compensation,* 3 Nat. Res. J. 1 (1963); Eugene J. Morris, *The Federal Navigation Servitude: Impediment to the Development of the Waterfront,* 45 St. John's L. Rev. 189 (1970).

b. Application of the Navigation Servitude

In *United States v. Chandler-Dunbar Water Power Co.*, 229 U.S. 53, 33 S.Ct. 667, 57 L.Ed. 1063 (1913), the U.S. Supreme Court found that no compensation was due Chandler-Dunbar for the removal of works in the river or the loss of the water power of the stream when the federal government condemned a portion of the upland riparian property for a navigation project which required the entire flow of the St. Marys River for improvement of navigation. The Court found that no private property rights could arise in the "running water in a great navigable stream." The Supreme Court followed this holding in *United States v. Twin City Power Co.*, 350 U.S. 222, 76 S.Ct. 259, 100 L.Ed. 240 (1956), in which the power company argued that the value of condemned upland property must include its value as a hydroelectric site. The Court found that no value derived from the flow of the stream itself was compensable.

Subsequently, the U.S. Supreme Court in *United States v. Rands*, 389 U.S. 121, 88 S.Ct. 265, 19 L.Ed.2d 329 (1967) refused to require the federal government to compensate an owner for the value of condemned property on the Columbia River as a port site. Congress responded by enacting section 111 of the Rivers and Harbors Act of 1970, 33 U.S.C.A. § 595(a). The section provides that in condemnation proceedings to acquire riparian property for river, harbor, and waterway improvement, "the compensation to be paid . . . shall be the fair market value of such real property based upon all uses to which such real property may reasonably be put, . . . any of which uses may be dependent upon access to or utilization of such navigable waters." Clearly overruling *Rands,* Congress has demonstrated that the navigation servitude does not constitutionally compel it to follow the no compensation rule.

c. Geographic Scope of the Navigation Servitude

The geographic scope of the navigation servitude is not coextensive with the reach of the Commerce Clause. In *Kaiser Aetna v. United States*, 444 U.S. 164, 100 S.Ct. 383, 62 L.Ed.2d 332 (1979), developers had dredged channels in a privately owned, non-navigable waterbody (Kuapa Pond—now Hawaii Kai Marina), increased the clearance of a bridge, and connected the pond by an eight-foot deep channel to a navigable bay. The U.S. Army Corps of Engineers (Corps) later asserted that permits had to be obtained for further excavation or development in the pond and that public access to the pond was required.

The U.S. Supreme Court held that Kuapa Pond clearly lies within the definition of navigable waters delimiting the reach of the Corps' regulatory authority under the Commerce Clause, but the Court also explained that the navigation servitude did not apply to the Corps' attempt to turn the privately owned pond into a "public aquatic park" and amounted to a taking of private property without compensation. The navigation servitude was described as "the important public interest in the flow of interstate waters that in their natural condition are in fact capable of supporting public navigation." The Court also emphasized that the pond was private property under Hawaiian law and not a "great navigable stream [incapable] of private ownership," quoting *United States v. Chandler-Dunbar Water Power Co.*, 229 U.S. 53, 33 S.Ct. 667, 57 L.Ed. 1063 (1913). See also *Dardar v. Lafourche Realty Co., Inc.*, 985 F.2d 824 (5th Cir. 1993).

d. State Navigation Servitudes

Many states also assert navigation servitudes, based on the state police power or the public trust doctrine, which are subordinate to the federal servitude. In *Wernberg v. State*, 516 P.2d 1191 (Alaska 1973), the Alaska Supreme Court reviewed three general approaches to state navigation servitudes. The general rule requires compensation to the riparian for interference with property rights unless the harm is caused in aid of navigation. The public purpose rule requires no compensation for harm if the project is for any public purpose. See, e.g., *Colberg, Inc. v. State ex rel. Dep't of Pub. Works*, 67

Cal.2d 408, 62 Cal.Rptr. 401, 432 P.2d 3 (1967). The Louisiana exception extends the servitude to projects in aid of navigation even if located a great distance from the water body. Although the Alaska Supreme Court found that the state applies the public purpose rule, it refused to apply the state navigation servitude to the particular case. In the factual situation where a bridge project cut off a right of access that had been exercised for twenty years, the court held that the Alaska constitution required compensation for taking such littoral property rights. See generally Daniel J. Morgan & David G. Lewis, Comment, *The State Navigation Servitude,* 4 Land & Water L. Rev. 521 (1969).

CHAPTER II

PUBLIC ACCESS TO BEACHES AND SHORES

As commercial, industrial, residential, and recreational uses of the coasts create a wall of development along the ocean's edge, the public not only loses the view of the beach and ocean, but also often loses the ability to access navigable waters, the publicly-owned beach seaward of the mean high tide line, and many dry sand beaches where the public may have gained rights. It takes only a brief Internet search to become aware of the increasing conflicts over access to and use of the nation's beaches. Amazon and Ebay have thriving businesses selling "Private Beach" signs, and local conflicts and legal cases involving some aspect of beach access have multiplied. As the amount of undeveloped beachfront property has dwindled, developers have sought to maximize the value of coastal properties by creating "private" beaches; owners paying premium prices for beach property believe they have purchased the right to exclude the public as well. Conflict on some beaches is intensified by the lack of adequate public accessways to the beach, creating disproportionate crowding near the few access points. The access problem is exacerbated by loss of beaches due to erosion and sea level rise.

Preserving the rights of the public as coastal populations continue to grow and beaches disappear is one on the most challenging problems faced by coastal communities and managers.

A. USE OF THE BEACH SEAWARD OF THE MHWL

The beach seaward of the mean high tide line, also referred to as the mean high water line (MHWL), the wet sand, is part of the public trust—open to the public for swimming, recreation, and fishing. As a general proposition, lateral or horizontal access along the wet sand area is unquestionably a public right. (Even in most of the states that recognize the low tide line as the boundary of private property, public access to the wet sand area is allowed for fishing and navigation). See, e.g., Gunderson v. Indiana, 90 N.E.3d 1171, 1188 (Ind. 2018). ([W]e hold that, at a minimum, walking below the natural [highwater boundary] along the shores of Lake Michigan is a protected public use in Indiana.").

The MHWL is a poorly conceived boundary from both a physical and legal perspective to apply to assure that the public does not stray onto private upland beach. The physical indeterminacy of the MHWL "on the ground" was discussed supra at Chapter I.B.3. In State v. Ibbison, 448 A.2d 728 (R.I. S.Ct. 1982), participants in a beach clean-up project were convicted of criminal trespass. After clarifying that the mean high tide is the boundary in the state, the Rhode Island Supreme Court dismissed the charges, stating that

basic due process provides that no man shall be held criminally responsible for conduct that he could not reasonably understand to be proscribed. Although this situation most often occurs when statutes are challenged for vagueness, we find that the facts of this case are such that these defendants are entitled to similar protection. (Citation omitted.)

In the future, any municipality that intends to impose criminal penalties for trespass on waterfront property above the mean-high-tide line must prove beyond reasonable doubt that the defendant knew the location of the boundary line and intentionally trespassed across it.

Id. at 732.

The impracticality of enforcing trespass complaints led one Florida community to adopt a policy of allowing beachgoers to use the beach up to twenty feet landward of the MHWL. Of course, twenty feet from the MHWL is just as indeterminate as the MHWL itself, so the city has at times used the debris line or the wet sand line as a surrogate for the MHWL. The policy has not provided a resolution to more than two decades of disputes between the public beachgoers and landowners.

In Crystal Dunes Owners Ass'n Inc. v. City of Destin, Fla., 476 F. App'x 180 (11th Cir. 2012), the 11th Circuit Court of Appeals rejected an argument of the condominium owners that the failure of police to enforce trespass on their privately-owned beach violated the Equal Protection Clause.

In their complaint, Owners allege that "they are not protected by law enforcement in the same manner as [ ] all other landowners in the City." However, "[d]ifferent treatment of dissimilarly situated persons does not violate the Equal Protection Clause." As the City and Sheriff's Office have argued, and we agree, *beachfront property is different from nonbreachfront property* under Florida law. . . . [S]atisfaction of the similarly situated prong requires a high degree of specificity. Appellants, as owners of beachfront condominiums, therefore, cannot allege that they are similarly situated to every landowner in the City and expect to meet that high burden of specificity. Having failed to establish the first element of their equal protection claim, we need not address the remaining elements of Owners' equal protection claim.

Id. at 185 (citations omitted)(emphasis added).

The Michigan Supreme Court has held that the scope of state shoreline ownership and the scope of the public trust rights are not necessarily the same. In Glass v. Goeckel, 703 N.W.2d 58 (Mich. 2005), the Michigan court found that even where statutory provisions may have affected the boundary between privately-owned, littoral land and state-owned, submerged lake-bottom, the private title of littoral landowners remains subject to the public trust below the historic ordinary high water mark. The court held that the land up to the historic ordinary high water remained subject to the jus publicum—the public rights preserved under the public trust doctrine— even if the title to the land (jus privitum) had passed into private ownership. The court also reaffirmed that "walking along the lakeshore is inherent in the exercise of traditionally protected public rights." See, id. at 75.

B. COMMON LAW THEORIES RECOGNIZING BEACH ACCESS LANDWARD OF THE MHWL

Common law property and public trust principles continue to play an important role in balancing public and private interests in the dry sand beach, because few states have addressed the public access issue comprehensively in legislation.

1. PUBLIC EASEMENTS BY PRESCRIPTION

A prescriptive easement is acquired by continuous, uninterrupted, exclusive use that is open and notorious and adverse under claim of right. See, e.g., *Jesurum v. WBTSCC Limited Partnership*, 169 N.H. 469 151 A.3d 949 (N.H. S.Ct. 2016) (finding a public prescriptive easement in a parking area and path for beach access). Most states recognize that easements by prescription may arise when the public makes continual use of beach property for the prescriptive period, which may range from as little as five years to as much as thirty years depending on a state's law. In *Gion v. City of Santa Cruz*, 465 P.2d 50, 56–57 (1970), the California Supreme Court explained: "Litigants . . . must also show that various groups of persons have used the land. If only a limited and definable number of persons have used the land, those persons may be able to claim a personal easement but not [an easement in] the public."

a. An Easement in "the Public"

The notion of establishing a prescriptive easement by public use is conceptually problematic. It can be argued that seasonal use by diverse members of the public can never meet the requirements of continuous or exclusive use. See, e.g., *Ivons-Nispel, Inc. v. Lowe*, 347 Mass. 760, 200 N.E.2d 282 (1964) (the general public is too broad a group to acquire a prescriptive easement to use a private beach for recreation); *State ex rel. Haman v. Fox*, 100 Idaho 140, 594 P.2d 1093 (1979). Beachfront owners have also maintained that because it is impossible to bring an ejectment or trespass action against the general public, the public should not be able to gain rights through prescription. See, e.g., *State ex rel. Thornton v. Hay*, 254 Or. 584, 462 P.2d 671 (1969). In spite of these conceptual hurdles, most states have recognized that an easement can be established by the public.

b. Adverseness

Establishing adverse use can be the greatest obstacle to overcome in acquiring a public prescriptive easement. Permissive use can never ripen into an easement. In recreational resort areas, a court may find, for example, that use of the beach by the public actually promotes the interests of the ocean front owner. See *City of Daytona Beach v. Tona-Rama, Inc.*, 294 So.2d 73 (Fla. 1974) (finding public use of the beach around the owner's recreational pier was not adverse, but was in furtherance of the owner's interest).

The so-called "open fields doctrine," which creates a presumption that unenclosed and undeveloped areas are used by the public by license of the owner, is applied in many jurisdictions. In *Gion v. City of Santa Cruz*, 465 P.2d 50 (1970), the California Supreme Court rejected the presumption of permissive use of open beaches. The "preferable view" the court found was to treat the question of adverse use as "ordinarily one of fact, giving consideration to all the circumstances and inferences that can be drawn therefrom." Id. at 58.

Some courts have rejected the principle that public use must be adverse in the same sense as in adverse possession cases, finding that a claim of right, adverse to the owner, is established when "whoever wanted to use [the beach] did so continuously . . . when they wished to do so without asking permission and without protest from the landowners." *Seaway Co. v. Attorney Gen. of Texas*, 375 S.W.2d 923, 937 (Tex. Civ. App. 1964); see also *Gion v. City of Santa Cruz*, supra.

c. Continuous Use by the Public

Landowners attempting to interrupt the continuous use by the public and prevent the ripening of an easement by prescription have occasionally faced significant hurdles. In *Concerned Citizens v State ex rel. Rhodes,* 329 N.C. 37, 404 S.E.2d 677 (1991), signs, fences, gates and guardhouses failed to stop the public from using the property, and the owner's futile attempts established the adverseness of the public's use. At trial, the frustrated agent of the owner asked: "[W]hat does it take to keep somebody out of the place [?] . . . [H]ave you got to set a tank up, a machine gun or what [?]" Id. at 51, 404 S.E.2d at 686.

d. "Substantial Identity" Requirement

Concerned Citizens was also interesting because the N.C. Supreme Court did not preclude a public prescriptive easement that shifted with fluctuating, windswept sand dunes, because the traveled way varied as the topography of the dunes changed. In general, prescriptive easements must be static and follow basically the same route continuously to give the owner notice of adverse use. The court found, however, that this requirement of "substantial identity" for a prescriptive easement must take into account the dynamic nature of the landscape. But see, *In re Banning*, 832 P.2d 724, 731–732 (1992) (holding that an easement by prescription or dedication must be confined to a "definite and specific line," even in the context of a dynamic beach).

2.   DEDICATION

Easements for the public can also be created by dedication. In *Trepanier v. County of Volusia*, 965 So.2d 276 (Fla. 5th DCA 2007), the court described dedication as follows:

. . . The public may acquire a right to use upland property by dedication. The dispositive issue in determining whether or not property has been dedicated appears to be whether the private property owner has expressed "a present

intention to appropriate his lands to public use."
City of Palmetto v. Katsch, 86 Fla. 506 (1923). In
Katsch, the court said:

The means generally exercised to express
one's purpose or intention to dedicate his lands
to the public use are by a (1) written instrument
executed for that purpose; (2) filing a plat or map
of one's property designating thereon streets,
alleys, parks, etc., (3) platting one's lands and
selling lots and blocks pursuant to said plat
indicating there in places for parks, streets,
public grounds, etc., (4) recitals in a deed by
which the rights of the public are recognized; (5)
oral declarations followed by acts consistent
therewith; (6) affirmative acts of the owner with
reference to his property such as throwing it
open in a town, fencing and designating streets
thereon; (7) acquiescence of the owner in the use
of his property by the public for public purposes.
[*Katsch*] at 511–12.

Trepanier, at 285.

a. Dedication by Acquiescence or Adverse Use

Unlike prescriptive easements, dedication of
property to public use does not necessarily require a
specific time period, but does depend on intent. In
Gion v. City of Santa Cruz, 465 P.2d 50 (1970), the
California Supreme Court held that "dedication of
property to the public can be proved either by
showing acquiescence of the owner in use of the land
under circumstances that negate the idea that the
use is under a license or by establishing open and

continuous use by the public for the prescriptive period." Id. at 56. In the case of dedication by acquiescence, the owner's intent is the determinant factor, and the length of public use is not relevant. Maintenance or patrolling of a beach by municipal authorities and the expenditure of public funds is relevant to the owner's knowledge and intent to acquiesce to public use. In the case of implied dedication by adverse use for the prescriptive period, the intent of the public—the intent to use without asking or receiving permission—becomes the controlling factor. See also *Seaway Co. v. Attorney Gen. of Texas*, 375 S.W.2d 923 (Tex. Civ. App. 1964).

In *Gion,* the public had used the shoreline land involved since at least 1900. The city had paved a parking lot, installed landslide alarms, maintained the land against constant erosion, and had collected trash on the beach. Occasionally, an owner had posted private property signs that had quickly disappeared. In *Dietz v. King,* 465 P.2d 50 (Cal. 1970), a case considered concurrently with *Gion,* the public had used a beach and a beach access road for at least a hundred years. Although no previous owners of the land had excluded the public, the Kings attempted to block the road with timber and had put up "no trespassing" signs. Neither action was effective in deterring the public from using the land. In both cases, the California Supreme Court found that a dedication to the public had taken place.

The California court's approach in *Gion* and *Dietz* created a landowner's dilemma: As a matter of law, ineffective attempts to exclude public use would not negate intent to dedicate; and even when intent to dedicate could not be found because the landowner attempted to exclude the public, the same evidence could provide the basis for a prescriptive claim by establishing adverse use for the prescriptive period. Moreover, the same evidence that establishes that the public's use is permissive, which negates a finding of prescription or dedication by adverse use, may also support a finding of dedication by acquiescence. The California legislature reacted by allowing landowners to record an instrument declaring that public use of the described land is permissive and by providing that such a recording is conclusive evidence of consent that cannot ripen into dedication or a prescriptive public right. California Code, Civil Code—CIV § 813. (Of course, the recording does not terminate public rights that may have already vested.)

The Hawai'i Supreme Court has specifically rejected *Gion's* theory of implied dedication. In *In re Banning*, 73 Haw. 297, 832 P.2d 724 (1992), the Hawaii court held that while continuous adverse public use may raise a rebuttable presumption of implied dedication, if public use is the only evidence of dedication, it must continue for much longer than the prescriptive period. See also, *Trepanier*, supra. Application of *Gion* was also found to be inconsistent with state policy that not only encourages property owners to open their lands and waters to the public for recreational purposes, but also specifically prohibits the public from acquiring any rights by prescription in the property as a result of such use.

b. Acceptance of a Dedication

Acceptance of a dedication by the government can have consequences and costs related to maintenance of the easement. Acceptance can also be express or implied. In *Gold Coast Neighborhood Ass'n v. State*, 403 P.3d 214, 237 (Haw. 2017), the state no longer wanted to maintain a seawall used by the public and maintained by the state for "decades." Citing those facts as evidence of acceptance of the dedication, the Hawai'i Supreme Court found that the state had "an easement over and across the Seawall by implied dedication." Further, "[t]he State thus has 'the right and the duty' to maintain the surface of the Seawall over and across which it has an easement." Id. at 237.

3.   CUSTOMARY USE

Of the significant legal hurdles to overcome in using prescriptive easement or implied dedication to protect public beach access, perhaps the most overwhelming is the burden of establishing access by the public on a lot by lot basis. See, e.g., *Opinion of the Justices*, 139 N.H. 82, 649 A.2d 604, 610 (1994) ("prescriptive easements, by their nature, can be utilized only on a tract-by-tract basis . . . ."); *Almeder v. Town of Kennebunkport*, 106 A.3d 1099, 1110 (2015) ("in order to obtain a prescriptive easement over a parcel of property, the claimant must demonstrate the requisite use of *that parcel*" (emphasis added)).

a. *Thornton v. Hay*: Kindling the Doctrine of Customary Use

In *State ex rel. Thornton v. Hay*, 254 Or. 584, 462 P.2d 671 (1969), the Oregon Supreme Court opted to apply the English common law doctrine of custom to the public beach access case, rather than "fill the courts for years with tract-by-tract litigation" to establish prescriptive easements. The court noted that the doctrine could be proven with reference to larger regions (or the entire state) and was consistent with the unique nature of dry sandy beaches in the state. Further, "the custom of the inhabitants of Oregon and of visitors in the state to use the dry sand as a public recreation area is so notorious that notice of the custom on the part of persons buying land along the shore must be presumed." Id. at. 462 P.2d 676–77.

Referring to Blackstone's Commentaries, the Oregon court in *Thornton* defined the requirements of custom to be public use that is ancient, exercised without interruption, reasonable, peaceable, obligatory, and not repugnant to other custom or law. The use of the dry-sand area of the Pacific shore by the public was found to be "an unbroken custom running back in time as long as the land has been inhabited." Id. 676–677. Application of this decision to all the state's ocean beaches has subjected the Oregon court to criticism for adjudicating the rights of coastal property owners in Oregon who were not parties to the litigation. See also *Stevens v. City of Cannon Beach*, 317 Or. 131, 854 P.2d 449 (1993). The Oregon court later refused to extend the custom doctrine to areas not actually adjacent to the high tide line and not customarily used by the public. See *McDonald v. Halvorson*, 308 Or. 340, 780 P.2d 714 (1989).

b. Adoption of Custom in Other States

A number of other states and courts have adopted the doctrine of custom to protect public access to beaches. The Texas Open Beaches Act provides expressly in its definition of public beach that public rights can arise through custom. A public beach is defined as any beach area "extending inland from the line of mean low tide to the line of vegetation . . . to which the public has acquired an easement . . . by prescription, dedication, presumption, or *has retained a right by virtue of continuous right in the public since time immemorial, as recognized in law and custom.*" Tex. Nat. Res. Code Ann. § Sec. 61.001(2) (Vernon 1978).

In Hawai'i, the state's supreme court has held that long-standing public use of the state's beaches to a recognizable boundary, the seaweed or debris line, has ripened into a customary right. *In re Ashford*, 50 Haw. 314, 50 Haw. 452, 440 P.2d 76 (1968); see also *County of Hawaii v. Sotomura*, 55 Haw. 176, 182, 517 P.2d 57, 61 (1973); *Public Access Shoreline Hawaii v. Hawaii County Planning Commission*, 79 Hawaii 425, 903 P.2d 1246 (Haw. 1995), cert. denied, 517 U.S. 1163 (1996)(coastal zone management act requires protection of customary rights). The Florida Supreme Court has found that the public has customary rights to use the dry sand area of certain beaches in the state. *City of Daytona Beach v. Tona-Rama, Inc.*, 294 So.2d 73 (Fla. 1974). North Carolina courts have taken judicial notice of custom, noting that "public right of access to dry sand beaches in North Carolina is so firmly rooted in the custom and history of North Carolina that it has become a part of the public consciousness." *Nies v. Town of Emerald Isle*, 244 N.C.App. 81, 92 (N.C. Ct.App. 2015). A *Washington Attorney General's Opinion*, 1970 AGO No. 27, has also concluded that the public is entitled to free use of the wet and dry sand beaches of the state based on the doctrine of custom. In denying an oceanfront owner the right to fence off a beach, the federal court for the District of the Virgin Islands held that "custom" is part of federal common law. *United States v. St. Thomas Beach Resorts, Inc.*, 386 F.Supp. 769 (D.V.I. 1974).

4. THE PUBLIC TRUST DOCTRINE

Because the public's right to enjoy public trust uses of the area below the high water line may depend on access to and across the dry sand, New Jersey courts have allowed the public trust doctrine to creep landward. In *Borough of Neptune City v. Borough of Avon-by-the-Sea*, 61 N.J. 296, 294 A.2d 47 (1972) and *Van Ness v. Borough of Deal*, 78 N.J. 174, 393 A.2d 571 (1978), the New Jersey Supreme Court held that the public trust doctrine requires that municipal beaches must be open to all members of the public on equal terms. In *Avon-by-the-Sea,* the court explained that [t]he public trust doctrine, like all common law principles, should not be considered fixed or static, but should be molded and extended to meet changing conditions and needs of the public it was created to benefit." Id. at 54. The court consequently struck down a requirement for nonresidents to pay a much higher fee than residents to use a municipal beach. The court held in *Deal* that the public could not be excluded by a town's dedication of a beach for use by its residents only. Subsequently, in *Matthews v. Bay Head Improvement Ass'n*, 471 A.2d 355 (1984), the New Jersey court extended the public trust doctrine to include: (1) a right of feasible access to the beach dependent on the particular circumstances of an area; and (2) the public's use of the sandy beach "where use of the dry sand is essential or reasonably necessary for enjoyment of the ocean." Id. at 365.

The Bay Head Improvement Association owned, or leased from private owners, a substantial part of the beach in the Borough of Bay Head, New Jersey, and limited daytime access to members of the Association. There was no public beach in the borough. The Association carried out the same activities as a municipality and received significant funding from the borough. To assure that such a strategy was not adopted broadly to foreclose the public from local beaches, the New Jersey Supreme Court held that the public trust doctrine required that membership in the Association must be open to the public at large. The court did not hold that all privately owned beachfront property must be open to the public, but the court's rationale—"that the public must be given both access to and use of privately-owned dry sand areas as reasonably necessary"— supports that conclusion. The New Jersey Supreme Court reaffirmed this principle in *Raleigh Avenue*

Beach Association v. Atlantis Beach Club, Inc., 185 N.J. 40, 879 A.2d 112 (2005), (holding that the public had the right to use a privately owned, dry sand beach).

The North Carolina legislature and the state's courts have defined "public trust rights as including the 'right to freely use and enjoy the State's ocean and estuarine beaches and public access to the beaches'." N.C. Gen.Stat. § 1–45.1; and see *Nies v. Town of Emerald Isle*, 244 N.C.App. 81 (N.C. Ct.App. 2015). Public trust *rights* are specifically recognized as extending beyond public trust *lands* to ocean beaches. In *Nies*, the court noted, however, a potential ambiguity in the statutory definition of "ocean beaches," because of its reliance on "common law as interpreted and applied by the courts of this State," and the lack of any case holdings establishing the landward extent of state beaches. Acknowledging "both the long-standing customary right of access of the public to the dry sand beaches of North Carolina as well as current legislation mandating such," the court defined the landward extent of the public trust beach area based on the legislation describing the "natural indicators" of the ocean beach—e.g., "the first line of stable, natural vegetation; the toe of the frontal dune; and the storm trash line." N.C. Gen.Stat. § 77–20(e). The court noted that it adopted this definition, "because it most closely reflects what the majority of North Carolinians understand as a 'public' beach." *Nies* at 93.

The state of Maine attempted to statutorily broaden the scope of the public trust doctrine in the intertidal zone to include recreational use. Maine had originally been part of the Massachusetts Bay Colony, and intertidal ownership was governed by a colonial ordinance providing that a shoreline owner's title extends to the low water line subject only to the public's right to fish, fowl, and navigate. In a four-three opinion, the Maine Supreme Court found that by declaring the intertidal zone to be impressed with a public trust which included recreational use, the 1986 Public Trust in Intertidal Land Act constituted an unconstitutional taking of private property. See *Bell v. Town of Wells*, 557 A.2d 168 (Me. 1989). See also, *Opinion of the Justices*, 365 Mass. 681, 313 N.E.2d 561 (Mass. 1974)(an advisory opinion of the Massachusetts Supreme Court finding that a legislative expansion of the public trust doctrine in that state would be unconstitutional). More recently, however, the Maine court held that the public's rights in the intertidal area were not strictly limited to fishing, fowling and navigation. In extending public trust rights in Maine to include the public's right to walk across intertidal lands for purposes of scuba diving, the court recognized a necessity to "strike a reasonable balance between private ownership of the intertidal lands and the public's use of those lands." *McGarvey v. Whittredge*, 28 A.3d 620, 636 (Me. 2011). See also *Ross v. Acadian Seaplants, Ltd.*, 206 A.3d 283 (Me. 2019)(harvesting seaweed from the intertidal land not within the public trust).

C. STATUTORY AND REGULATORY ACCESS REQUIREMENTS

Legislation or regulations creating new rights of public access to or across private lands to facilitate exercise of public trust use of beaches and waters is subject to challenge as a taking of private property by authorizing a permanent physical invasion. See, e.g., *Nollan v. California Coastal Comm'n*, 483 U.S. 825, 107 S.Ct. 3141, 97 L.Ed.2d 677 (U.S. 1987); *Bell v. Town of Wells*, 557 A.2d 168 (Me. 1989); *Opinion of the Justices (Public Use of Coastal Beaches)*, 139 N.H. 82, 649 A.2d 604 (1994). However, many states have statutes designed to protect existing public access and to mitigate the impacts of shoreline activities on existing access. For example, a Florida statute prohibits development or construction that interferes with public accessways created to the MHWL through public use, dedication, or other means unless a comparable, approved alternative accessway is provided. Fla.Stat. § 161.55(6). In *Ocean Harbor House Homeowners Assn. v. Cal. Coastal Comm'n*, 163 Cal.App.4th 215 (Cal.Ct.App. 6th Dist. 2008), cert. denied, 555 U.S. 1172 (2009), the court upheld the Commission's "broad discretion to adopt measures designed to mitigate all significant impacts [including beach access] that the construction of a seawall may have," and after critically examining the condition under *Nollan / Dolan* standards, see infra, also upheld a $5.3 million in lieu mitigation fee, calculated by an economic recreational value method, that was an "accurate reflection of what the state is actually losing as a result of this project." Id. at 225.

Coastal development regulatory programs, such as in California, and more general land use statutes regulating subdivision or planned unit development of land have routinely required, as a condition for development or subdivision approval, that the impacts of development on established public rights to the shoreline be mitigated. But reaching agreement on public access remains a contentious topic. For example, in 2018, California Coastal Commission officials reached a closed-door agreement providing access to a highly scenic portion of the California coast—the Hollister Ranch in Santa Barbara County—only to owners, guests, visitors with guides, and individuals who could kayak in from 2 miles away. In 2019, a California judge rejected this agreement as being inconsistent with the California Coastal Act in not considering adequately the public's rights to access the coast. *Tom Pappas v. State Coastal Conservancy*, Case No. 1417388 (Sup.Ct.Cal., Cty. of Santa Barbara). Negotiation are underway for a new access plan.

Government regulations to protect existing access can be inherently ineffective, however, for protecting public accessways established by common law principles: If the regulation is enforced at the state level, regulators may not be fully aware of local, customary uses that create public rights and easements; if regulation is implemented at the local level, municipalities may lack the incentive or resources to identify and enforce common law easements.

The Texas Open Beaches Act, Tex. Nat. Res. Code Ann. ch. 61, deals directly with the protection of existing beach access rights. The statute imposes penalties for obstructing access where the public has acquired a right to reach or use the sandy beach. It is also illegal to post signs indicating that the public has no right to use a public beach. Perhaps most importantly, the Texas legislature has found that the nature of the use of sandy beaches in the state justifies a rebuttable presumption that the beaches are public from the mean low tide line to the line of vegetation. See the beach diagram at Chapter I.B. In 2009, voters in Texas added access to public beaches to the state constitution's Bill of Rights. Art. I, sec. 33(b) provides: "The public, individually and collectively, has an unrestricted right to use and a right of ingress to and egress from a public beach. The right granted by this subsection is dedicated as a permanent easement in favor of the public."

North Carolina's legislation specifically recognizes "the right of the people to the customary free use and enjoyment of the ocean beaches, which rights remain reserved to the people of this State under the common law and are a part of the common heritage of the State recognized by Article XIV, Section 5 of the Constitution of North Carolina. These public trust rights in the ocean beaches are established in the common law as interpreted and applied by the courts of this State." N.C. Gen. Stat. Ann. § 77–20. See also *Nies*, supra (upholding a local government ordinance designating vehicle travel lanes on its beaches and excluding beach equipment in the lanes, as regulation of a long-established, customary use of the beach).

In Florida, several counties enacted legislation to attempt to protect the public's customary uses of their beaches. See *Alford*, No. 3:16CV362/MCR/CJK, 2017 WL 8785115, at *16 (N.D. Fla. Nov. 22, 2017) (finding that the county's customary beach ordinance was not *ultra vires*). In 2018, however, the Florida legislature passed a law, known as HB 631, striking down the latest local ordinance enacted in the state and providing that subsequent ordinances cannot go into force unless based on a judicial declaration affirming recreational customary use. All affected property owners must be given notice and the opportunity to intervene in the action. Two counties are currently implementing the process set out by the legislation, but the legislation remains controversial.

D. THE NATURE OF A PUBLIC EASEMENT

If the public establishes an easement to use a beach above the high tide line, what happens to the easement when natural forces move the beach? Does an easement follow the beach or dunes as they move due to erosion or avulsion? Generally, an easement is considered a "static real property concept." But the North Carolina Supreme Court did not reject a finding of a public easement over shifting, windswept sand dunes because the traveled way varied as the topography of the dunes changed. The court found that the requirement of "substantial identity" for a prescriptive easement must take into account the dynamic nature of the landscape. *Concerned Citizens v. State ex rel. Rhodes*, 329 N.C. 37, 404 S.E.2d 677 (1991).

Similarly, Texas appellate courts had posited that "[a]n easement fixed in place while the beach moves would result in the easement being either under water or left high and dry inland, detached from the shore. . . . The law cannot freeze such an easement at one place any more than the law can freeze the beach itself." *Matcha v. Mattox ex rel. People*, 711 S.W.2d 95 (Tex.Civ.App.1986). This concept, called a "rolling easement," had been applied in Texas to prevent rebuilding and to require removal of structures that obstruct beach access, even when the beach had moved substantially due to an avulsive event, such as a hurricane. The Texas Supreme Court did not, however, address the rolling easement as a matter of Texas law until 2012.

In *Severance v. Patterson*, 370 S.W.3d 705 (2012), the Texas Supreme Court held in an advisory opinion[1] that Texas does not recognize a "rolling" public beachfront access easement. Texas recognizes that the MHW boundary between state submerged lands and private upland moves with the changing shoreline; it is irrelevant whether the change is caused by erosion or avulsion. The court held that

---

[1]   A federal court adjudicating a 5th amendment takings claim resulting from application of the concept of rolling easements sought an advisory opinion from the Texas Supreme Court concerning whether the concept was part of state law. All state cases that applied rolling easements were at the intermediate court level. Severance v. Patterson, 566 F.3d 490, 503–04 (5th Cir.2009), certified questions accepted, 52 Tex.Sup.Ct.J. 741 (May 15, 2009).

easement boundaries, however, may only shift when gradual changes alter the location of the beach. Id. at 723 ("It would be impractical and an unnecessary waste of public resources to require the State to obtain a new judgment for each gradual and nearly imperceptible movement of coastal boundaries exposing a new portion of dry beach"). If an avulsive event, such as a hurricane, moves the MHW line and vegetation line suddenly and perceptibly, causing the former dry beach to become part of state-owned wet beach or become completely submerged, the adjacent private property owner is not automatically deprived of her right to exclude the public from the new dry beach. The land "encumbered by the easement is lost to the public trust, along with the easement attached to that land." Id. at 723–24. See also *Trepanier v. County of Volusia*, 965 So.2d 276 (Fla. Dist. Ct. App. 2007) (finding that the migration of the public's customary use with the movement of the beach is a matter of proof).

The Hawai'i Supreme Court impliedly rejected the concept of a "rolling" or shifting public easement in *In re Banning*, 832 P.2d 724 (1992). The court refused to extend a public easement to adjacent accreted lands in spite of state arguments that because the beach is subject to constant change, specifically bounded descriptions of public access easements are insufficient. The court maintained that an easement by prescription or dedication must be confined to a "definite and specific line," and that "vague description of the easement literally allows members of the public to redefine its location each time they use the land." Id. at 732.

E. PUBLIC BEACH ACCESS AND TAKINGS JURISPRUDENCE

Beach access statutes and public access conditions on development have been subject to continual challenges alleging that such access requirements are unconstitutional conditions or 5th amendment takings of property, particularly when the owner's right to exclude is implicated. In some instances, the public's right of access may even preclude any development of a parcel of property, reducing its value to the point that the owner may also base a takings claim on the severe or total reduction in the value of the property.

1. PROTECTION OF EXISTING PUBLIC BEACH ACCESS

Clearly, laws that do no more than protect existing public beach easements do not effect a taking of private property. In *Lucas v. South Carolina Coastal Council*, 505 U.S. 1003, 112 S.Ct. 2886, 120 L.Ed.2d 798 (1992), discussed fully infra at Chapter IV.E.2, the U.S. Supreme Court found that even in cases where regulation left the property with no economically viable use, government enforcement of a limitation on property rights based on background principles of law does not constitute a compensable taking of property, because the right to such use was never part of the owner's rights. Justice Scalia's majority opinion noted specifically that the Court "assuredly would permit the government to assert a permanent easement that was a pre-existing limitation on the landowner's title." Id. at 505 U.S. 1028–1029.

Governments regularly protect existing access along and access to beaches in land use regulations and permitting. California, for example, interprets its Coastal Act as requiring a coastal development permit under section 30106 of the Coastal Act to close an existing access road to a beach. In *Surfrider Found. v. Martins Beach 1, LLC*, 14 Cal. App. 5th 238, 221 Cal. Rptr. 3d 382 (Ct. App. 2017), review denied (Oct. 25, 2017), cert. denied, 139 S.Ct. 54, 202 L.Ed.2d 19 (2018), the California Court of Appeals upheld an injunction barring billionaire Vinod Khosla from closing a road used for beach access, pending his applying for and acquiring the necessary coastal development permit.

In spite of his specific language in *Lucas,* Justice Scalia wrote a strong dissent to the Court's denial of certiorari for *Stevens v. City of Cannon Beach*, 317 Or. 131, 854 P.2d 449 (1993). Stevens sought review of an Oregon Supreme Court decision finding that Stevens did not suffer a compensable taking when he was denied permits to build a seawall on the dry sand beach that was necessary to further develop his land. The Oregon court found that the doctrine of custom was a background principle of state property law, and that Stevens never had the right to obstruct the dry sand beach that was subject to public use based on custom. Justice Scalia found the reliance on *Thornton v. Hay*, 254 Or. 584, 462 P.2d 671 (1969), problematic both substantively and procedurally:

I believe that petitioners have sufficiently preserved their due process claim, and believe further that the claim is a serious one. Petitioners, who owned this property at the time Thornton was decided, were not parties to that litigation. Particularly in light of the utter absence of record support for the crucial factual determinations in that case, whether the Oregon Supreme Court chooses to treat it as having established a "custom" applicable to Cannon Beach alone, or one applicable to all "dry-sand" beach in the State, petitioners must be afforded an opportunity to make out their constitutional claim by demonstrating that the asserted custom is pretextual. If we were to find for petitioners on this point, we would not only set right a procedural injustice, but would hasten the clarification of Oregon substantive law that casts a shifting shadow upon federal constitutional rights the length of the State.

Stevens v. City of Cannon Beach, 510 U.S. 1207 (1994) (Scalia, J. dissenting).

Justice Scalia's strong objection to the application of the doctrine of custom to Oregon's beaches suggests that what he considered novel application of common law theories, such as custom or the public trust doctrine, may meet resistance in some courts. While these common law doctrines may be within the realm of "background principles of law," courts may find that newly-devised applications of the doctrines to further public access to beaches do not meet the requirements of the Fifth Amendment. But see, *Nies*

v. *Town of Emerald Isle*, 244 N.C.App. 81 (N.C.
Ct.App. 2015)(upholding regulation based on the
public trust rights of the public to ocean beach access
that arise from longstanding customary use).

2.   BEACH ACCESS CONDITIONS ON DEVELOPMENT PERMITS

To protect public access to beaches in furtherance
of California's constitutional provisions and the
state's coastal management program, the California
Coastal Commission routinely includes public access
as a condition for approval of coastal development
permits. For example, on a segment of Faria Beach,
forty-three of fifty-seven permits for development on
beachfront properties included easements for lateral
public access across the properties above the mean
high water mark, facilitating the public's use of the
public beaches at each end of Faria Beach. In *Nollan
v. California Coastal Commission*, 483 U.S. 825, 107
S.Ct. 3141, 97 L.Ed.2d 677 (1987), the owners of a lot
on Faria Beach objected to the Coastal Commission's
imposition of a similar easement on their lot as a
condition for receiving a permit to demolish a small
bungalow and replace it with a larger house.
Analogizing the factual situation to *Kaiser Aetna v.
United States*, 444 U.S. 164, 100 S.Ct. 383, 62
L.Ed.2d 332 (1979), see supra Chapter I.E.2.c,
Justice Scalia stated that the requirement of a public
easement across the beachfront would undoubtedly
constitute a permanent physical occupation, and
therefore a *per se* taking of the Nollan's property,
unless the condition furthered a land use regulation
that "substantially advance[s] legitimate state

interests." The Commission argued that it could have exercised its police power to deny the permit based on the interference with visual access and the "psychological barrier" to public use of the beach presented by the wall of development along the beach. This being the case, the Commission maintained that a permit condition serving the same legitimate purposes should not be found to be a taking. The Court agreed, but could not understand how lateral access to the beachfront related to visual access from the street and found that "the condition substituted for the prohibition utterly fails to further the end advanced as the justification for the prohibition." Id. at 483 U.S. 836–837. Conditions not related to the legitimate purposes underlying the authority to restrict development were depicted by the Court as "an out-and-out plan of extortion." Id.

Although *Nollan* found that there must be an "essential nexus," id. at 837, between the exaction and the effects of the development, the Court did not explain how close the fit must be. In *Dolan v. City of Tigard*, 512 U.S. 374, 114 S.Ct. 2309, 129 L.Ed.2d 304 (1994), the Court reaffirmed *Nollan's* standard and further explained that the "essential nexus" required is a "rough proportionality" between the dedication of property rights and the "nature and extent" of the impact of the proposed development. This scrutiny of whether the regulation substantially advances a legitimate state interest goes well beyond the traditional consideration by the courts of land uses measures, i.e., consideration of whether the conclusions of the government are "fairly debatable."

Euclid v. Ambler Realty, 272 U.S. 365, 47 S.Ct. 114, 71 L.Ed. 303 (1926).

In *Lingle v. Chevron*, 544 U.S. 528, 125 S.Ct. 2074, 161 L.Ed.2d 876 (2005), the Supreme Court clarified *in dicta* that *Nollan's* heightened scrutiny and more rigorous analysis of the fit between the burden and the exaction applies only in adjudicative decisions where the government imposes conditions requiring dedication of land or access—requirements that would be found to be per se compensable takings outside the permitting context. Although *Lingle* limits the scope of the *Nollan/Dolan* analysis to cases involving an application of the doctrine of "unconstitutional conditions," the application of the standard to beach access easements is clear. The Court noted in *Nollan* that where property rights, such as the right to exclude, are abridged, the police power must "substantially advance" a legitimate state interest and that this requirement is not just a matter of semantics. The Court will "be particularly careful about the adjective where the actual conveyance of property is made a condition to the lifting of a land-use restriction." See also *Koontz v. St. Johns River Water Management District*, 133 S.Ct. 2586 (2013) (holding that the government's demand for property from a land-use permit applicant must satisfy the requirements of *Nollan* and *Dolan even when the government denies the permit and even when its demand is for money*).

CHAPTER III

MANAGEMENT FRAMEWORK FOR OCEAN AND COASTAL RESOURCES

A. FEDERAL AND STATE BOUNDARIES IN THE COASTAL OCEANS

Managers and planners today support theories of ecosystem management and comprehensive, integrated planning for ocean areas and resources. Unfortunately, our institutions, agencies, and laws have evolved in a manner that often frustrates attempts to approach management of coastal and ocean resources in a coherent and cooperative fashion. Rather than dealing directly with the issue of cooperative management of ocean and coastal resources that are of mutual importance, the state and federal governments have waged legal battles for over seventy years over proprietary interests and preemption. Immeasurable funds and resources have been expended in endless controversies over ownership, jurisdiction, and boundaries of coastal land, waters and resources.

1. THE TIDELANDS CONTROVERSY

Until the 1940s, little doubt seemed to exist that the coastal states, rather than the federal government, "owned" the lands under the territorial sea. These lands and waters were presumed to be encompassed within the definitions of navigable waters or tidelands that belonged to the colonies upon becoming sovereign and to the subsequently admitted states under the equal footing doctrine. See Chapter I.A.

Most coastal states had legislation establishing offshore marine boundaries prior to 1940, and many state constitutions and federal acts admitting states to the Union described state boundaries as extending a marine league or more offshore. See, Gordon Ireland, *Marginal Seas Around the States,* 2 La. L. Rev. 252 (1940) (reviewing the offshore claims and law of each coastal state as of 1940). Numerous state courts had early concluded that the original colonies succeeded to the King's interest in the tidelands and adjacent seas and, therefore, title vested in the original colonies. Decisions of federal courts, including the U.S. Supreme Court, impliedly, if not expressly, supported the presumption of state ownership of the seabed and the territorial sea. See, e.g., *Manchester v. Massachusetts*, 139 U.S. 240, 11 S.Ct. 559, 35 L.Ed. 159 (1891); *The Abby Dodge v. United States*, 223 U.S. 166, 32 S.Ct. 310, 56 L.Ed. 390 (1912). Even Franklin Roosevelt's Secretary of the Interior, Harold L. Ickes, charged with administering United States public lands, stated that the federal government had no authority to lease the seabed for mineral exploration. In the now famous 1933 Proctor Letter, Ickes explained to a lease applicant that "[t]itle to the soil under the ocean within the 3-mile limit is in the State of California, and the land may not be appropriated except by authority of the State." Letter from Harold Ickes, Secretary of the Interior, to Olin S. Proctor (Dec. 22, 1933), reprinted in Ernest Barkley, The Tidelands Oil Controversy 129 (1953).

In the late 1930s, controversies emerged within California concerning oil recovered from submerged lands by shore-based slant drilling and ownership of mineral rights in submerged lands granted by the state to coastal cities for harbor and recreational development. Apparently instigated by Secretary Ickes and supported by the oil industry and by individuals from California interested in settling the offshore ownership issue, Congress in 1938 began a series of hearings and attempted to pass resolutions addressing federal interests in the lands below the territorial sea. These efforts culminated in 1946 in House Joint Resolution 225, which quitclaimed any rights of the federal government in lands beneath tidelands and navigable waters to the states. President Truman vetoed the resolution on August 2, 1946, citing the fact that the issue was currently before the Supreme Court.

On October 19, 1945, the United States Attorney General had filed an original jurisdiction suit in the Supreme Court against the state of California. *United States v. California*, 332 U.S. 19, 67 S.Ct. 1658, 91 L.Ed. 1889 (1947). The suit sought to have the United States declared the owner of the seabed and minerals from the mean low water line to three nautical miles seaward. California argued that because the original colonies had acquired from the Crown of England all lands under navigable waters, including all marginal seas within their boundaries, these lands also vested in California upon admission into the Union by virtue of the equal footing doctrine as an element of sovereignty.

The Court quickly dismissed California's arguments, concluding that "acquisition . . . of the three-mile belt [had] been accomplished by the national Government," rather than the English Crown or the colonies. Id. at 332 U.S. 35. The Court depicted the federal government's role not as merely a property owner, but as the entity responsible for the security and defense of the marginal seas and for the conduct of foreign relations:

> The ocean, even its three-mile belt, is thus of vital consequence to the nation in its desire to engage in commerce and to live in peace with the world; it also becomes of crucial importance should it ever again become impossible to preserve that peace. And as peace and world commerce are the paramount responsibilities of the nation, rather than an individual state, so, if wars come, they must be fought by the nation. The state is not equipped in our constitutional system with the powers or the facilities for exercising the responsibilities which would be concomitant with the dominion which it seeks.

Id. at 332 U.S. 35–36. (citations omitted). These vital interests apparently did not, however, necessitate ownership by the United States of the territorial sea. Instead, the Court held only "that California is not the owner of the three-mile marginal belt along its coast, and that the Federal Government rather than the state has *paramount rights* in and power over that belt, an incident to which is full dominion over the resources of the soil under that water area, including oil." Id. at 332 U.S. 38–39. (Emphasis added.)

On the heels of the *United States v. California* holding, the United States brought suit against both Texas and Louisiana on the basis that the broad principles of the *California* case also dictated federal ownership or control of the oil fields of the Gulf of Mexico. See *United States v. Texas*, 339 U.S. 707, 70 S.Ct. 918, 94 L.Ed. 1221 (1950) and *United States v. Louisiana*, 339 U.S. 699, 70 S.Ct. 914, 94 L.Ed. 1216 (1950). The Louisiana case, with little to distinguish the state's history from California, was found by the Supreme Court to be controlled by *United States v. California*, 332 U.S. 19, 67 S.Ct. 1658, 91 L.Ed. 1889 (1947). The Texas case, however, presented a clearly unique circumstance because of the state's preadmission history as a sovereign republic with a boundary and dominion extending three marine leagues into the Gulf of Mexico. The Court disposed of the case through application of the equal footing doctrine, finding that relinquishment of any "claim that Texas may have had to the marginal sea" to be incidental to the transfer of Texas' external sovereignty to the United States v. Texas, 339 U.S. 718.

2.   THE SUBMERGED LANDS ACT

The Supreme Court cases created great controversy in Congress about the ownership of the marginal seas and its resources. Following another vetoed attempt at quitclaim legislation, Congress passed the 1953 Submerged Lands Act (SLA), 43

U.S.C.A. §§ 1301–1315, which was signed into law by newly elected President Eisenhower. The SLA quitclaimed to the coastal states all federal proprietary rights in the three-mile territorial sea and confirmed federal government rights in the seabed and subsoil beyond that. The SLA accomplished three objectives: (1) it established state title to the lands below the territorial sea and its resources; (2) it decreed the limit of state ocean boundaries; and (3) it reserved federal rights in relation to commerce, navigation and foreign affairs both within and beyond state territorial limits.

a. Extent of State Ocean Ownership and Boundaries Under the SLA

Although one of the purposes of the SLA was to relieve both the state and federal governments of the "interminable litigation" provoked by *United States v. California,* the boundary provisions of the Act created additional legal problems. Section 1312 of the SLA confirmed title of the original coastal states to three geographic miles and recognized the authority of subsequently admitted states to extend boundaries to that distance. However, the section went on to provide the basis for states to continue to assert claims beyond three miles:

> Any claim heretofore or hereafter asserted either by constitutional provision, statute, or otherwise, indicating the intent of a State so to extend its boundaries is hereby approved and confirmed, without prejudice to its claim, if any it has, that its boundaries extend beyond that

line. Nothing in this section is to be construed as questioning or in any manner prejudicing the existence of any State's seaward boundary beyond three geographical miles if it was so provided by its constitution or laws prior to or at the time such State became a member of the Union, or if it has been heretofore approved by Congress.

43 U.S.C.A. § 1312. Congress left it to the courts to determine whether a state could establish a historic or congressionally-approved claim beyond three miles. Because the SLA did not address the methodology for establishing the seaward boundary lines, the courts also had to address the legal problems of boundary delimitation.

Only Texas and Florida have been able to establish claims beyond three miles. In 1960, the Supreme Court recognized the three marine league boundaries in the Gulf of Mexico of both Florida, based on Congressional approval of its 1868 constitution, and Texas, based on its historic claim. See *United States v. Florida*, 363 U.S. 1, 363 U.S. 121, 80 S.Ct. 961, 4 L.Ed.2d 1025, 4 L.Ed.2d 1096 (1960); *United States v. Louisiana*, 363 U.S. 1, 363 U.S. 121, 80 S.Ct. 961, 4 L.Ed.2d 1025, 4 L.Ed.2d 1096 (1960). In 1969, the United States brought an action against the Atlantic seaboard states in which the Supreme Court upheld the reasoning in *California* and precluded claims beyond three miles. *United States v. Maine*, 420 U.S. 515, 95 S.Ct. 1155, 43 L.Ed.2d 363 (1975). Florida's 3-mile Atlantic seabed boundary was addressed in a separate consent decree. United States v. Florida, 425 U.S. 791 (1976).

b. Boundary Issues Raised by the SLA

The Supreme Court's dismissal of the claims to extended jurisdiction in the Atlantic settled finally the question of the extent of coastal state boundaries, but litigation has continued for decades over the exact position of the 3-mile seaward boundaries of coastal states.[1] Because the SLA did not provide a legal or technical basis for delimiting boundaries, the Supreme Court adopted the provisions of the 1958 Convention on the Territorial Sea and Contiguous Zone to deal with boundary delimitation questions. *United States v. California*, 381 U.S. 139, 85 S.Ct. 1401, 14 L.Ed.2d 296 (1965).

The most fundamental issue in boundary extension is identification of the baselines or basepoints from which the territorial sea is measured. As a general proposition, the boundary is measured from the mean low water line. Waters within baselines or closing lines of bays and the mouths of rivers, and between some fringe islands and the coast are internal or inland waters and not part of the territorial sea. See, e.g., *United States v. Alaska*, 521 U.S. 1, 117 S.Ct. 1888, 138 L.Ed.2d 231 (1997). In the case of rivers and bays, the limit of the

---

[1]   See Aaron L. Shalowitz, Boundary Problems Raised by the Submerged Lands Act, 54 Colum. L. Rev. 1021 (1954). See also Aaron L. Shalowitz, 1–2 Shore and Sea Boundaries (United States Government Printing Office 1962, 1964); Michael W. Reed, 3 Shore and Sea Boundaries (United States Government Printing Office 2000).

territorial sea must be measured from closing lines across the mouth of the water body, not from the low water line. A true bay, as opposed to a mere indentation in the coastline, is identified by applying the semicircle, twenty-four mile closing line test. In order to qualify as a closed bay, a body of water must have an area larger than a semicircle that uses the closing line of the bay as its diameter. In no event, however, can the closing line be more than twenty-four miles.

Historic bays are an exception to the semicircle, twenty-four mile closing line rule. For example, in the *Alabama and Mississippi Boundary Case,* the U.S. Supreme Court found that Mississippi Sound qualifies as a historic bay. See *United States v. Louisiana,* 470 U.S. 93, 105 S.Ct. 1074, 84 L.Ed.2d 73 (1985). The Court identified factors that are taken into account in determining whether a water body is a historic bay to include: (1) continuous exercise of authority over the area; (2) acquiescence by foreign nations; and (3) the vital interests of the country, including geographical configuration, economic interests, and national security. In the *Louisiana Boundary Case, United States v. Louisiana,* 394 U.S. 11, 89 S.Ct. 773, 22 L.Ed.2d 44 (1969), the Court rejected Louisiana's claim to a historic bay, but it did recognize that a state could conceivably establish such a historic claim to internal waters even in the absence of an international claim by the United States. See also *Alaska v. United States,* 545 U.S. 75, 125 S.Ct. 2137, 162 L.Ed.2d 57 (2005); *United States v. Alaska,* 422 U.S. 184, 95 S.Ct. 2240, 45 L.Ed.2d 109 (1975).

As a technical matter, it should be noted that ocean boundaries are not generally measured by lines running parallel to the coast but are enclosed by an "envelope of arcs." The envelope is created by connecting the outer limits of arcs extended from basepoints along the coast at a radius based on the breadth of the jurisdictional claim. The envelope of arcs method assures that, for example, a state seaward boundary is always three miles from the *nearest* point on the coastline. Through modern developments this method has been further enhanced. See William E. Ball and Albert J. Doughty, Three-Dimensional Coastline Projection Computational Techniques for Determining Offshore Boundaries (MMS 1999) https://www.boem.gov/ uploadedFiles/BOEM/Oil_and_Gas_Energy_ Program/Mapping_and_Data/99-0044.pdf.

c. Lingering Issues Raised by Extension of the U.S. Territorial Sea

The United States continued to assert and recognize only a three-mile territorial sea, because of national security concerns, long after most countries had claimed 12-mile territorial seas based on customary international law. On December 27, 1988, the United States radically changed its policy when President Reagan announced the extension of the United States territorial sea to twelve miles by Presidential Proclamation No. 5928. 3 C.F.R. 547 (1988). The proclamation explains that it applies only to the United States' position internationally and does nothing to alter domestic law. Congress has amended very few domestic laws to reflect this international claim. The extension of the United States territorial sea from three miles to twelve miles, however, has raised questions about the nature of the ownership of this area and has reopened the question of what should be the extent of state waters. For a complete discussion of the issues surrounding the twelve-mile territorial sea extension, see 1–2 Territorial Sea Journal (1990–92).

B.   COASTAL ZONE MANAGEMENT

1.   THE COASTAL ZONE MANAGEMENT ACT AND RELATED LEGISLATION

The federal Coastal Zone Management Act of 1972 (CZMA), 16 U.S.C.A. §§ 1451–1464, embodied the recognition by Congress that the "coastal zone"—the coasts and adjacent marginal seas—were areas of both state and national concern and could be best managed through a cooperative approach to planning and management of the area. The CZMA's original purposes were "to preserve, protect, develop, and where possible, to restore or enhance, the resources of the Nation's coastal zone for this and succeeding generations." Enacted during the same period as other major federal environmental legislation, the CZMA differed substantially from legislation like the Clean Air Act or the Clean Water Act. First, state participation in coastal zone management planning was completely voluntary. Federal standards or management would not be imposed if the state did not develop a plan following federal guidelines. Second, although there was a recognized national interest in effective coastal management, Congress also recognized that the type of land use planning and management required by the CZMA was traditionally within the domain of state and local governments.

The CZMA provides federal funding for states to develop and administer coastal programs according to guidelines set out in the Act. While the funding for program development and administration is a traditional incentive to encourage state cooperation, The CZMA provides an additional incentive for state participation—the so-called federal consistency requirement. This provision creates a kind of reverse preemption that assures a state that, with certain exceptions, federal agency activities and activities that are sponsored or permitted by the federal government will be consistent with the state-created and federally approved coastal management plan.

The states are given great flexibility in their approaches to coastal management and even in determining the area to be covered by the program. The CZMA only generally defines the coastal zone to include the territorial sea and adjacent lands "to the extent necessary to control shorelands, the uses of which have a direct and significant impact on the coastal waters." 16 U.S.C.A. § 1453(1). Each state defines the landward limits of its coastal zone for purposes of its management program.

The Washington coastal program was the first to receive federal approval in 1976. With approval of the Illinois program in 2012, all thirty-five eligible states and territories (including the Northern Marianas, Puerto Rico, the Virgin Islands, Guam, and American

Samoa) had successfully developed federally approved programs. In 2011, however, the legislature of Alaska failed to extend the state program and officially withdrew from the federal program on July 1. 2011. An initiative added to the 2012 ballot to reinstate the program in Alaska failed.

The CZMA has been amended a number of times. The 1973 Arab oil embargo and energy crisis of the mid-1970s led to major amendments to the CZMA in 1976 to facilitate energy facility siting and other energy development. The 1980 amendments continued to focus attention on coastal states incorporating national interests in coastal planning. With the original development period ending, funding for the CZMA was substantially reduced and new program goals and policies were introduced to enhance coastal management. The Coastal Management Reauthorization Act of 1985 included new procedures for the review and amendment of state coastal programs. The Coastal Zone Act Reauthorization Amendments of 1990 made major changes in the federal consistency provision to clarify its scope and application. A new Coastal Zone Enhancement Grant Program was created to encourage states to improve their plans in one or more of eight areas of coastal concern, including: (1) coastal wetlands protection, (2) management of development in high hazard areas, (3) public access, (4) control of marine debris, (5) studying cumulative and secondary impacts of coastal development, (6) special area management planning, (7) ocean resources planning, and (8) siting of coastal energy and government facilities. 16 U.S.C.A. § 1456b(a).

The 1990 amendments also created a major new requirement for state coastal programs, a Coastal Nonpoint Pollution Control Program, for protecting coastal waters from pollution from shoreline land uses. See id. at § 1455b(a). The 1996 CZMA amendments did not make major substantive changes.

The latest reauthorization expired in 1999; although several new provisions have been introduced, Congress has repeatedly been unable to pass reauthorization language. A 2010 report outlines why this has been the case and why reauthorization has become controversial:

> 1. Numerous stakeholders (participants, use and development interests, and environmentalists); and

> 2. Changing context, including events (like Hurricane Katrina and the BP oil spill), new scientific information (like knowledge concerning marine dead zones), economic trends (like rising energy prices), and climate change.

See generally Harold F. Upton, Coastal Zone Management Background and Reauthorization Issues (Congressional Research Service Report 10–16, Sept. 29, 2010).

The National Estuarine Sanctuaries Program, which was created in 1972 as a part of the Coastal Zone Management Act, has evolved into the current National Estuarine Research Reserve System. 16 U.S.C.A. § 1461. The purpose of the reserve system is to provide natural field laboratories of representative estuarine types for research and to enhance public understanding of estuaries and their functions by creating opportunities for education and interpretation. NOAA is responsible for developing estuarine research guidelines to establish common research principles and objectives for the national reserve research system. Financial assistance may be available to the states to acquire lands for management, educational, and interpretive purposes.

Twenty-eight estuarine research reserves have been designated nationally that are characteristic of different coastal regions and estuarine types. State governors nominate areas for inclusion in the program. NOAA designates an estuarine area upon finding that it is a representative estuarine ecosystem suitable for long-term research and that state laws provide sufficient protection to "ensure a stable environment for research."

Area-based coastal management is also carried out under the National Estuary Programs (NEP) established under § 320 of the Clean Water Act administered by the federal Environmental Protection Agency (EPA). State governors nominate estuaries of national significance for preparation of non-binding management plans by private and public stakeholders. Congress specified 16 estuaries to which EPA was to give priority in administering the program. One expert has summarized the NEP this way:

> The NEP is a watershed-based management approach to protecting our nation's estuaries.

Acceptance into the NEP leads to a comprehensive evaluation of all the problems in a given estuary and the development of strategies to address the most serious problems threatening the long-term health of the estuary. Public participation in this effort is one of the conceptual cornerstones of the NEP, although meaningful participation by the public may not be fully realized in all cases. Management plans created under the NEP do not have the force of law, but they can and do motivate federal, state and local regulators into action.

Matthew W. Bowden, *An Overview of the National Estuary Program*, 11 Natural Resources & Environment 35 (1996).

The Chesapeake Bay Program authorized by Clean Water Act § 117 served as a model for the NEP. That program proceeded one significant step further to a multi-party agreement in which the member states have agreed to watershed level regulation of land use and water quality to meet agreed ecosystem performance goals such as a 40% reduction in controllable nitrogen and phosphorus loadings to the bay toward which there has been significant progress. Maryland, Virginia, Pennsylvania, the District of Columbia; over 50 federal agencies, and more than 2,000 local governments have implemented the program without laws that mandate such cooperation. See Harry R. Hughes and Thomas W. Burke, Jr., *The Cleanup of the Nation's Largest Estuary: A Test of Political Will*, 11 Natural Resources & Environment 30 (1996).

On the west coast, the state-federal CALFED Bay-Delta Program (now the Delta Stewardship Council) focused on San Francisco Bay and its tributaries with goals of improving statewide water supply reliability, and protecting and restoring the Delta ecosystem. The process has led to adoption of a Delta Plan in 2013 and state legislation, the Delta Reform Act, which requires state and local agencies to be consistent with the Delta Plan.

Also, under the Estuary Restoration Act of 2000, 33 U.S.C.A. § 2901, EPA, NOAA, Fish and Wildlife Service, Army Corps of Engineers, and Department of Agriculture, work in concert to restore estuaries. The purpose of the Act is to promote the restoration of estuary habitat; to develop a national Estuary Habitat Restoration Strategy for creating and maintaining effective partnerships within the federal government and with the private sector; to provide federal assistance for and promote efficient financing of estuary habitat restoration projects, and to develop and enhance monitoring, data sharing, and research capabilities. The final Estuary Habitat Restoration Strategy was approved in 2012. The Strategy attempts to focus program efforts and limited resources on areas not addressed by other federal programs.

2. DEVELOPMENT AND APPROVAL OF STATE CZM PROGRAMS

The development stage for state coastal management programs turned out to be a long, arduous process in most states. In general, states lacked statutory bases to implement coastal management programs, and local governments often balked at what was perceived as state usurpation of local planning and zoning functions.

The CZMA currently sets out the requirements for a state management program to receive federal approval at 16 U.S.C.A. §§ 1455–1456. The requirements can be broadly categorized as (1) informational and definitional, (2) institutional and organizational, (3) procedural, and (4) planning. Informational and definitional requirements include identifying boundaries of the coastal zone, defining permissible land and water uses, inventorying areas of particular concern, and defining "beach." Institutionally, the program must identify the means and legal authorities by which the state can carry out the program and the organizational structure to implement the program. The program must include procedures for intergovernmental coordination and public participation. Planning processes must be developed for prioritizing uses in the coastal zone, identifying and preserving areas of special "conservation, recreational, ecological, historical, and esthetic values," and for dealing with shoreline erosion and sea level rise. See id. at § 1452(2)(B) and (3). Finally, the program must include a planning process for energy facilities that "provides for adequate consideration of the national interest."

The Secretary of Commerce, currently through the National Oceanic and Atmospheric Administration's (NOAA) Office for Coastal Management, has the responsibility for determining whether a program meets the requirements of section 1455 and the purposes and policies of the CZMA. Programs are generally submitted in the form of an environmental impact statement meeting the requirements of the National Environmental Policy Act (NEPA), 42 U.S.C.A. § 4332. Program approval must include a determination that the views of federal agencies affected by the program have been "adequately considered."

In *American Petroleum Institute v. Knecht*, 456 F.Supp. 889 (C.D.Cal. 1978), the American Petroleum Institute (API) challenged the approval of the California Coastal Zone Management Program (CZMP). API's primary arguments were that the CZMP lacked the specificity necessary to meet the CZMA's requirements and that the program did not adequately consider the national interest. API contended that the program should "include detailed criteria establishing a sufficiently high degree of predictability to enable a private user of the coastal zone to say with certainty that a given project [meets the standards of the CZMP]." The federal district court first considered Congress' definition of a "management program," which emphasized that the program set "forth objectives, policies and standards to guide public and private uses of . . . the coastal zone." The court determined that there was no intent to require a "zoning map" or a predictive device for private users to rely upon. Instead, the program is intended to create a framework within which the state can make rational decisions balancing competing interests. The court also rejected API's argument that adequate consideration of the

national   interest   entailed   "affirmative
accommodation of energy facilities [as] a quid pro quo
for [program] approval."

Approved coastal programs are subject to
continuing review by NOAA to determine the extent
to which the state is implementing and enforcing the
program. Program approval may be withdrawn, or
financial assistance may be suspended under certain
circumstances. See16 U.S.C. § 1458(a).

In the 1987 review of California's coastal program,
NOAA required that the California Coastal
Commission, as California's implementing agency
under the California Coastal Act of 1976, prepare and
submit for approval guidelines that would provide
greater predictability for parties seeking consistency
determinations for proposed activities affecting the
Outer Continental Shelf. The Commission refused,
and NOAA withheld most of the program's
administrative funding. Congress enacted legislation
restoring the funds, but the NOAA grant continued
to be conditioned on the state adopting consistency
guidelines to be submitted to NOAA "for review and
approval as a program change." In *California v.
Mack*, 693 F.Supp. 821 (N.D.Cal. 1988), the state
challenged NOAA's authority to coerce modification
of a previously approved program by conditioning
further federal funding. The federal district court
held that NOAA does not have the authority to revisit
the provisions of an approved plan or to coerce,
through its power over funding, an alteration of the
approved program itself. The court viewed NOAA's
action as a reversal of its position in *American*

Petroleum Institute v. Knecht concerning the specificity of state programs and an attempt "to manipulate the coastal policy of the states ... by forcing a state to choose between modifying the program and losing federal financial assistance under the CZMA." Id. at 826. The court enjoined NOAA from withdrawing program approval or withholding funds based on the unlawfully imposed condition.

The 1990 amendments to the CZMA clarify the procedures necessary for NOAA to withdraw funds or approval of a state coastal program. If a state fails to adhere to its approved program or the terms of a grant, financial assistance may not be suspended until NOAA provides the state's governor with specifications and a schedule for compliance. Program approval may not be withdrawn unless the state fails to take the actions required for compliance. See 16 U.S.C.A. § 1458(c)–(d).

States may amend or modify an approved coastal program by submitting the amendment to the Secretary for review. In general, the Secretary must approve or disapprove the amendment within a maximum of 120 days unless additional time is necessary to meet NEPA requirements. If the amendment is not disapproved within that period, it is conclusively presumed to be approved. Id. § 1455(e)(1)–(2). Until the amendment is approved, it cannot be considered an enforceable policy for purposes of consistency determinations. Id. § 1455(e)(3)(B). NOAA regulations distinguish between a program amendment and routine program implementation. See 15 C.F.R. § 923.80–923.84. An "amendment" involves "substantial changes in, or substantial changes to, enforceable policies or authorities related to" certain aspects of a coastal management plan, 15 C.F.R. § 923.80(c), and requires approval under section 1455(c). "Routine program implementation," however, is a "[f]urther detailing of a State's program that is the result of implementing" the approved program and is not subject to the amendment approval process. 15 C.F.R. § 923.84(a).

In *AES Sparrows Point LNG, LLC v. Smith*, 527 F.3d 120 (4th Cir. 2008), Baltimore County had attempted to stop development of an LNG terminal by passing a categorical ban on LNG terminals in the Chesapeake Bay Critical Area that the CMP did not previously contain. The legislation was, however, never presented to NOAA for approval as part of the CMP. The court found that "[t]his, in our view, constitutes a 'substantial change' in the 'uses subject to management' by the CMP. It also implicates the 'national interest' because it involved 'the siting of facilities such as energy facilities which are of greater than local significance.'" 16 U.S.C. § 1455(d)(8). Without the submission and approval of the change by NOAA, the ban could not become part of the CMP.

3.   OPERATION OF THE CZMA

a. Program Approaches

Some states, such as North Carolina, South Carolina, Washington, and California, have passed comprehensive legislation to create their coastal management programs; other states, such as Oregon and Florida, have "networked" existing legislation and regulations under the umbrella of an executive order or policy statement. See Gilbert L. Finnell, Jr., Coastal Land Management in Florida, 1980 Am. B. Found. Res. J. 307. The CZMA gives states a great deal of flexibility in programmatic approaches. The Act recognizes three general approaches a state may adopt:

(A) State establishment of criteria and standards for local implementation, subject to administrative review and enforcement.

(B) Direct State land and water use planning and regulation.

(C) State administrative review for consistency with the management program of all development plans, projects, or land and water use regulations, including exceptions and variances thereto, proposed by any State or local authority or private developer, with power to approve or disapprove after public notice and an opportunity for hearings.

16 U.S.C.A. § 1455(d)(11).

b. Coastal Zone Boundaries

The definition of "coastal zone" in the CZMA at 16 U.S.C.A. § 1453(1) reads as follows:

(1) The term "coastal zone" means the coastal waters (including the lands therein and

thereunder) and the adjacent shorelands (including the waters therein and thereunder), strongly influenced by each other and in proximity to the shorelines of the several coastal states, and includes islands, transitional and intertidal areas, salt marshes, wetlands, and beaches. The zone extends . . . seaward to the outer limit of State title and ownership under the Submerged Lands Act. . . . The zone extends inland from the shorelines only to the extent necessary to control shorelands, the uses of which have a direct and significant impact on the coastal waters, and to control those geographical areas which are likely to be affected by or vulnerable to sea level rise. Excluded from the coastal zone are lands the use of which is by law subject solely to the discretion of or which is held in trust by the Federal Government, its officers, or agents.

The 1990 CZMA amendments changed the seaward boundary provisions to include all state ocean waters to correct the anomaly in Florida's coastal zone program. Although Florida's state waters in the Gulf of Mexico extend nine nautical miles, the CZMA had formerly limited its "coastal zone" to three miles. The definition of the landward boundary of the coastal zone allows major variation from one state to another. For example, North Carolina's Coastal Area Management Act defines the inland portion of the coastal zone as the area encompassed by all the counties bounded by coastal waters; Hawaii's coastal zone includes the entire state; California, on the other hand, defines the land portion of its coastal zone as a 1,000-yard strip extending inland from its coastal waters; Massachusetts' coastal zone extends landward 100 feet beyond the first major land transportation route encountered (e.g., a road, highway, or rail line), and also includes all of Cape Cod, Martha's Vineyard, Nantucket, and Gosnold.

Federal lands are excluded from the definition of "coastal zone." This does not mean, however, that activities on federal enclaves within a state's coastal zone are not subject to any state regulation. In *California Coastal Commission v. Granite Rock Co.*, 480 U.S. 572, 107 S.Ct. 1419, 94 L.Ed.2d 577 (1987), a mining company asserted that the California Coastal Commission had no authority to impose environmental permit conditions upon its mining activities on unpatented mining claims located in a national forest. Granite Rock argued that the Commission's permit requirements were preempted by several federal statutes including the CZMA's exclusion of federal lands from the definition of "coastal zone." The U.S. Supreme Court did not decide whether the federal lands involved were in fact excluded from the definition of "coastal zone," but concluded "that even if all federal lands are excluded from the CZMA definition of coastal zone, the CZMA does not automatically preempt all state regulation of activities on federal lands." In *Secretary of the Interior v. California*, 464 U.S. 312, 104 S.Ct. 656, 78 L.Ed.2d 496 (1984), the Supreme Court pointed out that the CZMA's consistency provisions were intended "to reach at least some activities conducted

in those federal enclaves excluded from the ...
definition of the coastal zone."

c. The CZMA and the Commerce Clause

State coastal management plans can significantly
obstruct industrial and energy development. For
example, Delaware prohibits all new heavy industry
within two miles of the coast, and a number of states
ban oil drilling in all or part of the coastal zone. In
Norfolk Southern Corp. v. Oberly, 822 F.2d 388 (3d
Cir. 1987), Norfolk Southern's plan to initiate a coal-
lightering service in Delaware Bay ran afoul of the
Delaware Coastal Zone Act (CZA) provisions banning
bulk product transfers in the coastal zone. In
response to Norfolk Southern's claim that the CZA
violates the dormant Commerce Clause, Delaware
argued that approval of its coastal program under the
federal CZMA constitutes Congressional consent for
the ban or, alternatively, that the ban does not offend
the Commerce Clause.

The Third Circuit Court of Appeals found that
although Congressional consent may be a defense to
a Commerce Clause challenge, neither the language
of the CZMA, the legislative history, nor case law
indicates an intent in the CZMA to expand or to alter
state authority in relation to the Commerce Clause.
However, in applying a deferential standard of
review to balance the incidental burdens on
interstate commerce with the "putative local
benefits," the court found that the nondiscriminatory
burden does not violate the Commerce Clause.

In *Ray v. ARCO*, 435 U.S. 151, 98 S.Ct. 988, 55 L.Ed.2d 179 (U.S. 1978), the U.S. Supreme Court summarily rejected the state of Washington's arguments that approval of its coastal management plan, which incorporated the Washington Tanker Safety Law, precluded the law's preemption by the federal Ports and Waterways Safety Act. Id. fn. 28.

4.   INTERGOVERNMENTAL COOPERATION AND THE CZMA—THE FEDERAL CONSISTENCY REQUIREMENT

a. Evolution of the Consistency Requirement

Federal grants to assist states in developing and administering coastal management programs provided an initial impetus for states to participate in coastal zone planning. But the so-called federal consistency requirement provides the major incentive for states to continue and maintain their programs. Prior to the 1990 amendments, CZMA section 307(c)(1), 16 U.S.C.A. § 1456(c)(1), provided that federal actions and activities "directly affecting the coastal zone" must be conducted "in a manner which is, to the maximum extent practicable, consistent with approved state management programs." In addition, federally permitted activities "affecting land or water uses in the coastal zone" had to be "conducted in a manner consistent with the program." Specific provisions required outer continental shelf (OCS) exploration and development plans to be consistent with state programs. Id.

(1) The Limiting Effect of Secretary of the Interior v. California

In *Secretary of the Interior v. California*, 464 U.S. 312, 104 S.Ct. 656, 78 L.Ed.2d 496 (1984), the state of California and others sued the Secretary of Interior on the ground that a proposed sale of oil and gas leases on outer continental shelf (OCS) tracts off the California coast could not be conducted without the Department of Interior making a consistency determination as required by CZMA section 307(c)(1). The Secretary argued that because the proposed lease sale was not an "activity directly affecting" the California coastal zone, no consistency determination was required.

The Outer Continental Shelf Lands Act (OCSLA), 43 U.S.C.A. §§ 1331–1356, divides the process for development of oil and gas OCS resources into four stages. A fifth stage, decommissioning, has been created by Interior Department regulations. 30 C.F.R. Parts 250, 256. The first is the five-year leasing plan prepared by the Department of Interior. Id. at § 1344. The second stage is the lease sale itself. Id. at § 1337. A lease purchaser acquires only the right to conduct limited preliminary activities on the OCS, such as geophysical and other surveys. The issue in *Secretary of the Interior v. California* was whether these preliminary activities "directly affect" the coastal zone. The third stage, exploration, and the fourth stage, development and production, cannot take place until after plans have been submitted for review and approved by the Secretary of the Interior. At these stages, the Outer

Continental Shelf Lands Act, 43 U.S.C.A. § 1340(c)(2), itself, as well as section 307(c)(3)(B) of the CZMA, refer to the CZMA consistency requirement, and a consistency determination is specifically required.

In a five-four decision of the Supreme Court, Justice O'Connor delivered a majority opinion that left the consistency doctrine in a state of confusion. The Court rejected the state's argument that "leasing sets in motion a chain of events that culminates in oil and gas development, and that leasing therefore 'directly affects' the coastal zone within the meaning of Section 307(c)(1)." The Court noted that the lease sale authorized only preliminary exploration "that has no significant effect on the coastal zone" and is only one "in a series of decisions that may culminate in activities directly affecting that zone." The Court went on to suggest that only federal activities conducted "in" the coastal zone could have direct effects. "Section 307(c)(1)s 'directly affecting' language was aimed at activities conducted or supported by federal agencies on federal lands physically situated in the coastal zone but excluded from the zone as formally defined by the Act." Ultimately, however, the Court was persuaded by the fact that although consistency of OCS activities during the exploration and development stages is addressed in both the OCSLA and CZMA, neither act specifically requires consistency review at the lease sale stage. The Court stated:

As we have noted, the logical paragraph to examine in connection with a lease sale is not

Sec. 307(c)(1), but Sec. 307(c)(3). . . . [L]ease sales can no longer aptly be characterized as "directly affecting" the coastal zone. Since 1978 the sale of a lease grants the lessee the right to conduct only very limited, "preliminary activities" on the OCS. . . .

It is argued, nonetheless, that a lease sale is a crucial step. Large sums of money change hands, and the sale may therefore generate momentum that makes eventual exploration, development, and production inevitable. On the other side, it is argued that consistency review at the lease sale stage is at best inefficient, and at worst impossible: Leases are sold before it is certain if, where, or how exploration will actually occur.

The choice between these two policy arguments is not ours to make; it has already been made by Congress. In the 1978 OCSLA amendments Congress decided that the better course is to postpone consistency review until the two later stages of OCS planning, and to rely on less formal input from State Governors and local governments in the two earlier ones. It is not for us to negate the lengthy, detailed, and coordinated provisions of CZMA Sec. 307(c)(3)(B), and OCSLA Secs. 1344–1346 and 1351, by a superficially plausible but ultimately unsupportable construction of two words in CZMA Sec. 307(c)(1).

Id. at 464 U.S. 343.

The Court's specific holding was that section 307(c)(1) did not mandate consistency review for OCS lease sales, but some agencies read the case more broadly. The U.S. Army Corps of Engineers, for example, adopted the interpretation that federal activities must be conducted "in" the coastal zone to have direct effects. See, e.g., Corps Ocean Dumping Regulations, 53 Fed. Reg. 14,902 (1988).

(2) Revitalizing the Consistency Requirement

After several years and a number of proposed amendments to CZMA section 307 to reverse *Secretary of Interior v. California,* the 1990 Coastal Management Act Reauthorization Amendments readdressed the federal consistency requirement. The federal consistency provision of CZMA section 307(c)(1)(A), 16 U.S.C.A. § 1456(c)(1)(A), currently provides:

(1)(A) Each Federal agency activity *within or outside* the coastal zone that *affects* any land or water use or natural resource of the coastal zone shall be carried out in a manner that is consistent to the maximum extent practicable with the enforceable policies of approved State management programs. A Federal agency activity shall be subject to this paragraph unless it is subject to paragraph (2) [federal development projects] or (3) [federally licensed or permitted activities and OCS exploration and development plans]. (Emphasis added.)

Overview of Federal Consistency Review

	Federal Agency Activities and Development Projects	Federal License or Permit Activities	Outer Continental Shelf Plans	Federal Assistance to State and Local Governments
Proposed action subject to participant review if it...	Affects any land or water use or natural resource of state coastal zone, regardless of location of activity.	Affects any land or water use or natural resource of state coastal zone and activity is listed in participant's CMP or NOAA approves review of unlisted activity.	Affects any land or water use or natural resource of state coastal zone.	Affects any land or water use or natural resource of state coastal zone and activity is listed in participant's CMP or participant reviews unlisted activity.
Consistency Requirement	*Consistent to the maximum extent practicable* with participant CMP enforceable policies.	Consistent with participant CMP enforceable policies	Consistent with participant CMP enforceable policies	Consistent with participant CMP enforceable policies
Participant Review Period	60 days (plus 15-day extension or alternative period agreed to by participant and federal agency)	6 months	3 months (participant may extend to 6 months)	Participant clearinghouse schedule
Impact of Participant Objection	Federal agency may proceed only if it provides legal basis for being *consistent to the maximum extent practicable*	Federal agency may not authorize activity unless Secretary overrides objection	Federal agency may not authorize activity unless Secretary overrides objection	Federal agency may not authorize activity unless Secretary overrides objection
Conflict Resolution	Mediation by Secretary of Commerce or OCM. (voluntary process and nonbinding decision)	Applicant may appeal to Secretary of Commerce to override participant objection (binding decision)	Applicant may appeal to Secretary of Commerce to override participant objection (binding decision)	Applicant may appeal to Secretary of Commerce to override participant objection (binding decision)

Source: Congressional Research Service, Report 45460, Coastal Zone Management Act (CZMA): Overview and Issues Congress 9 (January 15, 2019).

Note that the amendments do not specifically address OCS lease sales. The section does, however, specifically negate the interpretation that only activities conducted within the coastal zone are subject to consistency review. It remains possible for the Secretary of Interior to find that a particular lease sale does not "affect" a certain state's coastal zone.

b.   Limitations on State Consistency Review

The CZMA imposes certain limitations on state exercise of a "veto power" over federal agencies by use of the federal consistency requirement. First, a state must demonstrate that the activity is inconsistent with "enforceable policies" of its coastal management plan. Enforceable policies are "[s]tate policies which are legally binding through constitutional provisions, laws, regulations, land use plans, ordinances, or judicial or administrative decisions, by which a [s]tate exerts control over private and public land and water uses and natural resources in the coastal zone." 15 U.S.C.A. § 1453(6a). Through the phrase "to the maximum extent practicable," federal laws applicable to the agencies' operations can limit federal agency compliance with state programs. The CZMA also provides a mechanism to exempt inconsistent elements of a federal agency's activity from compliance "if the President determines that the activity is in the paramount interest of the United States." 16 U.S.C.A. § 1456(c)(1)(B). A finding by a state that OCS plans or a federal permittee's activities are not consistent with the state coastal plan may also be overridden by the Secretary of Commerce if the activity is "consistent with the objectives of [the CZMA] or is otherwise necessary in the interest of national security." Id. at § 1456(c)(3)(A)–(B).

Finally, states have a limited time to exercise consistency review to prevent delaying federal actions or issuance of federal permits or approvals. For example, if a state fails to respond within six months of receiving a complete consistency certification in regard to a federal license or permit, the state's concurrence will be "conclusively presumed." 16 U.S.C. § 1456(c)(3)(A). See also *Weaver's Cove Energy Llc. v. Rhode Island Coastal Resources Management Council*, 583 F.Supp.2d 259 (D. R.I. 2008), affirmed 589 F.3d 458 (1st Cir. 2009).

c. What Is a Federal Agency Action?

NOAA's 2006 regulations provide that:

The term "Federal agency activity" means any functions performed by or on behalf of a Federal agency in the exercise of its statutory responsibilities. The term "Federal agency activity" includes a range of activities where a Federal agency makes a proposal for action initiating an activity or series of activities when coastal effects are reasonably foreseeable, e.g., a Federal agency's proposal to physically alter coastal resources, a plan that is used to direct future agency actions, a proposed rulemaking that alters uses of the coastal zone. . . . 15 C.F.R. § 930.31 (a).

In *State of California v. Norton*, 311 F.3d 1162 (9th Cir. 2002), the 9th Circuit Court of Appeals required the Department of Interior to provide consistency determinations for lease suspensions it issued for 36 OCS leases off the California coast. NOAA's view is that "Federal agency activities do not include interim or preliminary activities incidental or related to a proposed action for which a consistency determination has been or will be submitted and which do not make new commitments for actions with coastal effects. Such interim or preliminary activities are not independent actions subject to federal consistency review." 71 Fed. Reg. 788, 807 (2006). NOAA distinguished the decision in *California v. Norton* as follows:

> The heart of the Ninth Circuit's decision is that lease suspensions cannot be categorically exempt from CZMA review. Applying the CZMA "effects test," the Ninth Circuit found that the 36 lease suspensions at issue had coastal effects. It is NOAA's view that the Ninth Circuit's coastal effects determination is limited to the 36 leases in that case. NOAA believes that in all other foreseeable instances, lease suspensions would not be subject to federal consistency review since (1) they do not generally authorize activities with coastal effects, and (2) if lease suspensions did result in activities with coastal effects, they should be addressed in a State's consistency review of the lease sale, EP [exploration program] or DPP [development and production program].

Id. at 807.

Note that the original lease sales in *California v. Norton* had not been subject to consistency review. Without the suspension, the leases would have expired.

d. Effects Triggering Consistency Review

Courts have disagreed as to what kinds of effects will trigger consistency review by a federal agency. The primary controversy has arisen in considering the effects of offshore oil and gas exploration and development. In *Kean v. Watt*, 1982 WL 170985 (D.N.J. 1982), the only significant effect of potential OCS development in the coastal zone was the financial burden on commercial fishermen that destruction or obstruction of an OCS fishery would have. There was no evidence that the development would have any environmental effects on resources in the coastal zone. The federal district court held that federal activities outside the coastal zone that affect only commercial activities in the coastal zone, and not the natural environment, do not directly affect the coastal zone and trigger the federal consistency requirement.

The federal district court in *Conservation Law Foundation v. Watt*, 560 F.Supp. 561 (D.Mass. 1983), specifically rejected the *Kean* court's conclusion. In a challenge to an OCS lease sale by the state of Massachusetts, the Conservation Law Foundation, and ten other environmental groups, the court found that the CZMA, by its own terms, recognized economic development within the Act's purposes and that the legislative history supported the consideration of both the social and economic effects in the coastal zone.

The 1990 amendments changed the language of section 307(c)(1) from "directly affecting the coastal zone" to "affects any land or water use or natural resource of the coastal zone." This change was not particularly illuminating and can be read to support either court's position. The only legislative history concerning the provision seems to support the broader reading of the statute. The chairman of the House Merchant Marine and Fisheries Committee explained:

> The question of whether a specific federal agency activity may affect any natural resource, land use, or water use in the coastal zone is determined by the federal agency. The Committee intends this determination to include effects in the coastal zone which the federal agency may reasonably anticipate as a result of its action, including cumulative and secondary effects. Therefore, the term "affecting" is to be construed broadly, including direct effects which are caused by the activity and occur at the same time and place, and indirect effects which may be caused by the activity and are later in time or farther removed in distance, but are still reasonably foreseeable.

136 Cong. Rec. H8068, 8075–76 (daily ed. Sept. 26, 1990).

Current regulations provide that:

[t]he term "effect on any coastal use or resource" means any reasonably foreseeable effect on any coastal use or resource resulting from a Federal agency activity or federal license or permit activity (including all types of activities subject to the federal consistency requirement under

subparts C, D, E, F and I of this part.) Effects are not just environmental effects but include effects on coastal uses. Effects include both direct effects which result from the activity and occur at the same time and place as the activity, and indirect (cumulative and secondary) effects which result from the activity and are later in time or farther removed in distance but are still reasonably foreseeable. Indirect effects are effects resulting from the incremental impact of the federal action when added to other past, present, and reasonably foreseeable actions, regardless of what person(s) undertake(s) such actions.

15 C.F.R. § 930.11(g) (2006). See also, *Entergy Nuclear Operations, Inc. v. New York State Dep't of State*, 28 N.Y.3d 279, 292, 66 N.E.3d 1062, 1070 (2016) ("application for a license to operate the Indian Point nuclear reactors for an additional 20 years is a new federal action, involving a new project, with different impacts and concerns than were present when the initial environmental impact statements were issued over 40 years ago" and requires consistency review).

e. Interstate Consistency

The consistency provisions can also lead to interstate conflicts when an activity that requires a federal permit or approval is not consistent with the coastal program policies of another state that may be affected by the activity. See 15 C.F.R. § 930.150(a); *In the Consistency Appeal of Islander East Pipeline*

Company, L.L.C. From an Objection by the State of Connecticut (2004). The CZMA does not specifically address whether consistency applies in such situations. In *In the Consistency Appeal of the Virginia Electric and Power Company from an Objection by the North Carolina Department of Environment, Health and Natural Resources* (1994), the state of North Carolina objected to water being drawn from Lake Gaston, on the boundary of the two states, to provide water to Virginia Beach. On the appeal of North Carolina's determination that the activity is inconsistent with its coastal program, the Secretary of Commerce found that the plain language of the statute required that the federal government apply the consistency provision to such activities. Specifically addressing the sensitive issue of allowing one state an effective "veto" over another state's activities, the Secretary stated:

> While the CZMA does not give one state direct authority to control activities in another state, the CZMA does grant to states with federally approved coastal management programs the right to seek conditions on or prohibit the issuance of federal permits and licenses that would "affect" their state. Thus, Congress has, in effect, granted states with a federally approved coastal management program, in exchange for their protecting the nation's coasts, the right to ensure that federal permittees and licensees will not further degrade those coasts. The ability to prevent the granting of federal permits and licenses is a federal authority which has been granted to coastal states, not a state

authority which has been usurped from the
states. However, as a safeguard to a state's
unrestrained use of this authority, an applicant
can, as the City has, appeal for an override by
the Secretary of Commerce.

Id.

Regulations adopted in December 2000 also
recognize the requirement of consistency for
"interstate coastal effects." 15 C.F.R. § 930.150(a)
provides:

A federal activity may affect coastal uses or
resources of a State other than the State in
which the activity will occur. Effective coastal
management is fostered by ensuring that
activities having such reasonably foreseeable
interstate coastal effects are conducted
consistent with the enforceable policies of the
management program of each affected State.

The regulations also impose limitations on
application of the consistency requirement in the
interstate context. 15 C.F.R. § 930.154 requires
states to list the kind and geographic location of
activities for which they intend to conduct interstate
consistency review. States must also demonstrate the
effects of such activities, as well as "include evidence
of consultation with States in which the activity will
occur, evidence of consultation with relevant Federal
agencies, and any agreements with other States and
Federal agencies regarding coordination of
activities." The list must be approved by NOAA as a

routine program change in order for a state to subject a federal action to interstate review.

f.   Federal License or Permit

The consistency requirement applies to applicants for federal licenses or permits. See *Mountain Rhythm Resources v. FERC*, 302 F.3d 958 (9th Cir. 2002); *United States v. San Juan Bay Marina*, 239 F.3d 400 (1st Cir. 2001). But different statutes also refer to a wide range of other types of federal "approvals" that may be required for particular activities. The term "license or permit" has been defined broadly in NOAA's regulations to include:

> any authorization that an applicant is required by law to obtain in order to conduct activities affecting any land or water use or natural resource of the coastal zone and that any Federal agency is empowered to issue to an applicant. The term ... does not include OCS plans, and federal license or permit activities described in detail in OCS plans ... or leases issued pursuant to lease sales conducted by a Federal agency (e.g., outer continental shelf (OCS) oil and gas lease sales conducted by the Minerals Management Service [now BOEM] or oil and gas lease sales conducted by the Bureau of Land Management). Lease sales conducted by a Federal agency are Federal agency activities under subpart C of [the CZMA].

15 C.F.R. § 930.51(a).

The definition of "license or permit" was modified in consistency regulations issued in 2006 to assure the term is not "overly-inclusive." Discussion of the regulation states that the definition creates a four-part test "to capture *any form* of federal license or permit that is: (1) Required by Federal law, (2) authorizes an activity, (3) the activity authorized has reasonably foreseeable coastal effects, and (4) the authorization is not incidental to a federal license or permit previously reviewed by the State." 71 Fed. Reg. 787 (2006).

g. Maximum Extent Practicable

While federal permittees and OCS developers must carry out their activities in a manner consistent with an affected state's coastal plan, federal agencies are only charged with consistency "to the maximum extent practicable." 16 U.S.C.A. § 1456(c)(1). This is not an escape clause for federal agencies to invoke when consistency with state programs is inconvenient but is an affirmative obligation. NOAA regulations explain the phrase as follows:

> The term "consistent to the maximum extent practicable" means fully consistent with the enforceable policies of management programs unless full consistency is prohibited by existing law applicable to the Federal agency.

15 C.F.R. § 903.32(a)(I).

In many cases it is not clear whether other federal statutory provisions preempt the CZMA's consistency requirement. For example, the eighth circuit Court of Appeals held in *Minnesota v. Hoffman*, 543 F.2d 1198 (8th Cir. 1976), that section 404 of the Clean Water Act exempts the Corps of Engineers from any state requirements relating to the discharge of dredged spoil. The Corps has also maintained that the Ocean Dumping Act, 33 U.S.C.A. §§ 1401–1445, may preempt the CZMA. See 33 C.F.R. § 336.2(C). The Ninth Circuit Court of Appeals held, however, that the Navy was required to obtain a state permit under Washington's Shoreline Management Act, part of the state coastal program, before continuing with dredging for a homeport project. *Friends of the Earth v. United States Navy*, 841 F.2d 927 (9th Cir. 1988); accord, *California Coastal Commission v. United States*, 5 F.Supp.2d 1106 (S.D.Cal. 1998).

h. "Positive" Consistency

In *Cape May Greene, Inc. v. Warren*, 698 F.2d 179 (3d Cir. 1983), the Third Circuit Court of Appeals addressed the issue of whether the federal government can deny, limit, or condition assistance to an activity that is consistent with a state's coastal management program. The court found that federal Environmental Protection Agency (EPA) could not condition funding for an indispensable sewage treatment plant on the denial of new hookups to development in the contiguous floodplain and other sensitive lands. The condition effectively precluded development in areas that had been designated as development areas in both the local comprehensive plan and the state coastal management plan. The court held that the EPA had acted arbitrarily and capriciously, particularly in failing to act consistently with the state's coastal program to the maximum extent practicable as required by the CZMA.

In a case remarkably similar to *Cape May Greene,* the Fourth Circuit Court of Appeals upheld a condition on a federal grant for a municipal sewage collection plant that limited access by new development to the federally funded project. The court in *Shanty Town Associates Ltd. Partnership v. Environmental Protection Agency,* 843 F.2d 782 (4th Cir. 1988), noted that the CZMA specifically provides that nothing in the federal consistency provisions diminishes or modifies existing federal laws or "shall in any way affect any requirement" imposed by the Clean Water Act. See 16 U.S.C.A. § 1456(e)–(f). The EPA was not interfering in local land use decisions but acting on specific findings that limitations were necessary to prevent a decline in water quality. See also, *Loveladies Harbor v. Baldwin,* 751 F.2d 376 (D.N.J. 1984)(upholding the denial of a Corps of Engineers permit to fill a wetland although the property owners in had received a state permit and water quality certification).

NOAA regulations now attempt to preclude an interpretation that the CZMA imposes a "positive consistency" requirement by providing that federal agencies may continue to impose stricter standards notwithstanding more permissive criteria in a state coastal program. See 5 C.F.R. § 930.39(d).

i. Appealing Consistency Determinations

The CZMA provides two procedures for dealing with disagreements concerning consistency determinations: 1) a mediation process for disagreements between federal agencies and coastal states, 16 U.S.C.A. § 1456(h); and 2) a Secretarial appeal process for federal permits and OCS exploration and development plans that are found by a state to be inconsistent with the state program. 16 U.S.C.A. §§ 1456(c)(3)(A)–(B). Technically, the term "appeal" is a misnomer. The Secretary examines the state's objection for compliance with the CZMA and conducts a *de novo* inquiry of whether the activity is consistent with the objectives of the CZMA or necessary in the interest of national security. The Secretary does not review whether the state was correct in its determination that the proposed activity was inconsistent with its coastal management program.

The fact that states that are dissatisfied with the mediation process can appeal consistency determinations in the courts and seek to enjoin agency actions that do not meet the requirements of CZMA section 307 has led to some concern that the federal consistency requirement may not serve the national interest. The 1990 amendments to the CZMA dealt with that contingency by providing a Presidential exemption in certain circumstances. After a court judgment finding a federal agency has not complied with the consistency provisions and a certification by the Secretary of Commerce that mediation is unlikely to resolve the compliance problem, the Secretary may request presidential intervention. Certain elements of the agency's action may be exempted from compliance if the President finds the activity is "in the paramount interest of the United States." 16 U.S.C.A. § 1456(1)(B). This presidential exemption was exercised by President Bush in 2008 to allow "the use of mid-frequency active sonar in [naval] exercises in the paramount interest of the United States."

Federal permit applicants or OCS developers who are denied permits or plan approval because of a state's negative determination on consistency can appeal the decision to the Secretary of Commerce. The Secretary can override the state decision and allow the permit to be issued if she or he finds that the activity is "consistent with the objectives of the [CZMA] or is otherwise necessary in the interest of national security." In order for the Secretary to override a state's consistency determination on the former grounds, the applicant must meet all three criteria set out at 15 C.F.R. § 930.121:

(a) The activity furthers the national interest as articulated in § 302 or § 303 of the Act, in a significant or substantial manner.

(b) The national interest furthered by the activity outweighs the activity's adverse coastal effects, when those effects are considered separately or cumulatively.

(c) There is no reasonable alternative available which would permit the activity to be conducted in a manner consistent with the enforceable policies of the management program. The Secretary may consider but is not limited to considering previous appeal decisions, alternatives described in state objection letters and alternatives and other information submitted during the appeal. The Secretary shall not consider an alternative unless the State agency submits a statement, in a brief or other supporting material, to the Secretary that the alternative would permit the activity to be conducted in a manner consistent with the enforceable policies of the management program.

The Secretary will not override a state determination if the applicant fails to establish all the above criteria, unless necessary on national security grounds. The national security exception requires that "a national defense or other national security interest would be significantly impaired if the activity were not permitted to go forward as proposed." 15 C.F.R. § 930.122.

Section 930.121(a) was revised in 2000 to add the requirement that the activity "further the national interest . . . *in a significant or substantial manner."* This change was intended to exclude from the appeal process projects with only minimal connection to the national goals of the CZMA, and to focus the process on assuring that national interests are fully considered in the state certification process. NOAA's discussion of the 2000 regulations notes that "a project can be of national import without being quantifiably large in scale or impact on the national economy. . . . To determine whether a project significantly or substantially furthers the national interest, NOAA encourages appellants and States to consider three factors: (1) The degree to which the activity furthers the national interest; (2) the nature or importance of the national interest furthered as articulated in the CZMA; and (3) the extent to which the proposed activity is coastal dependent." 65 Fed. Reg. 77150 (2000). Consistency determinations that are fundamentally local land use decisions are no longer matters for appeal to the Secretary.

Related to the appeal process is the question of who has authority to appeal or even enforce consistency decisions. The Secretarial appeal process, for example, is not available to disgruntled individuals or to local governments who would like to challenge a state's positive determination of consistency of an activity with the coastal program. And courts disagree as to whether the CZMA creates a right for private citizens or local governments to challenge developments that are inconsistent with an approved state coastal management plan. Compare *City of Sausalito v. O'Neill*, 386 F.3d 1186 (9th Cir. 2004) (city had standing to challenge consistency) with *Town of North Hempstead v. Village of North Hills*, 482 F.Supp. 900 (E.D.N.Y. 1979) (finding the CZMA "is neither a jurisdictional grant, nor a basis for stating a claim upon which relief can be granted," the court dismissed a CZMA claim against village by neighboring town). See also, *George v. NYC Dep't of City Planning*, 436 F.3d 102 (2d Cir. 2006)(CZMA creates no private right of action against city agencies); *Save Our Dunes v. Alabama Dep't of Envtl.*

Management, 834 F.2d 984 (11th Cir. 1987) (holding plaintiffs had no standing to appeal a coastal permit decision); *Serrano-Lopez v. Cooper*, 193 F.Supp.2d 424 (D.P.R. 2002) ("The zone of interests regulated by the CZMA includes a state's protection of their coastal zones and not an individual's attempt to seek further protection once the CZMA requirements have been complied with.").

Perhaps more frustrating to the purposes of the CZMA is a decision holding that the CZMA creates no implied right of action for a state to enjoin a federal permittee's activities that are inconsistent with the state coastal plan. In February 1986, John DeLyser applied to the Corps of Engineers for a permit to build a dock and boathouse on pilings. The permit was issued, but DeLyser instead began construction of a two-story residence with sanitary facilities. The Corps issued a cease and desist order and required DeLyser to submit an after-the-fact permit application. Because the state of New York found the project inconsistent with its coastal management program, the Corps denied the permit. DeLyser's appeal to the Secretary of Commerce was also unsuccessful. Despite the adverse rulings, DeLyser completed the building and took up residence. The Corps declined to enforce its order citing consideration of funding allocations and the failure of any party other than the state to object to the structure. The court held that the state had no authority under the CZMA to require DeLyser to remove the structure. See *New York v. DeLyser*, 759 F.Supp. 982 (W.D.N.Y. 1991). See also, *State of N.J., Dep't of Envtl. Prot. & Energy v. Long Island Power*

Auth., 30 F.3d 403 (3d Cir. 1994)(CZMA creates no right of action in favor of state against private parties for failure to submit consistency certifications).

CHAPTER IV

MANAGEMENT AND REGULATION OF COASTAL DEVELOPMENT

Intensive use and development of the nation's coastlines have contributed to loss of land and other coastal resources. The most sensitive and dynamic areas of the coastline—beaches, dunes, and barrier islands—are also the most attractive areas for recreation and development. Climate change and sea level rise have added an additional dimension to coastal development regulation as communities attempt to adapt to the sea's encroachment and more intense storm events.

Federal, state, and local governments have, often inadvertently, encouraged growth in these sensitive areas by providing infrastructure, flood insurance, and disaster relief. See Dana Beach, Coastal Sprawl: The Effects of Urban Design on Aquatic Ecosystems in the United States (Pew Oceans Commission 2002).

There are two primary approaches that have been taken to manage development on the coasts. First, because federal, state and local government subsidies and infrastructure spending have stimulated coastal growth, withholding such governmental support for development in coastal areas may provide an indirect means of controlling development. Resources can be directed toward infrastructure that optimizes coastal resilience. In addition, growth can be regulated directly through land use planning and by strictly regulating or prohibiting structures that will contribute to destruction of habitat or erosion of the shore, that will cause damage to public resources or other private property, or that will be located in unsafe or unstable areas.

A. LIMITING INFRASTRUCTURE FUNDING AND OTHER SUBSIDIZATION OF COASTAL DEVELOPMENT

Much of the exploding development on the nation's coasts could not have taken place without federal and state assistance and subsidies. Federal and state programs, infrastructure and other spending, including flood insurance, flood control projects, highway programs, sewage treatment facility funding and disaster relief, have rarely taken into account effects like encouraging growth in sensitive areas or long term issues like sea level rise (SLR). Such development involves tremendous public costs beyond the original expenditures: Average annual storm damage to coastal property, for example, amounts to billions of dollars, but continued coastal development without consideration of coastal resilience and adaptation to SLR will be catastrophic.

1.   NFIP: SUBSIDIZING COASTAL GROWTH?

One of the best examples of government incidentally subsidizing coastal development is the National Flood Insurance Program (NFIP), which was created by Congress in 1968 and is administered by the Federal Emergency Management Agency (FEMA). The NFIP was intended to reduce federal flood disaster relief by providing guaranteed, affordable flood insurance coverage for communities that adopt minimum federal building standards and land use controls that minimize flood damage and property losses.[1] NFIP insurance is typically sold through private insurers and any claims to recover are handled by these insurance companies who are paid by FEMA to handle the claims. Any issues on NFIP coverage for a privately-issued NFIP policy must be either appealed to FEMA[2] or filed in a federal court within one year of receiving denial of coverage. Even claims of "bad faith" will be waived because NFIP rules pre-empt State law, *Woodson v. Allstate Ins. Co.*, 855 F.3d 628, 631 (4th Cir. 2017).

The exponential growth in coastal areas subsequent to the passage of the program is often attributed to the availability of inexpensive flood insurance. Several cases have highlighted the environmental impacts of development facilitated by the NFIP and FEMA's obligations to take these impacts into account. In *Fla. Key Deer v. Paulison*, 522 F.3d 1133 (2008), the Eleventh Circuit Court of Appeals upheld an injunction prohibiting FEMA from issuing flood insurance for new developments in habitats suitable for the endangered Key deer species in Monroe County, the county encompassing the low-lying Florida Keys, on the basis that FEMA failed to fulfill its consultation obligations under section 7 of

---

[1] See generally, Christine A. Klein, The National Flood Insurance Program at Fifty: How the Fifth Amendment Takings Doctrine Skews Federal Flood Policy, 31 Georgetown Envtl L. Rev. 285 (2019); see also Part IV.B.2.

[2] If appealing to FEMA, a written notice must be filed within 60 days of an insurer's denial of a claim. FEMA will have 90 days from receipt of the appeal to make a decision.

the Endangered Species Act (ESA). But see, *Nat'l Wildlife Fed'n v. FEMA*, 345 F. Supp. 2d 1151, 1155 (W.D. Wash. 2004) (holding that the issuance of flood insurance is a nondiscretionary act and not subject to section 7 of the ESA). In *Coalition for a Sustainable Delta v. FEMA*, 812 F.Supp.2d 1089 (U.S. E.D. Cal. 2011), the court denied FEMA's motion for summary judgment in regard to its practice of allowing persons to artificially fill the floodplain to actually remove it from its floodplain status, and thus from regulations and requirements associated with the NFIP. The court found that such action could trigger the ESA duty to consult because it allowed land to be removed from the floodplain and could jeopardize certain endangered species.

Hurricanes and coastal storms since 2005 have strained the NFIP with unprecedented numbers of insurance claims. In July 2012, the U.S. Congress passed the Biggert-Waters Flood Insurance Reform Act of 2012 (BW-12) in an attempt to reduce the debt of the NFIP after claims outpaced revenue following Hurricane Katrina, Hurricane Ike, Tropical Storm Debby, and super-storm Sandy. BW-12 affects all the major components of the NFIP, including insurance rates, flood maps, grant programs, and flood plain management plans. Key provisions of the legislation require the NFIP to raise rates to reflect true flood risk, making the program more financially stable and changing how Flood Insurance Rate Map (FIRM) updates impact policyholders. Other provisions eliminate subsidies for vacation homes and non-primary residences. The changes have been controversial, however, and the future of the program remains the subject of debate and legislative proposals and even litigation by states seeking to delay flood insurance rate hikes.[3] Ultimately, however, the goal of NFIP reform is not to limit subsidization that encourages coastal growth, but to limit the impact of that growth on the federal budget. Earlier legislation more directly addressed the issue of the effects of the program on rampant coastal development.

2. THE COASTAL BARRIER RESOURCES ACT

To stem the impact of the NFIP and other federal subsidies on still undeveloped areas of the nation's coast, Congress enacted the 1982 Coastal Barrier Resources Act (CBRA), 16 U.S.C.A. §§ 3501–3510 (reauthorized by P.L. 109–226 in May 2006), the second generation of a program that coordinates environmental protection with federal fiscal policy. CBRA's purposes include preserving the natural resources of coastal barrier islands, minimizing loss of human life from hazardous coastal development, and restricting federal support for such development. Within Congressionally designated, undeveloped coastal barrier areas called the Coastal Barrier Resources System (CBRS), the Act restricts federal assistance or expenditures for new development. This includes NFIP coverage, government loans, non-emergency disaster relief, new bridges, roads and

---

[3]   See e.g., Rawle O. King, *The National Flood Insurance Program: Status and Remaining Issues for Congress*, Congressional Research Service Report No. 7–5700 (February 6, 2013); Arthur D. Postal, Mississippi Sues to Stop NFIP Rate Hikes, Credit Union Times (Sept. 30, 2013).

other infrastructure, and other forms of federal assistance and subsidies. The intent is that the expense and the risks of new development must be borne by the developer of coastal barrier island property. It is not clear at this time whether the approach has actually inhibited growth in the affected areas. See Elise Jones, *The Coastal Barrier Resources Act: A Common Cents Approach to Coastal Protection,* 21 Envtl. L. 1015 (1991). As developable coastal land becomes more and more scarce, however, developers are more likely to be willing to bear the increased private cost of development.

In *Bostic v. United States*, 753 F.2d 1292 (4th Cir. 1985), developers and landowners of property on Topsail Island, North Carolina, asserted that CBRA had wrongly designated their land as part of an undeveloped coastal barrier, making them ineligible for federal flood insurance. The *Bostic* court held, however, that since the map adopted by Congress specifically designated the island as an undeveloped coastal barrier, Congress unquestionably intended to include it in the CBRS, and the designation was not a reviewable agency action. The court also found that inclusion of the property in the CBRS was substantially related to the purposes of CBRA.

3.   GOVERNMENT FLOOD CONTROL PROJECTS

Government infrastructure spending to protect vulnerable areas from storm impacts and floods, such as New Orleans' system of levees, also leads to development in sensitive or dangerous areas of the coast. Litigation surrounding the failure of the U.S. Army Corps of Engineers (the Corps) to armor susceptible areas in a timely manner and the breaching of existing levees during Hurricane Katrina may lead to less reliance by property owners on these government protections when building in coastal areas. In the protracted litigation against the Corps for damages, the Fifth Circuit Court of Appeals applied the immunity provisions of the Flood Control Act of 1928 ("FCA"), 33 U.S.C. § 702, to deny claims of the residents of New Orleans' Lower Ninth Ward for levee breaches and held that "discretionary function" immunity further protected the Corps from liability. *Robinson v. United States (In Re Katrina Canal Breaches Litig.)*, 696 F.3d 436 (2012). The court read the FCA's immunity provisions broadly, recognizing "immunity for any flood-control activity engaged in by the government, even in the context of a project that was not primarily or substantially related to flood control." Id. In the case of damages not subject to FCA immunity, i.e., damage due to the Corps' failure to armor certain areas, the court found the discretionary function exception (DFE) "completely insulates the government from liability." Id. The DFE bars suit on any claim that is "based upon the exercise or performance or the failure to exercise or perform a discretionary function or duty on the part of a federal agency or an employee of the Government, whether or not the discretion involved be abused." 28 U.S.C. § 2680(a). Id., quoting the Federal Tort Claims Act. See also, St. Bernard Parish Government v. U.S., 887 F.3d 1354 (Fed.Cir. Ct.App. 2018)(holding that the U.S. cannot be held liable for a taking of property by inaction, and that government flood control projects that reduced the risk of flooding, although inadequate, were not shown to be the cause of the flooding).

Individual states such as Texas are investing state funds in providing better flood control for communities through the creation of a Flood Infrastructure Fund and a Texas Infrastructure Resiliency Fund (allows cities, counties and other political subdivisions to apply for grants and low or zero-interest loans for specific projects through the Texas Water Development Board).

B. COASTAL CONSTRUCTION REGULATION

Indiscriminate development on the coastline has created a multitude of problems. Development on beaches, dunes and floodplains is more vulnerable to storms and flooding and has already caused serious erosion of these areas, resulting in loss of recreation areas, public facilities, and the storm protection the coastal features had provided. Such development even exacerbates these problems by damaging the beach and dune system, causing increased erosion and potentially damaging adjacent lands and public access. Structures not designed or built to withstand coastal hazards subject the owners to the threat of loss of life and property and create a hazard to others when parts of the structure are driven by wind or water. Poorly designed and located coastal construction leads to major expenditures of public funds for flood and disaster relief. Intense coastal development also creates hurdles to effective adaption to sea level rise.

Inadequately regulated coastal construction has also interfered with the habitat values of beaches. For example, eroded Atlantic and Gulf coast beaches are critical nesting sites for threatened and endangered sea turtles. On the Pacific coast, marine mammals are losing beach habitat important for calving. Coastal development has also displaced or disrupted vital nesting areas for shore birds.

It is clear that the needs and public purposes served by strict coastal construction regulation go far beyond the normal purposes served and advantages created by orderly land use planning and regulation in inland areas.

1.   SETBACK LINES

a. Evolution of Setback Line Requirements

Historically, coastal setbacks, a kind of retreat strategy, have been a primary tool in coastal planning and construction regulation. See also, Part IV.C.3. for further discussion of retreat strategies. At least half of the coastal states have implemented a setback policy of some degree by creating zones at the ocean's edge where development is prohibited or strictly regulated. See John Houlahan, *Comparison of State Construction Setbacks to Manage Development in Coastal Hazard Areas,* 17 Coastal Mgmt. 219 (1989). Early setback lines generally prohibited or limited construction in areas within a prescribed distance from a baseline, usually the mean high water line, the vegetation line, or a line associated with the primary dune. See *Buechel v. State Dept. of Ecology*, 123 Wash.2d 1019, 875 P.2d 635 (1994). The distances were relatively arbitrary and generally ranged from 40 feet to 100 feet. As understanding of beach and dune processes increased and monitoring of shoreline erosion rates became common, and as coastal engineering became more sophisticated, delineation of setback lines also became more sophisticated and highly technical.

Many states now use a second type of setback line based on complicated calculations of seasonal shoreline fluctuations, vulnerability to storms and storm surges, and the rate of shoreline erosion or sea level rise (SLR).

Some examples of setbacks based on erosion rates or SLR include the following state regulations.

- The Maine Sand Dune Rules require that structures greater than 2,500 square feet be set back a distance based upon the future shoreline position considering two feet of SLR over the next 100 years. [ME Admin. Code, 2. 06–096 ch. 355, § 5 (2010).

- North Carolina allows for a tiered setback based upon the size and type of structure. The setback is determined by the vegetative line and the annual average rate of erosion. Smaller structures (less than 5,000 square feet) must be set back 30 times the erosion rate; larger structures must be set back 60 to 90 times the erosion rate based upon the size of the structure. NC Admin. Code tit. 15A, r. 7H.0306 (2010).

- Florida's Coastal Zone Protection Act of 1985, Fla. Stat. §§ 161.52–.58, restricts construction seaward of the seasonal high water line as it will exist thirty years after the construction permit application to certain single-family dwellings that can be constructed landward of the frontal dune. See generally Donna R. Christie, *Growth Management in Florida: Focus on the Coast*, 3 J. Land Use & Envtl. L. 33 (1987).

See Jessica Grannis, Adaptation Tool Kit: Sea-Level Rise and Coastal Land Use: How Governments Can Use Land-Use Practices to Adapt to Sea-Level Rise 25–27(2011).

Some state setback regulations still use fixed distances from a feature like the MHWL or dune ridge, but allow construction in parts of the zone if it meets strict requirements to protect or minimize harm to the structure and the environment, e.g., building codes with height requirements, wind standards and limits on impermeable surface. This kind of approach is often called "accommodation," because it increases coastal resilience to flooding and storms *and* allows continued use of the property. There are engineering and design limits to this approach, however, and it impedes habitat migration.

Hawai'i still uses the first type of setback line for controlling coastal development. Construction must be located landward of "[s]etbacks along shorelines [that] are established of not less than twenty feet and not more than forty feet inland from the shoreline." The "shoreline" is defined as the highest wash of the waves during high season, typically a debris or vegetation line. See Haw. Rev. Stat. § 205A–43. See also, *Diamond v. Dobbin*, 319 P.3d 1017, 132 Haw. 9 (2014)(demonstrating that determination of the shoreline from which the setback is measured, however, can still be a complicated process). The use of this method is more useful for Hawaii's beaches, which have not been subjected to the high rate of erosion that the Atlantic coast beaches, for example, have experienced.

South Carolina's 1988 Beachfront Management Act (BMA), S.C. Code Ann. §§ 48–39–270 to 48–39–360, was one of the country's most comprehensive coastal construction laws and used both types of setbacks. Under the state's coastal management program, the South Carolina Coastal Council has jurisdiction to regulate beachfront construction. The BMA required the Coastal Council to establish and record a baseline on the Atlantic coast at the "crest of an ideal primary oceanfront sand dune." From this baseline, a setback line was calculated at a distance of forty times the average annual erosion rate, but at a minimum distance of twenty feet landward of the baseline. The area within twenty feet landward of the baseline was a "dead zone" in which major structures were not permitted. In the remaining area between the baseline and the setback line, construction is limited to habitable structures not larger than 5000 square feet, located as far landward on a lot as possible, and meeting other demanding conditions. In the wake of Hurricane Hugo and a host of legal challenges, the BMA was amended in 1990 to eliminate the twenty-foot dead zone, making all construction between the baseline and setback line subject to the same standards.[4]

b. Setbacks and Existing Development

Setback lines, and other retreat strategies discussed further in Part IV.C.2, generally apply only to undeveloped beachfront property. Existing development is usually "grandfathered in" to lessen the immediate economic impact of the regulation. There is also some underlying rationale that these existing structures are temporary, i.e., until the next big storm. Existing structures may become subject to new regulation if they are expanded, improved, or destroyed. Two major problems have arisen in relation to grandfathering of existing structures. First, in areas that were almost fully developed prior to the new regulation, new prohibitions on development that apply only to the remaining undeveloped lots may appear to be unreasonable (leading to 5th amendment takings challenges). See *Lucas v. South Carolina Coastal Council*, 505 U.S. 1003, 112 S.Ct. 2886, 120 L.Ed.2d 798 (1992); but see,

---

[4]   See Newman Jackson Smith, *Analysis of the Regulation of Beachfront Development in South Carolina*, 42 S.C.L. Rev. 717 (1991). See also *Esposito v. South Carolina Coastal Council*, 939 F.2d 165 (4th Cir. 1991); *Beard v. South Carolina Coastal Council*, 304 S.C. 205, 403 S.E.2d 620 (1991); *South Carolina Coastal Conservation League v. South Carolina Dept. of Health*, 345 S.C. 525, 548 S.E.2d 887 (2001).

Fla. Stat. § 161.053(5)(b) (creating a variance from some coastal construction permitting requirements where existing adjacent structures form a "reasonably continuous and uniform construction line" seaward of the regulatory line and the existing structures have not been "unduly affected by erosion").

A second problem concerning existing structures relates to the determination of when they may become subject to the new regulatory scheme. South Carolina's Beachfront Management Act places new limitations on rebuilding structures that are "destroyed beyond repair" and originally banned their reconstruction within the dead zone or seaward of the baseline. Destroyed beyond repair means "more that sixty-six and two-third percent of the replacement value of the habitable structure . . . has been destroyed." See S.C. Code Ann. § 48–39–270(11). Such standards can undoubtedly trigger a "battle of the experts." Reacting to the widespread impact of the Act on beachfront homeowners in the wake of Hurricane Hugo, the South Carolina legislature amended the BMA in 1990 to give the Coastal Council the authority to issue special permits to allow reconstruction of habitable structures under certain conditions, even if they were located seaward of the baseline.

The Florida Coastal Zone Protection Act provides that its Coastal Construction Control Line (CCCL) and thirty-year erosion zone requirements will apply to all new construction except "modification, maintenance, or repair to any existing structure within the limits of the existing foundation which does not require . . . any additions to, or repair or modification of, the existing foundation." See Fla. Stat. § 161.053).

2. BUILDING CODES

Storms like Sandy, Katrina, Ike, Hugo and Michael have highlighted the need for strict building codes for coastal construction. Substandard housing is not only subject to greater damage in a storm, but also creates a hazard for other nearby properties. The creation of the National Flood Insurance Program (NFIP) by the National Flood Insurance Act of 1968, 42 U.S.C.A. §§ 4001–4128, has led to widespread adoption of minimum federal building standards for flood-prone areas, including beaches. The NFIP is intended to reduce federal flood disaster relief by supplying guaranteed flood insurance coverage to communities that adopt building standards and land use controls that minimize flood damages and property losses. State and local regulation may be stricter than federally imposed safety and building standards, and governments are encouraged to adopt land use regulations that guide development away from flood hazard areas.[5]

In addition to guaranteeing flood insurance for communities participating in the program, the NFIP

---

[5] See, e.g., N.C. Residential Code, Chap. 46 Coastal and Flood Plain Construction Standards; see generally, Texas A&M Agrilife Extension, *Coastal Resilience: State and Local Building Codes*, https://coastalresilience.tamu.edu/home/introduction-to-coastal-resilience/legal-framework-for-planning/stateandlocal/building-codes/.

also imposes penalties for nonparticipation. If a community with areas susceptible to flooding does not join the program, federal agencies, like the Small Business Administration and the Veterans Administration, are prohibited from providing federal assistance for development in flood-prone areas. See 42 U.S.C.A. § 4106(a). The NFIP has been held neither to be an unconstitutional coercion or imposition of strict federal building standards on the states, nor to be a taking of private property as a result of diminished property values in nonparticipating communities. See *Adolph v. Federal Emergency Management Agency*, 854 F.2d 732 (5th Cir. 1988); *Texas Landowners Rights Ass'n v. Harris*, 453 F.Supp. 1025 (D.D.C. 1978).

C.   BEACH EROSION, SEA LEVEL RISE, AND SHORELINE PROTECTION

According to a 2000 report by the Heinz Center for FEMA, "80 to 90 percent of the sandy beaches in the United States are eroding." The Atlantic coast has an average annual erosion rate of about 2 to 3 feet/year, while the Gulf coast states average 6 feet/year. Major storms events can produce erosion of as much as 100 feet of shoreline. On the Pacific coast, cliff erosion, although "site specific and episodic," can remove "tens of feet at one time." The report estimates that without additional beach restoration or structural protections, as many as 1,500 homes per year (and the land they stand on) could be lost to coastal erosion. Sea level rise exacerbates shoreline erosion: "a sustained rise of 10 cm in sea level could result in 15 meters of shoreline retreat. This amount of erosion is more than an order of magnitude greater than would be expected from a simple response to sea level rise through inundation of the shore." See H. John Heinz III Center for Science, Economics and the Environment, *Evaluation of Erosion Hazards* (2000).

The response to the retreat of the shoreline due to erosion and adaption to sea level rise are two of the most important issues for coastal managers today. Government strategies can be generally categorized as restoration, structural armoring, and retreat.

1.   BEACH RESTORATION

a. The Pros and Cons of Restoration

The economic importance of beaches to many coastal economies has led governments to conclude that restoration is an economic necessity. The process is not only expensive, however, but also perpetual. New beach engineering technologies may mean that a restored beach may last 5–10 years without renourishment—or it may be washed away the next week by a storm. The high cost of this management technique is argued to be justified by the revenues generated by the beaches and the protection afforded to upland properties. In a comprehensive study, the National Research Council (NRC) supports beach renourishment as a viable method for protecting the shoreline from erosion and for restoring lost beaches. The report also contains important warnings:

> Although proven engineered shore protection measures exist, there are no quick, simple, or inexpensive ways to protect the shore from

natural forces, to mitigate the effects of beach erosion, or to restore beaches, regardless of the technology or approach selected. Available shore protection measures do not treat some of the underlying causes of erosion, such as relative rise in sea level and interruption of sand transport in the littoral systems, because they necessarily address locale-specific erosion problems rather than their underlying systemic causes.

National Research Council, *Beach Nourishment and Protection* (1995).

b. Challenges to Beach Restoration

Beach restoration projects now go on routinely, and most coastal states, by statute or interpretation of the common law, provide for ownership of the created beach by the state and protection of the littoral owners' access rights. In spite of the protection of and enhancement of upland property values afforded by government restoration projects, some beachfront owners have brought legal challenges charging that projects have devalued or "taken" their property by obstructing their ocean view, see *City of Ocean City v. Maffucci,* 326 N.J.Super. 1, 740 A.2d 630 (N.J.Sup.Ct., App. Div. 1999) (holding that severance damages must include the loss in the value due to the obstruction of view by dunes associated with a beach restoration project); but see *Borough of Harvey Cedars v. Karan*, 70 A.3d 524 (N.J. S.Ct. 2013) (holding that calculation of severance damages must also include the value added to retained property attributable to the protective dune system); by restricting beach access routes to protect sea turtle habitat after a restoration project, see *Slavin v. Town of Oak Island*, 160 N.C.App. 57, 584 S.E.2d 100 (N.C. Ct.App. 2003) (holding that a littoral property owner's right of access to the ocean is a qualified one, subject to reasonable regulation that does not require compensation); by "taking" the riparian right to accretion, see *Walton County v. Stop the Beach Renourishment*, 998 So.2d 1102 (Fl. S.Ct. 2008) (holding that the right to accretions is a contingent right and not implicated in beach restoration); and by claiming state ownership of land created by the restoration project, see *Michaelson v. Silver Beach Improv. Asso.*, 342 Mass. 251, 173 N.E.2d 273 (1961) (holding that shoreline land created by the commonwealth belonged to the littoral owners) and *City of Long Branch v. Liu*, 363 N.J. Super. 411, 833 A.2d 106 (Law Div. 2003) (holding that the sand beach created by a government restoration project belongs to the state).

The issue of state beach restoration efforts as a "taking" of riparian rights has gone to the U.S. Supreme Court and is discussed infra in Section IV.E.4. *Stop the Beach Renourishment v. Florida Department of Environmental Protection*, 560 U.S. 702, 130 S.Ct. 2592, 177 L.Ed. 184 (2010).

Older cases dealing with ownership of the created beach tended to focus on whether the activity was accretion or avulsion. A better approach for courts may be to analyze modern beach restoration statutes is to consider beach restoration as *sui generis* and evaluate whether the statute reasonably balances the important the public and private interests involved.

2.   STRUCTURAL ARMORING

a. Solution or Source of Additional Problems?

Armoring or coastline "hardening" are terms that encompass seawalls, bulkheads, revetments, rip-rap, groins, and other fixed structures intended to stabilize the shoreline. Although armoring can provide short-term protection to endangered land and structures, it is not a preferred management tool. Evidence indicates that armoring increases the rate of erosion of adjacent beaches and causes damage to adjacent properties, loss of habitat, and loss of beach access. When a seawall is used, the beach seaward of the wall often completely disappears, eliminating beach habitat and intertidal area as well as the public's access and use of the beach. Because the seawall causes land at each end of the wall to erode at a greater rate, the seawall can also be considered a private nuisance.

Seawall construction can also interfere with the habitat values of a beach. Many states strictly regulate the construction of vertical walls and the placement of riprap on the beaches in turtle nesting areas and limit other coastal construction (including beach restoration) during the nesting season. See, e.g., *Sierra Club et al. v. von Kolnitz*, No. 2:16-CV-03815-DCN, 2017 WL 3480777 (D.S.C. 2017) (requiring the removal of temporary plastic seawalls in a turtle nesting area).

b. Can/Should Seawalls Be Prohibited?

One can argue that all hard armoring should be prohibited because shoreline property owners have assumed the risk of erosion, and armoring is an unsustainable solution for long-term management. In fact, a number of states now generally ban new hard armoring. South Carolina, North Carolina, Massachusetts, Rhode Island, Maine, Texas and Oregon have bans or near-bans on seawalls. (The Hawai'i prohibition on new private shoreline protection structures has apparently been swallowed up by its "exception" for structures that "result in improved aesthetic and engineering solutions to erosion at the sites.") Most coastal states have legislation that clearly prioritizes other alternatives as preferable means of shore protection. Property owners, on the other hand, counter that they have a right to protect their property.

(1) Do Owners Have a Right to Protect Property from Erosion?

In *Shell Island Homeowners Ass'n v. Tomlinson*, 134 N.C. App. 217, 517 S.E.2d 406 (1999), condominium owners challenged North Carolina's "hardened structure rule" which prohibited use of permanent erosion control structures, including bulkheads; seawalls; revetments; jetties, groins and breakwaters. The owners had been denied permits to attempt to stop the erosion of their property which

was threatening the destruction of the nine-story
condominium building. The court dismissed the
owners' non-constitutional claims for failure to
pursue administrative remedies but addressed
whether the rule effected a 5th Amendment taking of
their property. The plaintiff's primary argument was
that "the protection of property from erosion is an
essential right of property owners. . . ." The court
refused to recognize this proposition as a "legally
cognizable property interest" and stated that it has
"no support in the law." The court attributed any
losses on naturally occurring migration of the
beach—a "consequence of being a riparian or littoral
landowner." The takings claim was dismissed. (As an
aside, a suit by the Shell Island Resort Homeowner's
Association against state agencies and the Coastal
Resources Commission for negligence in granting a
permit to the developers of the Shell Island Resort
was also dismissed.)

Seawalls for protection of endangered property are
the source of major controversy on California's
crumbling coastline. California Constitution, art. 1,
section 1, entitled Inalienable Rights, provides: "All
people are by nature free and independent and have
inalienable rights. Among these are enjoying and
defending life and liberty, acquiring, possessing, and
protecting property. . . ." Further, California's
Coastal Act section 30235 states: "Revetments,
breakwaters, groins, harbor channels, seawalls, cliff
retaining walls and other shoreline construction that
alters natural shoreline processes *shall be permitted
to protect existing structures* . . . in danger from
erosion when designed to minimize or mitigate

adverse impacts to shoreline sand supply . . . ." (Emphasis added.) The law is not clear, however, whether the term "existing structures" refers to ones that existed at the time of enactment—1977—or at the time of the permit application. See Jesse Reiblich & Eric H. Hartge, The Forty-Year-Old Statute: Unintended Consequences of the Coastal Act and How They Might Be Redressed, 36 Stanford Envtl. Law J. 63 (2016)). In *Lynch v. California Coastal Com.*, 3 Cal.5th 470 (2017), the California Supreme Court had the opportunity to address the issue, but dodged the question by finding that the plaintiffs could not challenge the seawall permit conditions since they had already taken advantage of the permit by rebuilding the damaged protection structure. The court refused to recognize an "under protest exception" that could "potentially swallow the general rule that landowners must take the burdens along with the benefits of a permit." Id.

In spite of seemingly strong constitutional and statutory provisions addressing protection of property, California courts have held that

[t]here is no constitutional right to own property free from regulation. Neither the state nor the federal Constitution guarantees any person absolute liberty of action. "We do not consider lightly the importance of the constitutional guarantee attaching to private ownership and use of real property. . . . However, more than 50 years ago, it was clearly established that property ownership rights, reserved to the individual by constitutional provision, must be

subordinated to the rights of society. It is now a fundamental axiom in the law that one may not do with his property as he pleases; his use is subject to reasonable restraints to avoid societal detriment. . . ." (citations omitted).

Whaler's Village Club v. California Coastal Com., 173 Cal.App.3d 240, 252–53 (Cal.Ct.App. 2nd Dist. 1985). The Appeals Court also noted that neither the California Constitution nor the Coastal Act created a "vested right" to undertake their project in the sense of a vested right in the land use context which applies to projects that have already undergone government approval.

(2) The Common Enemy Doctrine

The "common enemy doctrine" is sometimes cited as a basis of a property owner's right to protect land from the encroaching sea. Although the doctrine primarily applied to diffuse surface waters, in his 19th century treatise, John M. Gould, noted:

The owners of lands exposed to the inroads of the sea . . . may erect walls and embankments to prevent the wearing away of the land or to protect it from overflow. *It is lawful to embank against the sea*, even when the effect may be to cause the water to beat with increased violence against the adjoining land. . . .

Gould, A Treatise on the Law of Waters 320–21 (Chicago, Callaghan & Co. 2d ed. 1891) (Emphasis added). Recently, the state of Washington, which had apparently applied the common enemy rule to seawalls, rejected the language of an 1896 case, *Cass v. Dicks*, 44 P. 113, 114 (Wash. 1896), as *dicta* and held that the common enemy rule does not apply to sea water. *Grundy v. Thurston County*, 155 Wn.2d 1, 117 P.3d 1089 (Wash. 2005). Because the issue in the *Grundy* case was whether the doctrine provided a defense for damage to a neighbor's property, however, it is not clear whether the case addresses other language in *Cass v. Dicks* recognizing a landowner's right to erect a seawall as a matter of self-defense, "having a right to protect his land and his crops from inundation." Id.

In *United States v. Milner*, 583 F.3d 1174 (9th Cir. Wash. 2009), coastal erosion had caused the tideland property boundary to intersect with shore defense structures erected by Washington homeowners. The United States, who holds the tidelands in trust for the Lummi nation, brought suit for removal of structures that were seaward of where the MHW boundary *would be* if the shore defenses had not been erected. The Ninth Circuit Court of Appeals adopted a novel approach advocated by Professor Joseph L. Sax in *Some Unorthodox Thoughts about Rising Sea Levels, Beach Erosion, and Property Rights*, 11 Vt. J. Envtl. L. 641 (2009). The dispute was characterized as one between two adjacent landowners. This view made the common enemy doctrine "inapposite because the water is not acting as a 'common enemy' of the parties involved." One party's loss was the other's gain. The common enemy doctrine could, therefore, not provide a basis for one party to permanently fix the boundary by erecting a seawall. The court found that both parties have a vested right to an ambulatory boundary and seemed to adopt a reasonable use doctrine. Although the homeowners were recognized as having a right to build structures to prevent erosion and storm damage, they "cannot use their land in a way that would harm the Lummi's interest in the neighboring tidelands." The court found that even though the shore protection structures were legal when erected, this was not a defense to the trespass action and could not justify unilaterally fixing the ambulatory boundary. *Milner* at 1188–1191.

3.   RETREAT

The third management option is one that is necessary where beach and dune systems are so dynamic that neither restoration nor armoring is feasible, when the economic costs of restoration cannot be justified, and when environmental concerns, e.g., preservation of coastal wetlands, outweigh justifications for armoring or restoration. It is also a strategy for planning for sea level rise. Retreat may involve strict construction regulations within the sensitive beach/dune system or complete construction prohibitions within particularly sensitive or hazardous areas. The use of setback lines is discussed in Chapter IV.B.1.

A version of the retreat strategy, called the rolling easement (not to be confused with the Texas beach access rolling easement) has been advocated by many commentators, but the current version of the concept is attributed to James G. Titus, a project manager for sea level rise in the Climate Change Division of the

U.S. EPA. Titus's strategy allows areas that could eventually become submerged to be developed or continue to be used until the use must be abandoned. No efforts would be allowed to protect the shore or hold back the sea. A rolling easement would further require removal of structures as they became seaward of a specifically designated migrating boundary, such as the dune vegetation line, mean high water, or the upper reaches of tidal wetlands. Ecosystems would be allowed to migrate inland, protecting access and habitat in the long term.

The idea is that there must be clear, definitive planning about what lands will be subject to the rolling easement so markets and investors have the certainty necessary to incorporate and manage the risk of sea level rise. "If some lands must give way to the rising sea, the economic, environmental, and human consequences could be much less if the abandonment occurs according to a plan rather than unexpectedly." See James G. Titus, *Rolling Easements* 4–10 (U.S. Environmental Protection Agency 2011), available at http://water.epa.gov/type/oceb/cre/upload/rollingeasementsprimer.pdf.

Titus's rolling easement is not an "easement" at all, but a range of strategies, including both regulatory and property rights approaches, to accomplish the goals of the rolling easement described above. His 2011 report provides a comprehensive "primer on more than a dozen approaches for ensuring that wetlands and beaches can migrate inland, as people remove buildings, roads, and other structures from land as it becomes submerged" as a guide for governments in planning for sea level rise. Titus, *Rolling Easements*, id.

The rolling easement has emerged in other forms, e.g., rolling land use regulations and rolling conservation easements, in numerous studies addressing adaption to sea level rise. See, e.g., Jessica Grannis, *Adaptation Tool Kit: Sea-Level Rise and Coastal Land Use: How Governments Can Use Land-Use Practices to Adapt to Sea-Level Rise* (2011), available at https://www.georgetownclimate.org/reports/adaptation-tool-kit-sea-level-rise-and-coastal-land-use.html (analysis of the economic, environmental, and social costs and benefits of each tool, and the legal and administrative feasibility of implementing them) and Center for Ocean Solutions, *The Public Trust Doctrine: A Guiding Principle for Governing California's Coast Under Climate Change* (July 2017). See also, Michael Wolf, Strategies for Making Sea-Level Rise Adaption Tools "Taking-Proof," 28 J. Land Use & Envtl. Law 157 (2013)

D. PROTECTING COASTAL WETLANDS

Coastal wetlands are among the world's most productive ecosystems, comparable to coral reefs or rainforests. In addition to providing resting, feeding and nursery habitat for 75% the nation's waterfowl and migratory birds, and breeding habitat for many marine species, wetlands are also vital for food chain production, water quality, aquifer protection and recharge, storm protection and flood control. See 33 CFR 320.4(b)(2). As much as 45 percent of the endangered and threatened species in the U.S.

depend on wetlands. But coastal wetlands have disappeared and continue to disappear, at staggering rates. The latest assessment found coastal wetland loss of over 80,000 acres per year—up 25% over the previous study period. US FWS and NOAA, Status and Trends of Wetlands in the Coastal Watersheds of the Conterminous United States 2004 to 2009 (2013). Put in perspective, that's about seven football fields every hour. Coastal development, silviculture and agriculture are responsible for most of the loss. Now wetlands are also in jeopardy by inundation as sea level rises, but arguably they can survive if allowed to "migrate" landward as the shoreline changes.

1.   AN OVERVIEW OF CWA § 404 PERMITTING

Clean Water Act, 33 U.S.C. § 1344 (CWA § 404), provides a nationwide scheme for controlling alteration of wetlands by discharges. Section 404 permitting authority is in the U.S. Army Corps of Engineers (Corps). The EPA, which implements all other sections of the CWA, has joint responsibility to administer § 404 and ultimate authority to interpret the statute. EPA also has authority to veto a permit issued by the Corps. 33 U.S.C.A. § 1344(c). See James City County v. Environmental Protection Agency, 12 F.3d 1330 (4th Cir. 1993).

a. CWA § 404 Jurisdiction—Navigable Waters

A threshold issue in wetlands permitting is what constitutes a wetland, i.e., what is the scope of the Corps' jurisdiction? Interestingly, CWA § 404 does not mention the term "wetland." Instead, the Act creates a permitting system for discharges of dredged and fill material into navigable waters. "Navigable waters" are defined as "the waters of the United States, including the territorial seas." 33 U.S.C.A. § 1362(7). This lack of preciseness in the statute has led to continuing controversy over § 404 jurisdiction. See, e.g., *United States v. Riverside Bayview Homes, Inc.*, 474 U.S. 121, 106 S.Ct. 455, 88 L.Ed.2d 419 (1985) (holding the Corps has permitting jurisdiction over wetlands that are adjacent to, but not directly connected to or flooded by, a navigable water body); *Solid Waste Agency of Northern Cook County (SWANCC) v. U.S. Army Corps of Engineers*, 531 U.S. 159, 121 S.Ct. 675, 148 L.Ed.2d 576 (2001) (holding that isolated wetlands are not subject to Corps jurisdiction); and *Rapanos v. United States*, 547 U.S. 715, 126 S.Ct. 2208, 165 L.Ed.2d 159 (2006). In the case of coastal wetlands, however, it is clear that tidally-affected water bodies are subject to § 404 at least as far inland as the mean high tide line and the head of tide on coastal rivers, see, e.g., *Leslie Salt Co. v. Froehlke*, 578 F.2d 742 (9th Cir. 1978). The principle coastal impact of *SWANCC* and *Rapanos* is to exclude from CWA § 404 isolated, non-tidal wetlands that have no significant nexus to tidal coastal wetlands. It should be noted that the new regulations are currently proposed to define navigable waters of the United States.

b. What Is a "Discharge"?

Once an area is determined to be within the definition of a wetland constituting waters of the United States, the issue becomes whether the activity involved requires a permit. The § 404 permit system regulates only the "discharge of dredged and fill material." Before 1993 the Corps had not required a permit for dredging that did not involve disposing of the material in a wetland. Likewise, draining of a wetland without a discharge (by pumps or channels, for example) had not been regulated. See *Save Our Community v. United States EPA*, 971 F.2d 1155 (5th Cir. 1992). Land clearing is another activity that does not clearly fit within the plain meaning of "discharging." See *Avoyelles Sportmen's League v. Marsh*, 715 F.2d 897 (5th Cir. 1983). Since 1993, there has been significant controversary concerning whether de minimus discharges, incidental fallback and sidecasting require permits. See, e.g., *United States v. Wilson*, 133 F.3d 251 (4th Cir. 1997)("[s]ide-casting from ditch-digging . . . effects no addition of a pollutant, and if the ditching successfully dries out the wetland prior to the addition of other materials, no violation of the Clean Water Act results because adding fill to dry land cannot be construed to be polluting the waters of the United States"), and *National Mining Association v. U.S. Army Corps of Engineers*, 145 F.3d 1399, 330 U.S.App.D.C. 329 (D.C.Cir. 1998)(Corps exceeded its jurisdiction by defining incidental fallback as an "addition" to waters of the United States and upheld a nationwide injunction on application of the regulation); but see, *United States v. Deaton*, 209 F.3d 331, 337 (4th Cir. 2000)(definition of discharge which includes "any addition of any pollutant to navigable waters" encompasses sidecasting in a wetland). In the latest version of the rule, the Corps made no bright line rule distinguishing incidental discharge from regulable discharge, did not define "incidental," and left jurisdiction over an activity to case by case determination. 40 C.F.R. § 232.2 (2018). The ability of § 404 to protect coastal wetlands continues to be vulnerable to a potential loophole if the wetland can be drained without a "discharge". See Kim Connolly, Stephen Johnson, and Douglas Williams, *Wetlands Law and Policy: Understanding Section 404* 128–130 (2005).

c. Exemptions

Some activities in wetlands are specifically exempted from § 404. Most significantly, § 404(f)(1) exempts "normal farming, silviculture, and ranching activities." 33 U.S.C.A. § 1344(f)(1)(A). Courts have generally applied this exemption narrowly to ongoing activities and not to activities that bring wetlands into a new use. See, e.g., *United States v. Brace*, 41 F.3d 117 (3d Cir. 1994).

d. Individual and General Permits

If a regulated activity occurs in waters of the United States, the applicant must qualify for either an individual or general permit. A dredge and fill activity having "potentially significant impacts" on waters of the United States requires an individual § 404 permit. The Corps may issue general permits for broad categories that the Corps determines will have "minimal adverse environmental effects," individually and cumulatively. Section 404(b)(1) of the CWA requires the Corps to apply guidelines developed by the EPA, as well as its own regulatory review standards.

e. Criteria for Permits

The EPA's § 404(b)(1) Guidelines create a presumption against filling waters for non-water-dependent purposes by prohibiting a permit if there is "a practicable alternative to the proposed discharge which would have less adverse impact on the aquatic ecosystem, so long as the alternative does not have other significant adverse environmental consequences" and presuming practicable alternatives exist unless an applicant clearly demonstrated otherwise. See 40 C.F.R. § 230.10.[6] The public interest test, set out at 33 C.F.R. § 320.4(a), is the focus of the Corps' regulatory review. Determining whether a project should be permitted involves balancing broad standards and cumulative impacts that range from economic and social factors to "the national concern for both protection and utilization of important resources" and "considerations of property ownership and, in general, the needs and welfare of the people." See also 33 CFR 320.4(b)–(*l*).[7]

---

[6]   See also *Bersani v. United States EPA*, 850 F.2d 36 (2d Cir. 1988); *Sylvester v. United States Army Corps of Eng'rs*, 882 F.2d 407 (9th Cir. 1989); *Sierra Club v. Van Antwerp*, 41 ELR 20346 (D.C. Cir. 2011); Jon Schutz, *The Steepest Hurdle in Obtaining A Clean Water Act Section 404 Permit: Complying with EPA's 404(b)(1) Guidelines' Least Environmentally Damaging Practicable Alternative Requirement*, 24 UCLA J. Envtl. L. & Pol'y 235 (2006).

[7]   See also Daniel R. Mandelker, *Practicable Alternatives for Wetlands Development Under The Clean Water Act*, 48 Envtl. L.

2.   NWP 13, SEAWALLS AND WETLANDS ADAPTATION TO SLR

In 2017, a controversial nationwide general permit, NWP 13, was again reissued. (NWPs must be reissued every 5 years.) See Nat'l Wildlife Fed'n v. U.S. Army Corps of Engineers, 170 F. Supp. 3d 6 (D.D.C. 2016)(dismissing a suit by environmental groups challenging NWF 13 on its face). Innocuously labelled "bank stabilization," NWP 13 allows coastal owners to build hard armoring structures, like bulkheads and seawalls, up to 500 feet without individualized, site specific permitting or impact review, and in most cases, even without pre-construction notice (PCN) to the Corps. Such structures can destroy wetlands and prevent any possibility of preserving wetlands through their migration. Without a PCN requirement, it is not possible to know how much armoring has been facilitated by NWP 13 or its past and future impacts.

A more positive step for wetland survival was the issuance of new NWP 54, also in 2017, that creates an alternative procedure to NWP 13 for creating "living shoreline." This "soft" armoring technique creates a shoreline fringe of wetland that both reduces erosion and provides or enhances wetlands services. The 500-foot limit for NWP 54 is waivable, and groups of adjacent homeowners can cooperate to

Rep. News & Analysis 10894 (October 2018)(reviewing the "practical alternatives" test and public interest review, and making recommendations for revising the practicable alternatives requirement that would improve its role in the protection of wetlands resources).

create larger project areas. The Corps does not, however, create any priority or preference for this technique. See Travis O. Brandon, *A Wall Impervious to Facts: Seawalls, Living Shorelines, and the U.S. Army Corps ff Engineers' Continuing Authorization of Hard Coastal Armoring in the Face of Sea Level Rise*, 93 Tul. L. Rev. 557 (2019).

3.   COASTAL WETLANDS AND THE STATES

Corps of Engineers' federal permits issued under either the Rivers and Harbors Act or the CWA are also subject to state veto under the state water quality standard compliance certification requirements of CWA section 401, 33 U.S.C.A. § 1341, see *Friends of the Earth v. Hall*, 693 F.Supp. 904 (W.D.Wash. 1988); and the state coastal program consistency certification requirements of CZMA § 307(c)(3)(A), 16 U.S.C.A. § 1456(c)(3)(A). See *Anton v. South Carolina Coastal Council*, 321 S.C. 481, 469 S.E.2d 604 (1996); *Ogburn-Matthews v. Loblolly Partners*, 332 S.C. 551, 505 S.E.2d 598 (1998).

In addition, many states regulate coastal wetlands alterations either through their CZM programs, see *Kirkorowicz v. California Coastal Commission*, 100 Cal.Rptr.2d 124 (Cal. App. 2000); *1000 Friends of Oregon v. LCDC*, 85 Or.App. 18, 735 P.2d 645 (Or. App. 1987); or specific dredge and fill legislation that requires permits for wetland alteration. See, e.g., Conn. Gen. Stat. §§ 22a–28 to 22a–35; Fla. Stat. §§ 373.403–373.443; Me. Rev. Star. Ann. tit. 12, §§ 4751–4758; N.J. Star. Ann. §§ 13:9A–1 to 13:9A–10; Or. Rev. Stat. §§ 196.800–196.990.

Section 404 of the CWA provides for delegation of some, but not all, wetland permitting authority to states that meet statutory requirements. 33 U.S.C.A. § 1344(g)–(*l*). However, only Michigan (1984) and New Jersey (1994) have been delegated § 404 permitting authority. 40 C.F.R. §§ 233.70, 71. (Florida, Oregon and Minnesota are in the process of assuming § 404 permitting authority). State permits issued under delegated § 404 authority are also subject to EPA veto.

Finally, Corps administration of the Rivers and Harbors Act and CWA § 404 is subject to the environmental impact assessment requirements of NEPA (see, e.g., *Ocean Advocates v. U.S. Army Corps of Engineers*, 402 F.3d 846 (9th Cir. 2004); *Shoreacres v. Waterworth*, 420 F.3d 440 (5th Cir. 2005)); the Endangered Species Act and Marine Mammal Protection Act discussed infra; and the permit coordination and consistency requirements of the CZMA discussed above. See, e.g., *Florida Marine Contractors v. Williams*, 378 F.Supp.2d 1353 (M.D.Fla. 2005). In the case of activities pursuant to a general permit like NWP 13, where the activity is not subject to individual action by the Corps,

> . . .[i]f the State agency's conditions are not incorporated into the general permit or a State agency objects to the general permit [as inconsistent with its coastal management program], then the Federal agency shall notify potential users of the general permit that the general permit is not available for use in that State unless an applicant . . ., who wants to use

the general permit in that State provides the State agency with a consistency certification . . . and the State agency concurs. 5 C.F.R. § 930.31(d).

E. COASTAL MANAGEMENT AND THE TAKINGS ISSUE

1. AN OVERVIEW OF THE TAKINGS ISSUE

The Fifth Amendment of the United States Constitution provides that private property "shall [not] be taken for public use without just compensation." When there has been a permanent physical invasion or physical appropriation of land by the government, it is generally incontrovertible that there has been a taking of property requiring compensation. *Loretto v. Teleprompter Manhattan CATV Corp.*, 458 U.S. 419, 102 S.Ct. 3164, 73 L.Ed.2d 868 (1982) (holding that even a slight, permanent physical invasion under government authority is a compensable *per se* taking). However, the question of when a regulation that severely affects the value or utility of land constitutes a "taking" has become one of the most complicated and pervasive questions in land use and environmental law.

The genesis of modern regulatory takings analysis is *Pennsylvania Coal Co. v. Mahon*, 260 U.S. 393, 43 S.Ct. 158, 67 L.Ed. 322 (1922), in which Justice Holmes stated: "The general rule at least is, that while property may be regulated to a certain extent, if regulation goes too far, it will be recognized as a taking." The U.S. Supreme Court described the conundrum of regulatory taking as follows:

> Government hardly could go on if to some extent values incident to property could not be diminished without paying for every such change in the general law. As long recognized, some values are enjoyed under an implied limitation and must yield to the police power. But obviously the implied limitation must have its limits. . . . One fact for consideration in determining such limits is the extent of the diminution [of value]. When it reaches a certain magnitude, in most if not all cases there must be an exercise of eminent domain and compensation to sustain the act.

Id. at 260 U.S. 413.

In *Pennsylvania Coal,* the Court found that a Pennsylvania statute that made it unlawful for mining operations to cause subsidence of public buildings, public streets, and private residences had "gone too far." The support estate is an interest in land that is recognized in Pennsylvania separate from the surface and mineral estates. The statute effectively barred the coal company's exercising its rights to the mineral and support estates, interests owned by the coal company that had not been transferred by the deed to the Mahons, the private owners of the surface estate. The Court found that the law had "very nearly the same effect for constitutional purposes as appropriating or destroying" the coal company's property. Id. at 260 U.S. 414.

In *Penn Central Transportation Co. v. City of New York*, 438 U.S. 104, 98 S.Ct. 2646, 57 L.Ed.2d 631 (1978), the Court acknowledged its inability to develop a set formula to evaluate regulatory taking claims, but set out "several factors that have particular significance": The economic impact of the regulation and the extent to which it interfered with distinct or reasonable investment-backed expectations must be balanced against the "character of the government regulation." Id. at 438 U.S. 125–126. In *Andrus v. Allard,* 444 U.S. 51, 65, 62 L.Ed.2d 210, 100 S.Ct. 318 (1979), the Court noted that "government regulation—by definition—involves the adjustment of rights for the public good." Government action that "merely affects property interests through 'some public program adjusting the benefits and burdens of economic life to promote the common good,' " is less likely to be found a regulatory taking. See also *Lingle v. Chevron*, 544 U.S. 528, 125 S.Ct. 2074, 161 L.Ed.2d 876 (2005). The Supreme Court considered Penn Central's expectations and concluded that, at least where the regulation does not interfere with existing use of the property, such long use constitutes the "primary expectation concerning the use of the parcel." Even though New York's landmark legislation prohibited the development of the air space above Grand Central Terminal, the terminal could continue to be used profitably as it had been for 65 years.

Most recent takings cases have placed emphasis on the economic impact of the regulation on the property owner. See *Lucas v. South Carolina Coastal Council*, 304 S.C. 376, 404 S.E.2d 895 (1991) (creating a

second category of *per se* taking in cases where a
regulation destroys all economic use or value of the
property). The outcome of a case often turns,
however, on the methodology used to determine the
economic impact or the extent of diminution in value
caused by the regulation. When the property retains
some economically viable use, courts will usually find
that there has been no taking. In *Penn Central,* the
Supreme Court made it clear that diminution of
value would be determined on the basis of the value
of the property as a whole as affected by the
regulation.

> 'Taking' jurisprudence does not divide a single
> parcel into discrete segments and attempt to
> determine whether rights in a particular
> segment have been entirely abrogated. In
> deciding whether a particular governmental
> action has effected a taking, this Court focuses
> rather both on the character of the action and on
> the nature and extent of the interference with
> rights in the *parcel as a whole. . . . Penn Central,*
> *id.* 130–131. (Emphasis added.)

The Court refused to consider whether all the
value of the air space above the terminal had been
taken by the regulation, focusing instead on the total
value of the property, including the transferable
development rights provided by the regulation.

In *Palazzolo v. Rhode Island,* 533 U.S. 606, 121
S.Ct. 2448, 150 L.Ed.2d 592 (2001), the U.S. Supreme
Court confronted the takings issues raised by permit
denials for proposed filling of Rhode Island coastal
wetlands protected under Rhode Island's coastal zone

management program. The case was remanded for reconsideration by the state supreme court based on the *Penn Central* analysis because the property still retained value and economic use. Upon remand, the trial court ruled that there had been no taking. *Palazzolo v. State*, 2005 WL 1645974 (R.I.Super.Ct. 2005). See also *Gove v. Zoning Board of Appeals of Chatham*, 444 Mass. 754, 831 N.E.2d 865 (Sup.Ct. 2005) (building prohibition on coastal lot subject to flooding held not a taking based on *Penn Central*).

Because so many major takings cases have focused on use of coastal lands and wetlands, these areas will be considered individually.

2. COASTAL CONSTRUCTION REGULATION

Beachfront property is often wedged between a coastal highway and the mean high water mark, leaving little flexibility for locating structures on the land. Setback lines and other restrictive zones may incorporate an entire shoreline lot. Coastal land has always been in jeopardy from storms and erosion, and is now the target of sea level rise. In addition, new coastal construction regulations may disproportionately affect unimproved lots in developed coastal areas. All of these factors make regulation of coastal construction particularly susceptible to claims that the regulation "goes too far" in impairing the use and value of the land when regulation affects development or protection of the property.

South Carolina's Beachfront Management Act (BMA), as passed in 1988, created a "dead zone" landward of a baseline at the crest of the primary dune within which no development would be permitted. The statute precluded the development of two lots on an extensively developed beach on the Isle of Palms that had been purchased in 1986 by David Lucas. Lucas filed suit in state court contending that the BMA had taken his property without compensation. The trial court found that the BMA deprived Lucas of all economically viable use of the land, rendering it "valueless." The South Carolina Supreme Court reversed, holding that the BMA was intended to prevent a serious public harm and required no compensation regardless of the effect on property value. *Lucas v. South Carolina Coastal Council*, 304 S.C. 376, 404 S.E.2d 895 (1991).

Although the BMA was amended in 1990 to provide for special permits for development in the former "dead zone," the U.S. Supreme Court granted certiorari to determine whether the BMA effected a "temporary taking" of the Lucas property. See *First English Evangelical Lutheran Church of Glendale v. Los Angeles*, 482 U.S. 304, 107 S.Ct. 2378, 96 L.Ed.2d 250 (1987) (holding that compensation is due for the period during which a regulation that effects a taking is in place, even if the regulation is subsequently withdrawn). Justice Scalia, writing for the majority, identified two categories of regulatory actions that required compensation without any balancing of the public interests served. The first category comprises regulations that authorize a permanent physical invasion. The situation in *Lucas v. South Carolina Coastal Council*, 505 U.S. 1003, 112 S.Ct. 2886, 120 L.Ed.2d 798 (1992), fell within the second category—

"where regulation denies all economically beneficial or productive use of land." The Court rejected the notion that no compensation is required in situations that can be characterized as preventing a harmful or "noxious" use. Justice Scalia asserted that the distinction between preventing a public harm and creating a public benefit is meaningless—dependent primarily upon a subjective determination of the values of competing uses of property. Noting that although situations where a regulation confiscates all value of land would be rare, such regulations should be treated as "similar" to a physical occupation, i.e., as a *per se* taking of property without compensation.

The Court postulated that the only exception to the compensation requirement in the case of a regulation that deprives land of all beneficial use, is when the "proscribed use interests were not part of [the] title to begin with." The Court further stated:

Any limitation so severe cannot be newly legislated or decreed (without compensation), but must inhere in the title itself, in the restrictions *that background principles of the State's law of property and nuisance* already place upon land ownership. A law or decree with such an effect must, in other words, do no more than duplicate the result that could have been achieved in the courts—by adjacent landowners (or other uniquely affected persons) under the State's law of private nuisance, or by the State under its complementary power to abate nuisances that affect the public generally, or otherwise. Id. at 505 U.S. 1030. (Emphasis added.)

The Court described a "total taking inquiry" into state nuisance law as normally including:

an analysis of, among other things, the degree of harm to public lands and resources, or adjacent private property, posed by the claimant's proposed activities, the social value of the claimant's activities and their suitability to the locality in question, and the relative ease with which the alleged harm can be avoided through measures taken by the claimant and the government (or adjacent landowner) alike.

Id. at 505 U.S. 1031–1032. (Citations omitted). The history of nuisance law suggests that this balancing test is similar to, but perhaps even more complicated than, the balancing of public interests served and private burdens imposed as applied in *Penn Central*. This analysis adds very little certainty to the process of determining when a regulation denying all use effects a taking. The Court exacerbated the uncertainty by also recognizing that (as in nuisance law) "changed circumstances or new knowledge may make what was previously permissible no longer so." It seems that the major differences in the two balancing tests (the *Penn Central* test and the "total takings" test) is that in the total takings analysis the burden of proof is shifted to the government and the court's judgment is substituted for the legislature's.

In *Lucas,* the Court found it probative that similarly situated owners had made the same use of land and are permitted to continue to make residential use of the land. In remanding the case to the South Carolina Supreme Court to determine the relevant background principles of state law, the U.S. Supreme Court observed:

> It seems unlikely that common law principles would have prevented the erection of any habitable structure or productive improvements on petitioner's land; they rarely support prohibition of the "essential use" of land.

In the remand of the *Lucas* case, the South Carolina Supreme Court found no common law basis for prohibiting Lucas' proposed use of the land and remanded the case to the trial court for a determination of the actual damages Lucas sustained for the temporary taking of his property. Interestingly, the state supreme court determined that the temporary taking began with the 1988 enactment of the BMA and continued through the date of that court's order, rather than finding that the taking continued only to the time of the Amendment of the BMA in 1990. *Lucas v. South Carolina Coastal Council*, 309 S.C. 424, 424 S.E.2d 484 (1992).

Although the U.S. Supreme Court specifically discussed nuisance law in *Lucas,* the Court did not explain what is incorporated in the concept of "other background principles" of state property law, leaving state courts to decide the parameters of this exception in total takings analysis. The Oregon Supreme Court has held that the doctrine of custom in the context of public beach access is such a background principle. See *Stevens v. Cannon Beach*,

317 Or. 131, 854 P.2d 449 (1993) and Chapter II.E.1. And the public trust doctrine and federal navigation servitude have been identified as background principles justifying the denial of compensation to landowners denied permits to develop lands periodically overflowed by tidewaters. See *Esplanade Properties, LLC v. City of Seattle*, 307 F.3d 978 (9th Cir. 2002); *McQueen v. South Carolina Coastal Council*, 354 S.C. 142, 580 S.E.2d 116 (2003); *Palm Beach Isles Associates v. United States,* 58 Fed.Cl. 657 (2003).

The Virginia Supreme Court held that landowners could not base a total takings claim on the loss of value of land acquired subject to preexisting regulatory restrictions. The court reasoned that because the land was acquired with knowledge of the restrictions on development, the "risk of economic loss" was assumed by the landowners as part of their title. The court found it unnecessary to analyze the Coastal Primary Sand Dune Protection Act to determine whether the Act prevented a nuisance. "Such an inquiry is irrelevant" since the owner never acquired, as part of his title, the right to freely develop the property. See *Virginia Beach v. Bell*, 255 Va. 395, 498 S.E.2d 414 (1998). In *Palazzolo*, 533 U.S. 606, 121 S.Ct. 2448, 150 L.Ed.2d 592 (2001), however, the U.S. Supreme Court declined to interpret the Fifth Amendment as including such a limitation. "A regulation or common-law rule cannot be a background principle for some owners but not for others. . . . A law does not become a background principle for subsequent owners by enactment itself." Id. at 533 U.S. 632. Unfortunately, the Court gave no hint as to when a regulation (that does not simply codify a common law principle) can become a background principle.

The Supreme Court has, however, applied a different kind of "temporal" element to its takings analysis in a case involving a land use moratorium halting development in particularly sensitive waterfront areas pending the preparation of comprehensive plans controlling future development. The Court refused to combine the rationales of *First English* and *Lucas* to characterize a prohibition on development during a 3-year moratorium as a *per se* "temporary, total taking" requiring compensation. In *Tahoe-Sierra Preservation Council, Inc. v. Tahoe Regional Planning Agency*, 535 U.S. 302, 122 S.Ct. 1465, 152 L.Ed.2d 517 (2002), the Court found "total taking" analysis inapplicable. In considering the impact of a regulation on the property "as a whole," a temporary restriction on use of the property is not a permanent deprivation because the property will recover, and perhaps even increase, its value after the moratorium is lifted.

Within days of the *Lucas* decision, the U.S. Supreme Court denied certiorari in another takings challenge to South Carolina's Beach Management Act (BMA). In *Esposito v. South Carolina Coastal Council*, 939 F.2d 165 (4th Cir. 1991), owners of residences located at least partially within the "dead zone" argued that the restrictions on rebuilding if the structures were destroyed diminished the present value of the property and constituted a taking. The federal court of appeals found that the BMA allowed the owners to continue the existing use of their land and dwellings, consistent with their expectations. Diminution of market value alone was not enough to establish that a taking had occurred.

3.   WETLANDS REGULATION

If the U.S. Army Corps of Engineers denies a CWA § 404 permit, the validity of that denial may be challenged in federal district court. Because the Corps' jurisdiction and broad scope of review are generally well established, many permit denials are now taken directly to the U.S. Claims Court under the Tucker Act. The Tucker Act, 28 U.S.C.A. § 1491, gives the Claims Court jurisdiction to hear any constitutional claims against the United States for damages. By choosing the forum of the Claims Court, the permit applicant accepts the validity of the permit denial but alleges that the denial constitutes an uncompensated taking of private property.

The first such takings challenges to denials of section 404 permits were brought in 1981. In cases like *Deltona Corp. v. United States,* 228 Ct.Cl. 476, 657 F.2d 1184 (1981), and *Jentgen v. United States,* 228 Ct.Cl. 527, 657 F.2d 1210 (1981), the Claims Court followed traditional *Penn Central* analysis in considering the public purpose and legitimacy of the regulation, whether the property retained economic use, and the degree to which investment-backed expectations had been frustrated. The court held that the permit denials did not amount to takings. *Loveladies Harbor, Inc. v. United States*, 28 F.3d 1171 (Fed.Cir. 1994), however, reached a different conclusion on the takings issue in similar circumstances. The major difference in the case appears to be in the court's method of determination of diminution of value or degree of deprivation of use.

In footnote 7 of *Lucas v. South Carolina Coastal Council*, 505 U.S. 1003, 112 S.Ct. 2886, 120 L.Ed.2d 798 (1992), the Supreme Court noted the imprecision of determining when all economically viable use of property is taken. The result is dependent upon "the 'property interest' against which the loss of value is to be measured." Id. fn. 7. In *Penn Central Transportation Co. v. City of New York*, 438 U.S. 104, 98 S.Ct. 2646, 57 L.Ed.2d 631 (1978), the Court identified the "denominator in [the] deprivation fraction," *Lucas*, at fn.7, as the value of the property as a whole as affected by the regulation. *Penn Central*, 438 U.S. 131–132. Applying this approach in *Deltona* and *Jentgen,* supra, the court considered the value of applicants' entire development as the relevant denominator. In *Loveladies Harbor,* however, the Claims Court refused to consider the areas for which the permits were denied in the context of the applicants' larger holdings, resulting in determinations that over 95 percent of the value had been deprived. *Loveladies Harbor v. United States*, 21 Cl.Ct. 153 (1990). On appeal, the Federal Circuit upheld the trial court conclusion that only land developed or sold after the wetlands became subject to regulation could be included in the denominator. *Loveladies Harbor v. United States*, 28 F.3d 1171 (Fed.Cir. 1994). See also *Florida Rock Indus., Inc. v. United States*, 18 F.3d 1560 (Fed.Cir.1994). In *Good v. United States*, 189 F.3d 1355 (Fed. Cir. 1999), the

Federal Circuit found no taking had occurred through a Corps coastal wetland fill permit denial because the claimants could not have had reasonable expectations of receiving a permit when they acquired the property in 1973. Accord, *Norman v. United States*, 429 F.3d 1081 (Fed.Cir. 2005).

Mitigation is a common requirement of wetlands permits to offset impacts of the wetland loss. When such requirements involve dedication of land, *Nollan* and *Dolan* clearly require a "nexus" and "rough proportionality" between the exaction and the effects of the landowner's proposed action. See Chapter II.E.2. In *Koontz v. St. Johns River Water Management District*, 570 U.S. 595, 133 S.Ct. 2586 (2013), the Water Management District (WMD) denied a state wetlands permit when the applicant refused to agree to any of the mitigation options proposed by the WMD. In the 5–4 decision, the U.S. Supreme Court stated that *Nollan* and *Dolan*'s principles apply whether "the government *approves* a permit on the condition that the applicant turn over property or *denies* a permit because the applicant refuses to do so." Id. at 570 U.S. 619. The Court also found that monetary exactions or "in lieu" fees are "functionally equivalent to other types of land use exactions" and must also satisfy the *Nollan/Dolan* requirements. Id. In holding that "the government's demand for property from a land-use permit applicant must satisfy the requirements of *Nollan* and *Dolan* even when the government denies the permit and even when its demand is for money," id., the Court provided little guidance concerning a remedy. Just compensation under the Fifth

Amendment is not relevant "[w]here the permit is denied and the condition is never imposed, [because] nothing has been taken." The Court directs that "[i]n cases where there is an excessive demand but no taking, whether money damages are available is not a question of federal constitutional law but of the cause of action—whether state or federal—on which the landowner relies." Id. 609–610. The implications of the case are still not fully understood, but Justice Kagan expressed in her dissenting opinion that her main concern was with how *Koontz* will constitutionalize the entire regulatory process. If *Nollan/Dolan* is applicable to all proposals and suggestions made during permit application negotiations, governments might desist altogether from communicating with applicants. Justice Kagan observes: "[The decision] deprives state and local governments of the flexibility they need to enhance their communities—to ensure environmentally sound and economically productive development. It places courts smack in the middle of the most everyday local government activity." Id. at 636–637. See also John D. Echeverria, *The Costs of Koontz*, 39 Vt. L. Rev. 573 (2015)(*Koontz* "undermines the Supreme Court as an institution by departing from prior precedent and established principles of takings doctrine without rhyme or reason").

4.   THE SPECTRE OF JUDICIAL TAKINGS

Because of the indeterminacy and unpredictability of regulatory takings cases, property owners often lack a clear test for making claims for compensation when coastal regulations have affected the value of their land. This situation has led property rights advocates to advance new theories that may affect the development of takings analysis and, consequently, coastal management law. In *Stop the Beach Renourishment v. Florida Department of Environmental Protection*, 560 U.S. 702, 130 S.Ct. 2592, 177 L.Ed. 184 (2010)(*STBR*), the property owners claimed that the Florida Supreme Court had taken their right to accretions, a vested property interest, by changing the law applicable to the right to accretion in the context of beach restoration. Although the U.S. Supreme Court unanimously agreed that there had been no Fifth Amendment taking, the plurality, led by Justice Scalia, found that judicial opinions "effect a taking if they recharacterize as public property what was previously private property." Id. at 560 U.S. 713. Justice Scalia's test for a judicial taking focused on the effect on existing property rights: "If a legislature *or a court* declares that what was once an established right of private property no longer exists, it has taken that property. . . ." Id. at 560 U.S. 716. (Emphasis added). Justice Scalia explained judicial taking as follows: "Condemnation by eminent domain, for example, is always a taking, while a legislative, executive, *or judicial* restriction of property use may or may not be, depending on its nature and extent." Id. He did not suggest that judicial taking would constitute another type of categorical taking.

The four concurring justices in *STBR* did not adopt the concept of judicial taking, finding adoption of a novel constitutional concept unnecessary to disposition of the case. Justice Kennedy, joined by

Justice Sotomayor, however, addressed the problems associated with applying the Fifth Amendment to judicial decisions and suggested that courts could be constrained appropriately from making arbitrary and irrational decisions that eliminate established property rights through the Due Process Clause. It is notable that none of the justices, however, categorically denied the existence of the concept of a judicial taking, and that six justices agreed that state supreme court decisions that eliminated existing property rights might be unconstitutional either as a judicial taking or as a due process violation. See, e.g., Surfrider Found. v. Martins Beach 1, LLC, 14 Cal. App. 5th 238, 262; 221 Cal. Rptr. 3d 382, 403 (Ct. App. 2017), review denied (Oct. 25, 2017), cert. denied, 139 S.Ct. 54, 202 L.Ed.2d 19 (2018) ("The lesson we take from *Stop the Beach* is that where it has been determined that a court action eliminates an established property right and would be considered a taking if done by the legislative or executive branches of government, it must be invalidated as unconstitutional, whether under the takings or due process clauses"); see also, Archbold-Garrett v. New Orleans City, 893 F.3d 318, 322 (5th Cir. 2018)("The fair market value of the property taken is ordinarily the measure of damages for a takings claim, while a "broad array of common law remedies" is available for a procedural due process claim." In the case, the parties sought both economic damages and equitable relief, noting that a "due process claim does not "assert[ ] the same injuries [or] seek[ ] the same relief as a takings claim.").

5. A NEW TAKE ON TAKINGS: FOURTH AMENDMENT "SEIZURE" OF PROPERTY

Plaintiffs have recently asserted a novel Fourth Amendment claim to an unreasonable seizure of property, rather than a Fifth Amendment taking. In *Severance v. Patterson*, 566 F.3d 490 (5th Cir. 2009), the federal case that certified the question of "rolling" public beach access easements to the Texas Supreme Court, the federal Court of Appeals found that the Fourth Amendment claim was not subsumed in Severance's taking claim, stating:

> . . . The Fourth Amendment applies to civil as well as criminal seizures, and the Supreme Court holds that an interference with individual property rights may be found to breach more than one provision of the Constitution. . . . The Fourth and Fifth Amendments . . . both provide specific constitutional commands. That they may have evolved through caselaw to overlap in providing remedies for some deprivations of property interests does not authorize this court to fail to apply one or the other provision. . . . [T]he elements of a violation of the two amendments differ, with the touchstone of a takings claim being lack of just compensation and that of a seizure claim being its unreasonableness.

Id. at 501–502. (Citations omitted). The federal court also rejected the argument that "every ordinary taking of property for public use is to be hereafter actionable as a seizure," noting that regulatory takings may not usually "involve sufficient interference with possessory interests to constitute a seizure." Id.

The Fifth Circuit Court summarized the elements of a Fourth Amendment claim as (1) a meaningful interference with possessory interests in property, see *United States v. Jacobsen*, 466 U.S. 109, 113 (1984), that is (2) unreasonable because the interference is unjustified by state law or, if justified, is uncompensated. The court found that "[n]ot only has the State thus appropriated an easement over her property, but it denies owing any compensation. These facts state a potential claim under the Fourth as well as Fifth Amendments. *Severence*, at 501–502.

It is still too early to judge the effect of *Severance* or *Stop the Beach* in regulation of the coast. It seems unlikely, however, that these additional causes of action will provide property owners the "bright line" they seek to demarcate when a regulation "goes too far." They may, however, create further hurdles for management of the coasts to adapt to SLR. See, generally, John R. Nolon, *Regulatory Takings and Property Rights Confront Sea Level Rise: How Do They Roll?*, 21 Widener L.J. 735 (2012); J. Peter Byrne, *Rising Seas and Common Law Baselines: A Comment on Regulatory Takings Discourse Concerning Climate Change*, 11 Vt. J. Envtl. L. 627–642 (2010).

CHAPTER V

OCEAN ENERGY AND MARINE MINERALS MANAGEMENT

A. OIL AND GAS DEVELOPMENT ON THE OUTER CONTINENTAL SHELF

1. OVERVIEW OF THE OCSLA

In 1953, the year in which the Submerged Lands Act was enacted, Congress also passed the Outer Continental Shelf Lands Act (OCSLA), 43 U.S.C.A. §§ 1331–56. See Chapter III.A.2. The OCSLA codified the Truman Proclamation of 1945, an executive order that asserted U.S. sovereignty over the resources within and on the submerged land that constitute the "natural prolongation" of the country under the adjacent seas. The OCSLA reaffirmed the United States' sovereignty and exclusive jurisdiction over its continental shelf resources and created authority for the Department of the Interior (DOI) to encourage discovery and development of oil through a leasing program. The OCSLA defines the outer continental shelf (OCS) as the submerged lands seaward of state boundaries and which "appertain to the United States and are subject to its jurisdiction and control." Id. § 1331(a). Since coastal nation jurisdiction over OCS resources was still an evolving concept at the time, the Act basically left the seaward limit of the OCS to be determined as a matter of international law.

The OCSLA, as enacted in 1953, authorized the DOI to lease OCS lands to the highest bidder for mineral production. The Secretary of the Interior could adopt rules for conservation of natural resources that would be incorporated into leases. Imposing new rules on leases after their issuance on conservation and environmental grounds, however, subjected DOI to suits claiming a taking of private property and impairment or breach of contract. See, e.g., *Union Oil Co. of Cal. v. Morton*, 512 F.2d 743 (9th Cir. 1975); *Sun Oil Co. v. United States Marathon Oil Co. v. United States*, 215 Ct.Cl. 716, 572 F.2d 786 (1978). But see *Marathon Oil Co. v. United States*, 158 F.3d 1253 (Fed.Cir. 1998) (holding that delays due to a state Coastal Zone Management Act consistency objection to exploration under an OCS lease were not compensable), *reversed on other grounds, Mobil Oil Exploration v. United States*, 530 U.S. 604, 120 S.Ct. 2423, 147 L.Ed.2d 528 (2000). The disastrous 1969 Santa Barbara blowout and oil spill led to widespread recognition that the limited provisions in the OCSLA for emergency suspensions and the authority for the DOI to impose conditions only at the leasing stage were totally inadequate for protection of the environment.

The first "overhaul" of the OCSLA did not occur, however, until the 1978 amendments. Importantly, oil and gas leases became subject to subsequently-enacted OCSLA regulations. The amendments also established criteria for suspension and cancellation of leases, incorporated environmental safeguards, and created a role for coastal states in OCS planning and development.

Although not a statutory change, the introduction of areawide leasing during President Reagan's administration, fundamentally changed the leasing process. Areawide leasing opened up entire OCS planning areas, millions of acres of OCS, to lease sales. The approach was intended to accelerate lease sales, but it also minimized competition among bidders and reduced the amount of bids and revenue to the U.S. It also made assessment of impacts of a lease sale difficult, increasing tension between the federal government and the states.

Starting in 1982, Congress began regularly introducing limitations on leasing in areas of the OCS by restricting funding in DOI's appropriations bills. These Congressional moratoria continued for 27 years. In addition, presidential leasing withdrawals authorized under OCSLA section 12(a), 43 U.S.C.A. § 1341(a), limited new leasing primarily to the central and western Gulf of Mexico and the OCS off Alaska. President Bush implemented a moratorium in 1990 on lease sales for a large portion of the continental U.S. from 1990–2000, which was extended to 2012 by President Clinton and rescinded by the second President Bush in 2008. President Obama protected several OCS areas by withdrawals from leasing, including marine sanctuaries (2008), and areas off Alaska and the Atlantic coasts (2015 and 2016). In 2017, President Trump issued Executive Order 13795 revoking the Obama withdrawals off Alaska and the Atlantic, and limiting protection of marine sanctuaries to areas designated as of July 14, 2008.

In 2006 Congress passed the Gulf of Mexico Energy Security Act (GOMESA) which required leasing in 8.3 million acres in the Gulf, including 5.8 million acres that were previously under Congressional moratoria. GOMESA also established a new moratorium on leasing activities in a redefined Eastern Gulf planning area within 125 miles of the Florida coast, as well as a portion of the Central Gulf planning area within 100 miles of coastline of Florida, until June 30, 2022. A moratorium also applies east of the Military Mission Line in the Gulf of Mexico in an area that has been traditionally used for military testing and training activities. The Act further provided for exchanges, allowing companies to exchange certain leases in moratorium areas for bonus and royalty credits to be used on other Gulf of Mexico leases.

On March 29, 2019, the U.S. District Court for the District of Alaska vacated President Trump's attempt by Executive Order13795 to revoke leasing withdrawals issued by President Obama in 2015 and 2016 for parts of the OCS in Alaska's Beaufort and Chukchi seas and canyon areas in the Atlantic. In *League of Conservation Voters et al. v. Trump et al.*, No. 17-cv-101, 2019 WL 1431217 (D. Alaska 2019), the court found that OCSLA section 12(a) authorized only presidential *withdrawals* of areas of the OCS from leasing, and the EO was consequently "unlawful and invalid." Because the Obama withdrawals were "for a time period without specific expiration," the court ordered that they "remain in full force and effect unless and until revoked by Congress." Although the case is likely to be appealed, there will be immediate effects on lease sale plans and on development of President Trump's policies to open up most of the OCS for leasing in a new Five Year Plan.

BOEM lists the following areas that continue under moratoria or withdrawals as of early 2019:

(1) the areas restricted by GOMESA discussed above;

(2) the North Aleutian Basin Planning Area and Bristol Bay withdrawn by President Obama on December 16, 2014, for a non-specific period of time; and

(3) marine sanctuaries that existed as of 2008, and the Northeast Canyons and Seamounts Marine National Monument.

2. THE OCSLA LEASING AND DEVELOPMENT PROGRAM

The 1978 OCSLA amendments created a process for OCS development that now comprises five phases: (1) a five-year lease program; (2) the lease sale; (3) exploration; (4) development and production; and (5) decommissioning with removal of structures. The program is administered by the Bureau of Ocean Energy Management (BOEM), formerly the Marine Minerals Service (MMS), within the Department of the Interior (DOI).

a. The Five-Year Lease Program

The Secretary of the Interior is charged by the OCSLA with preparation of an oil and gas leasing program which consists of five-year schedules of proposed lease sales indicating, as precisely as possible, size, timing, and location of such activities. 43 U.S.C.A. § 1344(a). To facilitate preparation of the program, the OCS has been divided into 26 planning areas.

OCS Planning Areas

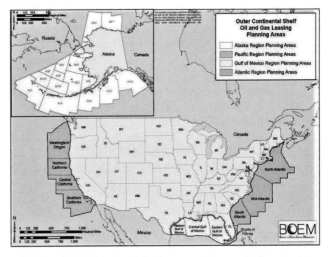

The 1978 amendments set out the considerations that must be taken into account in development of the lease program. In summary, these include: (1) the existing information for assessment, predictive, and environmental purposes concerning the geographical, geological, and ecological characteristics of such regions; (2) distribution of development benefits and environmental risks among regions; (3) the interest of potential oil and gas producers; (4) the relative environmental sensitivity and marine productivity of different areas and the potential for conflict with other ocean, seabed, and resource uses; and (5) laws and policies of affected states. Id. § 1344(a)(2)(A)–(H). The lease plan is intended to reflect, "to the maximum extent practicable ... a proper balance between the potential for environmental damage, the potential for the discovery of oil and gas, and the potential for adverse impact on the coastal zone." Id. § 1344(a)(3). See *Center for Biological Diversity v. U.S. Dep't of Interior*, 563 F.3d 466 (D.C. Cir. 2009) (vacating the leasing program and remanding the program to the Secretary of Interior to conduct adequate analysis of statutory factors and obtain the "proper balance" required).

Governors of affected states are given several opportunities to review and comment on the proposed leasing program both before and after publication of the proposed program in the Federal Register. An "affected state" includes: (1) a state connected to an artificial island or structure; (2) a state that will receive OCS oil for processing or transshipment; (3) a state designated by the Secretary of Interior because of the probability of significant impact or damage to the coastal, marine, or human environment from OCS development; or (4) a state that the Secretary finds is subject to considerable risk from oil spills, blowouts, or other releases because of such factors as prevailing winds or currents. 43 U.S.C.A. § 1331(f). The Secretary must reply to the governors in writing, explaining his decision to grant or deny the governors' requested program modifications. The submission of the lease program to Congress and the President must include copies of all correspondence between the Secretary and the governors of affected states. 43 U.S.C.A. § 1344(c).

Development and adoption of a Five-Year Lease Program also involves extensive review and consultation with other agencies, the oil and gas industry, the public, and local governments. The procedural requirements of both the OCSLA and the National Environmental Policy Act (NEPA), 42 U.S.C.A. §§ 4321–370, must be met. See *Natural Resources Defense Council, Inc. v. Hodel*, 865 F.2d 288, 275 U.S.App.D.C. 69 (D.C.Cir. 1988) (remanding the program to the Secretary for failure-to meet NEPA requirements, i.e., failure to consider the cumulative impact on migratory marine mammals); but see *Center for Biological Diversity v. U.S. Dep't of Interior,* 563 F.3d 466 (D.C. Cir. 2009) (Although the petitioners had standing to bring climate change claims, the NEPA-based claims are not ripe due to the multiple stage nature of the Leasing Program). NEPA provides states and the public an additional opportunity to participate in the OCS lease program by commenting on the draft and final EIS and through judicial review of the final EIS.

After publication of a proposed Five-Year Lease Program, states and local governments have an additional ninety days to make comments and recommendations. At least sixty days before approving the program, the Secretary must submit the program to Congress along with any comments and the Secretary's justification for rejecting the recommendations of a state or local government. 43 U.S.C.A. § 1344(d). The Secretary must review the leasing program yearly and may revise and reapprove it. A new program must be developed, however, every five years. Id. § 1344(e).

For sixty days after its approval by the Secretary, a five-year leasing program is subject to judicial review exclusively in the District of Columbia Court of Appeals through a suit by adversely affected or aggrieved persons who participated in the administrative proceedings related to the program. 43 U.S.C.A. § 1349(c)(1). But the reviewing court will accord the Secretary substantial deference. In *California v. Watt*, 668 F.2d 1290, 215 U.S.App.D.C. 258 (D.C.Cir. 1981), the court set out the standard of review for a five-year leasing program. In summary, the record must establish that: (1) the Secretary's factual findings are based on substantial evidence; (2) policy judgments are based on rational consideration of identified relevant factors; and (3) the Secretary's interpretation of the statute is a permissible construction. See also *Natural Resources Defense Council v. Hodel*, 865 F.2d 288, 275 U.S.App.D.C. 69 (D.C.Cir. 1988).

In *California v. Watt,* the D.C. Circuit Court of Appeals concluded that the Five-Year Lease Program approved in 1980 was deficient in specificity of areas and timing and in consideration of the OCSLA-mandated factors, including failure to quantify environmental costs and properly balance potential for environmental damage and adverse coastal impacts with potential for oil discovery. The court remanded the leasing program for reconsideration. Subsequently, the lease program for 1982–1987 opened virtually all the OCS, almost one billion acres, for leasing. Environmental groups challenged the program on the same grounds as the previous program and also on the grounds that it violated the court's 1981 decree. This time, however, the court rejected the arguments and upheld the entire lease plan. *California v. Watt*, 712 F.2d 584, 229 U.S.App.D.C. 270 (D.C.Cir. 1983).

Similarly, the five-year lease program for 2007–2012 was vacated for violations of the OCSLA and NEPA. In January 2007, President George W. Bush lifted the Presidential moratorium for Alaska's Bristol Bay and extensively expanded areas for leasing in the Beaufort, Bering and Chukchi Seas. The final program included a lease sale in Bristol Bay scheduled for 2011. See *Center for Biological Diversity v. U.S. Dep't of the Interior* (D.C.C. 2009). The U.S. Court of Appeals for the D.C. Circuit remanded the 2007–2012 Program, requiring the Secretary to consider the comparative environmental sensitivity and marine productivity of areas of the OCS and to reassess the timing and location of the leasing program to properly apply the balancing requirements of 43 U.S.C.A. § 1344(a)(2)(A)–(H). The court upheld, however, the program's limiting its analysis of the program's effects to "production activities on climate change generally, and the present and future impact of climate change on the local OCS areas," rejecting an argument that DOI should consider the broader climate change effects of consumption of the oil produced on the world. Id.

The most recently adopted Five-Year Program is the 2017–2022 National OCS Program, developed by the Obama Administration and finally approved by the Trump Administration's Secretary of Interior in January 2017. The 2017–2022 Program schedules 11 potential lease sales in 4 OCS planning areas, including10 sales in the Western and Central Gulf of Mexico Program Areas, and one sale in the Cook Inlet Program Area offshore Alaska. No lease sales were proposed for the Pacific or Atlantic OCS. In April 2017, however, President Trump issued Executive Order 13795, *Implementing an America-First Offshore Energy Strategy*, directing BOEM to develop a new National OCS Program for 2019–2024. The proposed 2019–2024 Program envisions opening up 90% of the OCS for leasing, including 47 lease sales (19 in Alaska and the Arctic) in 25 of the 26 OCS planning areas. The *League of Conservation Voters* litigation, supra, has, however, led the Trump Administration to put the program on hold pending appeals. See Part V.A.1.

b. The Lease Sale

(1) The Lease Sale Process

Before DOI may initiate a lease sale, environmental studies of the lease area must be conducted in cooperation with affected states. 43 U.S.C.A. § 1346. Data is used to predict, assess, and manage the possible effects of OCS development on human, marine, and coastal environments. The Secretary is to consider relevant environmental information in developing regulations, in issuing operating orders, and in making decisions relating to exploration, drilling, and development and production plans. The OCSLA also directs the Secretary to carry out post-development environmental studies to monitor changes resulting from OCS activities. Courts have required an additional EIS for individual lease sales. See, e.g., *Conservation Law Found. v. Andrus*, 623 F.2d 712 (1st Cir. 1979); *Natural Resources Defense Council, Inc. v. Morton*, 458 F.2d 827, 148 U.S.App.D.C. 5 (D.C.Cir. 1972).

The Secretary must provide notice and copies of documents for proposed lease sales to the governors of affected states. Governors of those states and executives of local governments may submit recommendations to the Secretary on the size, timing, and location of proposed lease sales. 43 U.S.C.A. § 1345. The OCSLA requires the Secretary to accept the timely recommendations of a governor on lease sales if he determines that the recommendations provide for "a reasonable balance between the national interest and the well-being of the citizens of the affected [s]tate." See *Massachusetts v. Clark*, 594 F.Supp. 1373 (D.Mass. 1984); *Conservation Law Found. v. Watt*, 560 F.Supp. 561 (D.Mass. 1983). The Secretary has, however, rejected the recommendations of governors of coastal states on several occasions. The deferential standard that courts have applied in reviewing the Secretary's rejection of such recommendations effectively eviscerates the section's obligatory language, i.e., "*shall* accept recommendations of the Governor." See *California v. Watt*, 520 F.Supp. 1359 (C.D.Cal. 1981) (finding that although the Secretary violated the spirit of the OCSLA by rejecting the governor's recommendations, giving due deference to the Secretary's judgment, the determination was not arbitrary and capricious); see also *Tribal Village of Akutan v. Hodel*, 869 F.2d 1185 (9th Cir. 1988) (holding that the Secretary's rejection of the governor's recommendations was not arbitrary and capricious). The Secretary must respond to a governor, in writing, concerning his reasons for accepting or rejecting the recommendations. 43 U.S.C.A. § 1345.

OCS leases are granted to the highest responsible, qualified bidder through a competitive bidding process. The bidding is done by sealed bids based upon a notice of sale published in the Federal Register. The lease term is for a five-to-ten year period depending on the depth of the water. Id. § 1337.

(2) The Nature of a Lease: Property or Contract?

Prior to the 1978 OCSLA amendments, courts had described the nature of an OCS lease as not conveying title but conveying a property interest enforceable against the government. See, e.g., *Union Oil Co. of Cal. v. Morton*, 512 F.2d 743 (9th Cir. 1975). However, in *Secretary of the Interior v. California*, 464 U.S. 312, 104 S.Ct. 656, 78 L.Ed.2d 496 (1984), the U.S. Supreme Court noted that, since 1978, "the purchase of a lease entitles the purchaser only to priority over other interested parties in submitting for federal approval a plan for exploration, production, or development." This interpretation leaves unclear what, if any, property interest a lessee receives. More recently, the Supreme Court described the interest as a "renewable lease contract." In *Mobil Oil Exploration & Producing Southeast, Inc. v. United States*, 530 U.S. 604 (2000), the Court held that Mobil was entitled to restitution for breach of the "contract" by Congress' enactment of new legislation (the Outer Banks Protection Act) that prevented Mobil from proceeding to the exploration stage of the lease.

Note, however, that both "lease contracts" and the OCSLA now provide that an OCS lease is issued subject to the OCSLA and not only all OCSLA regulations in force at the time of the lease, but also to all regulations issued pursuant to the statute in the future which provide for the prevention of waste and conservation of the natural resources of the OCS and the protection of correlative rights therein (and certain other statutes, such as the CZMA). See 43 U.S.C. § 1334. In *Century Exploration New Orleans, LLC v. U.S.*, 745 F.3d 1168, 44 ELR 20060, 78 ERC (BNA) 1482 (Fed. Cir. 2014), the Federal Circuit Court of Appeals held that stringent new operating regulations issued following the Deepwater Horizon oil spill did not breach the lease agreements. The court found that the regulations were issued under authority of the OCSLA (not the Oil Pollution Act) and that the "government has not breached its implied duty of good faith and fair dealing because the lease expressly authorized the government action at issue . . . , [i.e.,] changes to OCSLA regulatory requirements." Id. at 1180.

(3) Lease Suspension and Cancellation

DOI has the express power to temporarily suspend or cancel leases if the lessee fails to comply with the terms of the lease, or "if there is a threat of serious, irreparable, or immediate harm or damage to life (including fish and other aquatic life) . . . or to the marine, coastal, or human environment." 43 U.S.C.A. § 1334(1). A lease may be canceled only after suspension for a continuous period of five years and a hearing in which the Secretary determines that continuation would cause serious harm to the marine, coastal, or human environment and that the threat of harm will not be abated in a reasonable period. If a lease is canceled, the lessee is entitled to compensation based on the fair value of the canceled rights or the expenses incurred by the lessee, whichever is less. Moreover, a lease may be forfeited and canceled for failure to comply with the OCSLA, its regulations, or the lease conditions. Id.

Leases may also be suspended at the request of a lessee. Lease suspensions are routinely granted (and extended) when "in the national interest, to facilitate proper development of a lease or to allow for the construction or negotiation for use of transportation facilities." 43 U.S.C. § 1334(a). But see *Aera Energy LLC v. Salazar*, 642 F.3d 212 (2011), *cert. denied*, 132 S.Ct. 252 (2011) (holding the agency may, on the merits, allow a lease to expire despite lessee's request for suspension).

(4) Lease Sales and CZMA Consistency

In the 1990 amendments to the Coastal Zone Management Act (CZMA), Congress reacted to the U.S. Supreme Court's holding in *Secretary of the Interior v. California*, 464 U.S. 312, 104 S.Ct. 656, 78 L.Ed.2d 496 (1984), which found that lease sales are not subject to the federal consistency provisions of the Act. Although the amendments to the CZMA did not address lease sales specifically, it is clear that such sales are now among the category of federal activities that must be consistent with state coastal management programs to the maximum extent practicable if the activity affects the coastal zone. Lease suspensions also cannot be categorically excluded from consistency review. See *California v. Norton*, 311 F.3d 1162 (9th Cir. 2002). DOI delays in approving lessee exploration plans due to consistency review of suspended leases issued prior to the 1990 amendments, however, have been held to be a repudiation of the leases in *Amber Resources Co. v. United States*, 538 F.3d 1358, 1371 (Fed. Cir. 2008) (holding that the government had effectively "repudiated the lease agreements by putting into practice new [court-mandated] rules applicable to the availability of requested suspensions").

(5) Legal Challenges to Environmental Impacts of Lease Sales

Judicial challenges to lease sales are generally based on NEPA, the Endangered Species Act (ESA), 16 U.S.C.A. §§ 1531–1544, or the environmental provisions of the OCSLA itself. Challenges based on

NEPA usually focus on the adequacy of the EIS, either in the scope of the alternatives considered or in the analysis of the environmental impact. *Natural Resources Defense Council, Inc. v. Morton*, 458 F.2d 827, 148 U.S.App.D.C. 5 (D.C.Cir. 1972) is the leading case on the scope of alternatives the DOI must consider in the EIS. NRDC sought to enjoin a Gulf of Mexico lease sale because the EIS had failed to consider a number of conservation alternatives to the energy problem. The D.C. Circuit Court of Appeals rejected the DOI's argument that it was required to consider only alternatives within its jurisdiction. The court applied a "rule of reason" in holding that the degree of consideration of an alternative depends upon its likelihood of being implemented. While novel and evolving concepts should not be excluded from consideration, NEPA "does not require a 'crystal ball' inquiry." Id. at 837.

In analyzing the adequacy of the consideration of environmental impacts at the lease sale stage, courts have focused on the fact that the OCS leasing process confers no development rights. As a general principle, the amount and specificity of information on environmental impacts will vary at each stage of the OCS development process. Because the environmental impacts are largely speculative at the lease sale stage, courts have asserted that the Secretary does not need to consider in detail potential impacts that can be addressed with more certainty at the exploration or development stage. See *Tribal Village of Akutan v. Hodel*, 869 F.2d 1185 (9th Cir. 1988); *Village of False Pass v. Clark*, 733 F.2d 605 (9th Cir. 1984); *California v. Watt*, 683 F.2d 1253 (9th

Cir. 1982); *North Slope Borough v. Andrus*, 642 F.2d 589, 206 U.S.App.D.C. 184 (D.C.Cir. 1980).

Likewise, challenges to lease sales based on the failure of the Secretary to incorporate sufficient environmental protections to meet OCSLA requirements have also been found insufficient to stop a lease sale, because opportunities to impose additional conditions exist at later stages. *Village of False Pass v. Clark*, 733 F.2d 605 (9th Cir. 1984).

An EIS that omits speculative information at the lease sale stage is not the equivalent of an EIS that is "incomplete due to the omission of ascertainable facts, or the inclusion of erroneous information, violat[ing] the disclosure requirements of [NEPA]." See *Tribal Village of Akutan v. Hodel*, 869 F.2d 1185, fn.1 (9th Cir. 1988); see also, *Native Village of Point Hope v. Salazar*, 730 F.Supp.2d 1009, 1019 (D.Ct. Alaska 2010) (remanding an EIS that acknowledged significant information gaps as inadequate, because it "failed to determine whether missing information identified by the agency was relevant or essential" and "failed to determine whether the cost of obtaining the missing information was exorbitant, or the means of doing so unknown"). See also, *WildEarth Guardians v. Zinke*, No. CV 16–1724 (RC), 2019 WL 1273181, at *14 (D.D.C. Mar. 19, 2019) where the court found the BLM's EA and Finding of No Significant Impact (FONSI) regarding oil leases did not comply with NEPA for failing "to take a 'hard look' at GHG [greenhouse gas] emissions" at the lease sale stage, including production, "down-stream" and cumulative emissions. In regard to the argument that such analysis was premature, the court stated that

> [w]hile BLM could not, at the leasing stage, reasonably foresee the environmental impacts of specific drilling projects, it could reasonably foresee and forecast the impacts of oil and gas drilling across the leased parcels as a whole. "In determining what effects are 'reasonably foreseeable,' an agency must engage in 'reasonable forecasting and speculation,' with reasonable being the operative word." *WildEarth Guardians* at *14, citing *Sierra Club v. U.S. Dep't of Energy*, 867 F.3d 189, 198 (D.C. Cir. 2017).

Two provisions of the ESA are particularly relevant to the OCS oil leasing process. Section 7(a)(2) of the ESA, 16 U.S.C.A. § 1536(a)(2), requires federal agencies to "insure that any action authorized, funded, or carried out by such agency . . . is not likely to jeopardize the continued existence of any endangered species or threatened species or result in the destruction or adverse modification of habitat . . . determined by the Secretary . . . to be critical." ESA § 7(d), 16 U.S.C.A. 1536(d), prohibits any agency or applicant from making "any irreversible or irretrievable commitment of resources with respect to the agency action which has the effect of foreclosing the formulation or implementation of any reasonable and prudent alternative measures." In *Oceana v. Bureau of Ocean Energy Mgmt.*, 37 F. Supp. 3d 147 (D.D.C. 2014), the court concluded that

[a]ll courts considering lease sales under the OCSLA have concluded that "lease sales do not constitute an 'irreversible or irretrievable commitment of resources' within the meaning of section 7(d)." *Vill. of False Pass v. Watt*, 565 F.Supp. 1123, 1163 (D.Alaska 1983), aff'd sub nom. *Vill. of False Pass v. Clark*, 733 F.2d 605 (9th Cir.1984); see also *N. Slope Borough v. Andrus*, 642 F.2d 589, 611 (D.C.Cir.1980) ("Plainly, the preliminary activities permitted by this lease sale entail no 'irreversible or irretrievable commitment of resources with respect to the Agency action which has the effect of foreclosing . . . alternative measures which avoid jeopardizing the continued existence of any endangered or threatened species. . . .' "); *Conservation Law Foundation of New England, Inc. v. Andrus*, 623 F.2d 712, 714–716 (1st Cir.1979) (rejecting appellants' argument that the lease sale stage constituted an irreversible or irretrievable commitment of resources for purposes of a preliminary injunction); *Defenders of Wildlife*, 871 F.Supp.2d at 1326 ("Nothing in BOEM's mere approval of bids for Lease Sale 213 could reasonably be viewed as constituting an irreversible or irretrievable commitment of resources under § 7(d).")

Id. at 176.

The second important ESA provision applies when DOI proposes a lease sale that may adversely affect an endangered species or its critical habitat. The agency must consult with the U.S. Fish and Wildlife

Service (FWS) or the National Marine Fisheries Service (NMFS). The relevant service will issue a biological opinion concerning whether the proposed sale will jeopardize the endangered species or adversely modify its habitat. But see, *Oceana v. Bureau of Ocean Energy Mgmt.*, 37 F.Supp. 3d 147 (D.D.C. 2014)(BOEM was not required to complete consultation with NMFS under the ESA before approving leases; and NMFS's delay in preparing BiOp was not unreasonable).

If a finding of jeopardy or adverse modification of habitat is made, the service will suggest "reasonable and prudent alternatives" the agency can implement. However, the agency is not required to adopt the alternatives. But see *Village of False Pass v. Watt*, 565 F.Supp. 1123 (D.Alaska 1983) (noting that if the Secretary deviates from the alternatives, "he does so subject to the risk that he has not satisfied the standard of section (7)(a)(2)"). A court may set aside an agency's determination to reject the service's proposed alternatives, however, only if the decision was "arbitrary, capricious, an abuse of discretion, or otherwise not in accordance with the law" under the Administrative Procedure Act (APA).

In *Tribal Village of Akutan v. Hodel*, 869 F.2d 1185 (9th Cir. 1988), and in *Village of False Pass v. Clark*, 733 F.2d 605 (9th Cir.1984), DOI had failed to adopt completely the reasonable and prudent alternatives proposed by NMFS to reduce the risk of oil spills that might harm endangered (at that time) gray whales. In both cases, the Circuit Court of Appeals rejected the argument that DOI had violated section (7)(a) by not implementing all the alternatives at the lease sale stage. Again relying on the multistage nature of the OCS development process, the court found "no irreversible or irretrievable commitment of resources" at the time of the lease sale. See also *North Slope Borough v. Andrus*, 642 F.2d 589, 206 U.S.App.D.C. 184 (D.C.Cir. 1980); *Conservation Law Found. v. Andrus*, 623 F.2d 712 (1st Cir. 1979); cf., *Conservation Law Found. v. Watt*, 560 F.Supp. 561 (D. Mass. 1983) (enjoining a Georges Bank lease sale for violations of the ESA). The court's deferential standard of review and the "wait and see what happens" approach to ESA compliance disregards the impacts of preliminary activities on endangered species as well as the additional costs and conflicts associated with putting off such decisions to the final development stages.

When OCS activities are acknowledged to have potential effects on endangered species, the ESA provides various mechanisms that allow projects to proceed nonetheless. E.g., 16 U.S.C. §§ 1536(b)(4) and (o) (Secretary may issue biological opinions or incidental take permits setting out certain conditions that will minimize impacts to endangered species).

(6) Conflicts with Fisheries

Because oil and gas development on the OCS can cause direct user conflicts with fishermen, as well as the potential for destruction of fisheries resources by pollution, lease sales have also been challenged for the potential effects on fisheries resources. As a general proposition, a majority of states have taken a policy position that renewable resource development, such as fisheries, should be favored over nonrenewable resource development. States and environmentalists have also argued that the express language of the OCSLA requires that oil and gas development may only be conducted if there is no harm to fisheries. The OCSLA provides that the Act be "construed in such a manner that the character of the waters above the Outer Continental Shelf as high seas and the right to navigation and fishing therein shall not be affected." 43 U.S.C.A. § 1332(2). In *Massachusetts v. Andrus*, 594 F.2d 872 (1st Cir. 1979), the federal court of appeals rejected an interpretation of this section that imposed an absolute priority for fisheries over oil and gas development. Construing the Act as a whole and in conjunction with the Magnuson-Stevens Fishery Conservation and Management Act (MSA or Magnuson-Stevens Act) and NEPA, the court found that the legislation was concerned with "balanced use of all resources of the area." Id. 890. The court did find, however, that the Secretary has "a duty to see that gas and oil exploration and drilling is conducted without unreasonable risk to the fisheries. His duty includes the obligation not to go forward with a lease sale in a particular area if it would create unreasonable risks in spite of all feasible safeguards." Id.

(7) Conflicts with Aboriginal Rights

Conflict with the unextinguished aboriginal rights of Native Alaskans to occupy and use the OCS may prove to be a basis for challenging lease sales off

Alaska coasts. "Aboriginal title or right is a right of exclusive use and occupancy held by Natives in lands and waters used by them and their ancestors prior to the assertion of sovereignty over such areas by the United States. These rights are superior to those of third parties, including the states, but are subject to the paramount powers of Congress." *Village of Gambell v. Clark*, 746 F.2d 572, 574 (9th Cir. 1984) (*Gambell I*). Neither the SLA, the OCSLA, nor the Magnuson-Stevens Act address aboriginal rights to the OCS or the EEZ or their resources.

In 1983, the DOI began leasing over two million acres of the OCS lands off the west coast of Alaska. The tribal Villages of Gambell and Stebbins sought to enjoin the lease sale, claiming that oil leasing would adversely affect their aboriginal rights to hunt and fish on the OCS. The Villages further argued that the Secretary had failed to comply with § 810 of the Alaska National Interest Lands Conservation Act (ANILCA), 16 U.S.C.A. § 3120, which requires federal agencies to consider the effect of the "use, occupancy, or disposition [of public lands] on subsistence uses and needs" in Alaska. The district court granted summary judgment in favor of the Secretary and the oil company intervenors, denying the injunction and allowing the lease sale to go forward. While the appeal was pending, the Secretary approved exploration plans for the leased areas. On appeal, the Ninth Circuit Court of Appeals in *Gambell I* found: (1) that aboriginal claims by Native Alaskans had been extinguished by the Alaska Native Claims Settlement Act (ANCSA), 43 U.S.C.A. § 1603(b)(ANCSA extinguished aboriginal claims within the state of Alaska and authorized creation of 13 regional and tribal corporations to own in fee simple and manage 44 million acres of Alaska Native Lands); and (2) that the Secretary was required to comply with ANILCA. The Secretary made a post-sale evaluation of the impacts of the leases and found that neither exploratory activities nor oil production would significantly restrict subsistence uses.

In 1985, the Villages again sought to enjoin exploratory drilling and a further lease sale. The district court found that the Secretary did not comply with ANILCA, but did not issue an injunction. On appeal, the Ninth Circuit found that the Villages had established a strong likelihood of success on the merits and stated: "Irreparable damage is presumed when an agency fails to evaluate thoroughly the environmental impact of a proposed action." The court found that an injunction was the "appropriate remedy for a violation of an environmental statute absent rare or unusual circumstances." *Village of Gambell v. Hodel*, 774 F.2d 1414, 1424 (9th Cir. 1985) (*Gambell II*). The U.S. Supreme Court granted certiorari and held that ANILCA applies only to activities in Alaska and not to activities on the OCS and that the injunction had been improperly issued. *Amoco Prod. Co. v. Village of Gambell*, 480 U.S. 531, 107 S.Ct. 1396, 94 L.Ed.2d 542 (1987). On remand, the Ninth Circuit found that if ANILCA applied only *in* Alaska, ANCSA similarly only extinguished aboriginal rights *in* Alaska. The court also held that "aboriginal rights may exist concurrently with a paramount federal interest" in the OCS. The case was remanded to the district court for a determination of whether aboriginal rights on the OCS exist, whether oil and gas leasing and development interferes with such rights, and whether the OCSLA extinguishes aboriginal rights. *Village of Gambell v. Hodel*, 869 F.2d 1273 (9th Cir. 1989) (*Gambell III*).

By the time the case was before the federal district court again, the oil companies had completed exploration activities and relinquished the leases, and no further lease sales were scheduled. Upon appeal from the district court's summary judgment for the government without deciding any of the questions, the Ninth Circuit found the issue moot and that no basis for federal jurisdiction remained. *Village of Gambell v. Babbitt*, 999 F.2d 403 (9th Cir. 1993) (*Gambell IV*).

Subsequently, in *Native Village of Eyak v. Trawler Diane Marie, Inc.*, 154 F.3d 1090 (9th Cir. 1998) (*Eyak I*), the 9th Circuit held that the paramount rights of the United States in the offshore (the "paramountcy doctrine") barred aboriginal claims to *exclusive* rights to hunt and fish in the offshore area. See also *U.S. v. California*, 332 U.S. 19, 67 S.Ct. 1658, 91 L.Ed. 1889 (1947). In *Eyak II*, the 9th Circuit attempted to address the apparent conflict in *Gambrell III* and *Eyak I* concerning the relation of aboriginal rights and the paramount rights of the national government in the OCS. Applying a test that required the Village to show not only "continuous use and occupancy," but also "an exclusive and unchallenged claim to the disputed areas," the court, over a strong dissent, held that the Village had not provided sufficient evidence to establish aboriginal rights on the OCS. The court, therefore, had no need reach the issue of whether recognition of aboriginal rights creates a conflict with the federal paramountcy doctrine. *Native Village of Eyak v. Blank*, 688 F.3d 619 (9th Cir. 2012) *(Eyak II)*.

Most recently, the federal district court in Hawai'i addressed the federal paramountcy doctrine in regard to cultural fishing rights of native Samoans. See *American Samoa v. NMFS*, 2016 WL 6648921 (U.S.D. Hawaii 2016). Stating that the "paramountcy doctrine applies 'with equal force to all entities claiming rights to the oceans' including states, territories, and aboriginal groups [citing Eyak I, at 1096]," the court concluded that "[w]hile limited rights, *if established*, may exist concurrently with a paramount federal interest" [citing Eyak II at 62], no cultural or aboriginal rights were proved to exist. Id. (Emphasis in original). The relationship between aboriginal rights of use of the offshore and the paramount rights of the federal government consequently remains unresolved.

c. Exploration Plans

Before embarking on exploration, the lessee must submit an exploration plan to DOI for approval. The plan must include a schedule of exploration activities, description of the equipment to be used, location of the well, and other information. An oil spill contingency plan and an environmental report must accompany the plan. Id. § 1340(c); 30 C.F.R. §§ 250.30–250.33.

(1) NEPA Review

DOI may conduct an environmental assessment (EA) at this stage to determine whether it can make a Finding of No Significant Impact (FONSI) or if an EIS must be prepared. EAs are generally done for frontier areas, but for "mature areas" of the OCS, such as the Central and Western Gulf of Mexico, DOI had determined that EAs are generally not required. The agency had also adopted numerous "categorical exclusions"—categories of actions that do not, except in extraordinary circumstances, result in individually or cumulatively significant environmental effects. DOI also applies a tiering process, described as coverage of general matters in broad, programmatic impact statements with narrower, more focused environmental analyses at later and, ultimately, site-specific stages. 40 C.F.R. §§ 1502.20, 1508.28. The tiering process and the segmented nature of the OCS development process often result in environmental impacts not being addressed before the production and development stage of the process. Since the design of the program necessitates reevaluations, and at "preliminary" stages like 5-year plans, lease sales and even exploration plans, the process has not reached the critical stage of a decision which will result in "irreversible and irretrievable commitment of resources" to an action that will adversely affect the environment. See *Mobil Oil Corp. v. FTC*, 562 F.2d 170, 173 (2d Cir. 1977).

The Council on Environmental Quality (CEQ) in its *Report Regarding the Minerals Management Service's National Environmental Policy Act Policies, Practices, and Procedures as They Relate to Outer Continental Shelf Oil and Gas Exploration and Development* (August 16, 2010) detailed the failures of the NEPA process contributing to the Deepwater Horizon oil spill and proposed comprehensive recommendations, most of which were implemented for the 2012–2017 Five-Year Lease Program. Since 2010, CEQ has also issued a number of guidance documents intended to "modernize and reinvigorate" NEPA. See CEQ, *Steps to Modernize and Reinvigorate NEPA*, available at https://obamawhite house.archives.gov/administration/eop/ceq/ initiatives/nepa.

CEQ also criticized the OCSLA provision requiring DOI to approve, approve with modifications, or disapprove an exploration plan within 30 days once it is complete. 43 U.S.C. § 1340(c)(1). Whether Congress underestimated the potential impacts of exploration or simply intended to expedite OCS oil exploration, CEQ judged the time too short for proper evaluation of exploration plans and recommended elimination of the time limit. *Steps to Modernize*, supra.

(2) ESA Biological Opinion and Consultation

The abbreviated 30-day time for review of exploration plans also limits effective consultation related to impacts on endangered species. Although the ESA, like NEPA, applies to every stage of OCS development, the courts have applied an approach, like the NEPA review, that postpones detailed review until the stage where the agency's next decision may place a species may experience imminent "jeopardy."

In the Western and Central Gulf of Mexico planning areas, however, the high level of oil and gas development has led to a repetitive and duplicative process, prone to shortcuts, with little or no new review of impacts to the environment or endangered and threatened species. In 2002 and 2006–2007, the MMS (the predecessor of BOEM) engaged in ESA consultations with the NMFS on Gulf of Mexico oil and gas activities. In 2007, NMFS issued a biological opinion (BiOp) that the proposed activities would not jeopardize any listed species or adversely modify critical habitat. The BiOp required only two "reasonable and prudent alternatives," both directed toward minimizing sea turtle strikes. Because of the effects of the Deepwater Horizon oil spill, BOEM requested NMFS to reinitiate the ESA consultation in mid-2010. BOEM submitted a new biological assessment to NMFS in 2013. By the conclusion of *Oceana v. Bureau of Ocean Energy Mgmt.*, 37 F. Supp. 3d 147, 187 (D.D.C. 2014)(dismissing a challenge to further leasing because of unreasonable delay in issuing the BiOp), however, a new BiOp for Gulf of Mexico oil and gas activities had not been issued by NMFS. A recently filed case, *Gulf Restoration Network v. NMFS* (M.D. Fl., Case No. 8:18-cv-01504, June 21, 2018), continues to assert unreasonable delay in NMFS' issuance of a BiOp. According to the filing, [since 2013] BOEM has released a new five-year leasing program and proposed another, sold over 7 million acres of new leases through 13 lease sales in the Gulf of Mexico, and approved over 2,500 exploration plans and Development Operations Coordination Documents in the Gulf of Mexico. During that same period, BSEE [Bureau of Safety and Environmental Enforcement in DOI] has approved nearly 5,000 applications for permits to drill in the Gulf of Mexico.

All of these actions were taken without completion of ESA consultation and a BiOp taking account of what has been learned since the Deepwater Horizon oil spill.

(3) CZMA Consistency Review

DOI cannot, however, issue a permit for exploration until affected states have concurred, or are presumed to concur, with the consistency certification that must be submitted with the exploration plan. 16 U.S.C.A. § 1456(c)(3)(B). A consistency certification provided to affected states by the lessee asserts that the exploration plan is consistent with the states' coastal management programs. This process may involve an additional three to six months. (Concurrence by the state with the oil company's consistency determination is "conclusively presumed" if the state does not object within six months. 16 U.S.C. § 1456(c)(3)(A)–(B)).

d.   Development/Production Plans

Once a discovery has been made, a development/production plan must be submitted to DOI for approval before production activities can begin. The plan must include: a description of the activity; drilling facilities to be used; location and depth of wells; geological and geophysical data; environmental and safety standards; and a timetable for development and production. This plan must also be accompanied by an oil spill contingency plan and an environmental report. 43 U.S.C.A. § 1351(a), (c); 30 C.F.R. § 250.34.

There is only one provision in the OCSLA mandating the preparation of an EIS, and it is directed at development and production plans in frontier areas. 43 U.S.C. § 351(e)(1) provides that:

> [a]t least once the Secretary shall declare the approval of a development and production plan in any area or region . . . of the outer Continental Shelf, other than the Gulf of Mexico, to be a major Federal action.

Development plans are reviewed for environmental impacts to determine whether another EIS must be prepared. In mature areas, DOI generally finds it unnecessary to prepare an EA or an EIS because of the experience in that area. As in the case of exploration plans, however, the NEPA process has been substantially revised since the Deepwater Horizon oil spill to compel more adequate review.

DOI must disapprove or require modification of a development plan if it is determined that the lessee has failed to demonstrate compliance with applicable laws, that the activities threaten national security or defense, or that the activities pose serious harm to life (including aquatic life), property, or to the marine, coastal, or human environment. Id. § 1351(h)(1). The plan also cannot be approved if it is inconsistent with the coastal management program of an affected state. Id. § 1351(d). If a plan is disapproved for failure to comply with statutory requirements of the OCSLA, including the consistency requirements of the CZMA (which were also incorporated into the OCSLA), the lessee is entitled to no compensation. If a plan is disapproved for one of the other reasons specified in the section and an approvable, modified plan is not submitted within five years, the Secretary must cancel the lease and compensate the lessee. Id. § 1351(h)(2).

As in the case of a lease sale, the Secretary must provide notice and copies of documents for proposed exploration and development/production plans to the governors of affected states, who may submit recommendations to the Secretary with respect to a proposed development/production plan. Id. § 1345(c). The Secretary must accept a governor's recommendations if he determines that they provide for "a reasonable balance between the national interest and the well-being of the citizens of the affected [s]tate." Id.

e. Decommissioning

OCSLA regulations define decommissioning as: "(1) Ending oil, gas, or sulphur operations; and (2)

Returning the lease or pipeline right-of-way to a condition that meets the requirements of regulations of BSEE [in DOI] and other agencies that have jurisdiction over decommissioning activities." 30 C.F.R. § 250.1700. This definition applies to all forms of decommissioning covered by the regulations: permanently plugging wells, temporarily abandoned wells, removing platforms and other facilities, site clearance, and pipeline decommissioning. Id. at § 250.1703.

DOI regulations require that lessees "[p]romptly and permanently plug" their temporarily-abandoned oil wells if the government so orders, 30 C.F.R. § 250.1723, and they must in any event "permanently plug all wells on a lease within 1 year after the lease terminates." Id. § 250.1710. Generally, a lease is terminated when the last structure on the lease ceases production. A post-removal report is due within 30 days after removing a platform or other facility. After the decommissioning is complete, the agency must assess whether it has been undertaken properly.

In *Noble Energy, Inc. v. Salazar*, 671 F.3d 1241 (D.C. Cir. 2012), Noble Energy argued that it was not obligated to follow a DOI order to permanently plug and abandon oils well off the coast of California that had been temporarily plugged since 1985. Noble argued that because the government had been found to have repudiated their lease agreement, see *Amber Res. Co. v. United States,* 538 F.3d 1358 (Fed.Cir.2008), Noble was released from further compliance with statutory and regulatory obligations by the common law doctrine of discharge. The court remanded for determination of whether the decommissioning regulations applied when the government breached its contract. On remand, the court held that Noble's regulatory duty to permanently plug and abandon an exploratory well was not discharged by government's material breach of the lease. *Noble Energy, Inc. v. Jewell*, 110 F. Supp. 3d 5 (D.D.C. 2015), aff'd, 650 F. App'x 9 (D.C. Cir. 2016).

3.   OCS REVENUE SHARING

Revenues from OCS leasing include bonuses, royalties, and rentals. During the period from 2011 through 2016, the federal government revenues totaled almost $38 billion from OCS oil and gas activities. The revenues are deposited primarily in the general treasury, but some funds go to the Land and Water Conservation Fund and the National Historic Preservation Fund to be distributed to the states for relevant projects.

In spite of the substantial environmental risks to states from OCS development and the costs states bear for onshore impacts of OCS activities, there has been relatively little direct revenue sharing of OCS-generated funds with the coastal states. Unlike the policy for leasing activities on federally-owned lands within the inland areas of states, coastal states do not share directly in royalties, cannot impose severance taxes, and do not receive payments in lieu of taxes to mitigate the impact of federal OCS leasing activities.

Congress has begun to address the OCS revenue sharing issue in an incremental fashion.

Section 8(g) of the OCSLA, 43 U.S.C.A. § 1337(g), originally provided for states to claim a "fair and equitable share" of revenues if a federal lease within three miles of a state's seaward boundary may tap a resource pool that underlies both federal and state lands. Apparently, however, these funds are not intended to be a general sharing of OCS revenues, but are instead compensation to the adjacent state for recovery of oil resources from lands under state waters. A 1984 case, *Texas v. Secretary of the Interior*, 580 F.Supp. 1197 (E.D.Tex. 1984), held that determination of a fair and equitable share included issues such as onshore impacts in addition to the issue of how much oil was drained from state lands. The court awarded the state fifty percent of the revenues. Congress amended section 8(g) in 1986 to provide for states to receive a twenty-seven percent share of revenues from such future leases, unless the Secretary and the governor of a state enter into an agreement for unitization or revenue sharing. See *Alabama v. U.S. Dept. of Interior*, 84 F.3d 410 (11th Cir. 1996). The Energy Policy Act of 2005 further provides sharing of twenty-seven percent of revenue from renewable energy leases generated in the § 8(g) zone.

The Energy Policy Act of 2005 also created the Coastal Impact Assistance Program (CIAP) which allocated a portion of $250 million allocated annually in 2007–2010 to Alabama, Alaska, California, Louisiana, Mississippi, and Texas—the OCS oil-producing states. To qualify, the states had to develop approved CIAP plans and could use the funds for coastal conservation, restoration, mitigation, and public infrastructure.

When Congress enacted the 2006 Gulf of Mexico Energy Security Act (GOMESA), lifting Congress' leasing moratorium on 8.3 million acres of OCS and mandating sales in two areas of the Central and Eastern Gulf of Mexico planning areas, it also offered a new incentive for coastal state cooperation in OCS development in the Gulf of Mexico. The Act gives the Gulf oil-producing states—Texas, Louisiana, Alabama, and Mississippi—37.5% of the revenues from that newly opened territory. Since 2017, that same percent applies to all new production in the Gulf.

Neither the CIAP nor the GOMESA funds come with "no strings attached." Both programs require the funds to be spent on specified programs. GOMESA funds, for example, may only be used for:

- Projects and activities for the purposes of coastal protection, including conservation, coastal restoration, hurricane protections, and infrastructure directly affected by coastal wetland losses;

- Mitigation of damage to fish, wildlife, or natural resources;

- Implementation of a federally approved marine, coastal, or comprehensive conservation management plan;

- Mitigation of impacts of OCS activities through funding of onshore infrastructure projects; and

- Planning assistance and the administrative costs that do not to exceed 3%.

Arguably, these restrictions make the revenue-sharing less valuable to the states concerned. On the other hand, it can be argued that the program provides a dedicated source of funding directed at projects closely related to adaption to climate change and sea level rise, areas of great importance to coastal states. With the potential for expanded offshore leasing, legislation continues to be introduced to expand GOMESA-type revenue sharing programs to other states, but it remains a controversial issue. The Obama administration opposed revenue sharing; the Trump administration first called for the end of GOMESA revenue sharing–then changed position; environmentalists support the idea of funds for coastal restoration, but fear revenue sharing will lead to more OCS oil and gas development; and many coastal states want a share of the wealth if oil is produced off their coasts.

B. OCEAN RENEWABLE ENERGY

1. OCEAN WIND ENERGY (OWE)

Ocean windfarm development has had to overcome technical difficulties—inadequate port facilities and lack of specialized U.S. ships for construction—and legal hurdles, like the Jones Act and the almost 20-year litigation saga of Cape Wind Associates, the first, and ultimately unsuccessful, offshore wind project to receive a construction permit. Massachusetts' investment in port improvements, technological developments and tax incentives have been paving the way forward, however. The inefficiencies created by the gaps and overlaps in authority to regulate offshore wind siting and development have been addressed through new legislation, and state and regional planning are facilitating development. The Jones Act, 43 U.S.C. § 883, which requires that ships transporting goods between U.S. ports must be built in the U.S., owned primarily by U.S. entities and operated by US citizens, may still create hurdles, however. The act effectively prevents use of specialized foreign vessels for turbine construction. The first U.S. vessel is projected to be built by 2022. See generally, Joan Bondereff, et al., The Jones Act in US Offshore Wind: Challenge or Opportunity? (April 15, 2019)(available at https://www.offshorewind.biz/2019/04/15/jones-act-us-offshore-wind-challenge-opportunity/).

Prior to 2005, the OCSLA had no specific language authorizing DOI to permit offshore windfarms on the OCS. The Army Corps of Engineers (Corps) assumed jurisdiction under § 10 of the Rivers and Harbors Act (RHA), 3 U.S.C. § 403, which gives the Corps authority to permit obstructions to navigation in the "navigable waters of the United States" and on the OCS. The Corps' permitting involved no planning or siting process or authority to convey to wind companies the right to occupy and use an area the OCS exclusively. The Energy Policy Act of 2005, § 388 (EPAct; P.L. 109–58) amended the OCSLA to provide for federal review and permitting of offshore energy projects. The Secretary of the Interior, in consultation with other federal agencies, is authorized to grant leases, easements, or rights-of-way on the OCS for wind energy and other development not authorized by other applicable law. The Corps retained jurisdiction under the Rivers and Harbors Act in regard to obstructions to navigation. An April 2009 MOU between the DOI and the Federal Energy Regulatory Commission (FERC) recognized exclusive jurisdiction of DOI over "the production, transportation, or transmission of energy from non-hydrokinetic renewable energy projects on the OCS."

The EPAct requires the Secretary of DOI:

- to issue leases, easements, and rights-of-way on a competitive basis (with some limited exceptions);

- to provide for suspension and cancellation of any lease, easement, or right-of-way;

- to create a system of "royalties, fees, rentals, bonuses, or other payments" that will ensure a fair return to the United States:

- to ensure that activities under the EPAct amendments are carried out in a manner that adequately addresses environmental protection, safety, protection of U.S. national security, and protection of the rights of others to use the OCS and its resources and prevent interference with reasonable uses of the seas;

- to take into consideration other uses of the sea or seabed, including use for a fishery, a sea lane, a potential site of a deepwater port, or navigation;

- to "provide for the restoration of the lease, easement, or right-of-way," including financial assurances; and

- to impose "such other requirements as the Secretary considers necessary to protect the interests of the public and the United States."

See 43 U.S.C. § 1337(p).

In addition to requiring DOI to carry out these activities in consultation with other federal agencies, the EPAct provides for coordination and consultation with the governor of any state or the executive of any local government that may be affected by a lease, easement, or right-of-way. In addition, for projects that are located wholly or partially within 3 miles of state waters, states will receive 27% of the revenues generated. States within 15 miles of the geographical center of the project will receive an "equitable distribution" of the 27%, based on proximity to the project.

The renewable offshore energy program is administered by (BOEM), within DOI, through regulations adopted in 2009 by its predecessor agency, the Marine Minerals Service (MMS). In addition, in 2010, the DOI Secretary Salazar announced the "Smart from the Start" program to expedite Atlantic coast wind energy projects. In addition to identifying Wind Energy Areas for leasing and development, the Secretary sought to make the permitting process more efficient.

Among the states, Massachusetts and Rhode Island have been the most proactive in planning for OWE using the process of marine spatial planning. Rhode Island was an early innovator in addressing the need to respond to sea level rise and climate change through renewable energy, primarily OWE development. In 2010, Rhode Island adopted its Ocean Special Area Management Plan (Ocean SAMP), which comprehensively covers the ecology, cultural and historic resources, fisheries, recreation and tourism, marine transportation, and navigation of the state's offshore areas, as well as the effects of climate change. Applying this information to the process of marine special planning, the Ocean SAMP has provided a framework for assessment of offshore wind energy development that led to the nation's first offshore wind farm in waters off Rhode Island. A relatively small project, the five-turbine Block Island Wind farm went online in December 2016.

Rhode Island's Ocean SAMP was unique in applying not only to its state waters, but also to waters of adjacent states and areas of federal OCS and EEZ. NOAA approved the Ocean SAMP as a programmatic change to the RI Coastal Resources Management Program in 2011. The SAMP applies directly to its state waters and extends to review of federal projects and approvals of actions in the EEZ and in other states through the CZMA federal consistency provisions. The SAMP formed the basis for further coordination with federal agencies to facilitate OWE development.

NOAA approved a first of a kind Geographic Location Description (GLD) as part of the SAMP. The GLD describes how federal actions, permits or activities in the federal waters off Rhode Island covered by the Ocean SAMP may have a reasonably foreseeable impact on the state's coastal resources or uses, and automatically affords the state an opportunity to review federal projects out to 30 miles for consistency with the enforceable policies of its coastal program. The Federal Energy Regulatory Commission also recently approved the GLD.

In response to proposals for at least four more wind projects in the area, including the nation's first large-scale commercial wind project, Rhode Island requested (and received approval from NOAA) to extend its GLD to the federal OCS further offshore to incorporate new BOEM leases for renewable energy projects. The new GLD 2018 has been authorized separately from the GLD 2011 and applies only to BOEM authorizations for wind energy facilities, regardless of size, and associated cables for review within the GLD 2018. Through the Ocean SAMP and GLD 2018, Rhode Island successfully participated in the permitting process for Vineyard Wind, the world's largest windfarm, located 14 miles south of Martha's Vineyard, encompassing 166,886 acres (about 90 sq. miles) and involving 84 wind turbines. Through CZMA consistency review, the state could address its concerns for the state's fishing industry.

The move toward OWE is accelerating. There are currently ten active commercial BOEM leases off Massachusetts, Rhode Island, Virginia, Maryland, New York, New Jersey, and North Carolina, and two non-competitive leases issued off Delaware. But although the process has become more streamlined and planning attempts to take environmental and stakeholder interests into account, there will still be legal challenges. Most recently, fishermen failed in their attempt to enjoin a BOEM lease sale off New York to Statoil Wind US, LLC for development of a wind energy facility. In Fisheries Survival Fund v. Jewell, 2018 WL 4705795 (U.S.D. D.C. 2018), the court found that the fishermen had standing, but their NEPA claims were not ripe, and their OCSLA claims were precluded by failure to meet the notice requirement of the citizen suit provisions.

2.   WAVE, TIDAL AND THERMAL ENERGY

Wave and tidal forces, more reliable and predictable than wind, are additional potential sources of clean, renewable energy. Marine hydrokinetic energy projects are also expected to have a longer lifespan than offshore wind farms. Hydrokinetic energy uses the motion of the seas, whether waves, tides or currents, to, for example, turn turbines or to use the vertical movement of the water to generate electricity. Original tidal projects involved tidal barrages (dams) across bays, inlets or estuaries that used the flow of the water in and out through turbines to generate electricity. These barrages needed a tidal range of about 16 feet to function and had significant effects on coastal ecosystems. New tidal technologies can operate under a wider range of conditions and have fewer environmental effects. The most significant environmental effects of these new technologies are alteration of currents and waves and the effects of emissions of electro-magnetic fields (EMFs) on marine life.[1]

Although still far from commercial production, marine hydrokinetic prototypes and testing are going forward. Limited ocean thermal energy conversion technology is also being scaled up particularly in Hawai'i.

In the 1980s, Congress adopted legislation to promote the development of Ocean Thermal Energy Conversion (OTEC)—a technology that creates energy by using the gradient between cold deep waters and tropical surface waters. 42 U.S.C.A. §§ 9101–9168. This legislation was adopted before UNCLOS and authorized the U.S. to act consistent with the UN Convention on the High Seas to locate, construct, and operate OTEC facilities and plantships within what is today the territorial sea. OTEC facilities include any unit that is moored or fixed that uses the gradient in the ocean temperatures to generate energy and freshwater (byproduct of OTEC process) plus any cables or pipelines that convey electricity and water to the mainland. 42 U.S.C.A.§ 9102(11). OTEC plantships

---

[1]   See generally, Talal Husseini, Riding the renewable wave: tidal energy advantages and disadvantages (26 October 2018) (https://www.power-technology.com/features/tidal-energy-advantages-and-disadvantages/).

refer to vessels capable of using the ocean temperature gradient to generate energy. NOAA may issue licenses up to 25 years to OTEC facilities and plantships after an evaluation that includes consultations with the Coast Guard to avoid issues with freedom of navigation and with the EPA to ensure compliance with EPA administered regulations. 42 U.S.C.A.§ 9111(c). Any siting of an OTEC facility must avoid conflict with other ocean users such as oil and gas producers. Before issuing a license, NOAA must consult with the governor of any state that has been designated as an "adjacent state" that may be impacted by the OTEC activities. 42 U.S.C.A. § 9115(b) Proponents of OTEC facilities and plantships must prepare environmental impact statements. 42 U.S.C.A. § 9117(e). Such facilities and plantships are subject to the Clean Water Act. 42 U.S.C.A. § 9117(f).

Because the location of OTEC technology is limited to areas meeting its technical requirements and has been expensive to implement, the uptake of OTEC has been slow. In Hawai'i OTEC is being scaled up with at least one prediction that 12 commercial-scale OTEC plants could supply Hawai'i with all of its electricity needs. There are also proposals for exploring OTEC off the coast of the U.S. Southeast.

For ocean hydrokinetic or thermal projects on the OCS, leasing and development would be under the same BOEM ocean renewable energy program applicable to wind energy projects. See 30 CFR part 585—Renewable Energy and Alternate Uses of Existing Facilities on the Outer Continental Shelf.

There is also potential, however, that projects will be developed in state waters.

C. MARINE MINERALS MINING

1. OCS NON-ENERGY MINERAL MINING

United States jurisdiction over non-energy mineral resources of the outer continental shelf was also claimed in the 1945 Truman Proclamation and codified in the OCSLA. BOEM's Marine Minerals Program (MMP) is responsible for managing, leasing, exploration and development of these OCS resources. The majority of offshore minerals mining is for sand, gravel and shell for beach renourishment and other coastal restoration, but there is also commercial leasing of gold, manganese, and other hard minerals.

Increased attention to minerals mining of the OCS during the 1980s brought an increased awareness of the lack of comprehensive legislation or policy in the area. The OCSLA includes comprehensive authority for leasing and development of OCS lands for oil, gas, and sulfur exploitation. But only one sentence in the entire Act, section 8(k), mentions the leasing of "any mineral other than oil, gas, and sulphur." 43 U.S.C.A. § 1337(k). The extensive statutory framework that is in place for OCS oil and gas development does not exist for hard minerals mining. The major 1978 amendments to the OCSLA that provide for environmental protections, state participation in the leasing process, and state coastal plan consistency are specifically applicable only to oil and gas leases.

During the 1980s, the federal government began to encourage development of offshore minerals as part of the National Minerals and Materials Program Plan. The government's position was that the lack of comprehensive regulations for prospecting, leasing, and recovering of marine minerals had inhibited development of a domestic marine mining industry. In 1988, MMS (now BOEM) published rules on prelease prospecting of minerals other than oil, gas, and sulphur, 30 C.F.R. §§ 280.0–280.17, and in 1989, MMS issued rules for general leasing, 30 C.F.R. §§ 281.0–281.47, and for mining operations on the OCS, 30 C.F.R. §§ 282.0–282.50. Regulations adopted in 2017 at 30 CFR part 583 apply to any federal, state, or local government agency, as well as certain private individuals and corporations for negotiated, non-competitive leases for sand, gravel, and/or shell resources to be used only for coastal restoration projects.

Both commercial prospectors and certain scientific researchers are required to have a permit and an approved plan before conducting OCS prospecting activities. Lease sales may be initiated by the Secretary or by unsolicited requests for a lease sale. The rules generally provide for a competitive bidding system for leases. Section 8(k) was amended in 1994 and 1999 to eliminate the requirement of competitive lease sales when OCS sand and gravel resources are needed for public works projects such as beach and coastal wetlands restoration.

General environmental assessment and protection provisions are included at all three stages of the mineral development process. The regulations are most controversial in regard to coordination with affected or adjacent states. The regulations clearly intended that intergovernmental coordination and consultation would be carried out through six regional federal/state task forces, rather than through provisions comparable to the requirements for oil and gas development. See 30 C.F.R. § 281.13.

The governors of adjacent states will receive copies of permit applications and plans for prospecting upon submission, but states will not have the authority to comment upon the activities unless BOEM determines to prepare an environmental assessment. Id. § 280.11. At the lease sale and mining stages, governors will receive notice and documents and will have the opportunity to have their comments "considered." The federal consistency provisions of the CZMA are not addressed in the rules. This is likely because MMS was taking the position in its leasing regulations, issued prior to the 1990 CZMA amendments, that "coastal zone consistency concurrence is not required prior to a lease sale of OCS minerals"—a currently unsupportable position. 54 Fed. Reg. 2042, 2046 (1989).

The most fundamental objection to the OCS hard mineral mining regime is that the BOEM, lacks authority to promulgate the regulations under the OCSLA. Commentators have pointed out that the 1953 OCSLA and its amendments have dealt virtually exclusively with oil and gas development, and argue that one sentence in an act is inadequate to provide a statutory basis for a comprehensive regulatory program. One proposal is that hard mineral development should be addressed in comprehensive legislation for the U.S. Exclusive Economic Zone.

BOEM is currently implementing Executive Order 13817 of December 20, 2017, Federal Strategy To Ensure Secure and Reliable Supplies of Critical Minerals. DOI and the Department of Defense were instructed to identify minerals critical to national security and the nation's economy. The EO defines a "critical mineral" . . . "to be (i) a non-fuel mineral or mineral material essential to the economic and national security of the United States, (ii) the supply chain of which is vulnerable to disruption, and (iii) that serves an essential function in the manufacturing of a product, the absence of which would have significant consequences for our economy or our national security." DOI, in conjunction with the U.S. Geological Survey (USGS), is attempting to determine which 35 identified, critical minerals are located on the OCS. The EO further directs that DOI cooperate with a group of other federal agencies and entities to develop:

(i) a strategy to reduce the Nation's reliance on critical minerals;

(ii) an assessment of progress toward developing critical minerals recycling and reprocessing technologies, and technological alternatives to critical minerals;

(iii) options for accessing and developing critical minerals through investment and trade with our allies and partners;

(iv) a plan to improve the topographic, geologic, and geophysical mapping of the United States and make the resulting data and metadata electronically accessible, to the extent permitted by law and subject to appropriate limitations for purposes of privacy and security, to support private sector mineral exploration of critical minerals; and

(v) recommendations to streamline permitting and review processes related to developing leases; enhancing access to critical mineral resources; and increasing discovery, production, and domestic refining of critical minerals.

2. DEEP SEABED HARD MINERAL RESOURCES

The 1982 United Nations Convention on the Law of the Sea (UNCLOS or LOS Convention) creates a comprehensive international regime for the exploitation of the mineral resources of the deep seabed beyond coastal state jurisdiction. See Chapter 10. Based on the concept that the resources of the seabed are the common heritage of mankind, the principles proposed for governing the area met with strong opposition from the United States and from other developed countries.

The Deep Seabed Hard Mineral Resources Act (DSHMRA), 30 U.S.C.A. §§ 1401–1473, was enacted by the United States in 1980, prior to the conclusion of the UNCLOS negotiations. The Act set up a licensing scheme for mining of the seabed of the high seas beyond United States' jurisdiction. The licensing program was intended both as a spur to the UNCLOS negotiations and to provide an interim regime for seabed activities pending the Convention's coming into force that would provide a stable environment for U.S. investors. Other developed countries enacted similar legislation and entered into international agreements to deal with recognition of other countries' claims and to create mechanisms for conflict resolution.

The DSHMRA's "reciprocating states" provision allows the Administrator of NOAA to designate other nations as reciprocating states so their license and permit programs can be coordinated to respect each other's claims and to avoid conflicts. By 1983, France, Italy, Japan, the United Kingdom, and West Germany had enacted domestic seabed mining legislation and were designated by NOAA as reciprocating states The U.S. has subsequently negotiated agreements with Belgium, China, France, Germany, Japan, Russia, and the United Kingdom. The problem is that all these cooperative agreements were concluded before the LOS Convention came into force and were, generally, intended to be interim arrangements. It is not clear whether these arrangements are all now considered valid since the other countries involved are now subject to the UNCLOS regime.

The DSHMRA requires U.S. citizens and vessels to obtain a license from the Administrator of the National Oceanic and Atmospheric Administration (NOAA) to explore for nodules. Ten year exploration licenses are issued on a first-come, first-served basis for a specifically identified area. The license holder has a priority to receive a permit allowing commercial recovery. The permit gives the holder the exclusive right to explore or mine a specific area, but only as against other U.S. citizens. NOAA regulations recognize seabed mining as a freedom of the high seas, and issuance of licenses should "not unreasonably interfere with the exercise of the freedoms of the high seas by other nations, as recognized under general principles of international law." 15 C.F.R. § 970.503.

Prior to issuing an exploration license or recovery permit, the NOAA Administrator must make a number of specific findings concerning the exploration or recovery plan: (1) the activity will not interfere with the exercise of high seas freedoms by other nations or conflict with other international obligations of the United States; (2) the activity will not lead to a breach of international peace; (3) the activity will not adversely affect the environment; and (4) the activity will not endanger life at sea. Id. § 1415(a).

Several provisions of the act address environmental concerns. The DSHMRA extends Clean Water Act (CWA) jurisdiction to any discharge of a pollutant from vessels and other floating craft engaged in exploration or commercial recovery, extending jurisdiction to vessels even when on the high seas. NOAA must prepare programmatic environmental impact statements in certain circumstances and is required to prepare a site-specific EIS for each license or permit. If a license or permit may adversely affect a fishery resource, NOAA must consult with the relevant U.S. regional fisheries management council.

Because the Act requires any shore-based processing of minerals to take place in the U.S., deep seabed mining may have some effects on U.S. coastal areas. There is no provision, however, for approval by or consultation with coastal states prior to license or permit issuance. The commercial recovery regulations fill the gap by providing extensive state consultation provisions even though the act itself does not require them.

NOAA recently approved a five-year extension of two exploration licenses originally issued to Lockheed Martin Corporation (LMC) in 1984. LMC's current activities are being carried out in collaboration with a United Kingdom subsidiary. According to the notice in the Federal Register, the "extension maintains the proprietary interests that the licenses confer upon the Licensee but does not authorize LMC to conduct at-sea exploration activities pursuant to the licenses. Additional authorization and further environmental review by NOAA is required before at-sea exploration may be undertaken pursuant to these licenses." 82 FR 42327 (September 7, 2017). Commercial recovery, however, remains a distant prospect.

CHAPTER VI

OIL POLLUTION, OIL SPILL LIABILITY AND THE DEEPWATER HORIZON

A. INTRODUCTION

In 1989 the *Exxon Valdez* ran aground in Prince William Sound, Alaska, spilling more than 11 million gallons of crude oil. The oil spill provisions of the Clean Water Act (CWA) were woefully inadequate to deal with the cleanup, liability, natural resources restoration and other consequences of the spill. The Oil Pollution Act of 1990 (OPA) was passed to address the issues that the *Exxon Valdez* oil spill exposed. Many of the provisions of OPA had not been clarified or interpreted by the courts when, in April 2010, the *Deepwater Horizon* blowout on the Macondo Prospect spilled over 200 million gallons of oil into the Gulf of Mexico over 87 days. This time, much scrutiny focused on the inadequacies of technical, safety and environmental standards applicable to OCS oil development and production. The liability phase of the oil spill litigation was epic.

This chapter will review the background statutory and maritime common law applicable to oil spills, and the extent to which OPA 1990 has supplemented or supplanted this regime. In addition to discussing the oil spill cleanup process, the chapter reviews the status of OPA safety and construction requirements. The final section provides some of the highlights of the legal history of the *Deepwater Horizon* oil spill.

The international regime addressing oil pollution is discussed in Chapter VII.

B. OIL POLLUTION AND OIL SPILLS

Since 1972, section 311 of the CWA has been the primary mechanism for enforcing oil pollution control standards and establishing responsibility and liability for oil spill and hazardous substance clean up and damages. 33 U.S.C. § 1321. Congress passed 1990 Oil Pollution Act (OPA), 33 U.S.C. §§ 2701–761 after the Exxon Valdez oil spill "to streamline federal law so as to provide quick and efficient cleanup of oil spills, compensate victims of such spills, and internalize the costs of spills within the petroleum industry." Rice v. Harken Expl. Co., 250 F.3d 264, 266 (5th Cir.2001). However, section 311 of the CWA still provides the framework for civil and criminal enforcement by the federal government for oil spills and, along with admiralty law, is the basis for the potential liability of wrong-doers who are not defined as "responsible parties" in OPA. (Discussed infra). In general, the law that is not specifically displaced by OPA, e.g., cleanup, is still relevant to oil spills. Because many provisions of the OPA are similar to the prior law, cases interpreting section 311 are also useful. The Comprehensive Environmental Response, Compensation and Liability Act (CERCLA), 42 U.S.C. §§ 9601–675, creates a parallel scheme to section 311 and OPA for the hazardous substances to which it applies.[1]

---

[1]   CERCLA has a "petroleum exclusion" but this exclusion does not apply in the case of waste oil mixed with hazardous

1. PROHIBITIONS AND ENFORCEMENT UNDER CWA SECTION 311

a. Prohibition of the Discharge of Oil in Navigable Waters of the United States

Section 311(b)(1) of the CWA prohibits the "discharge[ ] of oil or hazardous substances into or upon the navigable waters of the United States." This policy is reinforced in section 311(b)(3) and (4) by a flat prohibition on oil or hazardous substance discharges in quantities which "may be harmful." Id. § 1321(b)(3)–(4). This prohibition forms the basis for civil and criminal penalties and for allocating responsibility and liability for discharges.

Section 311's prohibitions apply to the "navigable waters of the United States," adjoining shorelines, the contiguous zone, the 200-mile EEZ, and waters affected by outer continental shelf (OCS) activities, which may extend beyond 200 miles. The term "navigable waters" is limited only by the reach of the Commerce Clause and not by navigability in fact. Nonnavigable waters that are subject to the ebb and flow of the tide and wetlands that are adjacent to navigable waters are included within the scope of "navigable waters" for purposes of section 311. See, e.g., *United States v. Jones*, 267 F. Supp. 2d 1349 (M.D. Ga. 2003); *United States v. Texas Pipe Line Co.*, 611 F.2d 345 (10th Cir. Okla. 1979).

---

substances. City of New York v. Exxon Corp. 766 F. Supp. 177 (S.D.N.Y. 1991); United States v. Alcan Aluminum Corp.755 F. Supp. 531 N.D.N.Y 1991).

For purposes of CWA section 311, oil is broadly defined as "oil of any kind or in any form, including but not limited to petroleum, fuel oil, sludge, oil refuse, and oil mixed with wastes other than dredged spoil." 33 U.S.C. § 1321(a)(1). Hazardous substances are likewise construed broadly to include substances "which, when discharged in any quantity into or upon the navigable waters of the United States . . . or which may affect natural resources . . . present an imminent and substantial danger to the public health or welfare." Id. § 1321(b)(2)(A). However, until the Administrator of EPA designates a substance as hazardous, the provisions of section 311 do not apply. See *United States v. Ohio Barge Lines*, 410 F.Supp. 625 (W.D. La.1975). Hazardous substances subject to section 311 are designated at 40 C.F.R. § 117.1 17.23. Spills of hazardous substances, other than petroleum products, in navigable waters are also subject to regulation and liability under CERCLA.

b. What Are Harmful Quantities of Oil?

The discharge prohibition is limited to quantities of oil and hazardous substances that "may be harmful to the public health and welfare or environment of the United States" as determined by regulation. 33 U.S.C. § 1321(b)(4). Regulations identify "harmful quantities" to be amounts of oil or hazardous substances that:

(a) Violate applicable water quality standards, or

(b) Cause a film or sheen upon or discoloration of the surface of the water or adjoining shorelines or cause a sludge or emulsion to be deposited beneath the surface of the water or upon adjoining shorelines. 40 C.F.R. § 110.3. A "sheen" is "an iridescent appearance on the surface of water." Id. § 110.1.

c. The Spill Reporting Requirement

Spillers have an obligation, subject to criminal penalties, to report spills in harmful quantities. Obviously, a "sheen'" may be created by seemingly insignificant discharges, and the imposition of duties, penalties, and criminal liability based on the sheen test has been controversial.

In *United States v. Boyd*, 491 F.2d 1163 (9th Cir. 1973), the sheen test was upheld as a reasonable indicator of when a person must report a spill. The court noted that the test had advantages of simplicity and certainty over a quantitative test and was not unconstitutionally vague. But the question of what constitutes a spill of a reportable quantity lingered in other circuits and was the subject of a saga concerning Chevron that spanned 15 years.

An earlier version of section 311(b)(3) was written in terms of "harmful quantities," and Chevron challenged the sheen test, arguing that the statute required actual injury for a spill to be reportable or subject to a penalty. In *United States v. Chevron Oil Co.*, 583 F.2d 1357 (5th Cir. 1978), the Fifth Circuit Court of Appeals held that the sheen test created only a rebuttable presumption of harm to the environment. To alleviate any burden on the government to show actual harm in every case,

Congress amended section 311 to prohibit even quantities that "may be harmful." Chevron continued, however, to contest the imposition of civil penalties when a reportable spill nevertheless has little or no actual impact on the environment. In *Chevron, U.S.A., Inc. v. Yost*, 919 F.2d 27 (5th Cir. 1990), the court of appeals upheld the "sheen test" as the basis for imposing civil liability. "While it is apparent that such an approach sometimes overregulates, it is equally apparent that this imprecision is a trade-off for the administrative burden of case-by-case proceedings." Quoting *Orgulf Transport Co. v. United States*, 711 F.Supp. 344 (W.D.Ky. 1989), the court reasoned:

[t]hat Congress could have prohibited all discharges through a specific declaration and chose not to do so does not negate the effect of the amendment, a common sense reading of which illustrates that Congress chose to prohibit discharges which might not be harmful. Whether a spill resulted in actual harm to the environment is irrelevant to the determination of whether Section 311's prohibition of discharges of oil in quantities which may be harmful has been violated. The only pertinent inquiry is whether the spill was in a quantity that may be harmful as determined by the EPA. Because EPA has determined that a spill of oil which creates a sheen is a quantity which "may be harmful," such a spill is subject to the penalty provisions of 33 U.S.C. § 1321 and 40 C.F.R. Part 110.3.

d. Civil Penalties Under CWA § 311

Both civil and criminal enforcement and penalties are available for enforcement of section 311's prohibitions on discharges. Civil enforcement, through administrative orders and injunctive relief, is available to abate an actual or threatened discharge that "may be an *imminent and substantial threat* to the public health or welfare . . . and other living and nonliving natural resources." 33 U.S.C. § 1321(e)(1) (emphasis added). Although the Act does not define "imminent and substantial threat," the amendment to the provision that changed the word "is" to "may be" indicates that no actual harm need be shown. This is also consistent with interpretations of similar language in the Resource Conservation and Recovery Act (RCRA), 42 U.S.C. § 6973, and CERCLA, id. § 9606. See, e.g., *United States v. Conservation Chemical Co.*, 619 F.Supp. 162 (W.D.Mo. 1985) (holding that endangerment means risk of harm, considering the nature of the threat and its likelihood).

Civil penalties are imposed in federal court or administrative proceedings for discharging in violation of the Act and for failure to remove the discharge or to comply with an order or regulation. 33 U.S.C. § 1321(b)(7). OPA's amendments to the CWA substantially raised the limits for civil penalties and revised the criteria for consideration in assessing civil penalties. For example, civil penalties for discharges generally are raised from $5000 for each offense to an amount of up to $25,000 per day of violation or up to $1000 per barrel discharged. 33

U.S.C.A § 1321(b)(7)(A). For spills resulting from "gross negligence or willful misconduct" OPA requires a penalty of not less than $100,000 and not more than $3000 per barrel discharged. Id. § 1321(b)(7)(D). (Note that this means a minimum penalty of $100,000 will be imposed for the reckless discharge of only one barrel of oil.) The following factors are now considered in determining the amount of a civil penalty: (1) the seriousness of the violation; (2) the economic benefit to the violator resulting from the violation; (3) the degree of culpability; (4) other penalties involved in the same incident; (5) any history of prior violations; (6) the nature, extent, and degree of success of efforts by the violator in mitigating or minimizing the effects of the spill; (7) the economic impact of the penalty on the violator; and (8) other matters as justice may require. Id. § 1321(b)(8).

Several other aspects of civil penalties should be noted. First, they are in addition to, not in lieu of, any other removal costs and damages incurred by the government. Second, civil penalties may be imposed regardless of fault and even where the violator has reported the spill and taken total responsibility for its removal at his or her own expense. These strict liability penalties have been held to be constitutional. In *United States v. Atlantic Richfield Co.*, 429 F.Supp. 830 (E.D.Pa. 1977), for example, the federal district court found that imposition of penalties in such circumstances did not violate due process because there is a rational nexus between the behavior penalized and the purposes of the cleanup fund into which penalties are deposited. As noted above, penalties may also be imposed where the discharge causes no harm to the environment. See *Orgulf Transport Co. v. United States*, 711 F.Supp. 344 (W.D.Ky. 1989); *United States v. Jones (In re Jones)*, 311 B.R. 647, 2005 AMC 264 (Bankr. M.D. Ga. 2004); *In re Oil Spill by the Oil Rig*, 841 F. Supp. 2d 988, 2012 AMC 982 (E.D. La. 2012).

e. Criminal Penalties Under CWA § 311

Criminal prosecution under section 311 may relate to either the reporting requirements or to the spill itself. The decision of the federal government to pursue criminal prosecution is discretionary. A number of factors, including the prior history of the violator, the preventative measures that were taken, the need for deterrence, and the extent of cooperation, are considered by the government in deciding whether to bring criminal charges.

Section 311(b)(5) requires that a "person in charge" of a vessel or of an onshore or offshore facility must notify the National Response Center as soon as she or he knows of the oil or hazardous substance spill of a reportable quantity. 33 U.S.C. § 1321(b)(5) and part V.B.1.c, supra re "reportable quantity." Failure to report a spill or knowingly submitting false information in an oil spill report results in criminal liability. Id. § 1321(b)(5), (c)(4).

A person who knowingly or negligently discharges oil in violation of section 311's prohibitions or who knowingly endangers another person by such a violation is subject to criminal prosecution. See 33 U.S.C. § 1319(c). The penalties for such violations depend on the level of culpability. For example, negligent acts may be subject to fines of $2500 to $25,000 per day or no more than one year imprisonment or both, while knowing violations may incur fines of $5000 to $50,000 per day or be subject to no more than three years imprisonment or both. 33 U.S.C. § 1319(c)(1)–(2).

Reporting a spill does not insulate a violator from criminal prosecution for the discharge. However, section 311(b)(5), prior to OPA, created use immunity for the report by providing that "[n]otification received pursuant to this paragraph or information obtained by the exploitation of such notification shall not be used against any such person in any criminal case, except a prosecution for perjury or for giving a false statement." The "use immunity" provision protects against infringement of a defendant's privilege against self-incrimination. In *Hazelwood v. State*, 836 P.2d 943 (Alaska App. 1992), Joseph Hazelwood, captain of the *Exxon Valdez,* appealed his conviction on criminal charges for the negligent discharge of oil. Captain Hazelwood asserted that section 311's "use immunity" required suppression of evidence of his intoxication "obtained by exploitation" of his report and reversal of his conviction. The Court of Appeals of Alaska rejected the application of the "inevitable discovery doctrine" as inconsistent with the grant of immunity. The court also held that there was no evidentiary basis for finding the actual existence of an independent source for the state's evidence. In reversing Hazelwood's conviction, the court noted that its adherence to the law should not "be mistaken for enthusiasm." Id. at 954. The court went on: "But while we may feel sorely tempted, as individuals, to recast the law in a mold better suited to our personal sense of justice, we are bound, as judges, to resist this temptation. . . ." Id. Congress, on the other hand, can "recast the law" and has subsequently deleted the prohibition on the use for criminal prosecution of information gathered by further government investigation. As amended by the 1990 OPA, use immunity now applies only to the notification by the person in charge. See 33 U.S.C. § 1321(b)(5).

"Use immunity" applies only to criminal prosecutions, not to the use of reporting information for assessment of civil penalties. In *United States v. Ward*, 448 U.S. 242, 100 S.Ct. 2636, 65 L.Ed.2d 742 (1980), the U.S. Supreme Court held that the CWA's civil penalties are not "quasi-criminal" and that the Fifth Amendment's protection against self-incrimination does not apply to civil penalty proceedings.

2.   POLLUTION PREVENTION AND SPILL RESPONSE

As pointed out in the Introduction to this chapter, the *Exxon Valdez* oil spill revealed technical and operational issues that contributed to the disaster. In response, OPA 1990 incorporated new provisions for construction, manning and operations.[1] In addition, OPA addresses problems related to drug and alcohol abuse by broadening authority for drug and alcohol

---

[1]   No additional legislation was passed in the wake of the *Deepwater Horizon* oil spill.

testing of vessel personnel and for examination of criminal and traffic records in licensing merchant seamen. Procedures were established for relieving a captain of command when he is operating the ship under the influence of alcohol or drugs. The perception that vessels are poorly manned is addressed through new training, manning, and watch-keeping requirements. See 46 U.S.C. §§ 7101–114, 7701–705, 8101–104.

a. OPA Safety, Equipment and Construction Standards

OPA also required studies of tanker vessel safety standards and added new requirements for the minimum plating thickness of commercial vessels and for communication equipment. Undoubtedly the most controversial equipment standard of OPA was the requirement for double hulls. All new tankers over 5000 gross tons were required to have double hulls. OPA sets up a schedule for conversion of existing single hull tankers to double hulls. Single hull tankers were prohibited from operating in United States navigable waters or in the EEZ after 2010. By 2015, the prohibition extended to double-bottomed and double-sided vessels. 46 U.S.C. §§ 1274(a), 3703a, 3715(a). See *Maritrans v. United States*, 342 F.3d 1344 (Fed.Cir. 2003)(double hull requirement did not constitute a taking).

In *Ray* v. *Atlantic Richfield Co.,* 435 U.S. 151 (1978) and *United States v. Locke*, 529 U.S. 89 (2000), the Supreme Court affirmed that in areas like design, construction, alteration, repair, maintenance, operation, equipping, personnel qualification, and manning of tanker vessels, Congress has left no room for state regulation. OPA's savings clause, 33 U.S.C. § 2718, did not create new authority for the states to regulate in this field which had been preempted under other federal law. States retain "authority to regulate the peculiarities of local waters if there [is] no conflict with federal regulatory determinations." Id. See also, *United States v. Massachusetts*, 493 F.3d 1 (1st D. Ct.App. 2007).

OPA also addresses oil spill preparedness by expanding and strengthening the National Contingency Plan under the CWA. 33 U.S.C. § 1321(d). The President is ordered to prepare a plan "for efficient, coordinated, and effective action to minimize damage from oil and hazardous stance discharges." Id. § 1321(d)(2). The Plan must address the removal of a "worst case discharge of oil" and include: (1) creation of Coast Guard strike force teams; (2) establishment of a national center for coordination and direction of Plan implementation; (3) a system for surveillance and notice; (4) procurement and storage of removal and containment equipment; (5) procedures for identifying, containing, dispersing, and removing spills; (6) procedures to assure coordination of cleanup efforts; and (7) development of a fish and wildlife response plan. See id. Consistent with the Plan, the President must set up a National Response System (NRS), including a National Response Unit, District Response Groups, and Area Committees. Id. § 1321(j). Tank vessels and facilities must also submit response plans for worst case discharges and ensure the availability of personnel and equipment to carry out the response. Id. § 1321(j)(5). The effectiveness of the NCP, the NRS, and other aspects of the response to the *Deepwater Horizon* oil spill are subjected to review and critical analysis in the U.S. Coast Guard's *BP Deepwater Horizon Spill Incident Specific Preparedness Review*, available at https:// repository.library.noaa.gov/view/noaa/331.

b. Oil Well Safety After the *Deepwater Horizon*

Following the *Deepwater Horizon* spill, DOI requested a study of its causes by a National Academy of Engineering/National Research Council committee. The report also made "recommendations to industry and government [to] strengthen oversight of deepwater wells, enhance system safety, and improve the technical skills of industry and regulatory staff." See NAE/NRC, Macondo Well-Deepwater Horizon Blowout (National Academies Press 2011). DOI acted on these recommendations and in 2016 adopted the production safety systems rule (relating to drilling safety) and the well control rule (directed at blowout preventers) under OCSLA authority. However, responding to pressure from the oil industry, in 2018 the Trump administration rolled back these rules to "eliminate[ ] unnecessary regulatory burdens while maintaining safety and environmental protection offshore."

c. The Oil Spill Cleanup Response Under OPA

The primary liability for oil spill cleanup costs lies with the "responsible party." Responsible parties include owners, operators, and demise charterers of a vessel, terminal and pipeline owners and operators, offshore facilities, and licensees of deepwater ports. 33 U.S.C. § 2701(32).

But it is now the President who has primary responsibility for the cleanup process. Formerly, the language of CWA § 311 gave the President discretionary authority to intervene when a cleanup response was not conducted properly by the spiller. As amended by OPA, the provision now appears to create a mandatory duty: "The President shall . . . ensure effective and immediate removal of a discharge, and mitigation or prevention of a substantial threat of a discharge, of oil or a hazardous substance . . ." according to the National Contingency Plan (NCP). Id. § 1321(c)(1). In the case of a "Substantial Spill,"

> the CWA deletes the option of monitoring removal efforts. Instead, "[t]he President *shall direct all Federal, State, and private actions* to remove" a Substantial Spill. Id. § 1321(c)(2)(A) (emphasis added). Legislative history states that this provision was "designed to eliminate the confusion evident in recent spills where the lack of clear delineation of command and management responsibility impeded prompt and effective response." When addressing a Substantial Spill, the President may remove the discharge, arrange for the removal of the discharge, or destroy a discharging vessel, as he could for smaller spills; however, to "facilitate emergency response," the President may

perform these actions "without regard to any other provision of law governing contracting procedures or employment of personnel by the Federal Government." 33 U.S.C. § 1321(c)(2)(B).

In Re Oil Spill by the Oil Rig "Deepwater Horizon", 2012 WL 5960192 (Dist.Ct. E.D. La. 2012. The Federal Onsite Coordinator (FOSC) must direct all response efforts in the case of a Substantial Spill. A spill that "is so complex that it requires extraordinary coordination of federal, state, local, and responsible party resources to contain and clean up the discharge," may be declared a "spill of national significance" by the Coast Guard and place response efforts in the hands of a National Incident Commander. Id. §§ 300.5, 300.323.

Prior to OPA, a person who attempted to assist in the clean up or containment of an oil spill could be liable to the discharger if the efforts negligently contributed to further damage from the spill. OPA provides a "good Samaritan" exception to CWA § 311. A person or state will not be liable for removal costs and damages for assisting or rendering care consistent with National Contingency Plan (NCP) unless "the person is grossly negligent or engages in willful misconduct." The exclusion does not apply to personal injury or wrongful death actions, however. Id. § 1321(c)(4). The immunity does not extend to a responsible party; in fact, a responsible party must pay any additional costs that arise because of the exception. Id. The "good Samaritan" may also recover costs incurred in the assistance effort from the responsible party if the actions are consistent with the NCP.

Similarly, immunity extends to manufacturers of dispersants that are used in an oil spill cleanup in compliance with the NCP. The potentially toxic effects of dispersants have made their use controversial, but their use is contemplated by the CWA and incorporated in the NCP. In a case against Nalco, the manufacturer of the dispersant Corexit, the court found the exception from liability applies to the situation where the dispersant was listed on the NCP Product Schedule and pre-approved for use in a "spill of national significance." The court stated that the Act anticipated that there would have to be a balancing of the costs and benefits of the use of dispersants in a major spill, and the Act gives the government the responsibility to weigh the dangers of toxicity against the consequences of not using it. The court suggested that without immunity from liability, manufacturers not would be likely to provide or even produce a product necessary for effective oil spill response. The OPA provisions were found to preempt state as well as maritime law actions. *In re Oil Spill by the Oil Rig "Deepwater Horizon"*, 2012 WL 5960192 (Dist.Ct. E.D. La. 2012). Because the CWA also immunizes the federal government "for any damages arising from its actions or omissions relating to any response plan required by [Section 311 of the CWA]," the U.S. also has no liability for damage caused by toxic dispersants. See 33 U.S.C. § 1321(j)(8). See also Abby J. Queale, Responding to the Response: Reforming the Legal Framework for Dispersant Use in Oil Spill Response

Efforts in the Wake of Deepwater Horizon, 18 Hastings W.-Nw. J. Envtl. L. & Pol'y 63, 65 (2012).

When, from the standpoint of legal responsibility, is a spill site considered "clean"? Obviously, all the oil from a catastrophic spill is unlikely to be removed. In the case of the *Exxon Valdez*, thirty years after the spill pockets of oil remain trapped four to eight inches below sand and gravel deposits on the coastline. "Clean" can be an extremely subjective standard, depending on whether "how clean is clean" is determined by the government, environmentalists, scientists, the spiller, or the affected community. OPA gives the authority to determine when "removal . . . shall be considered completed" to the President, in consultation with governors of affected states and trustees that have been designated for purposes of natural resources restoration. Id. § 2711.

C.   THE *DEEPWATER HORIZON* LITIGATION: LIABILITY FOR CLEANUP COSTS AND DAMAGES

The litigation surrounding the *Deepwater Horizon* became as extensive and complex as the oil spill itself. In addition to the overwhelming nature of litigation concerning hundreds of thousands of claimants, the nature of marine oil pollution law added its own complexity with overlapping areas throughout a myriad of state statutory and common law, federal legislation and federal admiralty law. Even with so many laws potentially available to address oil spill cleanup and liability, the *Exxon Valdez* litigation highlighted the inadequacies of the existing scheme. In OPA of 1990, Congress attempted to address many of the issues, but rather than provide a single, comprehensive statute for liability, Congress has specifically retained certain available remedies and included "savings clauses," often leaving it to the courts to determine whether certain remedies have been preempted or displaced. In order to conceptualize the entire complex scheme, this section will begin with the common law and admiralty law background of maritime torts which still forms the primary basis for liability for "non-responsible" parties.

1. TRADITIONAL MARITIME TORT AND COMMON LAW REMEDIES

Traditional state common law torts of negligence, nuisance, and strict liability may be available sources of liability for spills of oil or hazardous substances in some circumstances. However, in the ocean and coastal context, if a cause of action is based on a maritime tort, admiralty law, must be applied as the substantive law.

a. Admiralty Jurisdiction and the Maritime Nexus

The U.S. Supreme Court set out the test for admiralty jurisdiction in tort cases in *Grubart, Inc. v. Great Lakes Dredge & Dock Co.*:

> [A] party seeking to invoke federal admiralty jurisdiction pursuant to 28 U.S.C. § 1333(1) over a tort claim must satisfy conditions both of location and of connection with maritime

activity. A court applying the location test must determine whether the tort occurred on navigable water. The connection test raises two issues. A court, first, must assess the general features of the type of incident involved to determine whether the incident has a potentially disruptive impact on maritime commerce. Second, a court must determine whether the general character of the activity giving rise of the incident shows a substantial relationship to traditional maritime activity.

513 U.S. 527, 534 (1995) (citations omitted). In *In re the Exxon Valdez*, 767 F.Supp. 1509 (D.Alaska 1991), the federal district court characterized the "oil spill from the *Exxon Valdez* as a classic maritime tort." The location test clearly was met, and because maritime commerce is the primary focus of admiralty law, the maritime nexus test was also met. Likewise, the *Deepwater Horizon* oil spill undoubtedly met the location test and had a disruptive impact on maritime commerce, and the operations of the *Deepwater Horizon* bore a substantial relationship to traditional maritime activity. See *In re Oil Spill by the Oil Rig "Deepwater Horizon"*, 808 F.Supp.2d 943 (Dist. Ct. E.D. La. 2011), citing *Theriot v. Bay Drilling Corp.*, 783 F.2d 527, 538–39 (5th Cir.1986) ("oil and gas drilling on navigable waters aboard a vessel is recognized to be maritime commerce"). On the final question of whether the *Deepwater Horizon* was a "vessel" subject to admiralty jurisdiction, the court stated that it "was at all material times a vessel in navigation. It was practically capable of maritime transportation." See *Stewart v. Dutra Constr. Co.*,

543 U.S. 481, 497 (2005). See also *Herb's Welding v. Grey*, 470 U.S. 414, 417 n.2 (1985) ('Offshore oil rigs are of two general sorts: fixed and floating. Floating structures have been treated as vessels by the lower courts.')." Id. See also *Offshore Co. v. Robison*, 266 F.2d 769, 779 (5th Cir.1959).

b. Courts and Jurisdiction

The admiralty jurisdiction of federal courts for maritime torts is not exclusive. Maritime tort actions may be brought in federal courts under diversity jurisdiction or in state courts, but regardless of the venue or how the tort is characterized, maritime law is still controlling unless displaced by a specific federal statute. State law has been held to be applicable in some limited situations where there are substantive gaps in maritime law. In addition, states may "create rights and liabilities with respect to conduct within their borders, when the state action does not run counter to federal laws or the essential features of an exclusive federal jurisdiction." *Romero v. Int'l Terminal Operating Co.*, 358 U.S. 354, 375 n. 42 (1959). But, in general, maritime law leaves few gaps in the regime for maritime torts that occur on the OCS and in the EEZ for state law to fill. The application of substantive maritime law has had significant ramifications in limiting both the amount and scope of a spiller's liability.

c. Limitations of Liability Under Maritime Law

The Limitation of Vessel Owner's Liability Act (Limitation of Liability Act), which is referred to in OPA as the Act of March 3, 1851, is an early enactment that was intended to promote commerce and shipping by limiting a shipowner's potential liability. 46 U.S.C. §§ 181–192. In summary, if a shipowner establishes that a loss caused by its vessel was not due to negligence within the owner's privity or knowledge, the owner's liability for the loss is limited to the value of the owner's interest in the vessel and her pending freight. In the case of a catastrophic accident without fault, the liability of the owner of a sunken vessel may be virtually nothing. In spite of a specific savings clause (see 33 U.S.C. §§ 2702, 2704), OPA effectively repeals the 1851 act's liability limits with respect to "responsible parties" for oil spill cleanup costs and for damages recoverable under OPA. See *Matter of MetLife Capital Corp.*, 132 F.3d 818 (1st Cir. 1997); *Seaboats, Inc. v. Alex C Corp. (In re Alex C Corp.)*, 56 ERC (BNA) 1498, 2003 AMC 256 (D. Mass. 2003). Non-responsible parties may still be able to take advantage of the limits, however.

Judge-made, general maritime law also limits liability by narrowly defining the parties entitled to recovery for damages. In *Robins Dry Dock & Repair Co. v. Flint*, 275 U.S. 303, 48 S.Ct. 134, 72 L.Ed. 290 (1927), the U.S. Supreme Court enunciated the rule that where negligence does not result in any physical harm and only economic injury is suffered, a plaintiff may not recover in maritime tort for the loss of the benefits of a contract or prospective trade (economic damages). In the context of an oil spill like the *Exxon Valdez* spill in Prince William Sound, the *Robins Dry Dock* rule precluded recovery in maritime tort for businesses, such as fish processors, boat charterers, and lodges and for use and enjoyment claims by recreational users, such as kayakers, photographers, and sport fishermen. Commercial fishermen fall within a controversial exception to the *Robins Dry Dock* rule. In *Union Oil Co. v. Oppen*, 501 F.2d 558 (9th Cir. 1974), the Ninth Circuit allowed the recovery of lost profits by commercial fishermen because even though they experienced no physical harm, they make direct use of a resource of the sea. Although it is not entirely clear that there exists a principled rationale to distinguish commercial fishermen from others who use the sea, this exception has been followed.

2. THE OIL POLLUTION ACT OF 1990

The massive damage done by the *Exxon Valdez* oil spill led Congress to accelerate its ongoing deliberations on modernizing liability laws. OPA represented the rejection of a new international liability scheme, the 1969/1992 International Convention on Civil Liability for Oil Pollution Damage discussed in Chapter VII, in favor of a stricter, unilateral approach to protection of our waters and shores.

a. Scope of OPA Regarding Marine Pollution

OPA applies only to oil spills. "[O]il means oil of any kind or in any form, including, but not limited to, petroleum, fuel oil, sludge, oil refuse, and oil mixed with wastes other than dredged spoil, but does not include petroleum, including crude oil or any fraction thereof, which is specifically listed or designated as a hazardous substance under . . . [CERCLA] . . . and which is subject to the provisions of that Act[.]" 33 U.S.C. § 2701(23).

b. Liability of Responsible Parties

Under OPA, each "responsible party" is strictly liable for cleanup costs and damages for discharges of oil. OPA defines responsible parties in 33 U.S.C. § 2701(32) to mean:

(A) VESSELS.—In the case of a vessel, any person owning, operating, or demise chartering the vessel. . . .

(C) OFFSHORE FACILITIES.—In the case of an offshore facility . . . the lessee or permittee of the area in which the facility is located or the holder of a right of use and easement granted under applicable State law or the Outer Continental Shelf Lands Act (43 U.S.C. 1301–1356) for the area in which the facility is located (if the holder is a different person than the lessee or permittee).

Note that, unlike for application of admiralty law, an oil rig does not have to be characterized as a "vessel" for OPA to apply.

(1) OPA Limits on Liability

Like the previous CWA 311 section that OPA replaced, OPA contains limits on liability and requires vessels to have evidence of financial responsibility sufficient to meet the maximum liability under the Act. Id. § 2716. The limits on liability are greatly increased over the levels set originally set by CWA section 311, however, and were also much greater than limits proposed in international schemes at the time.

The OPA limits on liability will be lifted in a number of circumstances. First, the limits will not apply if the incident was proximately caused by gross negligence, willful misconduct, or violation of a federal safety, construction, or operating regulation by the responsible party, his agent or employee, or a person acting pursuant to a contractual relationship with the responsible party. Id. § 2704(c)(1). In addition, the limit will not apply if the responsible party fails to report the incident, does not cooperate in removal activities, or refuses to comply with administrative or judicial orders issued pursuant to the Act's clean up authority. Id. § 2704(c)(2). In contrast to the Limitation of Liability Act, the burden of proof is on the government to establish that the responsible party is ineligible to have the limit on liability applied.

(2) Affirmative Defenses Under OPA

OPA provides a number of affirmative defenses that are a complete defense to liability for removal costs and damages. The responsible party must establish by a preponderance of the evidence that the discharge or substantial threat of a discharge of oil and the resulting damages or removal costs were caused solely by:

(1)   an act of God;

(2)   an act of war;

(3)   an act or omission of a third party, other than an employee or agent of the responsible party or a third party whose act or omission occurs in connection with any contractual relationship ... if the responsible party establishes ... that [she or he]

(A)   exercised due care with respect to the oil concerned, taking into consideration the characteristics of the oil and in light of all relevant facts and circumstances; and

(B)   took precautions against foreseeable acts or omissions of any such third party and the foreseeable consequences of those acts or omissions; or

(4)   any combination of paragraphs (1), (2), and (3).

Id. § 2703(a). The provisions continued the defenses available under the original section 311 except that OPA omits the defense of negligence by the United States. This exclusion may be significant since the government is responsible for maintaining navigation aids and publishing charts. The government may, however, be considered a third party for purposes of an affirmative defense. Much of

OPA's additional language merely codifies the narrow judicial interpretations of section 311. See, e.g., *Travelers Ins. Co. v. United States*, 2 Cl.Ct. 758 (1983) (holding that the owner of a vandalized oil storage facility was liable for cleanup costs where the owner failed to take reasonable security precautions). Because of the requirement that the act of God, war, or a third party must be the *sole cause* of the spill, the defenses are difficult to assert successfully.

The government will reimburse a responsible party for removal costs if the party establishes a complete defense. OPA now allows a responsible party entitled to this exception to liability to make a claim to the Fund for all costs and damages incurred that exceed the limit on liability. Id. § 2708. Cases under CWA section 311's limitation of liability provision had held that any initial costs incurred by a spiller in clean up or containment operations could not be offset against the moneys owed to the United States. These costs were, therefore, in addition to the limitation on liability for large spills. See *United States v. Dixie Carriers, Inc.*, 736 F.2d 18 (5th Cir. 1984); *Steuart Transp. Co. v. Allied Towing Corp.*, 596 F.2d 609 (4th Cir. 1979). These cases had undermined federal policy to encourage immediate and effective containment and removal.

(3) Indemnification Agreements

OPA does not prohibit indemnification agreements, i.e., agreements to insure or hold harmless a party. However, these agreements are only effective as between the parties and do not transfer liability under OPA. 33 U.S.C. § 2710. For example, a contract between an otherwise responsible party and an oil transporter to shift responsibility for any liability for a spill will act only as an indemnification and subrogation agreement and will not achieve a transfer of statutory liability.

c. Liability for Cleanup and Removal

The first category of liability for a spiller is removal cost. Removal costs include all costs of removal and containment incurred by the United States, a state, or an Indian tribe and any removal costs incurred by any person for acts taken by the person, state or agency that are consistent with the NCP. Section 2702(b) of OPA provides:

(a)   IN GENERAL.— . . .[E]ach responsible party for a vessel or a facility from which oil is discharged, or which poses the substantial threat of a discharge of oil, into or upon the navigable waters or adjoining shorelines or the exclusive economic zone is liable for the removal costs and damages specified in subsection (b) that result from such incident.

(b)   COVERED REMOVAL COSTS AND DAMAGES.—

(1)   REMOVAL COSTS.—The removal costs referred to in subsection (a) are—

(A)   all removal costs incurred by the United States, a State, or an Indian tribe under subsection (c), (d), (e), or (*l*) of section 311 of the Federal Water Pollution Control Act (33 U.S.C.

1321), as amended by this Act, under the Intervention on the High Seas Act (33 U.S.C. 1471 et seq.), or under State law; and

(B) any removal costs incurred by any person for acts taken by the person which are consistent with the National Contingency Plan.

d. Liability for Damages

(1) In General

The second category of liability for an oil spill is for the damages specified in OPA. Several categories of damages are recoverable only by governments. These include: (1) "[d]amages for injury to, destruction of, loss of, or loss of use of, natural resources;" (2) "[d]amages equal to the net loss of taxes, royalties, rents, fees, or net profit shares due to the injury, destruction, or loss of real property, personal property, or natural resources;" and (3) "[d]amages for net costs of providing increased or additional public services during or after removal activities, including protection from fire, safety, or health hazards, caused by a discharge of oil." Id. § 2702(b)(2)(A), (D), (F).

(2) Damages for Private Claimants

Neither the CWA section 311 nor CERCLA contains provisions for private claimants. Prior to the OPA, only the Deepwater Port Act, 33 U.S.C. § 1501 et seq., OCSLA, 43 U.S.C. § 1801 et seq., and Trans-Alaska Pipeline Authorization Act, 43 U.S.C. §§ 1651–1656, created statutory mechanisms for recovery of damages by individuals. When these laws were not applicable, claims had to be made under state law or maritime tort (admiralty law).

Private parties may claim three types of damages under OPA. First, owners and lessees may recover damages for "injury to, or economic losses resulting from destruction of, real or personal property." Id. § 2702(b)(2)(B). This is a straight-forward provision reflecting that both direct damage to property and consequential damages are recoverable. For example, damages to a resort's beach and facilities, as well as lost profits during closure resulting from the spill, would be recoverable.

A second category of private damages covers "subsistence use," but the term is not defined in the OPA nor is it expressly limited to aboriginal use of a resource. The provision covers "[d]amages for loss of subsistence use of natural resources, which shall be recoverable by any claimant who so uses natural resources which have been injured, destroyed, or lost, without regard to the ownership or management of the resources." Id. § 2702(b)(2)(C). The class of "subsistence claimant" identified for *Deepwater Horizon* oil spill settlement procedures has been defined as

> a person who fishes or hunts to harvest, catch, barter, consume or trade Gulf of Mexico natural resources, in a traditional or customary manner, to sustain basic personal or family dietary, economic security, shelter, tool or clothing needs, and who relied upon such subsistence resources that were diminished or restricted in

the geographic region used by the claimant due
to or resulting from the spill.

See *In re Oil Spill by Oil Rig Deepwater Horizon*, 910
F. Supp. 2d 891, 908 (E.D. La. 2012).

The final provision for private claims is for
"[d]amages equal to the loss of profits or impairment
of earning capacity due to the injury, destruction, or
loss of real property, personal property, or natural
resources." Id. § 2702(b)(2)(E). This section may have
been intended to codify the exception in maritime tort
law, created in *Union Oil Co. v. Oppen*, 501 F.2d 558
(9th Cir. 1974), that allows damages for purely
economic losses for commercial fishermen. See H.R.
Conf. Rep. No. 653, 101st Cong., 2d Sess. 103 (1990),
reprinted in 1990 U.S.C.C.A.N. 779, 781 (stating only
that a claimant need not be the owner of damaged
property or resources to recover lost profits and cites
the example of commercial fishermen). Some
commentators, however, have indicated that OPA
"deletes a limitation . . . under case law requiring
that the claimant show physical damage to a
proprietary interest before economic damage could be
awarded." Cynthia M. Wilkinson et al., *Slick Work:
An Analysis of the Oil Pollution Act of 1990*, 12 J.
Energy Nat. Resources & Envtl. L. 181, 204 (1992)
(The authors, who were counsels with the House
Merchant Marine and Fisheries Committee when the
provisions were enacted, assert that lost profits and
earnings "may be had by anyone").

The first case to interpret this provision did not
read it broadly. In *In re Cleveland Tankers, Inc.*, 791
F.Supp. 669 (E.D.Mich. 1992), the federal district

court dismissed claims for economic damages from an oil spill. Claimants included a trucking company that lost profits, commercial marinas that lost business because of the closing of the channel, a boat charterer, a steamship company whose trade was interrupted, and marine terminal and dock operators. First determining that the claims were not cognizable as maritime torts because of the "bright line" *Robins Dry Dock* rule, the court then held that damages were also unavailable under OPA because the claimants had not alleged "injury, destruction, or loss to *their* property." (Emphasis added.) The court basically read OPA as reaffirming the *Robins Dry Dock* rule. By way of dictum, the court in *Ballard Shipping Co. v. Beach Shellfish*, 32 F.3d 623 (1st Cir. 1994), reached the opposite conclusion.[2]

In the litigation surrounding the *Deepwater Horizon* oil spill, the court has unequivocally interpreted OPA as removing the *Robins Dry Dock* limitation from OPA claims. Judge Barbier of the U.S. District Court stated that "one major remedial purpose of OPA was to allow a broader class of claimants to recover for economic losses than allowed under general maritime law," and held that "OPA claims for economic loss need not allege physical damage to a proprietary interest." *In re Oil Spill by the Oil Rig "Deepwater Horizon"*, 808 F.Supp.2d 943 (Dist. Ct. E.D. La. 2011). This greatly expands the kinds of damage and classes of plaintiffs entitled to

---

[2]   See also Gregg L. McCurdy, *An Overview of OPA 1990 and Its Relationship to Other Laws*, 5 U.S.F. Mar. L.J. 423 (1993), and Francis J. Gonynor, *The Robins Dry Dock Rule: Is the "Bright Line" Fading?*, 4 U.S.F. Mar. L.J. 85 (1992).

compensation in the case of a major oil spill and does not provide the certainty provided by *Robins Dry Dock*'s "bright line rule."

(3) Relation of OPA to Punitive Damages

OPA does not provide for punitive damages, raising the question of whether OPA preempts punitive damages that were previously available under general maritime law. In the *Deepwater Horizon* litigation, Judge Barbier relied on the U.S. Supreme Court's reasoning in *Exxon Shipping Co. v. Baker*, 554 U.S. 471 (2008), that held that the CWA did not preempt the general maritime remedy available for punitive damages. As in the case of the CWA provisions analyzed in *Baker,* Congress demonstrated no intent or language in OPA to preempt maritime law punitive damages, and the availability of such punitive damages does not undermine OPA's remedial scheme. The court held, therefore, that claims for punitive damages are available for general maritime law claimants against both responsible parties and others responsible only under maritime law. Id. Note that in *Baker* the U.S. Supreme Court limited punitive damages in maritime cases, however, stating that it "consider[s] that [a] 1:1 ratio [between compensatory damages and punitive damages], is a fair upper limit in such maritime cases." *Baker* at 513.

(4) Damages in Foreign Waters

Recovery under CWA section 311 had been specifically limited to damages in United States waters. In *In re Oswego Barge Corp.*, 664 F.2d 327 (2d Cir. 1981), the court found that section 311 provided no remedies for pollution of foreign waters. OPA allows foreign claimants, including both governments and individuals, to recover removal costs and damages resulting from an oil spill from a vessel in United States' waters, from a tanker at a pipeline terminal or deepwater port, or from an OCS facility from responsible parties. 33 U.S.C. § 2707. OPA also does not bar general maritime law claims against non-responsible parties. But see, State of Veracruz v. BP, P.L.C. (In re Deepwater Horizon), 784 F.3d 1019 (5th Cir. 2015)(finding that the *Robin's Dry Dock* Rule applied in the case of criminal negligence as well as civil negligence and that Mexican states could not recover for ecological damages because the Government of Mexico is the owner of Mexico's coasts and waters).

(5) OPA's Natural Resources Damages

The natural resources damages provisions are perhaps the most revolutionary aspect of OPA. "Natural resources" are defined to include:

land, fish, wildlife, biota, air, water, ground water, drinking water, supplies, and other such resources belonging to, managed by, held in trust by, appertaining to, or otherwise controlled by the United States (including the resources of the exclusive economic zone), any State or local government or Indian tribe, or any foreign government.

Id. § 2701(20). "Damages for injury to, destruction of, loss of, or loss of use of, natural resources, including the reasonable costs of assessing the damage," are recoverable only by natural resources trustees designated for the United States, a state, an Indian tribe, or a foreign government. Id. § 2702(b)(2)(A). The primary duties of the trustees are: (1) to assess damages to the natural resources belonging to, managed by, or appertaining to their respective areas; and (2) to "develop and implement a plan for the restoration, rehabilitation, replacement, or acquisition of the equivalent, of the natural resources under their trusteeship." Id. § 2706(c). An assessment of damages by a trustee is entitled to a rebuttable presumption of appropriateness in any administrative or judicial challenge. Id. § 2706(e)(2). Problems clearly may arise involving duplicative or overlapping claims among trustees. OPA does not have a mechanism for resolving such conflicts. However, OPA does prohibit double recoveries from a responsible party for natural resource damages from the same incident. Id. § 2706(d)(3).

Determining appropriate values and methodologies for assessment of natural resources damages has been a ubiquitous problem. Prior to the OPA, natural resources damages arose under CERCLA. Working with very little guidance under CERCLA's natural resources damages provisions, the Department of the Interior's CERCLA regulations limited recoverable natural resource damages to "the lesser of' " (a) the cost of restoring or replacing the equivalent of an injured resource, or (b) the lost use value of the resource. In *Ohio v. United*

States Department of the Interior, 880 F.2d 432, 279 U.S.App.D.C. 109 (D.C.Cir. 1989), the D.C. Court of Appeals invalidated the regulations as directly contrary to the intent of Congress. Lost use value is a useful methodology for calculating damages such as commercial fishermen's lost profits. However, the court found that natural resources have values beyond, for example, the board feet of lumber in a forest or the value of a seal's or otter's pelt. Use value in such circumstances seriously undervalues the resource. The court endorsed the inclusion of passive values, such as existence values, in the calculation of damages. Existence values represent the value to individuals who make no active use of a beach, waterbody, or other natural resource, but still derive satisfaction from its existence.

The provisions of OPA provide a bit more guidance by identifying the following factors in calculating the measure of natural resource damages:

The measure of natural resource damages . . . is

(A) the cost of restoring, rehabilitating, replacing, or acquiring the equivalent of, the damaged natural resources;

(B) the diminution in value of those natural resources pending restoration; plus

(C) the reasonable cost of assessing those damages.

33 U.S.C. § 2706(d)(1). Congress expressed a preference for restoring resources when possible. Even this approach is controversial, however.

Although restoration is often the most cost effective approach, the restoration costs may still be disproportionate to the resource's value. On the other hand, many environmentalists and scientists would challenge man's ability to restore a natural resource to its previous pristine state. The Department of Commerce, as designated trustee for the federal government for most natural resources under OPA also incorporated lost use values in its regulations. See 15 C.F.R. pt. 990. The regulations largely were upheld in *General Electric Co. v. U.S. Dept. of Commerce*, 128 F.3d 767, 327 U.S.App.D.C. 33 (D.C.Cir. 1997).

(6) The Oil Spill Liability Trust Fund

Although all claims for cleanup costs and damages must be presented to the responsible party first, see the discussion of the presentment requirement discussed infra, the Oil Spill Liability Trust Fund (Fund) has been expanded under OPA to provide up to a billion dollars per incident, not only for federal costs and damages, but also for uncompensated private and state claims if "full and adequate compensation is not available." See 33 U.S.C. § 2713(d). The most obvious examples of when private claims would be paid by the Fund are when the spiller is not known, when the spiller has successfully asserted a complete defense, or when the spiller's liability exceeds the Act's limitations. The Fund is financed primarily by a five-cent per barrel tax on oil and penalties and fund transfers from other liability statutes.

3.   WHAT LAW?

Liability for damages from spills of oil or hazardous substances has proved to be an unending source of confusion. Rather than provide a single, comprehensive statute for liability, Congress has retained certain remedies in OPA, leaving it to the courts to sort out which remedies have been saved, preempted or displaced. The choice of law is often critical to who can recover damages, who is entitled to punitive damages, and what the limits of the polluter's liability may be. In addition to maritime law, state common law, and federal statutory law,[2] at least 24 states have passed oil spill legislation. Nearly all are strict liability statutes, and most impose unlimited liability. Further, in *Askew v. American Waterways Operators, Inc.*, 411 U.S. 325, 93 S.Ct. 1590, 36 L.Ed.2d 280 (1973), the U.S. Supreme Court held that CWA section 311 did not preempt a state statute imposing strict liability for state removal costs and for state and private damages for spills in the state's waters.

OPA contains a specific savings clause in regard to state law and federal maritime law. Section 1018(a) explains the relationship to state law, providing that nothing in OPA shall:

(1)   affect, or be construed or interpreted as preempting, the authority of any State or political subdivision thereof from imposing any

---

[2]   In *Middlesex County Sewerage Authority v. National Sea Clammers Ass'n*, 453 U.S. 1, 101 S.Ct. 2615, 69 L.Ed.2d 435 (1981), the U.S. Supreme Court held that "the federal common law of nuisance has been fully preempted in the area of ocean pollution."

additional liability or requirements with respect to—

(A)   the discharge of oil or other pollution by oil within such State; or

(B) any removal activities in connection with such a discharge; or

(2)   affect, or be construed or interpreted to affect or modify in any way the obligations or liabilities of any person under . . . State law, including common law. . . 33 U.S.C.A. 2718(a).

The *Deepwater Horizon* litigation created the necessity for Judge Barbier to determine the effect of this savings clause on state law claims. The court found that this language only protected existing state authority involving discharges "within such State," and in the case of oil spills on the OCS, state law had been preempted by federal maritime law. *In re Oil Spill by the Oil Rig "Deepwater Horizon"*, 808 F.Supp.2d 943 (Dist. Ct. E.D. La. 2011). In addition, the court found that the Supreme Court reasoning in *International Paper Co. v. Ouellette*, 479 U.S. 481 (1987), precluded application of state law. In that case, the CWA's savings provision did not allow application of state law to water pollution originating outside of the state because it would undermine the efficiency and predictability goals of the CWA. *Askew*, supra, was distinguished as applying only to spills that occurred in state waters, not to out-of-state polluters, and involved legislation that did not overlap with federal statutes. State law claims were, therefore, dismissed. See also, *In re Deepwater*

Horizon, 745 F.3d 157, 2014 WL 700065 (5th Cir. La. 2014) (affirming preemption of state law because the spill occurred on the OCS).

The *Deepwater Horizon* litigation also addressed the relation of general maritime law to OPA. It should be noted that general maritime law covers a much broader realm of liability than OPA: for example, OPA does not apply to products liability, personal injury or death claims, or punitive damages. But to the extent that claims against "responsible parties" are addressed by OPA, general maritime claims are preempted, and all claims against responsible parties are subject to OPA's presentment requirement.[3] See also *Gabarick v. Laurin Maritime (America) Inc.*, 623 F.Supp.2d 741, 747 (E.D.La.2009) (holding that OPA preempts general maritime law claims that are recoverable under OPA). Claims against non-responsible parties under maritime law, however, are not preempted by OPA. Maritime law continues to be subject to judge-made limitations, such as the *Robins Dry Dock* rule, and to the Limitation on Liability Act, which was specifically mentioned in OPA's savings provisions. Note, however, OPA effectively repeals the 1851 Act's liability limits with respect to oil spill cleanup costs and damages recoverable under OPA.

---

[3]   The statute provides that all claims for removal costs or damages shall be presented first to the responsible party, who is given 90 days to settle the claims. 33 U.S.C. § 2713. Presentment is a mandatory condition precedent to filing suit.

4. THE CULMINATION OF THE *DEEPWATER HORIZON* LITIGATION

The epic litigation spawned by the *Deepwater Horizon* oil spill included, inter alia, claims against BP for loss of life, civil and criminal penalties under the CWA, cleanup and removal costs, natural resources damages, property damages, economic damages resulting from the spill, lost revenues and lost taxes by government entities, costs for services rendered by governments, and products liability. It fell to Judge Barbier of the United States District Court for the Eastern District of Louisiana to sort out the law, the cognizable claims, and the plaintiffs eligible to claim damages.

a. Cognizable Claims and Eligible Plaintiffs

In an early phase of the case identifying the applicable law, the nature of cognizable claims, and OPA's procedural requirements. Judge Barbier's findings included:

1. The *Deepwater Horizon* was at all material times a vessel in navigation.

2. Admiralty jurisdiction is present because the alleged tort occurred upon navigable waters of the Gulf of Mexico, disrupted maritime commerce, and the operations of the vessel bore a substantial relationship to traditional maritime activity. With admiralty jurisdiction comes the application of substantive maritime law.

3. OCSLA jurisdiction is also present because the casualty occurred in the context of exploration or production of mineral on the Outer Continental Shelf.

4. The law of the adjacent state is not adopted as surrogate federal law under OCSLA, 43 U.S.C. § 1333(a)(2)(A).

5. State law, both statutory and common, is preempted by maritime law, notwithstanding OPA's savings provisions. All claims brought under state law are dismissed.

6. General maritime law claims that do not allege physical damage to a proprietary interest are dismissed under the Robins Dry Dock rule, unless the claim falls into the commercial fishermen exception. OPA claims for economic loss need not allege physical damage to a proprietary interest.

7. OPA does not displace general maritime law claims against non-Responsible parties. As to Responsible Parties, OPA does displace general maritime law claims against Responsible Parties, but only with regard to procedure (OPA's presentment requirement).

8. Presentment under OPA is a mandatory condition precedent to filing suit against a Responsible Party.

9. There is no presentment requirement for claims against non-Responsible Parties.

10. Claims for punitive damages are available for general maritime law claimants against Responsible Parties (provided OPA's presentment procedure is satisfied) and non-Responsible Parties. . . .

In re Oil Spill by the Oil Rig "Deepwater Horizon", 808 F.Supp.2d 943 (E.D. La. 2011).

b. Causation and Economic Damages

Judge Barbier addressed economic losses in regard to the claims of Moratorium Plaintiffs in *In re Oil Spill by the Oil Rig "Deepwater Horizon",* 168 F. Supp. 3d 908 (E.D. La. 2016). " 'Moratorium Plaintiffs' are described as 'deepwater drilling rig workers, rig support personnel, transport personnel,' . . . and others who suffered losses and damages as the result of the Six-Month Deepwater Drilling Moratorium issued by the United States Department of Interior on May 28, 2010, in response to the Spill." The court rejected a "but for" test, but rather based the "causation" test on two provisions of OPA. Based on text in Section 2702(a), the General Liability section (requiring that damages must "result from such incident") and Section 2702(b)(E) (requiring that any liability for a party's lost profits or diminished earning capacity be "due to" the incedent), the court concluded that "Plaintiffs must establish that their economic losses were "due to" the injury, destruction, or loss of property or natural resources that "result[ed] from" the discharge or threatened discharge of oil from the HORIZON/ Macondo well (i.e., the "incident")." The court found that "the Moratorium addressed the risk of possible future blowouts and oil spills from wells other than Macondo and was motivated by perceived weaknesses of industry-wide safety measures." The damages resulted from the perceived threat posed by other wells, not from Macondo. The court distinguished "shutdown" cases where damages arose from business interruptions caused by cleanup or containment operations. BP argued that the causation nexus should apply to claims under BP's Settlement Agreement reached in 2012. BP argued that the court-appointed administrator had misinterpreted the Agreement and dispersed funds to businesses without proof that the economic loss was "due to" the oil spill. A three-judge panel found that

> [i]n light of our reading of the Settlement Agreement, claim form, letter briefing, and the voluminous record in this appeal, we conclude the Settlement Agreement does not require a claimant to submit evidence that the claim arose as a result of the oil spill. Each claimant does attest, though, under penalty of perjury, that the claim in fact was due to the *Deepwater Horizon* disaster. . . . These requirements are not as protective of BP's present concerns as might have been achievable, but they are the protections that were accepted by the parties and approved by the district court. It was a contractual concession by BP to limit the issue of factual causation in the processing of claims. Causation, or in Rule 23 terms, traceability, was

not abandoned but it was certainly subordinated.

There is nothing fundamentally unreasonable about what BP accepted but now wishes it had not. . . .

The inherent limitations in mass claims processing may have suggested substituting certification for evidence, just as proof of loss substituted for proof of causation. Because the Settlement Agreement at least requires a formal assertion of the causal nexus, we conclude that what the certification panel relied upon in approving the class definition and Settlement Agreement remained in place during the processing of claims.

In re Deepwater Horizon, 744 F.3d 370, 376–377 (5th Cir. 2014).

c. Findings of Fault

In *In re Oil Spill by the Oil Rig "Deepwater Horizon" in the Gulf of Mexico, on April 20, 2010*, 21 F.Supp.3d 657 (E.D. La. 2014) [hereinafter *Phase One*], the court found BP, Transocean[3] and Halliburton[4] each liable under general maritime law for the blowout, explosion, and oil spill. See id. at para. 619. BP was "reckless" under general maritime law and a substantial cause of the blowout, explosion,

---

[3]   Transocean was the rig owner and operator who flagged the rig under the flag of convenience of the Marshall Islands.

[4]   Halliburton was the contractor who was responsible for providing the cement to seal the Macondo Well.

and oil spill. Id. para. 543. The court determined that while the Transocean drill crew's initial response "was incorrect, it hardly reflects a conscious disregard for a known risk or an extreme departure from the standard of care." Some of its later conduct "fell below the standard of care," but Transocean had limited time, in the context of a rapidly escalating situation, to react properly, unlike BP's misconduct for a much longer period and with "time to consider its choices." "For these reasons, the Court concludes that Transocean's conduct was negligent, and that Transocean's share of liability is considerably less than BP's." Id. at paras. 731–762. Because the court found Haliburton's defective cement was "not a cause of the blowout," Haliburton was not liable under strict products liability or for its "egregious behavior" concerning "cement tests and destroyed computer simulations." Its negligence for its "failure concerning well monitoring was relatively small." Id. paras. At 558–560.

d. Comparative Fault Under General Maritime Law

In the *Phase One* litigation, the court was required to determine the comparative fault of BP, Transocean and Halliburton for the blowout, explosions, and oil spill to allocate liability under general maritime law. (Recall that although BP is a responsible party under OPA, the company is also subject to general maritime law in areas not covered by OPA.) The court found that BP's conduct was reckless and that Transocean's and Halliburton's conduct was negligent. The court concluded that the comparative fault, expressed as a percentage of total liability, is BP: 67%; Transocean: 30%, and Halliburton: 3%. Id. at paras. 554–559.

e. Transocean and the Limitation of Liability Act

The *Phase One* court considered whether Transocean was entitled to protection under the Limitation of Liability Act. The Act does not apply if the negligence or unseaworthiness that caused the damage was within the "privity or knowledge" of the owner. The court found "that the drill crew's failure to divert flow overboard constituted a proximate cause of the explosion, fire, and oil spill that was within Transocean's privity and knowledge. To the extent this failure to act was negligent, Transocean was aware that its crews lacked training about the proper use of diverters, and therefore this negligence was within Transocean's privity and knowledge." In sum, Transocean was not entitled to limit its liability under the Act, because its maintenance failures constituted negligence and/or created an unseaworthy condition within its privity and knowledge. Id. at paras. 586–94.

f. BP and OPA's Liability Cap

Certain OPA limits may have been available to BP as a responsible party. No limits apply, however, if "the incident was proximately caused by . . . the violation of an applicable Federal safety, construction, or operating regulation by the responsible party, an agent or employee of the responsible party, or a person acting pursuant to a contractual relationship with the responsible party. . . ." In the *Phase One* case, the court found BP ineligible, because its failure to properly cement the well, in violation of a DOI regulation, was the proximate cause of the incident. See *Phase One*, at paras. 695–602.

g. Punitive Damages

In the *Phase* One litigation, the court found that although under general maritime law punitive damages may be imposed for reckless, willful, and wanton conduct, and that the conduct of BP's employees made punitive damages appropriate, BP cannot be held liable for punitive damages under general maritime law. The 5th Circuit rule is that operational recklessness or willful disregard is generally insufficient to visit punitive damages upon the employer. The conduct must emanate from corporate policy or from egregious conduct that a corporate official with policy-making authority participated in, approved of, or subsequently ratified. In the circumstances, the employees were not policy-making officials, nor did the reckless conduct emanate from corporate policy. Id. at paras. 561–567.

One of most important questions the court had to answer in the *Phase Two* litigation was "whether, considering both the Phase One and Phase Two evidence, any of the BP entities engaged in such extreme, extra-negligent conduct that would warrant punitive damages." In re Oil Spill by Oil Rig Deepwater Horizon in Gulf of Mexico, 77 F.Supp.3d 500, 520, para. 247. [Phase Two](E.D. La. 2015). The court concluded that (in spite of the fact that BP lied about the flow rate of the oil spill),

> punitive damages are not warranted. The Court finds that BP was not grossly negligent, reckless, willful, or wanton in its source control planning. A major factor in this determination is the fact that BP's source control plan complied with federal regulations and industry practice. Id. at para. 248. [The court noted that the findings did not change the Phase One findings, however.]

h. The Major Settlement Agreements

Phase One found that the operational reckless behavior of employees leading to the oil spill could not justify imposition of punitive damages on the employer (BP) based on 5th Circuit precedent. The conflict in circuits on this issue had the potential reach the Supreme Court. The *Phase One* case also found that Transocean's and Haliburton's misconduct did not exceed ordinary negligence; thus, these parties did not face punitive damages. But two days before the *Phase One* decision was announced, Haliburton entered into a $1.028 billion settlement agreement with the Plaintiffs' Steering Committee (PSC)(a court-appointed committee to represent bundled claims) in regard to punitive damages. HESI Punitive Damages and Assigned Claims Settlement Agreement (Amended as of November 13, 2014), *In re Oil Spill*, No. 2:10-md-02179 (E.D. La. Nov. 13, 2014), ECF No. 13646–1. In 2015, Transocean agreed to a similar agreement for $211.7 million that addressed punitive damages. *In re Oil Spill*, No. 2:10-md-02179 (E.D. La. May 29, 2015), ECF No. 14644–1.

The 2012 uncapped BP settlement agreement addressed "six categories of damage: (1) specified types of economic loss for businesses and individuals, (2) specified types of real property damage (coastal, wetlands, and real property sales damage), (3) Vessel of Opportunity Charter Payment, (4) Vessel Physical Damage, (5) Subsistence Damage, and (6) the Seafood Compensation Program." *In re Oil Spill by Oil Rig Deepwater Horizon*, 910 F.Supp.2d 891, 903 (E.D.La. 2012). Punitive damages were not directly addressed as a compensable category. The settlement agreement did, however, provide for many damage categories to be enhanced by risk transfer premiums (RTPs). "The RTP compensates class members for potential future loss, as well as pre-judgment interest, any risk of oil returning, any claims for consequential damages, inconvenience, aggravation, the lost value of money, compensation for emotional distress, liquidation of legal disputes about punitive damages, and other factors." Id. at 904. The RTP is expressed as a multiplication factor assigned to categories of claims, generally ranging from .25 to 3. One commentator argues that RTPs "incorporate an embedded societal punitive damages award" and "a surrogate or stand-in for punitive damages—which were not included as a separate component of the settlement." See Catherine M. Sharkey, *The BP Oilspill Settlements, Classwide Punitive Damages, And Societal Deterrence*, 64 DePaul L. Rev. 681 (2015).

i. Natural Resource Damages

In April 2016, the court approved a settlement with BP for natural resource damages based on the restoration plan proposed by the Natural Resources Trustees. See part VI.C.2.c(5), supra. Under this settlement, BP is liable to the Trustees for up to $8.8 billion for restoration to address natural resource injuries. The programmatic restoration plan is currently being implemented.

Related to OPA natural resources damages, additional funds paid by BP and other defendants paid to the federal government and states have been directed toward environmental and economic restoration of Gulf of Mexico. In 2012, Congress enacted the RESTORE Act (P.L. 112–141) to establish the Gulf Coast Restoration Trust Fund. Eighty percent of all administrative and civil CWA § 311 penalties, see infra, paid by *Deepwater Horizon* oil spill responsible parties are deposited in the fund. Approximately $5.5 billion in CWA penalties are expected to be available to support economic and environmental restoration activities in the five Gulf of Mexico states. See Congressional Resource Service, *Gulf Coast Restoration: RESTORE Act and Related Efforts*, CRS Report 43380 (updated July 24, 2017).

j. BP's Civil Liability

In the *Phase One* litigation, supra, the court found that BP was subject to enhanced civil penalties under the Clean Water Act because the discharge of oil was the result of BP's gross negligence and willful misconduct. See 33 U.S.C. § 1321. In the quantification stage of the *Phase Two* litigation, *supra*, the court found "that 4.0 million barrels of oil" were released from the reservoir. After deducting the Collected Oil from this amount per the parties' stipulation, the court found "for purposes of calculating the maximum possible civil penalty under the CWA that 3.19 million barrels of oil discharged into the Gulf of Mexico." After BP's petition for review of the almost $13.7 billion maximum CWA penalty based on this figure was denied by the U.S. Supreme Court, *BP Exploration & Prod. v. United States*, No. 14–1217, cert. denied (U.S. June 29, 2015), BP reached a settlement with the U.S. government and five states that included $5.5 billion for civil penalties. The final settlement represented a payment of $1,725 for each barrel of oil spilled. The total settlement also included $8.8 billion in natural resources damages and $4.9 billion to five states for economic losses and natural resource damages.

k. BP's Criminal Liability

Beyond cleanup costs, liability for damages and civil penalties, a polluter may also be liable for and criminal liability. Criminal liability may arise under a number of laws including the CWA, the Refuse Act and the Migratory Bird Treaty Act. In the case of the *Deepwater Horizon* spill, on November 15, 2012, BP agreed to pay $4 billion in criminal fines and penalties and pleaded guilty to eleven counts of felony manslaughter, one count of felony obstruction of Congress, and violations of the CWA and

Migratory Bird Treaty Act. In addition, a former BP executive was charged with obstruction of Congress and making false statements to law enforcement officials, and a Louisiana grand jury has returned indictments against the two highest-ranking BP supervisors on the well site for eleven felony counts of seaman's manslaughter, eleven felony counts of involuntary manslaughter and one violation of the CWA. See Department of Justice Press Release, BP Exploration and Production Inc. Agrees to Plead Guilty to Felony Manslaughter, Environmental Crimes and Obstruction of Congress Surrounding Deepwater Horizon Incident, available at https:// www.justice.gov/opa/pr/bp-exploration-and-production-inc-agrees-plead-guilty-felony-man slaughter-environmental (includes links to guilty plea and indictments). See also Environmental Law Institute, BP Criminal Plea Agreement Fact Sheet at http://eli-ocean.org/wp-content/blogs.dir/2/files/BP-Criminal-Plea-Agreement.pdf (detailing criminal charges and fines and identifying where the monies would go).

For a concise overview and summary, see Stephen L. Tatum, Jr., and Henrik Strand, The Deepwater Horizon Oil Spill: A Review of The Historic Civil and Criminal Liabilities, and Resulting Funding Streams, From America's Worst Environmental Catastrophe, 47 Tex. Envtl. L.J. 153 (2017).

CHAPTER VII

POLLUTION AND THE MARINE ENVIRONMENT

A. INTRODUCTION

Incidents like the oil spills from the *Torrey Canyon* in 1967, the *Amoco Cadiz* in 1978, the *Exxon Valdez* in 1989, and the *Deepwater Horizon* rig in 2010 focused worldwide attention on the devastation caused by accidental discharges of large quantities of oil. They have served as catalysts for the development of law relating to oil spill cleanup and damage liability. Although these disasters highlight the environmental tragedy of marine pollution, such accidents are not the primary, most widespread, or even most devastating source of pollution of the seas. Operational discharges of oil from vessels, ocean dumping of wastes, and discharge of sewage and wastes from land-based sources have contributed much more to the present level of marine pollution than the well known "disasters." Fortunately, both international and domestic regimes have been created to begin to deal more effectively with the prevention of marine pollution.

B. THE UNCLOS FRAMEWORK OF RESPONSIBILITIES FOR THE MARINE ENVIRONMENT

Part XII of the 1982 United Nations Convention on the Law of the Sea (UNCLOS), 21 I.L.M. 1261, addresses the marine environment. The basic obligation of every coastal nation is "to protect and preserve the marine environment." UNCLOS, art. 192. In addition to recognizing traditional rights of nations to control pollution and to protect the territorial sea environment, the treaty extends national jurisdiction for protection of the environment through the 200-mile EEZ. See id. art. 56(1)(b)(iii). The Convention adopts the basic principle of international law that activities should be conducted in a manner that does not cause damage by pollution to other countries and extends the principle to protect areas beyond national jurisdiction, i.e., the high seas and deep seabed. Id. art. 194(2).

1.   OBLIGATIONS IN REGARD TO MARINE POLLUTION

UNCLOS directs parties to "deal with all sources of pollution of the marine environment . . . [through measures] designed to minimize [pollution] *to the fullest possible extent.*" Id. art. 194(3) (emphasis added). The sources of pollution subject to control include vessels, offshore installations, and land-based sources. The drafters of UNCLOS envisioned that the treaty would serve as an "umbrella" and that nations would continue to regulate dumping and pollution from ships through regional and international agreements, such as the London Convention, the Cartagena Convention, and MARPOL 73/78. See arts. 197, 210, 211. The UNCLOS provisions for pollution control enforcement by coastal states in the EEZ do, however, substantially enhance the effectiveness of these treaties. See arts. 216–21.

UNCLOS is unique with regard to land-based sources of marine pollution, because it is the only global treaty that addresses this issue. The treaty calls on nations to control as much as possible:

> the release of toxic, harmful or noxious substances, especially those which are persistent, from land-based sources, from or through the atmosphere or by dumping[.]

Id. art. 194(3)(a). The Convention includes no provisions for enforcement, however, beyond calling upon nations to adopt and enforce laws that implement internationally recognized standards. Id. art. 213. The Convention encourages participation in international and regional efforts to control land-based sources of pollution, such as, the Barcelona Convention for the Mediterranean and the Lima Convention for the Southeast Pacific.

2. POLLUTION FROM DEEP SEABED MINING

UNCLOS is also the only treaty dealing with pollution of the seas resulting from exploration and exploitation of the deep seabed. Anticipating eventual mining of the deep seabed beyond national jurisdiction for manganese nodules, the treaty establishes an international obligation to protect the marine environment beyond national jurisdiction and obligates the Seabed Authority, an organization created under the treaty to oversee deep seabed mining, to develop regulations to assure that exploitation of the seabed does not harm marine or coastal flora, fauna, or natural resources. Id. art. 145. UNCLOS also provides that all contractors and applicants for contracts must have sponsoring States. Sponsoring States have the responsibility to ensure that seabed mining activities are carried out in conformity with the Convention.

In 2010, the Republic of Nauru submitted a request to the Seabed Authority to provide an interpretation of States' responsibilities. The Council—the executive and policy-making arm of the Authority—requested an advisory opinion from the specialized Seabed Disputes Chamber of the International Tribunal for the Law of the Sea (ITLOS), the judicial body created by the LOS Convention. This opinion provides the first judicial interpretation of the obligations and potential liability of States in regard to pollution and environmental damage from seabed mining operations. See Seabed Disputes Chamber of the International Tribunal for the Law of the Sea, Responsibilities and Obligations of States Sponsoring Persons and Entities with Respect to Activities in the Area (Case No. 17 (2011)).

The Chamber interpreted UNCLOS to impose two kinds of duties on a sponsoring State. First, the "responsibility to ensure" imposes a duty of "due diligence" on a sponsoring State to secure compliance by the sponsored contractors with the treaty and contract obligations—a duty the Chamber "characterized as an obligation 'of conduct' and not 'of result'." The due diligence obligation includes the duty to ensure that the contractor meets the requirement for adequate environmental impact assessment—a requirement the Chamber found to arise under both UNCLOS and customary international law. Due diligence also requires the sponsoring State to ensure that the obligations of a sponsored contractor are made enforceable through domestic laws and regulations. Id.

Second, the sponsoring State has direct obligations which include:

- an obligation to assist the Authority;
- the obligation to apply the "best environmental practices" set out in Authority's regulations;
- the obligation to apply a precautionary approach, made binding by inclusion in the Authority's regulations;
- the obligation to adopt measures to ensure the provision of guarantees; and
- the obligation to provide a system for compensation for damages. Id.

The liability of a sponsoring State arises from its failure to fulfill its obligations under the Convention and related instruments and the actual occurrence of damage. A sponsoring State's liability requires that a causal link be established between the failure to comply with its obligations and the damage. A sponsored contractor's failure to comply with its obligations does not in itself give rise to sponsoring State liability. Id.

The LOS Convention specifies neither what constitutes compensable damage nor who may be entitled to claim compensation. Although UNCLOS does not specifically entitle the Authority to make a claim, article 137(2) does provide that Authority acts "on behalf" of mankind. The Chamber also posited: "Each State Party may also be entitled to claim compensation in light of the *erga omnes* character of the obligations relating to preservation of the environment of the high seas and in the Area."

C. THE INTERNATIONAL REGIME FOR OIL POLLUTION AND OIL SPILLS

Recognizing that pollution of the seas by oil is a truly international issue, nations have negotiated a number of treaties to control intentional discharges and in an attempt to minimize accidental discharges. The effort began with the 1954 International Convention for the Prevention of Pollution of the Sea by Oil opened for signature May 12, 1954, 12 U.S.T. 2989, 327 U.N.T.S. 3, as amended in 1962, 1969, and 1971. This treaty, as amended in 1962, 17 U.S.T. 1523, 600 U.N.T.S. 332, prohibited the discharge of oil and oily mixtures into the sea in certain areas and required recordkeeping to document discharges of oil and the surrounding circumstances. Prohibited zones included all seas within fifty miles of a coast. The 1969 amendments, 28 U.S.T. 1205, 9 I.L.M. 1, added a rule that discharges, such as ballast discharges, must be *en route* and proscribed a rate of discharge in addition to a distance from land rule. Amendments in 1971, 11 I.L.M. 267, related to tank size and arrangement and created a fifty-mile prohibited zone around the Great Barrier Reef.

1.   INTERNATIONAL RESPONSE TO THE *TORREY CANYON*

The *Torrey Canyon* oil spill provoked the negotiation of a number of new treaties in the years following the 1967 disaster. First, the 1969 International Convention Relating to Intervention on the High Seas in Cases of Oil Pollution Casualties, done Nov. 29, 1969, 9 I.L.M. 25, 26 U.S.T. 765, 970 U.N.T.S. 211, and the 1973 Protocol (Intervention Convention), gave parties emergency response power beyond territorial waters. This treaty gives contracting parties the authority to "take such measures on the high seas as may be necessary to prevent, mitigate or eliminate grave and imminent danger to their coastline or related interests from pollution or threat of pollution of the sea by oil, following upon a maritime casualty . . . which may reasonably be expected to result in major harmful consequences." The 1973 Protocol, 34 U.S.T. 3407, 13 I.L.M. 605, extended intervention authority to hazardous substances other than oil. The Intervention Convention creates extraordinary coastal nation authority over vessels of other countries on the high seas. This authority must generally be exercised in consultation with and in consideration of the views of the flag state of the vessel and affected parties. Priority must be given to saving human lives.

The 1969 International Convention on Civil Liability for Oil Pollution Damage (CLC), done Nov. 29, 1969, S. Exec. Doc. G, 91st Cong., 2d Sess. 19 (1970), 9 I.L.M. 45, 973 U.N.T.S. 3, provides a legal basis for claims for damages to the territorial sea or coast of a nation. Shipowners are strictly liable for damages from an oil spill subject to certain defenses, such as an act of war, an act of God, or the act or omission of a third party. If the shipowner establishes that the spill occurred without his fault or privity, the CLC creates a limitation on liability and requires that all ships carrying over 2000 tons of oil have financial security or insurance to the limit of liability under the Convention. Claims under the CLC provide an exclusive remedy. But see *In re Oil Spill by the "Amoco Cadiz" Off the Coast of France on March 16, 1978*, 471 F.Supp. 473 (J.P.M.L. 1979) (rejecting Amoco's argument that the case should be dismissed because the CLC is an exclusive remedy and allows recovery only in the courts of countries that suffered the pollution damage or took steps to prevent it). The flag state is responsible for certifying that a vessel meets the financial responsibility requirements. Because vessel owners may attempt to avoid these requirements by flying "flags of convenience," parties to the CLC are required to enact domestic legislation requiring all vessels using its ports or terminals to have certificates of financial responsibility on board.

The 1971 International Convention on the Establishment of an International Fund for Compensation for Oil Pollution Damage (1971 Fund Convention), done Dec. 18, 1971, S. Exec. Doc. K, 92d

Cong., 2d Sess. 1 (1972), 1110 U.N.T.S. 57, was intended to supplement the inadequate liability compensation limits of the CLC and to provide compensation to individuals who suffer pollution damage not covered by the CLC. For example, damages from an oil spill in a country that is a party to the 1971 Fund Convention are recoverable even if the flag state of the offending vessel is not a party. The Fund is maintained by oil companies in each treaty nation rather than by the oil tanker owners and operators and increases the potential for recovery substantially.

Several protocols to the CLC and 1971 Fund Convention have been negotiated since 1984 to increase the liability and to broaden coverage of the conventions to include damage within the EEZ and reasonable environmental damages. The United States was criticized for acting unilaterally to impose additional levels and standards of liability after the *Exxon Valdez* oil spill and jeopardizing the viability and effectiveness of the international liability and compensation regime. See *U.S. Failure to Ratify Protocols Could Undermine Pollution Control, IMO Says,* 13 Int'l Envtl. Rep. (BNA) 240 (June 13, 1990). The 1992 Protocol to the CLC, however, incorporated many of the changes adopted by the U.S. (although the U.S. is not a party to the convention).

2.   MARPOL 73/78

The primary international agreement for prevention and control of oil discharges is now the 1973 International Convention for the Prevention of

Pollution from Ships, done Nov. 2, 1973, S. Exec. Doc. E, 95th Cong., 1st Sess. 1 (1979), 12 I.L.M. 1319, as modified by the 1978 Protocol, done Feb. 17, 1978, S. Exec. Doc. C, 96th Cong., 1st Sess. 1 (1979), 17 I.L.M. 546 (MARPOL 73/78). MARPOL 73/78 supersedes the 1954 convention on oil pollution prevention and extends the scope of the international pollution prevention effort to discharges of any harmful substance and to virtually all vessels and oil platforms. As of 2019 the Convention has 158 parties, including all major shipping countries and covering 99% of the world's shipping tonnage.

MARPOL 73/78 Annex II contains both operational and technological requirements. Operational discharges of oil are limited. For example, within "special areas" and fifty miles from land, only clean, segregated ballast may be discharged from tankers. More than fifty miles from land, discharges containing limited quantities of oil may be released while the vessel is *en route*. Tankers over 150 gross tons and other ships over 400 gross tons must have discharge monitoring equipment and be inspected and certified that they meet convention requirements. All discharges must be documented in an Oil Record Book. MARPOL 73/78 Annex II emphasizes improved technology, such as segregated ballasts and double hulls. Port reception facilities are required to eliminate the necessity of flushing tanks at sea. The United States implements MARPOL 73/78 Annex II with legislation entitled Prevention of Pollution from Ships, 33 U.S.C. §§ 1901–1913.

3. MARPOL REPORTING REQUIREMENTS AS AN ENFORCEMENT MECHANISM

Although international efforts have had a significant effect in the area of liability and cleanup costs for pollution from oil and hazardous substances, many commentators believe that the conventions have provided very little relief from chronic discharges from vessels. Enforcement is the responsibility of the flag country, and unfortunately, there is very little economic incentive for a country to engage in vigorous enforcement of the treaty obligations against its ships in distant waters. See Paul S. Dempsey, *Compliance and Enforcement in International Law—Oil Pollution of the Marine Environment by Ocean Vessels,* 6 Nw. J. Int'l L. & Bus. 459, 557–61 (1984). The United States has found a unique way to supplement enforcement against foreign ships calling in U.S. ports, however, by enforcing the requirement under MARPOL and U.S. implementing legislation that requires that ships maintain an Oil Record Book noting all discharges. See Act to Prevent Pollution from Ships (APPS), 33 U.S.C.A. § 1908. Several U.S. courts have upheld U.S. civil and criminal jurisdiction over vessels for falsification of and failure to maintain an oil record book, even when the underlying act of illegal discharge from the vessel occurred outside U.S. territorial jurisdiction. Maintaining a false oil record book and misrepresentation of the oil record book while in a U.S. port has provided a basis for U.S. jurisdiction independent of the discharge itself. See, e.g., *U.S. v. MST Mineralien Schiffarht Spedition Und Transp. GmbH,* 2018 WL 522764, at *1 (D. Me.

Jan. 22, 2018); *United States v. Oceanic Illsabe Ltd.,* 889 F.3d 178, 194 (4th Cir. 2018); *Giuseppe Bottiglieri Shipping Co. S.P.A. v. United States,* CIV.A. 12-0059-WS-B, 2012 WL 527619 (S.D. Ala. 2012). Cf. *U.S. v. Fafalios,* 817 F.3d 155 (5th Cir. 2016).

4.   UNCLOS, MARPOL AND PORT STATE CONTROLS

Provisions of UNCLOS were drafted with the expectation of a separate international regime, such as MARPOL, applying to vessel design and construction standards and operational rules. But UNCLOS offers increased opportunities for coastal state enforcement of international requirements. Port states are authorized to investigate and institute legal proceedings for discharges in violation of international standards against vessels voluntarily in port. UNCLOS, art. 218(1), 220(1). A coastal state may physically inspect and institute proceedings against a vessel navigating its territorial seas when there are "clear grounds for believing" that the vessel has violated international standards or the pollution control laws of the coastal state. UNCLOS, art. 220(2). A coastal state may only detain and institute proceedings against a vessel in the EEZ if there is "clear objective evidence" that a violation of international oil pollution control standards actually resulted in a "discharge causing major damage or threat of major damage to the coastline . . . of the coastal State, or to any resources of its territorial sea or [EEZ]." UNCLOS, art. 220(6).

Regional port state control agreements have led to more coordinated and regular inspections to assure vessels meet standards under MARPOL and other technical conventions. Originally intended as a back-up for flag state control, regional agreements have proved to be an efficient and effective way to identify and share information on sub-standard ships. Nine regional agreements or MOUs, now covering virtually all of the world's major ports, include: Europe and the north Atlantic (Paris MOU); Asia and the Pacific (Tokyo MOU); Latin America (Acuerdo de Viña del Mar); Caribbean (Caribbean MOU); West and Central Africa (Abuja MOU); the Black Sea region (Black Sea MOU); the Mediterranean (Mediterranean MOU); the Indian Ocean (Indian Ocean MOU); and the Riyadh MOU.

The U.S. Coast Guard maintains a port state control program to inspect, and sometimes detain, vessels for lack of seaworthiness and compliance with U.S. and international standards. In appropriate circumstances, sub-standard vessels may be banned from U.S. waters. See U.S. Coast Guard, Foreign & Offshore Compliance Division, available at https://www.dco.uscg.mil/Our-Organization/Assistant-Commandant-for-Prevention-Policy-CG-5P/Inspections-Compliance-CG-5PC-/Commercial-Vessel-Compliance/Foreign-Offshore-Compliance-Division/Port-State-Control/rso/.[1]

---

[1]   See also, Armando Graziano, Jens-Uwe Schroder-Henrichs, and Aykut I. Olcer, *After 40 years of regional and coordinated ship safety inspections: Destination reached or new point of departure?*, 143 Ocean Engineering 217–226 (2107).

5.   THE CARTAGENA CONVENTION

The United States and 24 other countries[2] are also parties to the Convention for the Protection and Development of the Marine Environment of the Wider Caribbean Region (Cartagena Convention), done Mar. 24, 1983, T.I.A.S. No. 11,085, 22 I.L.M. 227, and the Protocol concerning Co-operation in Combating Oil Spills in the Wider Caribbean Region, done Mar. 24, 1983, 22 I.L.M. 240. An additional sixteen countries are participating in a Caribbean Action Plan to implement the treaty. The Convention addresses a number of sources of marine pollution including vessels, dumping, seabed activities, airborne pollution, and land-based sources, and provides a dispute resolution procedure.

6.   MARPOL: BEYOND OIL POLLUTION

It should be noted that the MARPOL 73/78 regime now goes far beyond oil pollution, the subject of mandatory Annexes I and II of the convention. Additional voluntary annexes are: Annex III—Prevention of Pollution by Harmful Substances Carried by Sea in Packaged Form; Annex IV—Prevention of Pollution by Sewage from Ships; Annex—Prevention of Pollution by Garbage from Ships; and Annex VI—Prevention of Air Pollution from Ships. The U.S. has accepted Annexes I, II, III, V and VI. The U.S. has not ratified Annex IV, but has equivalent regulation for the treatment and

---

[2]   All the countries in the Caribbean Basin are parties except Suriname, Honduras and Haiti.

discharge standards of shipboard sewage. See 33 U.S.C. 1251; 33 C.F.R. 159.

[For a discussion of the U.S. domestic regime dealing with oil pollution and oil spills, see Chapter VI.]

D. OCEAN DUMPING

The intentional discharge of dredged spoil, sewage sludge, and industrial wastes into the ocean probably constitutes about ten percent of the pollutants in the ocean. Eighty to ninety percent of the deliberately dumped material is dredged spoil from navigation, waterway, and harbor projects. As much as ten percent of dredged materials are contaminated with oil, heavy metals, and organochlorine compounds. Industrial wastes may be obvious sources of hazardous or toxic contaminants, but sewage sludge may also contain heavy metals and organic chemicals. Ocean disposal has not only contributed to the general degradation of the marine environment, but also has direct effects on habitats and organisms at dumpsites. See Maritime Affairs: A World Handbook 240–41 (Edgar Gold ed., 2d ed. 1991).

1. THE LONDON CONVENTION

The Convention on the Prevention of Marine Pollution by Dumping of Wastes and Other Matter (London Convention), done Dec. 29, 1972, 26 U.S.T. 2406, 1046 U.N.T.S. 120, is the primary international agreement dealing with marine disposal of wastes. Ocean "dumping" is defined in the Convention as:

(i)   any deliberate disposal at sea of wastes or other matter from vessels, aircraft, platforms or other man-made structures at sea;

(ii) any deliberate disposal at sea of vessels, aircraft, platforms or other man-made structures at sea.

Id. art. 111(1).

The nations that are party to the London Convention originally agreed to prohibit the dumping of materials listed in Annex I of the Convention, unless they are "rapidly rendered harmless by physical, chemical, or biological processes in the sea . . . ." (Annex I, No. 8, 26 U.S.T. at 2465). Dumping of material specifically listed in Annex II and other material is allowed only on the issuance of a prior permit. The Convention set forth a number of factors in Annex III to be considered in granting permits, including the characteristics of the waste and site, method of disposal, effect on marine organisms, other uses of the sea, and the availability of alternative methods of dumping.

2.   THE 1996 PROTOCOL TO THE LONDON CONVENTION

The Convention's 1996 Protocol was intended to modernize and, at some point, replace the 1972 convention. It greatly restricted permissible dumping by prohibiting the ocean dumping of all wastes except those listed in a revised Annex I, the so-called "reverse list." Revised Annex I only allows the dumping of dredged material, sewage sludge, fish wastes, inert geological materials, natural organic materials, abandoned vessels and platforms, and other bulky items made of iron, steel, concrete, and similar nonharmful materials. Revised Annexes II and III to the 1996 Protocol deal with waste assessment and arbitral procedures. The 1996 Protocol provided that it would come into force upon its ratification by 26 nations, including at least 15 of the 76 nations who are parties to the London Convention. The 1996 Protocol entered into force in 2006. Currently, the Protocol has 57 parties. The United States is one of the current 87 parties to the London Convention, but has not ratified the 1996 Protocol.

3.   OCEAN CARBON SEQUESTION: DUMPING?

The fact that the oceans are natural "carbon sinks" has led to proposals to enhance that capability by "ocean fertilization" and to use the oceans and seabed for sequestration of carbon. Ocean fertilization does not technically involve "disposal" in the ocean, but the parties to the London Convention have agreed that a precautionary approach is called for in dealing with such projects and that "ocean fertilization activities other than legitimate scientific research should not be allowed." See Resolution LC-LP.1 (2008) on the Regulation of Ocean Fertilization and Statement of concern regarding the iron fertilization project in ocean waters west of Canada (adopted 2 November 2012, reaffirming the position of the London Convention adopted in 2008). In 2013, the London Protocol Parties adopted amendments to regulate marine geoengineering activities, including ocean fertilization. The amendments to regulate marine geoengineering under the London Protocol have not entered into force.

Carbon sequestration is more clearly within the scope of the London Convention. In 2006, Annex I of the 1996 Protocol was amended to allow CO_2 streams from CO_2 capture to be considered for dumping in sub-seabed geological formations if (a) disposal is into a sub-seabed geological formation; (b) they consist overwhelmingly of carbon dioxide with minimal incidental associated substances; and (c) no wastes or other matter are added for the purpose of disposal. The interpretation of the London Convention as prohibiting the export of CO_2 to other countries for injection into sub-seabed geological formations led to an amendment in 2009 to allow for cross-border transportation of CO_2 for sub-seabed storage. The requirement that the amendment be ratified by two thirds of Convention's parties to enter into force has slowed implementation.

4.   THE U.S. OCEAN DUMPING ACT

In 1972, Congress enacted the Marine Protection, Research and Sanctuaries Act of 1972 (MPRSA), 33 U.S.C. §§ 1401–445, to implement the London Convention. The first two titles of MPRSA are commonly known as the Ocean Dumping Act (ODA). The ODA was enacted "to regulate the dumping of all types of materials into ocean waters," and grants the Environmental Protection Agency and the Secretary of the Army, through the U.S. Army Corps of

Engineers (the Corps), the authority to regulate ocean dumping.

a. ODA Definition of Dumping

The ODA defines ocean "dumping" broadly as "a disposition of material." Id. § 1402(f). Material may include solid wastes, industrial waste, radioactive waste, sewage sludge, incinerator residue, and dredged materials. However, dumping does not include effluent from ocean sewage outfalls, construction of offshore structures or artificial islands, or the deposit of oyster shells or other materials for the purpose of developing fisheries resources. Id. In general, anything placed on the ocean floor for purposes other than disposal is excluded.

b. Administration and Permitting Under the ODA

As with the CWA, the Administrator of the EPA is charged with the ultimate responsibility of enforcing the provisions of the ODA. Under the ODA, the Administrator may grant permits for ocean dumping of nondredged materials except "radiological, chemical, and biological warfare agents, high-level radioactive waste, and medical waste," for which no permits may be issued. Id. § 1412(a). While an environmental impact statement may not be necessary for every case of open water dumping, the OPA requires a site specific survey of each disposal site. *Manatee County v. Gorsuch,* 554 F. Supp. 778, 787 and n. 18 (M.D. Fla. 1982). In general, the EPA may only allow disposal that "will not unreasonably degrade or endanger human health; welfare, or amenities, or the marine environment, ecological systems, or economic potentialities." Id. More specifically, EPA permit criteria include consideration of: (1) the effect of dumping on human health and welfare, including economic, esthetic, and recreational values; (2) the effect of dumping on fisheries resources, plankton, fish, shellfish, wildlife, shorelines, and beaches; (3) the effect of dumping on marine ecosystems, particularly the concentration and dispersion of such material; potential changes in marine ecosystem diversity, productivity, and stability; and species and community population dynamics; (4) the persistence and permanence of the effects of the dumping; (5) the effect of dumping particular volumes and concentrations; (6) the appropriate locations and methods of disposal or recycling, including land-based alternatives and the probable impact of alternatives upon the public interest; (7) the effect on alternate uses of the oceans, such as scientific study, fishing, and other living and non-living resource exploitation; and (8) the need for the proposed dumping. See 40 C.F.R. Pts. 227–228.

The EPA Administrator also designates sites and times for ocean dumping "that will mitigate adverse impact on the environment to the greatest extent practicable." 33 U.S.C. § 1412(c)(1). Because most long-term dumping sites are for dredged materials, the EPA must develop management plans for those sites that include monitoring and protections for the environment. Id. § 1412(c)(3).

c. Comparison of Jurisdiction Under the ODA and CWA § 404

The ODA authorizes the Corps of Engineers, with the concurrence of the EPA, to issue permits for the dumping of dredged material. Id. § 1413. Under section 404 of the CWA, the Corps also has authority to permit the discharge of dredged materials into navigable waters. Id. § 1344(a). Because ODA jurisdiction includes all ocean waters seaward of the territorial sea baseline and because "navigable waters of the United States" under the CWA includes waters three nautical miles seaward of that baseline, the Corps' programs for disposal of dredged material overlap in the ocean to three miles offshore. The Corps has published regulations addressing the issue of the overlapping jurisdiction of the CWA and the ODA in the 3-mile territorial sea. All disposal in the ocean or territorial sea of material that has been excavated or dredged from navigable waters will be evaluated under the ODA. Only materials determined to be deposited primarily for the purpose of fill will be evaluated under section 404 of the CWA. See 33 C.F.R. § 336.0; see also 53 Fed. Reg. 14,902, 14,905 (1988).

Whether a permit for dredged spoil disposal is evaluated under the CWA or the ODA can be significant. First, although the criteria for evaluation are virtually the same, the ODA requires that the Corps "make an independent determination as to the need for the dumping[,] . . . other possible methods of disposal[,] and . . . appropriate locations for the dumping." 33 U.S.C. § 1413(b). The CWA does not have a comparable requirement.

In permitting discharges under the CWA, both the CWA's requirement for state certification that a project does not violate state water quality standards and the federal consistency requirements of the Coastal Zone Management Act (CZMA) are applicable to activities with effects within three miles of the coast. In its ODA regulations, the Corps rejected comments by states that federal consistency requirements should apply to dumping beyond coastal waters and asserted that the ODA may preempt both the CWA certification provisions and the CZMA. For dumping material from federal projects in state ocean waters, the ODA does limit the authority of states to adopt or enforce any rule or regulation more stringent than the requirements of the ODA. Id. § 1416(d)(2). Otherwise, state authority over dumping in the state ocean waters is preserved. Id. § 1416(d)(1). But the Corps regulations state that it will continue to seek state water quality certification and consistency determinations for dredged spoil disposal within three miles of shore only as a matter of comity and specifically reserved its legal rights on the issue. 33 C.F.R. § 336.2(c). When one considers that the Corps itself generates almost ninety percent of the dredged spoil dumped in the sea, it is clear that the "checks and balances" of the CWA and CZMA may be appropriate to help reconcile the Corps' roles as both generator and regulator.

The EPA does have oversight authority over the Corps in issuing ocean-dumping permits for dredged spoils and over the Corps' use of disposal sites not designated by the EPA. 33 U.S.C. § 1413(c). The EPA must concur with the Corps' determination that a permit or alternative disposal site complies with the ODA's criteria and restrictions. If the EPA declines to concur, the Corps may not issue the permit. Id. If the Corps determines that there is no economically feasible method or other available site that will not violate ODA criteria, the EPA must grant a waiver unless it finds that the "dumping . . . will result in an unacceptably adverse impact on municipal water supplies, shellfish beds, wildlife, fisheries . . . , or recreational areas." Id. § 1413(d). The Corps does not administratively issue itself permits for dumping dredged spoils, but the same standards and criteria apply for federal dredged spoil disposal projects. Id. § 1413(e).

d. Dumping of Industrial Waste and Sewage

In 1977, Congress amended MPRSA to forbid the issuance of permits for dumping of sewage sludge into ocean waters after December 31, 1981. The amendment went on, however, to define sewage sludge as municipal waste "the ocean dumping of which *may unreasonably degrade or endanger* human health, welfare, amenities, or the marine environment, ecological systems, or economic potentialities." (Emphasis added). In *City of New York v. United States Environmental Protection Agency,* 543 F.Supp. 1084 (S.D.N.Y. 1981), the federal district court rejected the argument that the amendment required an absolute end to dumping. The court held that EPA could not deny the continuance of New York's sludge dumping permit without considering the effects of alternatives to ocean dumping, such as land-based disposal, in its determination of whether ocean dumping caused unacceptable harm. In the Ocean Dumping Ban Act of 1988, Congress amended MPRSA to reverse *City of New York*. All ocean dumping of both sewage sludge and industrial wastes was banned after December 31, 1991, and no permits were issued to "new entrants" during the interim period. 33 U.S.C. § 1414b(a).

e. Ocean Incineration

The prohibition on ocean dumping of industrial wastes had an interesting impact on a form of waste disposal that many thought was a promising concept for disposing of a number of highly toxic and hazardous substances. EPA had for a long time considered ocean incineration to be "dumping" both in the sense that smokestack emissions are deposited in ocean waters and in the sense that incinerator residue is also disposed of at sea. When EPA suspended development of ocean incineration regulations and barred consideration of new permit applications because of the ban on new entrants and the complete prohibition on dumping industrial wastes after 1991, Seaburn, a commercial waste disposal company, challenged EPA's characterization of ocean incineration as dumping. *Seaburn, Inc. v. United States EPA*, 712 F.Supp. 218 (D.D.C. 1989). Seaburn argued that smokestack emissions could not rationally be equated with dumping and that incinerator residue did not fit the definition of industrial waste. The D.C. federal district court found that this time Congress had unequivocally intended a moratorium on dumping of industrial wastes. Finding that "EPA's interpretation of the Ocean Dumping Ban Act [was] sufficiently rational to be entitled to the traditional deference accorded an agency interpretation of a statute," the court granted the EPA's motion for summary judgment and closed the door on research and development of ocean incineration technology.

The 1993 amendments to the London Convention and the 1996 Protocol have now also banned the ocean incineration and dumping of industrial wastes.

E. PERSISTENT MARINE DEBRIS—PLASTICS

Humans contribute large amounts of materials that can be categorized as persistent marine debris to ocean waters and beaches—oil tarballs, glass, metal—but over the last few decades, it has become clear that nondegradable plastics contribute the most significant long-term threat to the marine environment. Vessels and offshore facilities generate much of this plastic debris, which includes monofilament line, driftnets and other fishing nets, ropes, plastic sheeting, containers, and food packaging. But it is estimated that an average of 8 billion metric tons of plastic enter the oceans from land each year. People incur direct economic costs from marine debris on beaches and from debris that damages vessels. Perhaps more tragic, however, is the impact on marine wildlife. Inestimable numbers of fish, marine mammals, birds, and sea turtles die annually from entanglement with or ingestion of plastic debris. Relatively recently, it has been discovered that plastics and other debris have accumulated in five massive oceans gyres that concentrate the pollution and multiply the deleterious effects. See, e.g., *Tracking Ocean Debris,* 8 IPRC Climate 14 (2008); Jose G.B. Derraik, *The pollution of the marine environment by plastic debris: a review,* 44 Marine Pollution Bulletin 842 (2002).

1.   PLASTICS AND MARPOL ANNEX V

Under the London Convention, plastics cannot be dumped at sea. The Convention only applies, however, to materials that are transported for the purpose of disposal in the ocean. The scope of the London Convention does not reach "[t]he disposal at sea of wastes or other matter incidental to, or derived from the normal operations of vessels . . . and their equipment." London Convention, art. III(1). "Normal operations of vessels" have entailed the disposal of hundreds of thousands of tons per year of ship-generated plastic garbage and lost or abandoned fishing gear.

a. MARPOL Annex V

The international community addressed this gap in the regulation of vessel operational wastes in Annex V of MARPOL 73/78. Regulations for the Prevention of Pollution by Garbage from Ships

(Annex V of MARPOL 73/78), Oct. 31, 1973, S. Treaty Doc. No. 3, 100th Cong., 1st Sess. 1 (1987), 12 I.L.M. 1434. Annex V prohibits "the disposal into the sea of all plastics, including but not limited to synthetic ropes, synthetic fishing nets and plastic garbage bags." Id. reg. 3. Floatable, nonplastic materials may not be disposed of within twenty-five miles of land, and food wastes and other garbage must be discharged at least twelve miles from shore. Id. The only exemptions from the discharge prohibitions are: (1) disposal necessary for the safety of the ship or crew, or to save life at sea; (2) discharges resulting from damage to a ship or its equipment; and (3) accidental loss of synthetic fishing nets. Id. reg. 6. The third exemption continues to account for significant plastics pollution.

The at-sea disposal prohibition necessitates other waste disposal options. Annex V requires nations that are parties to provide garbage reception facilities at ports and terminals. Id. reg. 7.

The United States ratified Annex V in 1987; the Annex went into force internationally in 1988.

b. U.S. Implementation of Annex V: The Marine Plastic Pollution Research and Control Act

The United States implemented Annex V through the enactment of the Marine Plastic Pollution Research and Control Act (MPPRCA), which amended the Act on Prevention of Pollution from Ships, 33 U.S.C. §§ 1901–1912. MPPRCA extends Annex V's prohibitions on plastics and garbage disposal to all U.S. ships wherever they are located in the world. In addition, foreign ships operating in U.S. navigable waters or the EEZ, whether flying the flag of a party to MARPOL or not, are subject to Annex V requirements. Id. § 1902(a)(1), (3). Pursuant to Annex V, the MPPRCA also requires ports and offshore terminals to provide garbage reception facilities. Id. § 1905. Large ports and terminals that receive oil or cargo tankers or that receive more than 500,000 tons of fish annually must have certificates of adequacy from the U.S. Coast Guard in order to continue to receive ships. 33 C.F.R. § 158.135.

c. Enforcement of the MPPRCA

The MPPRCA contains a number of enforcement provisions. The Act mandates regulations for certain ships to maintain refuse record books to account for waste production and disposal. 33 U.S.C. § 1903(b). While in port or in U.S. navigable waters or in the EEZ, domestic and foreign ships subject to Annex V may be inspected for violations. Id. § 1907(c)–(d). U.S. ships may be inspected anywhere. Id. § 1907(e). Civil penalties are substantial and can be up to $25,000 for each violation. Knowing violations of the statute or Annex V constitute a class D felony. Id. § 1908. Ships are also subject to *in rem* actions for penalties and may be denied clearance to enter ports or permits to proceed from port. Id. § 1908(d).

To supplement enforcement, the MPPRCA contains a "whistle-blower" provision that allows a court to award up to one-half of a fine to persons providing information of violations. Id. § 1908(a). With the incentive of this provision, crew members and tourists with video cameras and smartphones have been providing evidence of illegal dumping of plastics and garbage by cruise ships. In 1993, Princess Cruise Lines pleaded guilty and paid a record $500,000 fine for illegally dumping plastics and garbage that had been videotaped and reported by passengers, who received one-half of the penalty. See *Vacationers Go Undercover at Sea to Film Dumping*, N.Y. Times (July 31, 1993). See also *United States v. Wallenius Ship Management Pte.*, No. 2:06-CR-00213 (D.N.J. Aug. 10, 2006) (court awarded one-half of a $5 million fine to four crew members who faxed information alleging that they were being ordered to engage in deliberate acts of pollution); *United States v. OMI*, No. 2:04-CR-00060 (D. N.J. 2004) (court awarded one-half of a $4.2 million criminal fine to a Second Engineer who upon arrival asked for directions to local police department and reported illegal discharges and falsified records); and *United States v. Regency Cruises, Inc.*, No. 94-245-CR-T-21(C) (M.D. Fla. Mar. 8, 1995) (court split one half of the $250,000 fine among two witnesses who reported the pollution). In 2019, Carnival Corporation paid $20 million in penalties for violations that included dumping of plastics.

2. LAND-BASED PLASTICS POLLUTION

In addition to marine-based sources such as passenger and fishing vessels and oil platforms, a sizable quantity of plastics originating on the coast are ending up as marine debris. In 2018, the United States passed the Save Our Seas Act reauthorizing the NOAA Marine Debris Program and giving the

NOAA administrator the power to declare a "severe marine debris event" arising from a severe storm and provide cleanup assistance. P.L. 115–265.

According to the UN, more than 60 countries have enacted bans, phaseouts or taxes on single-use plastics which contribute significantly to marine plastic pollution. The U.S. is a major contributor to ocean plastics pollution, but has not adopted a comprehensive policy addressing many of the types of disposable, one-use plastics that enter the environment and, eventually, the oceans. In this vacuum, New York, California and Hawai'i have enacted bans on one-use plastic bags, and several states have enacted charges or recycling measures. Other states have been slower to take action, and a significant number of cities have taken action: Boston, Boulder, Chicago, Montgomery Cty. (Md.), Los Angeles, New York, San Francisco, Portland (Maine), Seattle and Washington, D.C have plastic bag bans. See National Conference of State Legislators, State Plastic and Paper Bag Legislation (4/30/19) (at http://www.ncsl.org/research/environment-andnatural-resources/plastic-bag-legislation.aspx).

In some states, however, plastics bans have triggered preemption conflicts between state and local governments. The states of Minnesota, Pennsylvania and Michigan have preempted local government plastic bag bans. In 2018, the Texas Supreme Court held that Laredo's ban was preempted by the state's Solid Waste Disposal Act. The case affected similar bans in other Texas cities, including Austin. See City of Laredo v. Laredo Merchants Ass'n, 550 S.W.3d 586, 591 (Tex. 2018).

At the international level, the Global Partnership for Marine Litter involves UNEP, governments, businesses, and NGOs.[3] Regional partnerships have emerged from the Global Partnership in the Caribbean and the Northwest Pacific. The Partnership does not have any governance ability, but is primarily a forum for dialogue and education. At the business level, a number of companies have made pledges to redesign packaging or improve recycling of packaging. As of 2019, there is little evidence of system-wide changes in consumer products. There is clearly a long way to go to deal with one of the largest sources of marine plastics pollution.

F.   POINT SOURCE DISCHARGES FROM LAND AND OFFSHORE FACILITIES

At the same time the Ocean Dumping Act was pending, Congress was in the middle of a struggle to pass sweeping Federal Water Pollution Control Act (FWPCA, now known as CWA) amendments. This water pollution legislation, which passed into law over President Nixon's veto in October 1972, had as its original goal the elimination of polluting discharges into navigable waters by 1985. While much of this legislation was designed to deal with the

---

[3]   For more information about the partnership see Global Partnership Framework Document (October 2018), https://paper smart.unon.org/resolution/uploads/k1900241-framework_ document_for_the_gpml_-_advance.pdf.

nation's fresh and estuarine waters, it reached coastal waters in some cases. See, e.g., *California Public Interest Research Group v. Shell Oil Co.*, 840 F.Supp. 712 (N.D.Cal.1993)(involving oil refinery selenium discharges into San Francisco Bay) and *Northwest Env. Advocates v. U.S. EPA*, 2005 WL 756614 (N.D.Cal. 2005)(involving vessel ballast water discharges of invasive species). Two sections, however, deal specifically with ocean discharges: Section 403 (33 U.S.C. § 1343) regulates the offshore discharge of nondredged materials from onshore outfall pipes, and other point sources, except vessels. See, e.g., *United States v. Weitzenhoff*, 35 F.3d 1275 (9th Cir. 1993) (criminal prosecution for toxic sludge discharges into ocean waters off Honolulu). Section 404 (33 U.S.C. § 1344) regulates discharges of dredged materials into waters seaward to three nautical miles and authorizes the Corps of Engineers to issue permits for the discharge of dredged or fill materials at EPA-specified disposal sites in navigable waters.

CWA section 403 utilizes a precautionary approach where information is insufficient, calls for prevention of unreasonable degradation of the marine environment, and authorizes the use of effluent limitations established by the EPA. The section provides for a prohibition of discharges, if necessary, to achieve those requirements. Although section 403 of the CWA and section 102 of the ODA are similar, they are not identical. In essence, the ODA applies to dumping from vessels into ocean waters and does not apply to discharges from pipes and outfalls, which are subject to control under the CWA. All such discharges seaward of the inner boundary of U.S. territorial seas are subject to section 403 requirements.

Section 301 of the CWA makes unlawful the unpermitted discharge of any pollutant by any person except in compliance with the terms of that and other specifically enumerated sections. In short, section 301 prohibits the discharge of untreated sewage. Permit criteria developed pursuant to CWA section 403 supplement section 301 requirements and are applicable to permit proceedings authorized by section 402, as well as to municipal marine dischargers seeking a modification of the normally applicable secondary sewage treatment requirements as provided by section 301(h).

In a case that may become significant for States grappling with coastal pollution, certiorari has been granted by the U.S. Supreme Court regarding the question of whether pollutants that originate in a point source (injection wells) but are discharged to the ocean through groundwater require a CWA permit. The 9th Circuit decided in *County of Maui v. Hawai'i Wildlife Fund* that an NPDES permit was needed because the more than de minimis releases into the ocean were "fairly traceable" to the injection wells. 881 F.3d 754, 765 (9th Cir. 2018).

The administrative framework of the CWA differs fundamentally from that provided in the ODA. The ODA is a federal program explicitly preempting state regulatory activity. With certain exceptions, the CWA envisions state's developing pollution control programs that are reviewed and approved by EPA, thus giving states permit authority over point sources of pollution seaward to three nautical miles. See *Pacific Legal Foundation v. Costle*, 586 F.2d 650 (9th Cir. 1978). Beyond three nautical miles, EPA administers the discharge permit processes for outer continental shelf (OCS) oil and gas facilities (see, e.g., *BP Exploration & Oil, Inc. v. Environmental Protection Agency*, 66 F.3d 784 (6th Cir. 1995)), deepwater ports (see 33 U.S.C. § 1502(10)), ocean thermal energy conversion facilities (see 42 U.S.C. § 9117(f), and other offshore facilities (see 33 U.S.C. § 1316)). See also *Sierra Club, Lone Star Chapter v. Cedar Point Oil Co.*, 73 F.3d 546 (5th Cir. 1996) (EPA regulation of discharges from offshore oil and gas operations in state waters).

G. POLLUTION FROM OTHER LAND-BASED ACTIVITIES

Worldwide, it is estimated that about seventy to eighty percent of marine pollution comes from land-based sources (LBS) and activities rather than vessels. These activities include industrial and sewage point source discharges like those in the previous section and more dispersed runoff pollution into rivers, estuaries, and the ocean from agriculture, forestry, mining, and urban development. The international and United States legal responses to LBS pollution, especially the runoff type, are much less developed than for vessels. Articles 207(1) and 213 of the 1982 UNCLOS very generally obligate nations party to the convention to adopt laws to prevent, reduce, and control pollution of the marine environment from land-based point sources and runoff. Paragraphs 17.24 through 17.29 of Agenda 21 produced by the 1992 United Nations Conference on Environment and Development (U.N. Doc. A/CONF. 151/26 (1992)) contain recommendations for national action, as do the 1985 Montreal Guidelines for the Protection of the Marine Against Pollution from Land-Based Sources (UNEP/GC. 13/9/Add. 3, UNEP/ GC/DEC/13/1811, UNEP ELPG No. 7 (1985)) issued by the United Nations Environmental Program (UNEP). More detailed is the UNEP 1995 Global Programme of Action for the Protection of the Marine Environment from Land-Based Activities (UNEP (OCA)/LBA/IG.2/7).[4]

Nine multilateral regional conventions for specific ocean areas address LBS pollution, including the Cartagena Convention for the Caribbean Region to which the United States is a party. As of 2016, the United States and 11 other Cartagena Convention members are parties to the Protocol Concerning Pollution from Land-Based Sources and Activities (LBS Protocol) to the Cartagena Convention which entered into force in 2010. The LBS Protocol applies to the wider Caribbean region, including the Gulf of Mexico and Atlantic Ocean south of 30 degrees north latitude and out to 200 miles from shore.

The LBS Protocol comprises four annexes with the following provisions:

---

[4]   See J. Karau, D. VanderZwaag, & P. Wells, *The Global Programme of Action for the Protection of the Marine Environment from Land-Based Activities: A Cacophony of Sounds, Will the World Listen?* in Ocean Yearbook 13 (E. Borgese, A. Chircop, M. McConnell, & J. Morgan, eds., 1997).

- **Annex I** lists land-based sources and activities and their associated contaminants of greatest concern;

- **Annex II** establishes procedure to develop regional standards and practices for the prevention, reduction and control of the Annex I sources and contaminants;

- **Annex III** sets specific regional limitations for domestic sewage; and

- **Annex IV** requires each party to take measures, including plans, programs and other actions, to prevent, reduce and control agricultural non-point sources.

LBS Protocol parties must address Annex III and IV by creating legally-binding effluent limitations for domestic sewage and by developing plans for the reduction and control of agricultural non-point sources. See EPA, *Cartagena Convention and Land-Based Sources Protocol*; and the Caribbean Environmental Program, available at http://cep.unep.org.

In the United States, regulation of both the point source and the runoff components of LBS pollution occurs primarily under the CWA. CWA runoff regulatory programs include those for concentrated animal feeding operations (see *Waterkeeper Alliance, Inc. v. U.S. EPA*, 399 F.3d 486 (2d Cir. 2005)), combined sewer overflows (see *Northwest Environmental Advocates v. City of Portland*, 56 F.3d 979 (9th Cir. 1995)), and stormwater (see *Molokai Chamber of Commerce v. Kukui (Molokai) Inc.*, 891

F.Supp. 1389 (D.Hawaii 1995); see also *Decker v. Northwest Envtl. Def. Ctr.*, 133 S.Ct. 1326 (2013) (holding that NPDES permits are not required for stormwater runoff from logging roads)). Other runoff pollution sources are addressed as nonpoint sources (NPS) through the state-implemented land use planning and pollution prevention process of CWA section 319 (33 U.S.C. § 1329) and the coastal NPS control provisions of the federal Coastal Zone Management Act (CZMA) (16 U.S.C. § 1455b). The latter requires state design and implementation of enforceable NPS pollution management measures against a broad range of NPS sources and includes federal consistency requirements paralleling those of CZMA section 307 (16 U.S.C. § 1456).

When the cumulative impact of point and nonpoint source pollution in a particular water body results in a violation of its state-established CWA ambient water quality standards, the CWA's complex total maximum daily load (TMDL) process (see 33 U.S.C. § 1313(d)) can be invoked to force reductions in both types of pollution. See *Dioxin/Organoehlorine Center v. Clarke*, 57 F.3d 1517 (9th Cir.1995) (EPA-imposed TMDL for dioxin in Columbia River upheld); *Pronsolino v. Nastri*, 291 F.3d 1123 (9th Cir. 2002) (TMDL requirements apply to water bodies impaired solely by NPS pollution); *American Farm Bureau Federation v. U.S. E.P.A.*, 792 F.3d 281(3rd Cir. 2015) (upholding Chesapeake Bay TMDLs).

H. AIR POLLUTION AND THE SEAS

1. POLLUTION FROM OCEAN VESSELS

Rather than addressing air pollution impacts on the ocean, MARPOL 73/78, Annex VI, primarily addresses the impact of air pollution from ships on the health and environment of affected land areas and populations. Annex VI was first adopted in 1997 and limits sulphur oxides (SO_x) and nitrous oxides (NO_x)—the main air pollutants contained in ships exhaust gas—and prohibits deliberate emissions of ozone-depleting substances. MARPOL Annex VI was revised in 2008 to continue reductions in emissions of SO_x, NO_x and particulate matter (PM) and to provide for designation of emission control areas (ECAs) requiring additional reductions of SO_x pollutants.

The IMO approved a North American Emission Control Area (ECA) area including the U.S. continental EEZ and Hawaii's (and Canada's) EEZ that went into effect in 2012 and a United States Caribbean Sea ECA that went into effect in 2014. Within the ECAs, the United States can enforce strict SO_x emission limits from vessel fuel, and beginning in 2016, ships must also achieve an 80% percent reduction in NO_x.[5]

---

[5]   See *Pac. Merch. Shipping Ass'n v. Goldstene*, 639 F.3d 1154 (9th Cir. Cal. 2011) (upholding California regulations that require ships engaged in international and interstate commerce to use specific low-sulfur fuels whenever they are going to or from California ports or travelling within twenty-four miles of the California coastline. The Supreme Court denied certiorari based on a brief requested from the Solicitor General recommending denial in spite of the apparent conflict with the U.S. "paramount

NORTH AMERICAN EMISSION CONTROL AREA

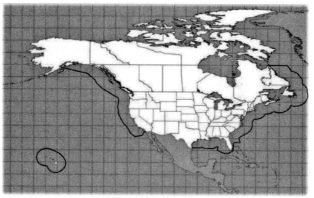

Source: US Environmental Protection Agency

2.   OCEAN ACIDIFICATION

The ocean is a "sink" for carbon dioxide. In fact, some scientists earlier thought that such ocean absorption of CO_2 would counter the greenhouse effect and climate change. The oceans absorb about one third of the CO_2 produced, but now the oceans have become of concern because the basic chemistry of the oceans is being changed by the process of ocean acidification. NOAA states that in the 200 years since the industrial revolution, ocean surface waters have increased 30% in acidity. Ocean acidification is

---

authority to regulate maritime commerce," because the California regulations are "largely consistent" with federal requirements and would "be overtaken" by federal requirements to implement the ECA.) See also Alaska v. Kerry, 972 F. Supp. 2d 1111 (D. Alaska 2013)(rejecting challenge to extension of the Emission Control Zone off Alaska because acceptance of amendment to MARPOL was not justiciable under political question doctrine).

referred to as the "other CO_2 problem," the "sleeper issue" of climate change and climate change's "evil twin." See *National Research Council, Ocean Acidification: A National Strategy to Meet the Challenges of a Changing Ocean* (2010). This report states that "[s]cientific research on the biological effects of acidification is still in its infancy and there is much uncertainty regarding its ultimate effects on marine ecosystems," but that whether decision makers focus on reducing greenhouse gases or mitigating ecological effects, the time take action is now. If legal action is pursued to "jog" action by the government, one might think the Clean Air Act would be the tool of choice, however, the Center for Biological Diversity sued under the CWA to challenge EPA approval of Washington's and Oregon's failure to identify waters experiencing ocean acidification as "impaired" and requiring the establishment of TMDLs to meet water quality standards. EPA was, however, granted summary judgment based on the court finding its decision was not arbitrary and capricious. See Ctr. For Biological Diversity v. U.S. E.P.A., 90 F. Supp. 3d 1177, 1183 (W.D. Wash. 2015). See also, Miyoko Sakashita (senior attorney for CBD), *Using the Clean Water Act to Tackle Ocean Acidification: When Carbon Dioxide Pollutes the Oceans*, 6 Wash. J. Envtl. L. & Pol'y 599 (2016) (describing the CWA as "one of the most powerful tools that we have to combat ocean acidification" and proposing a strategy).

CHAPTER VIII

PROTECTION OF SPECIAL MARINE AREAS AND MARINE CULTURAL HERITAGE

A. MANAGEMENT AND PROTECTION OF SPECIAL MARINE AREAS

In the terrestrial context, the United States has for more than a century set aside or specially managed lands for to preserve their beauty, grandeur and inspirational attributes, their environmental sensitivity and special habitats, and their cultural and historic value. Only relatively recently, however, have the same kind of considerations led to extending protection and management to areas of the seas that provide the same kind of contributions to our society.

1. NATIONAL MARINE SANCTUARIES

In 1972, Congress created the National Marine Sanctuaries Program as part of the Marine Protection, Research and Sanctuaries Act. 16 U.S.C.A. §§ 1431–1445a. The purpose of the program is to identify marine areas of special national or international significance due to their resource or human-use values and to provide authority for comprehensive conservation and management of such areas where existing regulatory authority is inadequate to assure coordinated conservation and management. Among the considerations in determining the national or international significance of a site are:

(A)   the area's natural resource and ecological qualities, including its contribution to biological productivity, maintenance of ecosystem structure, maintenance of ecologically or commercially important or threatened species or species assemblages, maintenance of critical habitat of endangered species, and the biogeographic representation of the site; [and]

(B) the area's historical, cultural, archaeological, or paleontological significance;

. . .

Id. § 1433(b)(1)(A)–(B). The Act particularly identifies the importance of maintaining and restoring "living resources by providing places for species that depend upon these marine areas to survive and propagate." Id. § 1431(b)(9). Designation of a marine area as a sanctuary, in itself, does not prohibit all development or use, but does require special use permits from the Department of Commerce (DOC) to authorize specific activities that are compatible with the purposes of the sanctuary. Id. § 1441. See *Craft v. National Park Service*, 34 F.3d 918 (9th Cir. 1994); *United States v. Fisher*, 22 F.3d 262 (11th Cir. 1994); *United States v. Fisher*, 977 F.Supp. 1193 (S.D.Fla. 1997) (injunctions and civil penalties imposed on divers and salvors for altering sanctuary seabeds without permits).

The national marine sanctuaries program got off to a slow start. The Secretary of Commerce did not designate the first sanctuary, the U.S.S. Monitor National Marine Sanctuary (NMS), until 1975. The designated sanctuaries encompassed relatively small areas of ocean space and were managed for narrowly defined purposes. Eight sanctuaries were designated during this period: the *U.S.S. Monitor,* Key Largo and Looe Key off Florida, Gray's Reef off Georgia, the Channel Islands, the Gulf of Farallones, and Cordell Banks in California, and Fagatele Bay in America Samoa. Criticism of both the designation process and the effectiveness of the NMS program led to a reassessment of the marine sanctuaries program.

In 1988 and 1992 the program was amended substantially. Federal agencies were required to consult with the Secretary of Commerce prior to taking actions within or outside an NMS that was likely to destroy or injure a sanctuary resource. Similar to the ESA consultation process, the Secretary may provide alternatives to the proposed agency action if the action is likely to affect sanctuary resources. Subsequent amendments provide that if an agency takes an action other than a recommended alternative that injures or destroys sanctuary resources, the agency must prevent or mitigate further damage, as well as restore or replace the sanctuary resources. 16 U.S.C.A. § 1434(d).

During this period, important provisions for enforcement and liability were added that give sanctuary designation and sanctuary management plans greater authority. The amendments provide that it is unlawful to:

(1) destroy, cause the loss of, or injure any sanctuary resource managed under law or regulations for that sanctuary;

(2) possess, sell, offer for sale, purchase, import, export, deliver, carry, transport, or ship by any means any sanctuary resource taken in violation of this section. . . .

Id. § 1436. A "Sanctuary resource" is "any living or nonliving resource . . . that contributes to the . . . value of the sanctuary." Id. § 1432(8). The amendments create a rebuttable presumption that all sanctuary resources on board a vessel were taken in violation of the act or regulations. Id. § 1437(d)(4). Enforcement authorities are granted broad powers to board, search, and seize vessels, and impose civil penalties of up to $100,000 per violation per day. Id. § 1437(b)–(c). In addition, persons damaging or injuring any sanctuary resources are strictly liable for response costs and damages. Id. § 1443. See *United States v. M/V Jacquelyn L.*, 100 F.3d 1520 (11th Cir. 1996); *United States v. Fisher*, 977 F.Supp. 1193 (S.D.Fla. 1997); *United States v. M/V Miss Beholden*, 856 F.Supp. 668 (S.D.Fla.1994); *United States v. Great Lakes Dredge & Dock Co.*, 259 F.3d 1300 (11th Cir. 2001).

The designation process for marine sanctuaries has been streamlined, but Congress has also accelerated the process by designating or ordering the designation of certain sanctuaries. During this second phase of sanctuary designation, the Florida Keys (which incorporated Key Largo and Looe Key NMSs), Monterey Bay, Stellwagen Bank, the Hawaiian Islands Humpback Whale, the Flower Garden Banks, the Olympic Coast, and Thunder Bay national marine sanctuaries have been created.

The National Marine Sanctuary System now comprises more than 170,000 square miles of marine and Great Lakes waters and includes thirteen sanctuaries as well as the Papahānaumokuākea (originally the Northwestern Hawaiian Islands) Marine National Monument, which is discussed in part 2 of this section, and the Pacific Remote Islands Marine National Monument.

The current generation of sanctuaries differs from those designated earlier in two ways: (1) their size, and (2) their management approach. The newest marine sanctuaries encompass extensive ocean areas of both federal and state jurisdiction. Designation of large ocean areas allows management of more of the activities that affect sanctuary resources and provides the opportunity to develop an ecosystem-based approach to resource management. Management plans can be developed that deal with direct and indirect, as well as primary and secondary, effects on sanctuary resources. Federal and state cooperative programs are encouraged, and advisory councils have become an integral part of both the plan development process and subsequent plan implementation. Because designation of such large areas affects numerous user groups, conflict management is an important part of plan development and implementation. See, e.g., *Personal Watercraft Industry Association v. Department of Commerce*, 48 F.3d 540, 310 U.S.App.D.C. 364 (D.C.Cir. 1995). This new kind of national marine sanctuary depends on a cooperative inter-governmental approach to management of large marine areas and has provided a model for development of other marine protected areas.

2. MARINE NATIONAL MONUMENTS

The Antiquities Act of 1906, 16 U.S.C.A. § 431, gives the president discretion to set aside "historic landmarks, historic and prehistoric structures, and other objects of historic or scientific interest that are situated upon the lands owned or controlled by the Government of the United States to be National Monuments. . . ." In cases involving conflicts with state government, the Supreme Court has recognized that the president has the right to reserve waters located over federal submerged lands. See *United States v. California*, 436 U.S. 32, 36 n. 9 (1978) (Channel Islands National Monument); and *Alaska v. United States*, 545 U.S. 75, 103 (2005) (Glacier Bay National Monument).

The language of the statute, which provides that the monuments encompass the "smallest area compatible with proper care and management of the objects to be protected," suggests that Congress was conferring this power on the president to be used to protect small, discrete areas. The language has not, however, deterred presidents since Theodore Roosevelt from declaring millions of acres of public lands to be national monuments.

On June 15, 2006, President George Bush proclaimed the largest national monument to date, the Northwestern Hawaiian Islands (NWHI) National Monument, comprising nearly 140,000 square miles of federal waters surrounding 10 islands and atolls in the Pacific Ocean and stretching more than 1,200 miles from Nihoa to Kure Atoll. Presidential Proclamation 8031 (71 F.R. 36443, June 26, 2006). At the time of its designation, the monument was the world's largest protected marine area. The Proclamation was amended in 2007 by Proclamation 8112 to rename the monument as Papahānaumokuākea National Monument (PNM), (72 F.R. 10031, February 28, 2007). By presidential proclamation of August 26, 2016, President Obama roughly quadrupled the size of PNM to an area of 582,578 square miles.

The PNM is a unique environment with over 7,000 species, one quarter of which are found only in the Hawaiian Archipelago. Among the most endangered of the resident species is the Hawaiian monk seal, and the islands are the breeding area for 90 percent of the threatened Hawaiian Island green sea turtles. Over 14 million birds inhabit these remote islands, and the waters teem with fish species and sensitive coral ecosystems. The islands are also of great cultural significance for native Hawaiians.

In 2005, the state of Hawaii had declared the state waters surrounding the NWHI as a marine reserve, prohibiting all extractive uses, including commercial and recreational fishing. President William Clinton, through two Executive Orders, had protected the federal waters in the area as a Coral Reef Ecosystem Reserve, and the area was under consideration for designation as a national marine sanctuary. Executive Order 13178 (December 4, 2000) and Executive Order 13196 (January 18, 2001). The proclamation of the national monument, however, confers a significantly higher level of protection on the PNM than the sanctuary status would have provided.

The protections provided to the monument are unprecedented. Vessels must have permission to access the monument and are required to use vessel-monitoring systems. Even vessels merely passing through monument waters are required to give notice at least 72 hours before transiting the waters. Among the prohibited activities are: exploring for, developing, or producing oil, gas, or minerals; using or attempting to use poisons, electrical charges, or explosives in the collection or harvest of a monument resource; introducing or otherwise releasing an introduced species from within or into the monument; and anchoring on any living or dead coral. Commercial lobster fishing was terminated immediately by the proclamation, and commercial fishing for bottomfish and associated pelagic species was phased out within five years. Sustenance fishing outside of special preservation areas may, however, be permitted. Other uses of the monument are to be strictly regulated to assure the activities are "compatible with the purposes for which the monument is designated and with protection of monument resources." See 71 F.R. 36443, June 26, 2006. The monument was the first to be under the jurisdiction of the Department of Commerce and NOAA, and is currently cooperatively managed by the Secretary of Commerce (NOAA) the Secretary of the Interior (U.S. Fish and Wildlife Service) and the State of Hawaii.

In January 2009, President Bush established three more marine national monuments in the Pacific totaling 195,274 square miles at the Marianas Trench, remote coral atolls designated as the Marianas Trench, the Pacific Remote Islands and Rose Atoll, and Rose Atoll in American Samoa.

President Obama, on September 25, 2014, further expanded the Pacific Remote Islands Marine National Monument in the central Pacific from around 87,000 square miles to approximately an additional 408,000 square miles. Incorporating the 200-mile U.S. exclusive economic zone (EEZ) adjacent to seven uninhabited islands and atolls, the monument is the largest marine protected area on earth. In 2016, President Obama proclaimed the Northeast Canyons and Seamounts Marine National Monument to protect 4,913 square miles of underwater canyon ecosystems off the New England coast.

Commercial users have unsuccessfully challenged the designation of Marine Monuments by disputing the exercise of presidential powers under the Antiquities Act. *Mass. Lobstermen's Ass'n v. Ross*, 349 F. Supp. 3d 48 (D.D.C 2018) (Finding that executive powers to declare national monuments extend to areas that are solely submerged lands citing Illinois Cent R.R. v. Chicago, 176 U.S. 646, 660 (1900)).

3.   OTHER MARINE PROTECTED AREAS

The National Marine Sanctuaries Act and the Antiquities Act both protect ocean areas but using different approaches. The D.C. Circuit in *Mass. Lobstermen* highlighted some of these differences when it deliberated on the status of the Northeast Canyons and Seamounts Marine National Monument noting that "[t]he Antiquities Act is entirely focused on preservation. The Sanctuaries Act, on the other hand, addresses a broader set of values including 'recreation [ ]' and the 'public and private uses of the [ocean] resources.'" Id. at 59.

In addition to these major statutes, there are numerous other ways for federal and state governments to protect and conserve marine areas and resources. For example, marine areas are being protected as national parks, national monuments, national wildlife refuges, fishery management zones, national estuarine research reserves and state reserves. In recent years, marine protected areas (MPAs), ranging from multiple-use areas to no-take reserves, have proliferated as a conservation and management tool. In California marine protected areas can be designated by law, administrative actions, or voter initiatives. Marine Life Protection Act, Cal. Fish & G. Code § 2852(c).

In 2000, President Clinton issued Executive Order 13158 on Marine Protected Areas (MPAs) directing federal agencies to work with state, local, and nongovernmental partners to create a comprehensive, nationwide network of marine protected areas. The Executive Order recognizes the need to integrate efforts to protect marine areas through an ecosystem-based approach to management and maximize opportunities for coordination of research and public education. The Executive Order defines "marine protected area" as "any area of the marine environment that has been reserved by federal, state, territorial, tribal, or local laws or regulations to provide lasting protection for part or all of the natural and cultural resources therein." As an initial step, the Marine Protected Areas Inventory (formerly the Marine Managed Areas Inventory), a comprehensive geospatial database designed to catalog and classify over 1,700 marine protected areas within US waters, was developed to contribute to the development of a national system of Marine Protected Areas. The Inventory revealed that 41% of all U.S. waters are in some form of MPA.

NOAA and the Department of Interior created the National Marine Protected Areas Center and a 30-member MPA Federal Advisory Committee to develop a framework for a national MPA system and to work with agencies and stakeholders to develop regional systems of MPAs that can achieve ecosystem-wide goals and objectives. In 2008, NOAA and the Department of Interior published Framework for the National System of Marine Protected Areas of the United States of America (2008), identifying goals and conservation objections and providing guidance for the development of a national system of MPAs. The *Framework* established eligibility criteria and created a nomination process for existing MPAs to be included in the national system. In addition, to creating a process for improving regional and ecosystem-based coordination of MPAs, the *Framework* developed science-based processes for identifying natural and cultural resource conservation gaps in the national system.

As of 2019, about 8% of all U.S. waters are in an MPA with a primary focus on conserving natural or cultural resources (not including fishery MPAs). Of these MPAs, only 3% of U.S. waters are "no take" areas. Approximately 86% of U.S. MPAs are multiple use.

B.   PRESERVATION OF UNDERWATER CULTURAL HERITAGE AND ADMIRALTY LAW CONFLICT

1.   BACKGROUND

Both the federal government and the coastal states view ancient shipwrecks off the coasts of the United States as having significance beyond the monetary value of the recoverable cargo. The historic importance of such shipwrecks is illustrated by the designation of the site of the wreck of the U.S.S. Monitor as the nation's first national marine sanctuary. Marine archaeologists portray private salvage of historic wrecks by treasure hunters as the equivalent of "looting" an archaeological, historic, or culturally significant site. Private salvors do not perceive themselves as looters and point out that without their investment of resources and capital, historic wrecks would never be located.

New technologies and improved research techniques have led to the discovery of an increasing number of vessels in recent years, and conflicts concerning jurisdiction and ownership of these vessels have led to complex court cases. During the last several decades, numerous shipwreck cases have addressed the appropriateness of the application of the maritime law of salvage or finds as well as issues of jurisdiction, preemption, ownership, and eleventh amendment immunity of states from suit. The courts have not been entirely consistent in their conclusions, and although a few principles have emerged, a myriad of issues are still unresolved.

2. ADMIRALTY LAW AND HISTORIC SHIPWRECKS

a. Federal Claims to Shipwrecks

To assert ownership or control of shipwrecks, the United States must make an express claim. After adjudication of the boundary between state and federal submerged lands in *United States v. Florida*, 420 U.S. 531, 95 S.Ct. 1162, 43 L.Ed.2d 375 (1975) established that the wreck of the treasure ship Atocha was located on the federal continental shelf rather than on state lands, the United States asserted title to the wreck and the recovered artifacts. The Fifth Circuit Court of Appeals held that it may be within the power of the federal government to exercise its "sovereign prerogative" to claim abandoned property found at sea, but the United States had never enacted legislation to assert such a claim. See *Treasure Salvors, Inc. v. Unidentified Wrecked and Abandoned Sailing Vessel*, 569 F.2d 330 (5th Cir. 1978). Specifically, the court found that the United States cannot claim ownership of wrecks on

the continental shelf based on the Abandoned
Property Act, 40 U.S.C.A. § 310, or on the Antiquities
Act, 16 U.S.C.A. §§ 431–433, because the wreck was
located beyond the jurisdiction of the Acts. The
United States also could not base a claim on the
Truman Proclamation or the Outer Continental Shelf
Lands Act, because they were not intended to extend
"control over non-resource-related material in the
shelf area," such as shipwrecks. The federal
government does, however, under the Antiquities
Act, 16 U.S.C.A. §§ 431–433, protect shipwreck sites
on lands owned or controlled by the federal
government, including national parks and national
marine sanctuaries. See also *Klein v. Unidentified
Wrecked and Abandoned Sailing Vessel*, 758 F.2d
1511 (11th Cir. 1985) (holding that the United States
was in constructive possession of a shipwreck
embedded in the soil in Biscayne Bay National Park).

b. Jurisdictional Conflict in State Waters

Historically, the most fundamental conflict in
cases of shipwrecks found within state boundaries
concerns whether federal admiralty law preempts
state salvage or archaeological recovery laws.
Although a majority of states had long ago enacted
legislation asserting ownership or the authority to
regulate and manage historic shipwrecks, courts
have failed to settle the question of whether such
statutes are enforceable. See *Zych v. Unidentified,
Wrecked and Abandoned Vessel, Believed to be the
Seabird*, 941 F.2d 525 (7th Cir. 1991). A number of
federal courts have held that cases involving
shipwrecks are within the federal courts' exclusive

admiralty jurisdiction. See *Martha's Vineyard Scuba Headquarters, Inc. v. Unidentified, Wrecked and Abandoned Steam Vessel*, 833 F.2d 1059 (1st Cir. 1987); *Platoro Ltd. v. Unidentified Remains of a Vessel*, 614 F.2d 1051 (5th Cir. 1980); *Treasure Salvors, Inc. v. Unidentified Wrecked and Abandoned Sailing Vessel*, 569 F.2d 330 (5th Cir. 1978). Other courts have specifically found that state regulation of such shipwrecks is inconsistent with federal maritime principles and is preempted by federal admiralty law. See, e.g., *Cobb Coin Co. v. Unidentified, Wrecked and Abandoned Sailing Vessel* (*Cobb Coin I*), 525 F.Supp. 186 (S.D.Fla. 1981). However, some federal courts, even within the same circuit as courts asserting exclusive admiralty jurisdiction, have upheld the exercise of state authority over wrecks. See *Jupiter Wreck, Inc. v. Unidentified, Wrecked and Abandoned Sailing Vessel*, 691 F.Supp. 1377 (S.D.Fla. 1988); *Subaqueous Exploration & Archaeology, Ltd. v. Unidentified, Wrecked and Abandoned Vessel*, 577 F.Supp. 597 (D.Md. 1983).

c. Fundamentals of Salvage Law

Under the law of salvage, the original owner retains title to goods saved from peril by a salvor. However, the salvor who meets certain requirements is entitled to a reward for rescuing the goods from marine peril. The admiralty court sits as a court of equity in determining the salvage award. The U.S. Supreme Court has identified six main factors to consider in determining a salvage award:

(1.) The labor expended by the salvors in rendering the salvage service. (2.) The promptitude, skill, and energy displayed in rendering the service and saving the property. (3.) The value of the property employed by the salvors in rendering the service, and the danger to which such property was exposed. (4.) The risk incurred by the salvors in securing the property from the impending peril. (5.) The value of the property saved. (6.) The degree of danger from which the property was rescued.

The Blackwall, 77 U.S. 1, 19 L.Ed. 870 (1869). The salvage award is intended not only to compensate the salvor, but also to reward "meritorious services" and serve as an inducement to others. Salvors do not get ownership of the ship or cargo unless the ship is found to be abandoned and the law of marine finds, rather than salvage, applies. When salvaged property is unique or has special intrinsic value, however, an award *in specie* is generally found to be more appropriate than a monetary salvage award.

d. Salvage Law v. the Law of Finds

Even when the application of federal maritime and admiralty law is clear, questions persist concerning whether the law of salvage or the law of finds applies to such shipwrecks. Under the law of finds, a finder who takes possession and exercises control over lost or abandoned property acquires title. In the case of ancient shipwrecks, some courts have rejected the legal fiction of salvage law that the "owner intends to return" and the application of salvage law. See, e.g.,

Treasure Salvors, Inc. v. Unidentified Wrecked and Abandoned Sailing Vessel, 569 F.2d 330 (5th Cir. 1978) (holding that "[d]isposition of a wrecked vessel whose very location has been lost for centuries as though its owner were still in existence stretches a fiction to absurd lengths"). Two exceptions to the law of finds are that the property is not considered legally lost if it is embedded in the soil or if the owner of the land has constructive possession of the property. See, e.g., *Klein*, supra (holding that a "finder" was entitled to no salvage award for a vessel embedded in the soil within a national park); and *Chance v. Certain Artifacts Found & Salvaged from The Nashville*, 606 F.Supp. 801 (S.D.Ga. 1984)(holding the state of Georgia to be the owner of a Confederate raider embedded in the state-owned submerged lands of the Ogeechee River).

In *Columbus-America Discovery Group v. Atlantic Mut. Ins. Co.*, 974 F.2d 450 (4th Cir. 1992), the Fourth Circuit Court of Appeals explained that the law of salvage is preferred over the law of finds, because it diminishes the incentive for secretive behavior and encouraged open, cooperative conduct to protect property. See id. at 460–62 & n. 2 (4th Cir. 1992) (discussing the few cases in which courts have applied the law of finds); see also *R.M.S. Titanic, Inc. v. The Wrecked & Abandoned Vessel*, 435 F.3d 521, 532 (4th Cir. 2006) (in stark contrast to the law of salvage, an ancient part of the jus gentium, the law of finds is a "disfavored common-law doctrine incorporated into admiralty but only rarely applied."). In the case of historic shipwrecks, applying salvage law preserves the court's equitable jurisdiction to impose standards on salvors that can insure that ancient shipwreck sites are excavated using proper methods and that artifacts are recovered in a manner that maintains their historic significance.

In *Columbus-America*, the law of salvage, rather than the law of finds, applied to the recovery of up to a billion dollars in gold from the 1857 wreck of the S.S. Central America on the high seas off the South Carolina coast. The Columbus-America Discovery Group, which located the vessel in 1988 and had been recovering the gold sought to be declared owner of the gold that the ship was transporting from California to New York. However, the insurance underwriters who had paid the claims for the disaster and who had been subrogated to the rights of the original owners of the gold also asserted ownership. The district court found Columbus-America to be the "finder" and owner of the gold. The appellate court reversed, summarizing the applicable law of as follows:

> [W]hen sunken ships or their cargo are rescued . . . courts favor applying the law of salvage over the law of finds. Finds law should be applied . . . where the previous owners are found to have abandoned their property. Such abandonment must be proved by clear and convincing evidence. . . . Should the property encompass an ancient and long lost [sic] shipwreck, a court may infer an abandonment. Such an inference would be improper, though, should a previous owner appear and assert his ownership interest; in such a case the normal

presumptions would apply and an abandonment would have to be proved by strong and convincing evidence.

Columbus America, supra at 465. The failure of the insurers to continue recovery efforts did not constitute abandonment of "long lost property that was involuntarily taken from [their] control," and the law of salvage was found applicable. Id. at 468.

3.   SALVAGE AND HISTORIC PRESERVATION

Maritime common law principles do not specifically address the issue of preservation of historical and archaeological artifacts during salvage operations, but admiralty courts have begun to fashion rules. For example, the court in *Columbus-America Discovery Group*, supra, stated that the degree to which salvors worked to protect the historical and archaeological value of the wreck and items salved is relevant to the salvage award. In *MDM Salvage, Inc. v. Unidentified, Wrecked and Abandoned Sailing Vessel*, 631 F.Supp. 308 (S.D.Fla. 1986), the federal district court considered the work that the salvors had done to protect the historical and archaeological integrity of the wreck and the salvaged items inadequate to award the salvor exclusive salvage rights. When the exclusive salvage rights to the Titanic were challenged, the court held that the preservation of the archaeological integrity of the wreck site as well as the preservation of the retrieved artifacts was evidence that the operation had been undertaken with due diligence. *R.M.S.*

Titanic Inc. v. Joslyn, 924 F.Supp. 714 (E.D.Va. 1996).

In *Chance v. Certain Artifacts Found & Salvaged from The Nashville*, 606 F.Supp. 801 (S.D.Ga. 1984), the federal district court refused any salvage award because the handling of the property by the salvors was increasing the likelihood of deterioration of the antiquities rather than "rescuing" them from marine peril. The federal court in *Cobb Coin Co. v. Unidentified, Wrecked and Abandoned Sailing Vessel* (*Cobb Coin II*), 549 F.Supp. 540 (S.D.Fla. 1982) held "that in order to state a claim for a salvage award on an ancient vessel of historical and archaeological significance, it is an essential element that the salvor document to the Admiralty Court's satisfaction that it has preserved the archaeological provenance of a shipwreck." In other words, courts have now found that evidence of preservation is not just a standard for determining the amount of or enhancing the salvage award, but a threshold requirement for determining the right to exclusive salvage rights or entitlement to any salvage award.

4. SALVAGE AND ENVIRONMENTAL PROTECTION

Exploration for shipwrecks and salvage operations can be destructive of more than just the historic value of the site and the artifacts that are discovered. Many shipwrecks have occurred on coral reefs and in productive, shallow water areas. A common exploration technique involves anchoring the boat and using the boat's prop-wash deflectors to direct the prop-wash into the ocean floor. The prop-wash creates craters in the seabed soil that expedite exploratory activities, but the technique also creates substantial turbidity in the water and destroys the habitat. Both state governments and the Army Corps of Engineers contend that this activity constitutes dredging and discharges that require permits. See, e.g., *Lathrop v. Unidentified, Wrecked and Abandoned Vessel*, 817 F.Supp. 953 (M.D.Fla. 1993) (holding that admiralty jurisdiction may be supplemented by necessary restrictions on salvage operations to ensure safety and to protect navigation and the environment). In the Florida Keys National Marine Sanctuary, exploration and salvage operations have been strictly limited to protect the Sanctuary's primary resource, the coral reefs. *United States v. Fisher*, 22 F.3d 262 (11th Cir. 1994); *United States v. Fisher*, 977 F.Supp. 1193 (S.D.Fla. 1997).

5. THE ABANDONED SHIPWRECK ACT (ASA)

Congress attempted to alleviate some of the confusion concerning the ownership and authority to regulate certain shipwrecks through passage of the Abandoned Shipwreck Act (ASA) of 1987, 43 U.S.C.A. §§ 2101–2106. To protect shipwrecks of historic significance, the Act asserts the title of the federal government and then transfers to the state:

. . . any abandoned shipwreck that is:

(1) embedded in submerged lands of a State;

(2) embedded in coralline formations protected by a State on submerged lands of a State; or

(3) on submerged lands of a State and is included in or determined eligible for inclusion in the National Register.

Id. § 2105(a). "Abandoned" is not defined in the legislation.

Congress found that abandoned shipwrecks of historical significance are the type of resources that states should manage, because they are "irreplaceable State resources for tourism, biological sanctuaries, and historical research," and they offer unique recreational and educational opportunities. Id. § 2103(a)(1). The ASA attempts to address the multi-use aspects of the resources by directing states to develop "appropriate and consistent" policies to:

(A) protect natural resources and habitat areas;

(B) guarantee recreational exploration of shipwreck sites; and

(C) allow for appropriate public and private sector recovery of shipwrecks consistent with the protection of historical values and environmental integrity of the shipwrecks and the sites.

Id. § 2103(a)(2). The ASA encourages states to create underwater parks to provide additional protection and provides funds under the National Historic Preservation Act for the "study, interpretation, protection, and preservation of historic shipwrecks and properties." Id. § 2103(b). Federal guidelines have been published "to assist" states in developing legislation and management programs for shipwreck sites covered by the legislation. See id. § 2104. The federal government is not given authority to review state programs, however, and the transfer of ownership of shipwrecks is not dependent on federal approval of state management schemes.

Finally, because Congress found both the law of salvage and the law of finds unsuitable for preservation of historic shipwrecks, the ASA specifically provides that neither shall apply to abandoned shipwrecks that have been transferred into state ownership. Id. § 2106(a).

In applying the ASA to newly discovered shipwrecks, a number of questions arise: (1) Is the wreck abandoned?; (2) Is the wreck embedded?; (3) Does Congress' attempt to carve out a limited exception to admiralty jurisdiction violate constitutional principles?; (4) Does the Eleventh Amendment preclude federal courts from adjudicating claims to ships that states may claim under the ASA?; and (5) Does the ASA preempt state statutes that make claims to wrecks beyond the rights bestowed by the ASA?

a. Meaning of "Abandoned" in the ASA

In *California and State Lands Comm. v. Deep Sea Research, Inc.* (*The Brother Jonathan*), 523 U.S. 491, 118 S.Ct. 1464, 140 L.Ed.2d 626 (1998), the U.S. Supreme Court addressed the ASA for the first time.

The Court clarified that the "meaning of 'abandoned' under the ASA conforms with its meaning under admiralty law." Thus, despite the statutory language rejecting the application of admiralty law to ships transferred to the states by the ASA, a large body of admiralty law concerning abandonment still remains relevant to determining, as a threshold issue, whether a vessel falls within the ASA. It was originally estimated that the ASA would only apply to about five percent of the more that 50,000 shipwrecks in United States waters, but narrowly defining abandonment under admiralty principles limits the Act even further. (See also, supra, concerning abandonment and the law of finds).

Fairport Int'l Exploration v. The Shipwrecked Vessel known as The Captain Lawrence, 177 F.3d 491 (6th Cir. 1999) comprehensively reviews the federal maritime law applicable to the term "abandonment." Abandonment can be express or by inference. Neither lapse of time alone nor the owner's failure to return to a shipwreck site necessarily establishes abandonment, but these aspects do contribute to circumstantial evidence from which abandonment may be inferred. The case specifically addressed the issue of the burden of proof borne by the party asserting abandonment under the ASA and found: "The uniform rule in admiralty is that a finding of abandonment requires proof by clear and convincing evidence."

b. Embeddedness

In *Zych v. Unidentified, Wrecked and Abandoned Vessel, Believed to be the Seabird*, 941 F.2d 525 (7th Cir. 1991), the Seventh Circuit Court of Appeals identified the issues of embeddedness and constitutionality as controlling in the case of an 1868 shipwreck discovered in Lake Michigan within Illinois state waters. The court remanded the case for a determination of whether the ship was "embedded" within the definition of the ASA. "Embedded" is defined as "firmly affixed in the submerged lands or in coralline formations such that the use of tools of excavation is required in order to move the bottom sediments to gain access to the shipwreck, its cargo, and any part thereof[.]" 43 U.S.C.A. § 2102(a). The term is to be interpreted consistently with the common law exception from the law of finds. The *Zych* court of appeals further directed that, if on remand the ship were found to be "embedded" and, therefore, within the scope of the ASA, the lower court should address the constitutionality of the ASA. The court of appeals identified two grounds for challenging statutes that alter admiralty jurisdiction: (1) exclusion of "a thing falling clearly within [admiralty jurisdiction];" or (2) alteration of jurisdiction so that admiralty jurisdiction is non-uniform. The uniformity challenge is directly dependent on the determination of the first challenge.

On remand to the district court, the court found Zych's admission of embeddedness sufficient to bring the shipwreck within the scope of the ASA, making the constitutionality of the ASA the controlling issue. *Zych v. Unidentified, Wrecked and Abandoned Vessel*, 811 F.Supp. 1300 (N.D.Ill. 1992). The court found that the ASA did not alter admiralty jurisdiction by precluding application of the law of salvage and finds to abandoned shipwrecks, because these cases were not clearly within admiralty jurisdiction. The court stated that:

> [b]ecause a salvor essentially had no claim in federal court for a salvage award against the state prior to enactment of the ASA, either because salvage law does not apply to claims against abandoned vessels [i.e., because they are subject to the law of finds], or because the eleventh amendment bars an award of salvage against the state as owner of the vessel, the [ASA] ... would have virtually no effect on federal admiralty jurisdiction.

Id. Similarly, elimination of the law of finds and the vesting of title in the state had no effect on admiralty jurisdiction, because it simply accomplished the same result as applying the embeddedness exception of the common law of finds. (Accord, *Sunken Treasure, Inc. v. Unidentified, Wrecked & Abandoned Vessel*, 857 F. Supp. 1129 (D.V.I. 1994)). The district court also found that the concept of embeddedness was sufficiently related to the historic significance of a shipwreck to withstand a constitutional due process challenge. *Id.*

c. State Claims and the Eleventh Amendment

In *Deep Sea Research*, supra, the state of California claimed that the Eleventh Amendment precluded the federal court from adjudicating the state's interest in the Brother Jonathan. The state relied on *Florida Department of State v. Treasure Salvors, Inc.*, 458 U.S. 670, 102 S.Ct. 3304, 73 L.Ed.2d 1057 (1982), where four members of the plurality and four dissenters had agreed that Treasure Salvors could not sue Florida in federal admiralty court to recover property owned by the state without the state's consent. In that case, however, the state official was found to have acted beyond his authority and the state did "not have even a colorable claim to the artifacts." Subsequent cases found federal courts to have no in rem admiralty jurisdiction where the state presents a "colorable claim" to the wreck. See, e.g., *Marx v. Government of Guam*, 866 F.2d 294 (9th Cir. 1989); *Maritime Underwater Surveys, Inc. v. Unidentified, Wrecked and Abandoned Sailing Vessel*, 717 F.2d 6 (1st Cir. 1983). The Supreme Court distinguished *Deep Sea Research* by the fact that the res in *Treasure Salvors* was in the possession of the state. Noting the constitutional underpinnings of admiralty jurisdiction, the Court held that "the Eleventh Amendment does not bar federal jurisdiction over the Brother Jonathan and, therefore, that the District Court may adjudicate . . . the State claims to the shipwreck." Four concurring justices in the case would have based the holding not on the lack of possession by the state, but on the premise that the Eleventh Amendment does not bar in rem admiralty actions. The concurring justices specifically noted that in admiralty cases, it is "evident that the issue [of Eleventh Amendment state immunity] is open to reconsideration." *Deep Sea Research*, at 510.

d. The ASA and State Law Preemption

The Supreme Court in did not resolve the issue of whether the ASA preempts state law claims to shipwrecks not covered by the ASA. The Ninth Circuit Court of Appeals had concluded that the California law was pre-empted because shipwrecks that do not meet the requirements of the ASA are exclusively within the admiralty jurisdiction of the federal government. *Deep Sea Research, Inc. v. Brother Jonathan*, 102 F.3d 379 (9th Cir. 1996). Because of the possibility that the issue would be moot after the application of the ASA on remand, the Supreme Court declined to address the preemption issue and that question remains unresolved.

6.   INTERNATIONAL ASPECTS OF U.S. SALVAGE AND MARINE CULTURAL HERITAGE LAW

a. The Need for Uniformity and Consistency

United States' admiralty jurisdiction extends not only to U.S. waters and U.S. vessels, but in the case of maritime casualties, also to U.S. and other shipwrecks in faraway locales beyond any nation's territorial jurisdiction. If a part of the shipwreck, the res, is brought into a U.S. federal court, the court can exercise constructive in rem jurisdiction over the wreck itself based on the presence within the judicial district of physical items salvaged from the wreck. For example, salvage operations of the RMS *Titanic*, a British-flagged vessel built in Ireland that sank in international waters in the north Atlantic in 1912 on its maiden voyage, were conducted under the jurisdiction of the U.S. District Court for the Eastern District of Virginia. In *R.M.S. Titanic v. Haver*, 171 F.3d 943 (4th Cir.1999), the court explained that salvage law is part of the maritime common law of nations, jus gentium, and is recognized among nations as a matter of comity. "The need for courts of admiralty to apply the law similarly is fundamentally important to international commerce and to the policies supporting order on the high seas. It is therefore prudent for [a U.S.] court sitting in admiralty, to assure enforcement in harmony with these shared maritime principles." Id. at 967. Further, the court explained that "maritime law has the force of law, not from extraterritorial reach of national laws, nor from abdication of its sovereign powers by any nation, but from acceptance by common consent of civilized communities of rules designed to foster amicable and workable commercial relations." Id. at 960–961.

In *Haver*, the 4th Circuit Court of Appeals found that while RMST, the salvor-in-possession designated by the district court, was entitled to an order to prohibit interference with salvage operations, RMST could not prohibit Haver from conducting tours and photographing images of the wreck. RMST had made the "novel" argument that because videos and photographic images of the Titanic could be marketed, that Haver was

improperly removing "property" from the site. The
Circuit Court rejected this claim as follows.

> . . . [I]f we were now to recognize, as part of
> the salvage law, the right to exclude others from
> viewing and photographing a shipwreck in
> international waters, we might so alter the law
> of salvage as to risk its uniformity and
> international comity, putting at risk the benefits
> that all nations enjoy in a well-understood and
> consistently-applied body of law. This risk is
> heightened when it is understood that such an
> expansion of salvage rights might not encourage
> salvage and might, additionally, discourage free
> movement and navigation in international
> waters. . . .

Id. at 970. This international component
highlights why uniformity and consistency critical
elements of admiralty law.

b. Salvage and Sovereign Vessels

Under U.S. law, sovereign vessels are treated
differently than private vessels regarding
abandonment. The US. And many other nations,
including Spain, take the position that sunken
military ships are never abandoned by their
governments out of respect for lost crews and because
the vessels are "honored graves." As owners of the
sovereign vessels, the nations can forbid any salvage
efforts. A State Department letter included in the
House Report on the ASA states, "the U.S. only
abandons its sovereignty over, and title to, sunken
U.S. warships by affirmative act; mere passage of

time or lack of positive assertions of right are insufficient to establish such abandonment." The letter goes on to say that the United States accords the same presumption of non-abandonment to sovereign vessels of other nations that have sunk in U.S. waters while on the noncommercial service of that state. H.R. Rep. No. 100–514(II), at 13 (1988).

In *Sea Hunt v. The Unidentified Shipwrecked Vessel*, 221 F.3d 634 (4th Cir. 2000), the state of Virginia claimed ownership under the ASA of the *La Galga* and the *Juno,* Spanish Navy frigates that sank in 1750 and 1802, respectively. The state issued permits to Sea Hunt, a maritime salvage company, to conduct salvage operations and recover artifacts from the wrecks. Spain asserted ownership over the shipwrecks. The court upheld the title of Spain to the vessels, finding that governments retain "ownership of foreign warships sunk in waters of the United States without being captured, and . . . that title to such sunken warships is not lost absent express abandonment by the sovereign." Id. at 643.

Congress subsequently codified the U.S. position in the Sunken Military Craft Act, Pub. L. No. 108–375, §§ 1401–08 (2004). To carry out U.S. policies concerning military vessels, U.S. admiralty courts will not exercise in rem jurisdiction over foreign military vessels discovered in international waters. In *Odyssey Marine Exploration, Inc. v. Unidentified Shipwrecked Vessel*, 657 F.3d 1159 (11th Cir. 2011), the Court of Appeals held that the Spanish military vessel, *Nuestra Senora de las Mercedes*, and its cargo were immune from judicial arrest under the Foreign

Sovereign Immunities Act (FSIA), 28 U.S.C.S. §§ 1602–1611, and that the cargo aboard the was not severable from the shipwreck, because other statutes, including the Sunken Military Craft Act which treats cargo as part of the shipwreck, would govern the salvage claims against the Spanish vessel. See 657 F.3d 1159 (11th Cir. 2011). As a result, Odyssey Marine had to turn over to Spain the $600 million treasure trove it had already recovered and brought to the United States. Odyssey Marine was subsequently also ordered to pay $1 million in attorney's fees to Spain, primarily because it had attempted to hide the identity and location of the vessel.

The United States has not become party the U.N. Convention on the Protection of Underwater Cultural Heritage, primarily because the treaty does not unambiguously require the consent of the flag nation before its military vessels can be the subject to recovery. Article 7, section 3 envisages the nation in whose waters a state vessel is found notifying the flag state "with a view to cooperating on the best methods of protecting State vessels and aircraft . . . ."

CHAPTER IX

FISHERIES MANAGEMENT: STATE, NATIONAL AND FOREIGN WATERS

A. STATE FISHERIES MANAGEMENT

Prior to 1977, states were the primary managers of the country's fisheries. By virtue of the police power, the states have regulated fisheries in inland waters and the three-mile territorial sea since colonial times. See *McCready v. Virginia*, 94 U.S. 391 (1876) (holding a state owns "the tide-waters . . . and the fish in them, so far as they are capable of ownership while running"). States have also regulated beyond the three-mile territorial sea. See *Skiriotes v. Florida*, 313 U.S. 69 (1941)(U.S. Supreme Court recognized the right of Florida to apply its state law prohibiting sponge fishing to Florida citizens taking sponges in international waters). Individual states can regulate citizens of other States when those citizens are fishing in state jurisdictional waters.

State fishing regulations have been challenged under the federal Equal Protection Clause, the Commerce Clause, and the Privilege and Immunities Clause. In general, State fishing laws have been upheld as long as the State can demonstrate a legitimate state interest. See e.g. *Davrod Corp. v. Coates*, 971 F.2d 778 (1st Cir. 1992)(finding that a vessel length limitation that only affected out of state vessels was a proper fisheries management regulation because conservation of fish stocks is a legitimate state regulatory concern.); *Raffield v.*

Florida, 565 So.2d 704 (Fla. 1990)(finding statute prohibiting the taking of fish with a purse seine was a valid exercise of state power to protect fisheries relied upon by residents even though the fisheries were beyond the territorial limits of the of the state); *Ampro Fisheries, Inc. v. Yaskin,* 127 N.J. 602, 606 A.2d 1099 (1992)(Commerce Clause challenge to state prohibitions of industrial menhaden fishing rejected); *New York State Trawlers Ass'n v. Jorling,* 16 F.3d 1303 (2d Cir. 1994)(Commerce Clause challenge to state ban on lobster trawling rejected); *Marilley v. Bonham,* 844 F.3d 841 (9th Cir. 2016) (Privileges and Immunities Clause challenge to higher fees being charged by California to nonresident commercial fishers rejected); *State v. Bundrant,* 546 P. 2d 530 (Alaska 1976)(holding that Alaska's state interest in conserving its crab fishery justified state regulation of offshore crab fishery beyond state boundaries).

When fishermen can demonstrate a discriminatory impact of a regulation, they have prevailed under the Equal Protection Act. In *Bateman v. Gardner,* 716 F.Supp. 595 (S.D.Fla. 1989), and *Southeastern Fisheries Ass'n, Inc. v. Martinez,* 772 F.Supp. 1263 (S.D.Fla. 1991), the federal district court found that Florida statutes placing shrimping and mackerel catch restrictions on Florida-registered vessels in federal waters violated equal protection rights because of the statute's discriminatory impact. The court implied that a state's *Skiriotes* jurisdiction is limited to circumstances in where a state fishery regulation mirrors federal regulations for the same area. But other federal courts have rejected Equal

Protection Clause claims. *Chinatown Neighborhood Ass'n v.* Harris, 33 F. Supp.3d 1085 (2015) (The Court rejected a claim that the implementation of the California statute prohibiting a person from possessing, selling, or distributing shark fins resulted in an equal protection violation for Chinese Californians). State courts have not been willing to find equal protection considerations on the basis of different rules applying to different fishing gear. *Puget Sound Harvesters Ass'n v. Dep't of Fish & Wildlife,* 182 Wn. App. 857 (Wash. App. 2014)(finding no equal protection violation in assigning different catch shares between gill-netters and purse seiners).

While States exercise broad jurisdiction over state waters, Congress can preempt state fishery laws. Preemption under the MSA is discussed in Part B.5 below. Other statutes such as the Atlantic Coastal Fisheries Cooperative Management Act may also displace state authority within state waters. 16 U.S.CA. § 5106(c). In other instances, federal acts such as the Halibut Act, 16 U.S.C.A. § 1801 contemplates state involvement in halibut fishery management in relation to landing fish. See also *State v. Dupier,* 118 P. 3d 1039 (Alaska, 2005)(finding that the Magnuson-Stevens Act does not preempt all aspects of state regulation of fish caught in the Exclusive Economic Zone).

B. FEDERAL FISHERIES MANAGEMENT

To protect fisheries from overexploitation in the zone beyond state waters between three and twelve miles, Congress passed the Bartlett Act in 1964 prohibiting any foreign vessel from fishing in those waters. (Public Law 88–308, May 20, 1964). The act was ineffective in protecting U.S. interests. In 1976, before negotiations at the Third UN Conference on the Law of the Sea (UNCLOS III) had reached substantial consensus, Congress passed the Fishery Conservation and Management Act, now named the Magnuson-Stevens Fishery Conservation and Management Act (Magnuson-Stevens Act or MSA), to protect offshore fisheries and the American fishing industry, 16 U.S.C.A. §§ 1801–1882. The MSA extended exclusive United States fisheries jurisdiction to 200 miles offshore. The offshore management area was originally designated the fishery conservation zone, but the MSA was later amended to reflect the 1983 United States' claim to a 200-mile exclusive economic zone (EEZ). For purposes of the MSA, the EEZ extends from state seaward boundaries (generally three miles offshore) out to 200 miles from shore.

The broad policies and purposes of the act are directed toward the conservation, development, and management of fishery resources, as well as the development of domestic commercial and recreational fishing. Id. § 1801. The MSA provides a comprehensive system for regulating domestic and foreign fishing in federal waters. States have unsuccessfully challenged the constitutionality of the MSA when disagreements arose over whether fishermen from different states are being treated fairly in regard to allocations. *Connecticut ex rel. Blumenthal v. United States,* 369 F. Supp. 2d 237 (Conn. 2005)(finding that the State is not a person for purposes of the 5th Amendment and that a 10th Amendment claim failed because the MSA provision was not directed at the States but at DOC Secretary).

In the 197-mile wide EEZ, the United States claims exclusive authority to manage and regulate all fisheries. A fishery is defined as "one or more stocks of fish which can be treated as a unit for purposes of conservation and management and which are identified on the basis of geographical, scientific, technical, recreational, and economic characteristics." § 1802(13)(A). Fisheries include highly migratory species like sharks and tunas. Id. § 1811(a), § 1802(20). Jurisdiction over anadromous species (e.g., salmon) is claimed throughout their migratory range beyond the EEZ. Id. § 1811(b).

The MSA established eight regional fishery management councils (RFMCs) to formulate fishery management plans for each of the regions that are enforced through regulations of the U.S. Department of Commerce (DOC). Id. § 1852(a).

The Act has been amended over a dozen times. The first amendments included the Processor Preference Act in 1978 and the American Fisheries Promotion Act in 1980 designed to strengthen American control over its fisheries. The second set of amendments focused on improving the RFMCs and implementing regulations under the fishery management plans. The third set of amendments involved extending U.S. jurisdiction over tuna, addressing driftnet fishing on the high seas, and managing the Bering Sea pollock fishery.

In 1996, the MSA was substantially amended by the Sustainable Fisheries Act (SFA) focusing on improving the biological conservation of fish stocks and the protection of habitat. These amendments added new standards to minimize both bycatch and adverse economic effects on fishing communities. The 1996 amendments also defined an individual fishing quota (IFQ) as a "Federal permit under a limited access system to harvest a quantity of fish, expressed by a unit or units representing a percentage of the total allowable catch of a fishery that may be received or held for exclusive use by a person." Id. § 1802(23)

The last substantial amendment to the Act was the Magnuson-Stevens Fishery Conservation and Management Reauthorization Act in 2006. (P.L. 109–479) This amendment clarified the requirement of RFMCs to combat overfishing and encouraged the use of more market-based fishery management mechanisms.

1. REGIONAL FISHERY MANAGEMENT COUNCILS

Regional Fishery Management Councils (RFMCs) implement the MSA by deciding which fisheries within a particular region require "conservation and management". *Id.* § 1852(h) To make this decision, the councils rely on guidance from two advisory committees: a scientific committee and a fishing industry advisory committee. *Id.* § 1852(g)(1) and 1852(g)(3).

REGIONAL FISHERY MANAGEMENT COUNCILS

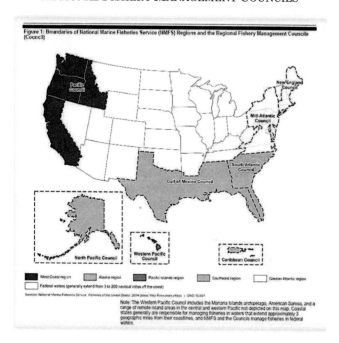

Figure 1: Boundaries of National Marine Fisheries Service (NMFS) Regions and the Regional Fishery Management Councils (Council)

The eight regional councils are composed of the regional director of the National Marine Fisheries Service (NMFS), state fishery management officers, and individuals from each state who are recommended by state governors and appointed by the Secretary of Commerce. The number of voting members ranges from 7 (e.g., Caribbean Council) –21 (Mid-Atlantic Council) with usually the majority of council members appointed by Department of

Commerce.[1] The appointed council members must be persons who are knowledgeable about fishery conservation and management, commercial or recreational fishing, or the fisheries resources of a region. Id. § 1852(b). In making appointments, the Secretary is also required to apportion council membership between recreational and commercial fishery representatives based on such factors as the type of fisheries managed, the quantity of fish harvested, fishing and processing methods used, and the number of participants in the fisheries. Id. §§ 1852(b)(2)(A)–(B). Appointed members may only serve three consecutive three-year terms. Id. at § 1852(b)(3). Councils usually meet four times a year and most meetings are open to the public.

In the first decades of the MSA, most of the RFMCs were dominated by commercial fishermen, leading to some commentators viewing the process as biased.[2] The 1996 Sustainable Fisheries Act amendments to the MSA began addressing some of the criticisms by requiring disclosure of financial conflicts of interest of commission nominees, id.§ 1852(j), and requiring councils to make conservation of fish stocks the first priority.

Responding to criticisms concerning the RFMCs, Congress instituted several changes through the 2006 MSA Reauthorization Act. New council

---

[1]   Non-voting members include representatives of the Coast Guard, State Department, and U.S. Fish and Wildlife Service.

[2]   See, e.g., T.A. Okey, *Membership of the Eight Regional Fishery Management Councils in the United States: Are Special Interests Over-Represented?*, 27 Marine Policy 193 (2003).

members are required to take a training course
designed to prepare the members to deal with the
scientific, social, economic, environmental, legal, and
conflict of interest requirements of the fishery
management process. Id. at § 1852(k). The
Reauthorization Act also strengthened and clarified
the MSA requirements concerning conflict of interest
and recusal. Id. at § 1852(j). Finally, the Act limited
the discretion of the councils very significantly in
setting annual catch levels that exceed scientifically
determined levels. See id. § 1852(h)(6).

The 2006 Reauthorization Act did not respond
comprehensively to the criticism that the councils are
dominated by the fishing industry and do not
adequately represent broader public interests.[3] The
appointment process for the Gulf of Mexico Fisheries
Management Council was changed significantly,
however, by requiring the nomination by the state
governors of three individuals representing the
commercial, recreational and charter fishing sectors,
as well as another individual "knowledgeable
regarding the conservation and management of
fisheries resources in the jurisdiction." If the
Secretary determines a governor's nominees do not
meet these requirements, the Act provides a process
for residents of a state to make nominations that the
Secretary may add to the list of nominees submitted
by a state governor. Id. § 1852(b)(2)(D).

The Reauthorization Act also purports to improve
the decision-making by RFMCs by providing more

---

[3]   Pew Oceans Commission, *America's Living Oceans:*
Charting a Course for Sea Change, 44–45 (2003).

consistency among councils. To provide more consistent application of the Act, the RFMCs are authorized to create a Council Coordination Committee consisting of the chairs, vice chairs, and executive directors of the councils (or other members or staff) to provide a forum for discussion of issues of relevance to all Councils in implementing the MSA. Id. § 1852(l).

Next, the Secretary is directed to revise agency procedures for compliance with the National Environmental Policy Act (NEPA). Id. § 1854(i)(1). In consultation with the Council on Environmental Quality (CEQ) and the Councils, and with public participation, the Secretary is to develop a uniform environmental review procedure for fishery management plans (FMPs) that integrates NEPA review, analysis and public input and conforms with time-lines for review and approval of FMPs under the MSA. Id. Once these new procedures are adopted, they "shall be the sole environmental impact assessment procedure for fishery management plans, amendments, regulations, and other action taken or approved pursuant to the [MSA]." Id. § 1854(i)(2). See also *Notice of Availability of Draft Revised and Updated National Environmental Policy Act (NEPA) Procedures for Magnuson Stevens Act Fishery Management Actions*, 79 Fed. Reg. 36726 (June 30, 2014).

2. FISHERIES MANAGEMENT PLANS

The MSA requires the creation of Fisheries Management Plans (FMPs) to prevent overfishing[4] by specifying the optimum yield for a given stock.[5]

RFMCs have the primary responsibility for preparing FMPs for EEZ fisheries, establishing management policies not only for how, when, where, and how many fish are caught, but also allocating the catch among users. Each FMP is expected to identify issues within a fishery and specific conservation and management measures to address the issues. As of 2019, there are forty-six fisheries management plans regulating both groups of species such as the coastal pelagic species and single species such as dogfish.

---

[4] Overfishing is defined as the "rate or level of fishing mortality that jeopardizes the capacity of a fishery to produce the maximum sustainable yield on a continuing basis." 16 U.S.C.A § 1802(29). Note "overfishing" is always a direct result of fishing activities.

Maximum Sustainable Yield is the largest long-term average catch or yield that can be taken from a stock under prevailing ecological and environmental conditions. 50 C.F.R. § 600.310(c)(1)(i).

[5] Optimum yield is defined to be the amount of fish which:

"(A) will provide the greatest overall benefit to the Nation, particularly with respect to food production and recreational opportunities; and taking into account the protection of marine ecosystems;

(B) is prescribed as such on the basis of the maximum sustainable yield from the fishery, as reduced by any relevant economic, social, or ecological factor; and

(C) in the case of an overfished fishery, provides for rebuilding to a level consistent with producing the maximum sustainable yield in such fishery."

16 U.S.C.A. § 1802(28).

Altogether NOAA Fisheries tracks the status of 474 fish stocks and has contributed to the rebuilding of forty-five fish stocks since 2000.[6] A RFMC cannot remove a fishery from an FMP and delegate it to the management of a state. *United Cook Inlet Drift Ass'n v. Nat'l Marine Fisheries Service,* 837 F.3d 1055 (9th Cir., 2016).

FMPs and plan amendments developed by the RFMCs must be submitted to NMFS acting on behalf of the Secretary of Commerce, who must approve a plan if it is consistent with applicable law. Id. § 1854(a)(3). The Secretary's approval is not reviewed de novo and will not be overturned unless it is inconsistent with the national standards or other applicable law, or if it is arbitrary and capricious or an abuse of the Secretary's discretion. See, e.g., *Associated Fisheries of Maine v. Daley,* 127 F.3d 104 (1st Cir. 1997); *C & W Fish Co. v. Fox,* 931 F.2d 1556, 289 U.S.App.D.C. 323 (D.C.Cir. 1991); *Fishermen's Dock Cooperative, Inc. v. Brown,* 75 F.3d 164 (4th Cir. 1996); *Pacific Marine Conservation Council v. Evans,* 200 F.Supp.2d 1194 (N.D.Cal. 2002).

If NMFS does not act to approve a plan within the statutory period of 30 days after the end of a 60 day notice and comment period, then the plan goes into effect. If NMFS disapproves of a plan, then the

---

[6]   NOAA tracks stocks subject to "overfishing" and "overfished" stocks. An "overfished" stock are stocks whose biomass falls below a certain scientific threshold because of a combination of factors including fishing but also habitat degradation, pollution, or climate change impacts. RFMCs have the discretion to determine the definition of "overfished" for each species.

council is given another opportunity to revise the plan based on NMFS' recommendations of how to bring the plan into conformity with the law.

FMPs are subject to NEPA. In consultation with the Council on Environmental Quality (CEQ) and the Councils, and with public participation, the Secretary is expected to develop a uniform environmental review procedure for fishery management plans that integrates NEPA review, analysis and public input and conforms with time-lines for review and approval of FMPs under the MSA.

While most FMPs are developed by RFMCs, the Secretary has independent authority to prepare FMPs for Atlantic highly migratory species, and in a limited number of other circumstances. Id. § 1854. For example, the Secretary has the discretion to prepare an FMP when a Council fails to develop and submit a plan for a fishery requiring management "after a reasonable period" and when a Council fails to resubmit a revised plan or amendment after the Secretary has disapproved or partially disapproved the plan or amendment. Id. § 1854(c). Further, when an RMFC is notified that a fishery is overfished by NOAA Fisheries and the RFMC does not submit a plan for rebuilding an overfished fishery within two years of notification, the Secretary of Commerce is required to prepare a plan or plan amendment. Id. § 1854(e)(5).

FMPs must be developed based on ten national standards set out in the MSA. Id. §§ 1851(a)(1)–(10). In addition, NMFS has issued National Standard

Guidelines to ensure that FMPs are consistent with the MSA. (50 C.F.R. §§ 600.305–600.355). Councils have some flexibility in how to implement the standards, which might include placing greater burden on certain members of the fishing sector. *Fishermen's Finest Inc. v. Locke,* 593 F.3d 886, 896 (9th Cir. 2010)("The National Standards do not require any particular outcome with respect to allocations; rather, they provide a framework for the Council's analysis."). Some of the National Standards are challenged more often than others, particularly, Standard 1, 2, 4, and 8. The ten National Standards are:

(1) Conservation and management measures shall prevent overfishing while achieving, on a continuing basis, the optimum yield from each fishery for the United States fishing industry.[7]

(2) Conservation and management measures shall be based upon the best scientific information available.[8]

(3) To the extent practicable, an individual stock of fish shall be managed as a unit

---

[7]   *Western Sea Fishing Co. v. Locke,* 722 F. Supp. 2d 126 (D. Mass. 2010); *Blue Water Fisherman's Ass'n v. Mineta,* 122 F. Supp. 2d 150 (D.D.C. 2000); *Ctr. for Biological Diversity v. Blank,* 933 F. Supp. 2d 125 (D.D.C. 2013); *NRDC v. Nat'l Marine Fisheries Serv.,* 71 F. Supp. 3d 35 (D.D.C. 2014)

[8]   *Gen. Category Scallop Fishermen v. United States DOC,* 720 F. Supp. 2d 564 (D.N.J. 2010); *Hadaja, Inc. v. Evans,* 263 F. Supp. 2d 346 (D.R.I. 2003); *Little Bay Lobster Co. v. Evans,* 352 F.3d 462 (1st Cir. 2003); *Or. Trollers Ass'n v. Gutierrez,* 452 F.3d 1104 (9th Cir. 2006); *Coastal Conservation Ass'n v. United States DOC,* 846 F.3d 99 (5th Cir. 2017).

throughout its range, and interrelated stocks of fish shall be managed as a unit or in close coordination.[9]

(4) Conservation and management measures shall not discriminate between residents of different States. If it becomes necessary to allocate or assign fishing privileges among various United States fishermen, such allocation shall be (A) fair and equitable to all such fishermen; (B) reasonably calculated to promote conservation; and (C) carried out in such manner that no particular individual, corporation, or other entity acquires an excessive share of such privileges.[10]

(5) Conservation and management measures shall, where practicable, consider efficiency in the utilization of the resources; except that no such measure shall have economic allocation as its sole purpose.

(6) Conservation and management measures shall take into account and allow for variations among, and contingencies in, fisheries, fishery resources, and catches.

---

[9]   *Or. Trollers Ass'n v. Gutierrez*, 452 F.3d 1104 (9th Cir. 2006).

[10]   *Western Sea Fishing Co. v. Locke*, 722 F. Supp. 2d 126 (D. Mass. 2010); *Fishing Rights Alliance v. Pritzker*, 247 F. Supp. 3d 1268 (M.D. Fla. 2017); *Yakutat, Inc. v. Gutierrez*, 407 F.3d 1054 (9th Cir. 2005).

(7) Conservation and management measures shall, where practicable, minimize costs and avoid unnecessary duplication.

(8) Conservation and management measures shall, consistent with the conservation requirements of this Act (including the prevention of overfishing and rebuilding of overfished stocks), take into account the importance of fishery resources to fishing communities in order to (A) provide for the sustained participation of such communities, and (B) to the extent practicable, minimize adverse impacts on such communities.[11]

(9) Conservation and management measures shall, to the extent practicable, (A) minimize bycatch[12] and (B) to the extent bycatch catch

---

[11] *Nat'l Coalition for Marine Conservation v. Evans,* 231 F. Supp. 2d 119 (D.D.C. 2002); *North Carolina Fisheries Ass'n v. Daley,* 27 F. Supp. 2d 650 (E.D. Va. 1998); *Little Bay Lobster Co. v. Evans,* 352 F.3d 462 (1st Cir. 2003); Or. Trollers Ass'n v. Gutierrez, 452 F.3d 1104 (9th Cir. 2006); *Pac. Coast Fedn. of Fishermen's Ass'ns v. Blank,* 693 F.3d 1084 (9th Cir. 2012); *Coastal Conservation Ass'n v. United States DOC,* 846 F.3d 99 (5th Cir. 2017).

[12] Bycatch" is "fish which are harvested in a fishery, but which are not sold or kept for personal use, and include economic discards and regulatory discards, [but] does not include fish released alive under a recreational catch and release fishery management program." 16 U.S.C. § 1802(2).

A catch can be both "bycatch" and a "target stock" if a desirable fish is, for example, undersized.

cannot be avoided, minimize the mortality of such bycatch.[13]

(10) Conservation and management measures shall, to the extent practicable, promote the safety of human life at sea.[14]

All FMPs must prevent overfishing while achieving an optimum yield. The 2006 MSA Reauthorization Act now requires that *all* FMPs set annual catch limits at a level that prevents overfishing. See 16 U.S.C. § 1852(h)(6); 16 U.S.C. § 1853(A)(15). Notably, the Reauthorization Act requires RFMCs to set the annual catch limits at a level that does not exceed the recommendations of the Councils' scientific and statistical committees or the new peer review process established by the Act to improve the scientific data available for management. See id. § 1852(h)(6); see also, id. § 1852(g).

Since the 1990 amendments to the MSA, the contents of an FMP have been required to include a "fishery impact statement" to "assess, specify, and describe the likely effects . . . [on] participants in the fisheries and fishing communities affected by the plan or amendment. . . ." Id. § 1853(a)(9). The protection of fishing communities was raised to a governing standard in 1996. In response, National Standard Eight focused on the interests of fishing

---

[13]   *Blue Water Fisherman's Ass'n v. Mineta*, 122 F. Supp. 2d 150 (D.D.C. 2000); *NRDC v. Nat'l Marine Fisheries Serv.*, 71 F. Supp. 3d 35 (D.D.C. 2014).

[14]   *Or. Trollers Ass'n v. Gutierrez*, 452 F.3d 1104 (9th Cir. 2006).

communities was added to the MSA by the SFA. Id.
§ 1851(a)(8).[15]

In *A.M.L. Int'l, Inc. v. Daley*, 107 F. Supp. 2d 90 (D.
Mass. 2000), in spite of arguments that the FMP
would result in the closure of the spiny dogfish
fishery for at least five years, the Court of Appeals
upheld the FMP. The court noted that a collapsed
fishery that would not be economically viable for
decades would create worse economic consequences
than implementing the FMP. The court emphasized
that the duty to prevent overfishing under Standard
One takes precedence over Standard Eight.
Regulations provide that the effect of Standard Eight
is that when two alternatives achieve similar
conservation goals, the agency will choose the
alternative that better achieves Standard Eight
goals. See 50 C.F.R. § 666.345(b).

The Secretary of Commerce must report annually
to Congress and councils on the status of fisheries
and identify fisheries that are overfished or are
approaching a condition of being overfished. 16
U.S.C. § 1854(e)(1). "A fishery shall be classified as
approaching a condition of being overfished if, based
on trends in fishing effort, fishery resource size, and
other appropriate factors, the Secretary estimates

---

[15]   See generally, Michael C. Laurence, *A Call to Action:
Saving America's Commercial Fishermen,* 26 Wm. & Mary Envtl.
Pol'y L. Rev. 825 (2002) (describing the implementation of
National Standard Eight and supporting government reduction of
fishing capacity as a final, viable option for saving fishermen and
fishing communities).

that the fishery will become overfished within two years." Id. § 1854(e)(1).

The MSA requires that within two years of notification that a fishery is overfished, the responsible RFMC must submit a FMP, plan amendment, or proposed regulations that will *immediately* end overfishing and rebuild affected stocks of fish within a specified time, which will normally not exceed 10 years. Id. § 1854(e)(3–4). See *Natural Resources Defense Council v. NMFS*, 421 F.3d 872 (9th Cir. 2005)(finding an FMP for a seriously overfished fishery with a 33-year rebuilding time that also called for an increased annual quota "patently unreasonable").

If the Council does not act within the required period, the Secretary must prepare an FMP or plan amendment and regulations within nine months to stop overfishing and rebuild affected stocks of fish. Id. § 1854(e)(5). See *Natural Resources Defense Council v. Daley*, 209 F.3d 747, 341 U.S.App.D.C. 119 (D.C.Cir. 2000)(holding that the level of take allowed under a rebuilding plan must have at least a 50% likelihood of achieving the goal of rebuilding the stock).

FMPs must also identify essential fish habitat (EFH) for the managed fishery. Id. § 1853(a)(7). EFH is defined as "those waters and substrate necessary to fish for spawning, breeding, feeding or growth to maturity." 16 U.S.C. § 1802(10). FMPs must include measures to minimize the adverse impacts of fishing on EFH and identify actions encouraging the conservation of EFH. Id. Federal agencies are required to consult with the Secretary on their actions that may adversely affect EFH. Id. § 1855(b)(2). The Councils are required to make recommendations to the Secretary on federal and state actions affecting anadromous fish habitat, including EFH, and may make recommendations on actions affecting the habitat of other species. Id. § 1855(b)(3). RFMCs must provide specific information about which EFHs need protection and why. *American Oceans Campaign v. Daley* 183 F. Supp. 2d 1 (D.D.C. 2000)

The MSA has provided authority for FMPs to protect designated areas by restricting or prohibiting fishing, types of fishing gear or types of vessels. Id. § 1853(3)(A). The establishment of marine reserves that prohibit all fishing, however, has become quite controversial. The 2006 Reauthorization Act requires that closure of an area to *all fishing* by an FMP must ensure that the closure:

(i)   is based on the best scientific information available;

(ii) includes criteria to assess the conservation benefit of the closed area;

(iii) establishes a timetable for review of the closed area's performance that is consistent with the purposes of the closed area; and

(iv) is based on an assessment of the benefits and impacts of the closure, including its size, in relation to other management measures (either alone or in combination with such measures), including the benefits and impacts of limiting access to: users of the area, overall fishing activity, fishery science, and fishery and marine conservation.

Id. § 1853(b)(2)(B).

FMPs can be amended. Seasonal management of fisheries is usually based on fisheries rules (also called "specifications") that are issued under the FMPs. An FMP created by a regional council is not considered the same as a plan created by an interstate compact. (*United States v. Saunders*, 828 F.3d. 198 (4th Cir. 2016)) (refusing to apply an exception under the Lacey Act, the Court distinguished between a regional council plan created under the MSA that applied to federal waters from a fisheries plan adopted by the Atlantic States Regional Fishing Commission which only regulated state waters.)

3.   INDIVIDUAL FISHING QUOTAS AND LIMITED ACCESS PRIVILEGE PROGRAMS

FMPs using limited entry or individual fishing quota (IFQ) systems as a management mechanism are acceptable under the national standards. In fact, the MSA includes such limited access systems among the discretionary measures a Council may include in an FMP. IFQs are also sometimes known as catch shares, Individual Transferable Quotas (ITQs), or Individual Vessel Quotas. The 2006 Reauthorization Act also created "limited access privilege programs" (LAPPs) which expands the concept of IFQs to fishing communities. Id. § 1853(a).

IFQs under U.S. federal law are by definition revocable permits, not property interests, that can be issued for a maximum period of ten years. The government has the power to modify any such permit without compensation. 16 U.S.C.A. § 1853(a)(3). Courts have not found fifth amendment takings. *Am. Pelagic Fishing Co. L.P. v. United States,* 379 F.3d 1363, 1377 (Fed. Cir. 2004)(finding the use of a vessel in an EEZ "does not equate to a cognizable property interest for purposes of a takings analysis" when a permit is revoked).

In designing a limited access system, a Council must take into account:

(A) present participation in the fishery;

(B) historical fishing practices in, and dependence on, the fishery;

(C) the economics of the fishery;

(D) the capability of fishing vessels used in the fishery to engage in other fisheries;

(E) the cultural and social framework relevant to the fishery;

(F) the fair and equitable distribution of access privileges in the fishery; and

(G) any other relevant considerations. . . .

16 U.S.C.A. § 1853(b)(6). Before creating a limited access system for an overfished fishery, the Council must be able to model that the program will assist in the rebuilding of the stock. Id. § 1853A(c)(1) Any Council that develops a limited access program must

also have a cost-recovery program for management, data collection, and enforcement. *Glacier Fish Co. v. Pritzker*, 832 F.3d 1113 (9th Cir. 2016)(discussing the right to collect cost-recovery fees from individual members to a "coop" permit).

Numerous decisions have upheld FMP limited access systems including IFQ systems. See *Alliance Against IFQs v. Brown*, 84 F.3d 343 (9th Cir. 1996); *Norbird Fisheries, Inc. v. National Marine Fisheries Service*, 112 F.3d 414 (9th Cir. 1997); *Hadaja, Inc. v. Evans*, 263 F.Supp.2d 346 (D.R.I. 2003); *Sea Watch Int'l v. Mosbacher*, 762 F.Supp. 370 (D.C.Cir. 1991); *Gen. Category Scallop Fishermen v. United States DOC*, 720 F. Supp. 2d 564 (D.N.J. 2010)(rejecting a 5th amendment taking claim when the Council reduced the number of boats given quotas within a particular fishery).

Many managed fisheries are now under some form of a limited license program.[16] Post-October 2002, IFQ programs must conform with recommendations from the National Academy of Science.

IFQ programs have been recently questioned as the "privatization" aspects of the programs have had

---

[16]   Examples of Catch Share Programs include New England Atlantic Sea Scallops, North Pacific Halibut & Sablefish, Bering Sea Pollock Cooperatives, Groundfish (non-pollock) cooperatives, Bering Sea King & Tanner Crab, Gulf of Alaska Rockfish, Pacific Sablefish, Pacific Groundfish Trawl Rationalization, Hawaii longline tuna, Gulf of Mexico Red Snapper, Gulf of Mexico Grouper & Tilefish, Gulf of Mexico Mackerel, Gulf of Mexico Red Snapper, South Atlantic Wreckfish, South Atlantic Golden Crab, Mid-Atlantic Golden Tilefish, Mid-Atlantic Surf Claim & Ocean Quahog, Caribbean Snapper and Grouper.

measurable economic impacts on rural, indigenous, and low-income participants in commercial fisheries.[17] There is concern based on empirical findings that power in a limited access fishery has been concentrated in the hands of only a few well-capitalized fishery participants.

The 2006 Reauthorization Act expands the concept of "limited access privilege programs" (LAPPs). Id. § 1853(a). Fisheries that are already subject to a limited access system may qualify for management under a LAPP system which expands the concept of IFQs to include allocation of harvesting privileges to fishing communities and regional fishing organizations. A fishing community is one that is "substantially dependent on or substantially engaged in the harvest or processing of fishery resources to meet social and economic needs. . . ." Id. § 1801(16). To participate in a LAPP as a fishing community, residents who conduct commercial or recreational fishing, processing or fishery-dependent support businesses must meet participation criteria developed by the relevant RFMC and develop a "sustainability plan." Id. The plan must "address the social and economic development needs of coastal communities, including those that have not historically had the resources to participate in the fishery." Id. § 1853a(c)(3).

Councils may also create LAPPs through their own initiative by petition by the majority of the fishermen

---

[17]   See Oran R. Young et al., "Moving beyond panaceas in fisheries governance." *Proceedings of the National Academy of Sciences*, 2018; 201716545 DOI: 10.1073/pnas.1716545115.

in a limited entry fishery, or in the case of the Gulf or New England regions, by a 2/3 vote in a referendum among eligible permit holders. Id. § 1853a(c)(6). See *Coastal Conservation Ass'n v. Blank*, 2011 WL 4530544 (M.D. Fla. Sept. 29, 2011)(upholding the Gulf of Mexico Council's eligibility criteria to participate in a referendum to create a grouper and tilefish IFQ program); *Newton v. Locke*, 701 F.3d 5 (1st Cir. Mass. 2012)(upholding an amendment to the FMP for the Northeast Multispecies Groundfish Fishery which, among other things, altered and expanded the fishery's preexisting "sector allocation program" and distinguished the program from an ITQ or LAPP program).

A regional fishery association is a specific form of limited access privilege program in the MSA. A regional fishery association is:

> an association formed for the mutual benefit of members—
>
> (A) to meet social and economic needs in a region or subregion; and
> (B) comprised of persons engaging in the harvest or processing of fishery resources in that specific region or subregion or who otherwise own or operate businesses substantially dependent upon a fishery.

Id. § 1802(13A). These associations are not eligible for allocations, but may hold members' allocations. Regional fisheries organizations, comprising participants who hold quota shares, may qualify for participation in a LAPP by developing and submitting a plan meeting criteria developed by the relevant RFMP. Id. § 1853a(c)(4).

In 2010, NOAA released its Catch Share Policy to clarify and simplify design and implementation of catch share programs and reduce impediments to adoption in appropriate fisheries. "Catch share" is a general term for fishery management strategies that allocate a specific portion of the annual catch limit of a fishery to individuals, cooperatives, communities, or other entities. This includes LAPPs, IFQs and "other exclusive allocative measures such as Territorial Use Rights Fisheries (TURFs) that grant an exclusive privilege to fish in a geographically designated fishing ground." The Policy contains criteria for Councils to apply to assess whether a fishery will benefit from a catch share program and guiding principles to apply in developing a catch share program. *NOAA Catch Share Program,* available at http://www.nmfs.noaa.gov/sfa/manage ment/catch_shares/about/documents/noaa_cs_policy. pdf. Each recipient of a catch share is directly accountable to stop fishing when its exclusive allocation is reached. But with a secure allocation of the catch, there is no pressure or need to race for fish. More time and flexibility to fish allows fishermen to fish more sustainably by avoiding bycatch, unwanted species, and reducing the amount of discards and more efficiently by avoiding derby fishing and maintaining the economies of coastal communities.

4.   FOREIGN FISHING IN THE U.S. EEZ

One of the primary goals of the 1976 Fishery Conservation and Management Act was to "Americanize" the waters off the U.S. coast. The Act allowed for foreign fishing in the U.S. EEZ, but only to the extent that fisheries allocations exceed domestic harvesting capacity and only when pursuant to a fishing treaty or Governing International Fishery Agreement (GIFA). A GIFA requires compliance with numerous conditions, including the foreign nation agreeing to acknowledge exclusive U.S. management authority, to abide by all fishery regulations, to allow boarding and inspection for enforcement of U.S. laws, to reimburse U.S. citizens for damages to vessels or gear caused by a fishing vessel of the nation, and to permit and pay the costs associated with a required onboard observer. 16 U.S.C.A. § 1821(c). Each foreign fishing vessel must have an annual permit and is subject to permit fees and poundage fees for fish caught. Id. § 1824. A vessel's permit can be revoked for violation of conditions, *United States v. Kaiyo Maru No. 53*, 503 F.Supp. 1075 (D.Alaska 1980), and the release of a nation's fishery allocation can be affected. 16 U.S.C.A. § 1821(e)(1)(D).

The total allowable level of foreign fishing (TALFF) is determined by the appropriate fishery management council for each fishery. The TALFF is calculated by determining the surplus of optimum yield after taking account of the harvest by U.S. vessels, the domestic annual harvest. The TALFF for each fishery is allocated to foreign nations by the

Secretary of State, in cooperation with the Secretary of Commerce, based on a number of factors, including the degree and extent of: (1) tariff barriers on the importation of or restricted market access for U.S. fish and fish products, particularly for the fish for which the allocation is requested; (2) cooperation to advance U.S. fishery exports; (3) cooperation in fisheries research and technology transfer, enforcement of fishery regulations, and minimization of gear conflict with U.S. fishermen; (4) traditional fishing by the foreign nation in a fishery and the nation's dependence on the fishery for domestic consumption; and (5) other matters the Secretary of State "deems appropriate." Id. § 1821(e)(1)(E). A TALFF allocation could also be affected by a nation's failure to allow reciprocal U.S. fishing or by a "certification" by the Secretary that the nation engaged in fishery or trade practices that undermine the International Convention for the Regulation of Whaling. See *Associated Vessels Servs., Inc. v. Verity*, 688 F.Supp. 13 (D.D.C. 1988)(holding that the court has no authority to invade the policy-making realm and order a reallocation of TALFF).[18]

Foreign countries enhanced their access to fish from the U.S. EEZ through so-called "joint ventures" in which U.S. fishermen deliver harvests directly to foreign fish processing vessels. These arrangements were perceived as a loophole in the law by onshore processors and as a new market opportunity by U.S.

---

[18]   Gary M. Shinaver, Comment, *Fishery Conservation: Is the Categorical Exclusion of Foreign Fleets the Next Step,* 12 Cal. W. Int'l L.J. 154 (1982).

fishermen. In an attempt to balance the interests of both domestic fishermen and processors, Congress amended the MSA to require permits for such joint ventures that limited transfers to the portion of the fishery harvest beyond U.S. onshore processing capacity. 16 U.S.C.A. § 1824(b)(6)(B).[19]

Since enactment of the MSA in 1976, the Congressional goal of Americanizing fishing in the U.S. EEZ largely has been achieved. No TALFF for foreign fishing has been set for the U.S. EEZ since 1991, and no foreign vessels have harvested any fish or participated in a joint venture since 2003.

With 2.25 million square miles of EEZ, some illegal fishing takes place in U.S. EEZs, however, particularly in the Pacific Ocean in the no-take areas set aside as marine national monuments.[20] These and other EEZ incursions into U.S. EEZs and the U.S. response are addressed in the *U.S. National Plan of Action to Prevent, Deter, and Eliminate Illegal, Unregulated, and Unreported Fishing* published by NOAA.

5.   STATE MANAGEMENT AFTER ENACTMENT OF THE MSA

MSA section 306(a)(1), 16 U.S.C.A. § 1856(a)(1), generally preserves state fisheries management

---

[19]   Donna R. Christie, *Regulation of International Joint Ventures in the Fishery Conservation Zone*, 10 Ga. J. Int'l & Comp. L. 85 (1980)

[20]   See Mark Richardson and the Marine Conservation Institute, *Protecting America's Pacific Marine Monuments: A Review of Threats and Law Enforcement Issues* (2012).

authority within its boundaries. An exception arises when state action or lack of action "substantially and adversely affect[s]" the implementation of an FMP for a fishery located predominately within the EEZ. The Act then allows the Secretary to directly regulate the affected fishery seaward of the state internal waters. 16 U.S.C.A. § 1856(b). Such preemption is infrequently used.

Section 1856(a)(3), as amended in 1996, preserves a *Skiriotes*-type jurisdiction for vessels registered in a state operating beyond state waters where: (1) the state laws are consistent with any applicable federal FMP, laws, or regulations, or there is no applicable federal FMP, laws, or regulations; or (2) a federal FMP delegates management to the state and the state laws are consistent with the FMP. Issues have arisen involving federal preemption and other constitutional challenges, the statutory meaning of "registered" and "consistent", and state enforcement mechanisms.

a. Interpretation of "Registered"

State registration for purposes of extraterritorial jurisdiction is not defined in the MSA, but courts have interpreted the term liberally. These interpretations either implicitly or explicitly start with the premise that Congress intended registration to be defined by local or state law. The idea that Congress intended section 1856(a)(3) to refer to federal registration requirements instead of state requirements has been rejected by at least two courts. See *State v. F/V Baranof*, 677 P.2d 1245

(Alaska 1984); *People v. Weeren*, 163 Cal.Rptr. 255, 607 P.2d 1279 (1980). Federal registration requirements may, however, provide a helpful background for the registration issue. To comply with federal registration requirements, vessels weighing more than five net tons are required to be enrolled and licensed or registered by the federal government. Ships engaged in foreign trade are "registered" to establish nationality. Ships engaged in domestic trade or fishing are "enrolled" as evidence of the national character of the vessel and "licensed" to regulate its use. See *Douglas v. Seacoast Products*, 431 U.S. 265, 97 S.Ct. 1740, 52 L.Ed.2d 304 (1977). Vessels weighing less than five tons are not required to register with the federal government, but instead can have a registration number issued by an appropriate state.

The state in which the vessel is principally used is deemed to be an appropriate state for state registration purposes. *United States v. Seafoam II*, 528 F.Supp. 1133 (D.Alaska 1982). In *People v. Weeren*, 163 Cal.Rptr. 255, 607 P.2d 1279 (1980), the California Supreme Court determined that state licensing for commercial fishing purposes sufficed as state "registration" under the MSA. The vessel in *Weeren* was arrested beyond state waters for violation of a state law prohibiting the use of aircraft for spotting swordfish. The vessel did not possess a state identification number because it was enrolled with a United States document number. The court analyzed the different purposes of federal licensing, registration, or enrollment and of state registration. The court reasoned that preventing a state from enforcing its regulations against a vessel that was not required to obtain a state identification because the vessel possessed a federal number would render section 1856(a) "virtually meaningless, limiting [state] jurisdiction to pleasure boats and those few commercial fishing vessels lighter than five net tons." The court concluded that its interpretation prevented "the anomalous result which would follow [if the state could enforce its laws against] those boats in which the state had asserted only a limited identification and record-keeping interest, but was precluded as to vessels ... which it has specifically licensed to engage in [a particular fishing activity]."

Some states have statutorily defined the term "registration" for purposes of extraterritorial jurisdiction over fisheries. For example, Maine's fishing license statute defines a registered vessel as one owned or operated by the possessor of a fishing license. In *State v. Hayes*, 603 A.2d 869 (Me. 1992), the Maine Supreme Court determined that possession of a Maine commercial fishing and lobster license meant that the defendant's vessel was registered within the meaning of section 1856(a). The vessel did not possess a state identification or registration number. Interpreting section 1856(a) to give effect to each state's definition of registration may subject a vessel to the simultaneous, and possibly conflicting, regulation of more than one state while fishing in the EEZ, leading to confusion for the vessel owner and enforcement authorities.

b. Meaning of "Consistent"

The MSA allows substantial confusion to continue by not entirely preempting state regulation beyond state waters when a federal plan and regulations are in place. States may still regulate state-registered vessels if no federal FMP is in place or if their laws and regulations are "consistent" with "the fishery management plan and applicable Federal fishing regulations." 16 U.S.C. § 1856(a)(3)(A). Further, the state can regulate other fishing vessels beyond state waters if the Secretary delegates management to a state with laws and regulations consistent with the applicable federal FMP. 16 U.S.C. § 1856(a)(3)(B). Significantly, the term, "consistent," was not defined in either case. It is clear that less restrictive regulation would not be consistent with the conservation regime of FMPs, but it is not entirely clear that more restrictive state regulations are consistent. Several courts have held that because the purposes of the MSA include development of the fishing industry, state regulations that restrict fishing in the EEZ beyond the level allowed in federal FMPs are not consistent. See, e.g., *Southeastern Fisheries Ass'n, Inc. v. Chiles*, 979 F.2d 1504 (11th Cir. 1992); *State v. Sterling*, 448 A.2d 785 (R.I. 1982); *Vietnamese Fishermen Assn. of America v. California Department of Fish and Game*, 816 F.Supp. 1468 (N.D.Cal. 1993); but see *Louisiana Seafood Mgmt. Council v. Foster*, 917 F. Supp. 439 (The "spirit and purpose of the Magnuson Act is to protect and conserve saltwater finfish" and does not preempt state regulation).

c. Federal Preemption

MSA 306(a)(3)'s approval of state EEZ fisheries regulations which are consistent with federal FMPs, laws, or regulations presents issues similar to federal preemption questions. A court's analysis of whether a federal law preempts state regulation generally focuses on three issues: (1) Did Congress intend to occupy the field?; (2) Is there a conflict?; and (3) Does the state regulation present an obstacle to the goals and purposes of the federal law? *Douglas v. Seacoast Products*, 431 U.S. 265, 97 S.Ct. 1740, 52 L.Ed.2d 304 (1977).

In the fisheries management context, the first issue involves the question of whether the mere enactment of the MSA preempts state fishery regulation in the EEZ. If by enacting the MSA Congress evidenced intent, either express or implied, to occupy the entire field of fishery regulation, then any state fishery regulation is preempted by the Act. *State v. F/V Baranof*, 677 P.2d 1245 (Alaska 1984) (holding that Alaska laws had not been expressly preempted by the MSA and that no federal regulations had impliedly displaced state regulation of the crab fishery). Most courts have determined that mere enactment of the MSA does not preempt state fishery regulations. E.g., *State v. Dupier*, 118 P.3d 1039 (Alaska 2005); *Louisiana Seafood Management Council, Inc. v. Foster*, 917 F.Supp. 439 (E.D.La. 1996); *Anderson Seafoods, Inc. v. Graham*, 529 F.Supp. 512 (N.D.Fla. 1982); *State v. Painter*, 695 P.2d 241 (Alaska App. 1985); *State v. F/V Baranof*, 677 P.2d 1245 (Alaska 1984); *Livings v. Davis*, 465

So.2d 507 (Fla. 1985). Although the enactment of the MSA manifests a strong federal interest in fisheries regulation, section 1856(a)(3) expressly precludes a finding that Congress intended for the MSA to preempt all state EEZ fishery regulations through complete occupation of the field.

Preemption can also occur when a state law conflicts with a federal FMP, laws, or regulations. Obviously, state regulations that are more lenient than a federal FMP, laws, or regulations present a conflict. The harder question has arisen in the context of more restrictive state regulation, and courts have come to inconsistent conclusions. Some courts find no conflict if it is possible to comply with both laws. See, e.g., *Skiriotes v. Florida,* 313 U.S. 69, 61 S.Ct. 924, 85 L.Ed. 1193 (1941)(a Florida statute regulating equipment used for sponge fishing did not conflict with a federal law regulating the size of sponges that could be taken); *Potter v. McCullers,* 505 So.2d 510 (Fla.Dist.Ct.App. 1987)(finding application of a Florida shrimping regulation constitutional when enforced beyond state waters but outside of a federally regulated shrimp sanctuary).

As a general proposition, federal environmental laws usually do not preempt more protective state legislation. However, some courts have found state regulations preempted by less restrictive federal rules for the same fishery. See, e.g., *Southeastern Fisheries Ass'n, Inc. v. Chiles,* 979 F.2d 1504 (11th Cir. 1992); *State v. Sterling,* 448 A.2d 785 (R.I. 1982). A slight deviation between a state and a federal regulation that are "substantially the same" will not lead to preemption. *State v. Painter*, 695 P.2d 241 (Alaska App. 1985)(finding no conflict between state and federal regulations when the only difference between the two regulations was that the state law provided criminal sanctions and the federal regulation provided civil sanctions).

Consistent with section 306(a)(3)(B), 16 U.S.C.A. § 1856(a)(3)(A), state regulation has been upheld because a federal FMP, law, or regulation expressly permits enforcement of the stricter state law. *State v. Hayes*, 603 A.2d 869 (Me. 1992)(finding no conflict when federal regulations contained language that retained local and state "fishing, catch and gear" requirements and permitted enforcement of more restrictive state lobster regulations); *Raffield v. State*, 565 So.2d 704 (Fla. 1990)(finding no conflict when the preamble to federal red drum fishery rules expressly stated that state landing laws were not superseded by the rules). However, in *Southeastern Fisheries Ass'n v. Mosbacher*, 773 F.Supp. 435 (D.D.C. 1991), the D.C. District Court struck down federal regulations for the Gulf of Mexico red drum fishery that provided for state landing and possession laws to continue to be enforced. The court found that failure to preempt state landing laws was arbitrary and capricious and an abuse of the Secretary's discretion. In effect, the FMP allowed fishermen to catch redfish within the EEZ, but not land them, since four of five Gulf States prohibited or restricted landing.

Finally, preemption may occur when a state fishery regulation presents an obstacle to the goals and purposes of the federal FMP, law, or regulation. When a state enforces regulations stricter than the federal FMP, without specific authorization in the FMP, state regulations may be viewed as presenting an obstacle to MSA goals of promoting domestic commercial fishing and preventing piecemeal extraterritorial state regulation. *Bateman v. Gardner*, 716 F.Supp. 595 (S.D.Fla. 1989); *Southeastern Fisheries Ass'n v. Martinez*, 772 F.Supp. 1263 (S.D.Fla. 1991).

d. Enforcement Issues

Enactment of the MSA has also created enforcement problems for the states, even for regulations that apply only within state waters. Landing or possession laws are the primary means for enforcing fisheries regulations. These laws can have the effect of regulating out-of-state citizens in the EEZ. Even enforcement against a state's citizen fishing in the EEZ of state gear restrictions by laws prohibiting possession can be problematic if the prohibited gear is expressly permitted by a federal FMP, law, or regulation. *Vietnamese Fishermen Ass'n v. California Fish & Game Dept.*, 816 F.Supp. 1468 (N.D.Cal. 1993). In *Southeastern Fisheries Ass'n v. Department of Natural Resources*, 453 So.2d 1351 (Fla. 1984), the Florida Supreme Court found that a Florida law prohibiting the use or possession of fish traps within state waters unconstitutionally limited the legal use of the traps in the EEZ. Although the state could continue to prosecute fishermen for unlawful possession of fishtraps, the state "must prove, as an element of possession, the intent to unlawfully use the fish traps" in Florida waters—a virtually impossible burden in the majority of field enforcement situations.

C.   UNITED STATES AND INTERNATIONAL FISHERIES LAW

While the Magnuson-Stevens Act (MSA) was adopted in 1976 before UNCLOS was concluded to address overexploitation of North Atlantic fisheries, the U.S. has been in full support of the UNCLOS fisheries management regime that was developed in part on the basis of MSA principles.

UNCLOS provides that EEZ fisheries should be managed and conserved by the coastal state using the best scientific information available to assure maintenance or restoration of populations at a level of maximum sustainable yield "as qualified by relevant environmental and economic factors." See UNCLOS Art. 61(2)–(3); see also, 16 U.S.C. §§ 1802(21), 1851. UNCLOS requires coastal nations to "promote the objective of optimum utilization" of EEZ fishery resources, but does not require full utilization. Because countries have total discretion in establishing allowable catch, limited only by the duty not to overexploit, the requirement that other countries have access to surplus stocks can be illusory. See UNCLOS, Articles 61, 62(2). Foreign fishing nations have no recourse under UNCLOS if a coastal nation sets the allowable catch at the same level as domestic harvesting capacity, leaving no surplus.

When a coastal country sets its allowable catch at a level that yields a surplus that is available to foreign fishermen, UNCLOS provides that all relevant factors should be taken into account in allocating the surplus, including the coastal nation's economic and other national interests, the rights and needs of geographically disadvantaged and land-locked countries, the requirements of developing countries in the region, and the "need to minimize economic dislocation in [countries] whose nationals have habitually fished in the zone or which made substantial efforts in research and identification of stocks." Id. art. 62(3).

1. ILLEGAL, UNREPORTED, AND UNREGULATED FISHING

UNCLOS does not explicitly prohibit illegal, unreported, and unregulated fishing (IUU Fishing) but does require States to cooperate in fisheries management. After UNCLOS went into effect, the FAO developed a voluntary international plan of action (IPOA) to deter Illegal, Unreported, and Unregulated (IUU) fishing that is not controlled by flag state or coastal state action. Nations are encouraged to develop national plans of action that use "all available jurisdiction in accordance with international law" and to adopt not only market-related measures, but also port state measures, coastal state measures, and measures to ensure that their nationals do not support or engage in IUU fishing. See *International Plan of Action to Prevent, Deter and Eliminate Illegal, Unreported and Unregulated Fishing* (FAO 2001).

a. U.S. Response to IUU Fishing

The U.S. first set out its response to the FAO's voluntary IPOA with a *National Plan of Action of the United States of America to Prevent, Deter, and Eliminate Illegal, Unregulated, and Unreported Fishing* (2004) (NPOA), an effort coordinated by the U.S. Department of State in conjunction with NOAA, NMFS, the U.S. Coast Guard, the Office of the U.S. Trade Representative, the U.S. Fish and Wildlife Service and the U.S. Customs Service. The NPOA also made recommendations for strengthening U.S. efforts to address IUU fishing. The 2006 Reauthorization of the MSA implemented many of these recommendations.

In 1992, Congress passed the High Seas Driftnet Fisheries Enforcement Act (1992) (building on the earlier Driftnet Impact Monitoring, Assessment, and Control Act of 1987), which bans imports of fish and sport fishing equipment from nations whose nationals are not respecting the United Nations' moratorium on large-scale high seas driftnet fishing and denies port privileges to offending vessels. 16 U.S.C.A. § 1826a; UNGA Resolution 46/215 (1991) (calling for a worldwide driftnet moratorium as of December 31, 1992). The legislation was strengthened by the High Seas Driftnet Fishing Moratorium Protection Act (Moratorium Act) in 1995.

The United States has also passed legislation to implement the Agreement to Promote Compliance with International Conservation and Management Measures by Fishing Vessels on the High Seas (the

Compliance Agreement), which was adopted by the Conference of the FAO in 1993. Under the Compliance Agreement, States parties that flag high seas vessels agreed to take such measures as may be necessary to ensure that their flagged fishing vessels do not engage in any activity that undermines the effectiveness of international conservation and management measures. The High Seas Fishing Compliance Act of 1995, 16 U.S.C. §§ 5501–5509, establishes a system of permitting, reporting and regulation for United States vessels on the high seas.

The 2006 Reauthorization of the MSA (amending the Moratorium Act) is the most far-reaching U.S. legislation on international fisheries. The Reauthorization set out directives for the U.S. to address illegal, unreported, and unregulated (IUU) fishing, and the related issues of strengthening international fisheries management organizations, and preventing bycatch of protected living marine resources.[21]   16   U.S.C.A.   §§ 1826i–1826k.   The Moratorium Protection Act was further amended in 2011 by the Shark Conservation Act, (Pub. L. 111–348), to extend the Act to domestic and international conservation of sharks. See 77 Fed. Reg. 40554 (July 10, 2012); see also the Shark Finning Prohibition Act, 16   U.S.C.A.   § 1822,   and   *United   States   v. Approximately 64,695 Pounds of Shark Fins*, 520 F.3d 976 (2008) (holding the Shark Finning Act inapplicable to vessels transshipping fins; case led to

---

[21]   NMFS has compiled a list of protected living marine resources for purposes of applying the Act, available at http:// www.nmfs.noaa.gov/msa2007/docs/list_of_protected_lmr_act_022 610.pdf.

amendment of the act). The Moratorium Act sets out guidelines for defining IUU fishing that are implemented at 50 CFR 300.201 as follows:

(1) Fishing activities that violate conservation and management measures required under an international fishery management agreement to which the United States is a party, including but not limited to catch limits or quotas, capacity restrictions, and bycatch reduction requirements;

(2) Overfishing of fish stocks shared by the United States, for which there are no applicable international conservation or management measures or in areas with no applicable international fishery management organization or agreement, that has adverse impacts on such stocks; or,

(3) Fishing activity that has a significant adverse impact on seamounts, hydrothermal vents, cold water corals and other vulnerable marine ecosystems located beyond any national jurisdiction, for which there are no applicable conservation or management measures, including those in areas with no applicable international fishery management organization or agreement.

NMFS is required to report biennially to Congress on nations identified as having vessels:

(1) engaged in IUU fishing,

(2) bycatch of Protected Living Marine Resources, and/or

(3) high seas fisheries targeting or incidentally catching sharks that are not regulated by a program for the conservation of sharks comparable to that of the United States, taking into account different conditions.

16 U.S.C.A. § 1826h. The U.S. consults with nations identified as IUU fishing nations to provide the opportunity for nations to comply with international fisheries management and conservation agreements and to adopt bycatch reduction methods in international fisheries that are comparable to methods used in U.S. fisheries. An identified nation that is not certified by the Secretary of Commerce as having taken appropriate measures to address IUU fishing or bycatch of protected living marine resources is subject to import prohibitions on certain fish products and port access limitations. In 2011, NMFS published a final rule creating procedures for the identification and certification of nations under the provisions of the act. See 76 Fed. Reg. 2100 (Jan. 14, 2011).

In 2014, the U.S. bolstered its authority to prohibit imports of fish caught by IUU fishing by ratifying the FAO's Port State Measures Agreement (PSMA). In November 2015, President Obama signed into law the Illegal, Unreported and Unregulated Fishing Enforcement Act. This act increased the enforcement authority of the U.S. Coast Guard and NOAA to deny both national and foreign vessels alleged to be IUU fishing port entry and services. The law also provided for the development and distribution of a list of known IUU vessels and established civil and criminal penalties for IUU vessels violating the Antigua Convention of 2003. The PSMA Agreement came into force June 2016.

In December 2016, NOAA began implementing the U.S. Seafood Import Monitoring Program requiring permitting, data reporting, and recordkeeping requirements for thirteen priority commercial species including tunas and king crab. 15 CFR Part 902 (December 9, 2016). The program was nearing full implementation by December 2018.

b. Future Challenges to Control of IUU Fishing

Attention continues to be focused on ending IUU fishing. For example, the Division of Sustainable Development of the U.N. Department of Economic and Social Affairs identifies IUU fishing as a major issue for action in the 2030 Agenda for Sustainable Development, which was adopted by all U.N. member states in 2015. Sustainable Development Goal 14 on conserving ocean resources includes Target 14.4 requiring States by 2020 to "effectively regulate harvesting and end overfishing, illegal, unreported and unregulated fishing and destructive fishing practices and implement science-based management plans" to restore fisheries. Other non-governmental organizations have also invested in improving the availability of information about potential IUU fishing and oil spills. Collecting data from a variety of sources including satellites, vessel monitoring systems, and vessel automatic identification systems, Global Fishing Watch provides the public near real-time data on marine fishing activity of over 65,000 commercial vessels. Several states including Indonesia, Peru, and Costa Rica have made its proprietary vessel monitoring data public.

A particular challenge for combating IUU fishing is tackling transshipment which involves the movement of fish from fishing vessels to cargo vessels. This practice decreases transparency and is likely to encourage the mixing of legal and illegally captured seafood.[22]

The FAO has developed Technical Guidelines for transshipment at sea to minimize illegal activities. FAO Technical Guidelines for Responsible Fisheries—Fisheries Management Suppl. 4 Marine Protected Areas and Fisheries (FAO 2011) There are no global regulations on transshipment, but five of the high seas Regional Fisheries Management Organizations have a partial ban on transshipment on the high seas, and the Southeast Atlantic Fisheries Organization has banned at-sea transshipments.

---

[22] See Anastasia Telesetsky, Laundering Fish in the Global Undercurrents: Illegal, Unreported, and Unregulated Fishing and Transnational Organized Crime, 41 Ecol. Law Q., 939 (2015)(describing further consequences of IUU fishing and proposals for control).

2. THE PROBLEM OF STRADDLING STOCKS AND "DONUT HOLES": THE BERING SEA POLLOCK

The 200 nautical mile EEZ jurisdictions of the Russia and the U.S. enclose a small area of the Bering Sea that is referred to as the "donut hole." Because the area is high seas and not subject to Russian or United States fishing regulation, exploitation of the pollock fishery by foreign vessels was uncontrolled for many years. The situation is a classic example of the problem of so-called "straddling stocks." In the 1980s, Japan, Korea, China, and Poland vessels severely overfished the area of the central Bering Sea creating severe conservation problems for pollock. Negotiations were initiated in 1991 to develop a multilateral regime for pollock exploitation in the central Bering Sea. During the three-year period of negotiations, all the parties voluntarily suspended fishing for pollock in the "donut hole" as well as in adjacent EEZs.

The Convention on the Conservation and Management of Pollock Resources in the Central Bering Sea, with Annex, *done* June 16, 1994, establishes an international regime for the conservation and management of pollock resources in the "donut hole." An Annual Conference will establish the allowable harvest level (AHL) and individual national quotas (INQs), as well as other conservation and management measures for pollock and define the plan of work for the Scientific and Technical Committee. The Convention contains strong enforcement provisions requiring that vessels fishing for pollock in the Convention area carry scientific observers and use real-time satellite position-fixing transmitters, and allowing boarding and inspection of all fishing vessels of any Party to the Convention by authorized officials of any other Party for compliance with the Convention.

3.   U.S. PARTICIPATION IN REGIONAL FISHERIES MANAGEMENT ORGANIZATIONS

The United States is a party to the 1995 UN Fish Stocks Agreement that empowers regional fisheries management organizations (RFMOs) to adopt appropriate fisheries management programs for the high seas and take effective measures against IUU fishing. The U.S. is a member of several existing RFMOs and has participated in the development of new regional fisheries arrangements. In November 1995 the United States joined the Northwest Atlantic Fisheries Organization (NAFO), the successor to International Commission of the Northwest Atlantic Fisheries (ICNAF) (1949–1978). The United States has also participated in negotiation of the recently concluded Western and Central Pacific Fisheries Commission, which establishes conservation and management measures for all countries and vessels operating in the region. In addition, the U.S. has been a member of the International Commission for the Conservation of Atlantic Tunas (ICCAT) since 1976. ICCAT has also incorporated important principles of the U.N. Fish Stocks Agreement into rules for members and for nonmembers fishing within the region.

The United States is a party to the South Pacific Tuna Treaty with 16 Pacific Island states. U.S. purse seine vessels are permitted to fish for a certain number of fishing days within the EEZ of Pacific Island states in exchange for a payment. Implementing the treaty has helped to improve monitoring, control and surveillance in the region's tuna fisheries. In 2016, the U.S. State Department announced that the U.S. would be withdrawing from the treaty with an end date in January 2017, because U.S. tuna vessels could not pay fees for the 8,250 fishing days that the U.S. had agreed to. The U.S. tuna fishing business has been economically contracting due to competition with fleets from other nations. In December 2016, a six-year extension to 2022 was agreed upon. The new arrangement specifies the number of potential fishing days the US fleet can purchase, the EEZs in which they can be used and the costs for each of those days (reportedly US$12,500/day for the first two years). The renegotiated agreement provides for more participation by Pacific Island Parties to maximize benefits related to the operation of the US fleet in the region. As part of the treaty arrangement, the U.S. government will continue to provide US$21 million annually as economic assistance to the Pacific Island region

The 2006 MSA Reauthorization called on the U.S. to "improve the effectiveness of international fishery management organizations in conserving and managing fish stocks under their jurisdiction." 16 U.S.C.A. § 1826i. The United States is currently a member of numerous RFMOs that cooperatively manage fisheries across the world's oceans. Some of these RFMOs are specific to tuna fishing while other RFMOs cover a broader set of commercial fisheries.

Pacific Ocean
<ul><li>Inter-American Tropical Tuna Commission (IATTC)</li><li>Western and Central Pacific Fisheries Commission (WCPFC)</li><li>North Pacific Anadromous Fish Commission</li><li>South Pacific Regional Fisheries Management Organization (SPRFMO)</li><li>International Pacific Halibut Commission</li></ul>
Atlantic Ocean
<ul><li>International Commission for the Conservation of Atlantic Tunas (ICCAT)</li><li>North Atlantic Salmon Conservation Organization (NASCO)</li><li>Northwest Atlantic Fisheries Organization (NAFO)</li><li>Western Central Atlantic Fisheries Commission</li></ul>
Southern Ocean
<ul><li>Commission for the Conservation of Antarctic Marine Living Resources (CCAMLR)</li></ul>
Indian Ocean
<ul><li>Indian Ocean Tuna Commission (IOTC)</li></ul>

Several of the RFMOs that the U.S. participates in use catch documentation and certification schemes to ensure compliance with and enforcement of their management programs. E.g., CCAMLR and the IATTC have adopted catch certification programs, and ICCAT has adopted statistical document programs for several species. The United States seeks to encourage RMFOs to increase their effectiveness through adoption and authorization of more market-based measures against IUU fishing, better identification and monitoring of IUU fishing vessels, and adoption of stronger port state controls. By working through these and other international organizations, the United States hopes to avoid unilateral action and take effective action against IUU fishing that is consistent with WTO obligations.

CHAPTER X

PRESERVING THE BIODIVERSITY OF THE SEAS

Not very long ago, the living resources of the oceans were considered inexhaustible—beyond the ability of humans to overexploit or destroy. The ingenuity of mankind and the advances in technology in the last century proved that those assumptions are far from true. While the world is far from adequately addressing preservation of biodiversity on an ecosystem scale, by the last few decades of the 20th century, the United States and other nations were beginning to address the rapid decline in populations of some key species. This chapter looks at protection of marine mammals, including whales, and legislation protecting endangered species.

A. THE MARINE MAMMAL PROTECTION ACT

The Marine Mammal Protection Act of 1972 (MMPA), 16 U.S.C.A. §§ 1361–1421h, includes protection of a diversity of species including whales, dolphins, porpoises, seals, sea otters, manatees, dugongs, walruses, and polar bears. Id. § 1362(6).[1] In 1972, Congress recognized the possibility that iconic

---

[1]   The Departments of Commerce and the Interior administer the MMPA. Through the National Marine Fisheries Service (NMFS), the Secretary of Commerce has responsibility for whales, porpoises, dolphins, seals, and sea lions. The Secretary of Interior, through the Fish and Wildlife Service (FWS), is responsible for other marine mammals, including walruses, polar bears, manatees, and sea otters. Id. § 1362(12)(A).

marine mammals were at risk of extinction unless human activities that were damaging the marine environment were controlled. As Congress noted:

> [M]arine mammals have proven . . . to be resources of great international significance, esthetic and recreational as well as economic, and . . . should be protected and encouraged to develop to the greatest extent feasible commensurate with sound policies of resource management and . . . the primary objective of their management should be to maintain the health and stability of the marine ecosystem. Whenever consistent with this primary objective, it should be the goal to obtain an optimum sustainable population keeping in mind the carrying capacity of the habitat.

Id. § 1361(6).

The MMPA takes a precautionary approach to protecting marine mammals by focusing on conserving sustainable populations. The key institution created by the MMPA is the Marine Mammal Commission, an independent scientific advisory body. The three-member Commission is appointed by the President, subject to Senate confirmation, and is charged with continuing review and assessment of marine mammal stocks, conservation methods, and research programs. The Commission's recommendations are directed to the development of both domestic policies and international arrangements for conservation of marine mammals. Id. §§ 1401–1402.

The FWS and NMFS are required to complete a stock assessment report for each marine mammal stock present in waters under U.S. jurisdiction on the basis of the best scientific information available. Stock assessments should be reviewed either annually for stocks, for which there is significant new information or that have been specified as "strategic stocks," or once every 3 years for other marine mammals.

1. THE MORATORIUM AND ITS LIMITATIONS

The heart of the MMPA is a moratorium on the taking and importation of marine mammals and marine mammal products. Id. § 1371(a). "The term 'take' means to harass, hunt, capture, or kill. . . ." Id. § 1362(13). The moratorium applies to actions of United States citizens on the high seas, but does not apply extraterritorially to the taking of marine mammals in the territorial waters of other nations *United States v. Mitchell*, 553 F.2d 996 (5th Cir. 1977). A "take" that is knowing and intentional violates the MMPA, while an action that accidentally or unintentionally harms a marine mammal may be an excepted "incidental take." *Pac. Ranger, LLC v. Pritzker,* 211 F. Supp. 3d 196 (D.D.C. 2016) (Characterizing the MMPA as a "strict liability" statute requiring no mens rea, the Court found fishermen who set nets and a fish aggregating device in an area with knowledge that whales were present in the area in violation of the MMPA. Such action could not be considered "accidental" and "unintentional").

The moratorium is not absolute and contains a waiver provision, a number of exceptions, and an exemption for Alaskan natives.

a. Moratorium Waiver

To authorize a waiver of the moratorium, the Secretary generally must determine that a species or stock is at its optimum sustainable population (OSP) and that the waiver will not reduce the population below that level. The concept of OSP is unique and is presumably something different from the principle of maximum sustainable yield (MSY), which is often used in the management of commercially exploited wildlife. However, the definition of OSP is ambiguous, factoring in the carrying capacity of the environment and the health of the ecosystem, as well as the maximum productivity of the species. Id. § 1362(9). Taking marine mammals subject to a waiver of the moratorium requires a permit setting the number and kind of animals to be taken, the time period and place, and other conditions. Waivers on the importation of marine mammals or products require the Secretary to certify that the program for taking marine mammals in the country of origin is "consistent" with the MMPA. Id. § 1371(a)(3)(A).

b. Exception to the Moratorium for Scientific Research, Public Display, or Enhancing Survival and Recovery of a Species of Stock

(1) Scientific Research Permits

The first statutory exception to the moratorium is the authorization for the Secretary to issue permits "for purposes of scientific research, public display, or enhancing the survival or recovery of a species or stock." 16 U.S.C.A. § 1371(a)(1). Applicants for scientific research permits must demonstrate the bona fide, nonduplicative research need for taking the animal. Permits for lethal research are issued only in limited circumstances when alternatives are not feasible. Captive maintenance of an animal requires a showing that removal is necessary and that the animal will be returned to the ocean as quickly as feasible. Permits for scientific or public display purposes are subject to the environmental assessment procedures of NEPA. See *Jones v. Gordon*, 792 F.2d 821 (9th Cir. 1986) (permit for capture of killer whales for scientific and public display purposes invalid for failure to prepare an environmental impact statement).

(2) Public Display

The MMPA may authorize the issuance of permits to take or import marine mammals for a public display to applicants who offer "a [public] program for education or conservation purposes ... based on professionally recognized standards of the public display community." Id. § 1374(c)(2)(A)(i). See also *Animal Protection Inst. of Am. v. Mosbacher*, 799 F.Supp. 173 (D.D.C. 1992) (Secretary had not abused his discretion in issuing import permits for public display of whales without determining OSP when evidence indicated that stocks of the species were abundant). A permit to take a marine mammal for public display, however, may not be issued for a stock that has been designated by the Secretary as depleted. "Depleted" means that the population is below OSP or that the species is listed as endangered or threatened under the Endangered Species Act. Id. § 1362(1). If a species is listed as threatened or endangered under the Endangered Species Act (ESA), a scientific research or enhancement permit is necessary for the marine mammal to be held at a public display facility.

In *Georgia Aquarium, Inc. v. Pritzker*, 135 F. Supp. 3d 1280 (N.D. Ga. 2015), the court upheld NMFS's denial of a permit to import eighteen beluga whales from Russia for public display. Georgia Aquarium sought to import the beluga whales "to enhance the North American beluga breeding cooperative by increasing the population base of captive belugas to a self-sustaining level and to promote conservation and education." NMFS stated it was unable to make the required finding that the proposed activity, by itself or in combination with other activities, would not likely have had a significant adverse impact on the species or stock. See 50 C.F.R. § 216.34(a)(7). Because of continuing marine capture operations in Russia and other issues raised by NMFS with regard to subsistence hunting, pollution, climate change and more, Georgia Aquarium could not carry its burden to demonstrate that the permit "would [not] contribute to the demand to capture belugas from this stock for the purpose of public display worldwide, resulting in the future taking of additional belugas from this stock." See also Megan E. Boyd, Georgia Aquarium v. Pritzker: The Beginning of the End for Belugas in Captivity in the United States, 25 Animal L. 93, 118 (2019)("[I]t is not clear what else the

Aquarium could have done to meet its strict burden of proof.").

(3) Regulation of Marine Mammals in Captivity and Swim-with-Dolphin Programs

Prior to the 1994 amendments to the MMPA, NMFS shared authority over marine mammals while in captivity with the Department of Agriculture (DOA). The 1994 MMPA amendments delegated primary authority to DOA to manage the care of marine mammals in public display facilities under the Animal Welfare Act (AWA) and removed the requirement for an MMPA permit to hold an animal for public display, 7 U.S.C.A. §§ 2131–2159. DOA developed rules for such facilities through a negotiated rulemaking process. Scientists and animal welfare advocates have expressed concern that the regulations do not meet the needs of the animals, that existing rules need stronger enforcement, and that the regulated facilities should exert less influence in standard setting.

DOA currently allows numerous programs for dolphin/human interaction including feeding pools and swim-with-dolphin programs. Critics claim these programs put the dolphins and humans at risk. DOA developed rules in 1998 to regulate such programs, but "suspended enforcement" of the rules in 1999. See 9 C.F.R. 3.111 and 64 FR 15918. Allowing such programs sends mixed signals to the public who are prohibited from having similar interactions with dolphins in the wild.

(4) Feeding Dolphins in the Wild

Congress amended the MMPA in 1992 to direct the Secretary to carry out studies to determine if the feeding of dolphins in the wild had adverse effects on their health or behavior, but it did not require that vessel operators who take tourists to offshore sites to feed dolphins get a waiver or permit to take dolphins. NMFS regulations requiring a permit were upheld in *Strong v. Secretary of Commerce,* 5 F.3d 905 (5th Cir.1993). Current regulations categorize feeding marine mammals in the wild as prohibited harassment and taking under the MMPA. See 50 C.F.R. pt. 216.

(5) Rehabilitation Facilities

Stranded, sick, or injured marine mammals are often rehabilitated in private facilities. Through the Marine Mammal Health and Stranding Response Program, 16 U.S.C. §§ 1421, 1421b.2, NMFS has created a network of private and governmental stranding organizations to rescue and rehabilitate marine mammals. These organizations must apply for an MMPA permit. The organizations are deemed custodians of stranded marine mammals and are authorized to "take" stranded animals, attempt to rehabilitate them, and reintroduce them into the wild. Animals in rehabilitation are required to be released within six months unless they are determined to be unreleasable because of injuries, medical conditions, and behavioral issues.

Prior to releasing a rehabilitated animal into the wild, the custodian is required to provide a release

plan to NMFS for approval. 50 C.F.R. § 216.27(a).
NMFS has discretion concerning animals considered
non-releasable, including allowing the custodian to
keep the animal or transfer it to an approved facility,
or requiring the custodian to euthanize it. 50 C.F.R.
§ 216.27(b). NMFS may require that rehabilitated
marine mammals be used for public display and
educational purposes in lieu of animals taken from
the wild. 50 C.F.R. § 216.27(b)(4); § 216.27(c)(1). See
NMFS Procedural Directive, *Process for Placing Non-
Releasable Marine Mammals from the Stranding
Program into Permanent Care Facilities* (2012),
available   at   http://www.nmfs.noaa.gov/op/pds/
documents/2/308/02–308–02.pdf. See also *Inst. of
Marine Mammal Studies v. Nat'l Marine Fisheries
Serv.*, 23 F.Supp.3d 705, 2014 WL 2154348
(S.D.Miss. 2014) (remanding denial of a take permit
for a releasable, stranded sea lion, because NMFS
improperly delegated federal authority to a stranding
organization).

c. Exceptions to the Moratorium for Incidental Take in Commercial Fishing Operations and Take Reduction Plans

The second exception to the moratorium is for
permits for taking marine mammals incidental to
commercial fishing operations. Id. § 1371(a)(2). What
constitutes an incidental take has been the subject of
both regulation and litigation.

Taking of marine mammals incidental to fishing
operations can potentially be authorized under three
provisions of the MMPA: (1) The Secretary can issue

permits under a waiver; (2) the Secretary can issue a permit for marine mammals taken incidental to commercial fishing operations under the MMPA, 16 U.S.C.A. § 1371; or (3) under a 1981 amendment to the MMPA, id. § 1371(a)(4), the Secretary can issue general permits through formal rulemaking to allow the taking of "small numbers" of nondepleted marine mammals incidental to commercial fishing by U.S. citizens if the total taking has "negligible impact" on the species or stock. Importantly, none of these sections provides authority for permitting a taking in fishing operations of depleted species, i.e., species that are not at or above optimum sustainable population (OSP) or that are threatened or endangered. See *Earth Island Institute v. Brown*, 865 F.Supp. 1364 (N.D.Cal. 1994).

NMFS has properly interpreted the exception to only apply to unintentional and incidental takes of marine mammals. *Black v. Pritzker,* 121 F. Supp. 3d 63 (D.D.C. 2015) (Finding that defendant captains and owners of vessels failed to comply with MMPA Certificate of Authorization permitting "the incidental, but not intentional, taking of marine mammals").

In *Kokechik Fishermen's Ass'n v. Secretary of Commerce*, 839 F.2d 795, 268 U.S.App.D.C. 116 (D.C.Cir. 1988), fishermen and environmentalists challenged the issuance of a permit to the Japan Salmon Fisheries Cooperative Association to take Dall's porpoises in the course of their salmon fishing in the North Pacific. The permit did not include northern fur seals and other marine mammals that would also foreseeably be taken. The Secretary had concluded that it was not possible to make a finding as to whether certain northern fur seal populations were at or above OSP. The federal court of appeals held that issuance of the permit was contrary to the MMPA, because "it allowed incidental taking of various species of protected marine mammals without first ascertaining as to each such species whether or not the population of that species was at the OSP level." Id.

The court's decision conflicted with the agency's past practice and had a number of immediate ramifications for both domestic and foreign fishermen. With no authority in the MMPA for issuing permits for the incidental take of depleted species, the Secretary's ability to issue *any* incidental take permits was questionable. First, no permit could be issued if it was known that even small numbers of depleted species would be taken in a fishery. Second, in almost any fishery, the Secretary would be unlikely to be able to make the findings required by the court in order to issue a permit either because information was inadequate to determine which animals were likely to be taken incidentally or because data was insufficient to determine whether the population of such species was at OSP and would not be disadvantaged.

While Congress adopted the MMPA to prevent the excessive dolphin mortality caused by environmentally damaging fishing techniques such as those deployed by the tuna purse seiners in East Pacific Ocean, Congress also recognized that it was extremely difficult to commercially fish with zero bycatch. When the MMPA was drafted, Congress provided a special two-year exemption for commercial fishing of tuna after the MMPA was enacted. After the initial two-year period, continued incidental take was by permit and subject to the same type of regulations governing issuance of permits for a waiver. Before issuing a permit, NMFS is required to determine the impact of a take on a species "optimum sustainable population." The "immediate goal" was that incidental kill of marine mammals be "reduced to insignificant levels approaching a zero mortality . . . rate." 16 U.S.C.A. § 1371(a)(2).

In 1981, the MMPA was amended to provide that the goal of achieving "insignificant levels" of marine mammal mortality would be satisfied "in the course of purse seine fishing for yellowfin tuna by a continuation of the application of the best . . . safety techniques and equipment that are economically and technologically practicable." 16 U.S.C.A. § 1371(a)(2). The MMPA was again amended in 1988 to put additional restrictions on incidental take of dolphins and porpoises. Tuna boats are now required to carry officials observers. § 1374(h).

Amendments in 1984 and 1988 to the MMPA required the Secretary to impose bans on importation of tuna from nations that did not regulate incidental take of marine mammals to produce a rate of taking comparable to U.S. vessels. These amendments eventually became the basis for the Tuna/Dolphin international trade disputes discussed in Section X.A.4 infra.

Because so little information was available about marine mammal interactions with fishing, other than with tuna fishing, Congress responded to the *Kokechik* case in 1988 by enacting a five-year interim exemption to allow commercial fisheries to operate while information necessary for management of interactions was compiled. See 16 U.S.C.A. § 1383a. This was followed by 1994 amendments requiring NMFS to prepare stock assessments for all marine mammal species under U.S. jurisdiction whether healthy or in decline. 16 U.S.C.A. § 1386.

The assessments must include a determination of the stock potential biological removal (PBR) level and a recovery factor and are subject to review by regional scientific review groups. The amendments reaffirmed the Act's overall goal of reducing the incidental kill or serious injury rate from commercial fishing operations to insignificant levels approaching zero, and for the first time set a specific deadline of seven years after enactment for its achievement. 16 U.S.C.A. § 1387. These new provisions require the Secretary to issue a general authorization for the incidental lethal takes occurring during fishing to those vessels that register under an extension of the existing vessel registration system provided by the Act in section 1383a. Mandatory fishing vessel reporting program for vessels with frequent and occasional interactions with marine mammals, a mandatory observer program for those vessels to verify data on mortality and injury, a prohibition on intentional lethal takes, and emergency authority for the Secretary to intervene when particular stocks are declining were also included in the 1994 provisions.

The Secretary has also established take reduction teams, composed of industry, government, and non-resource user group representatives, to prepare take reduction plans for marine mammal populations most affected by commercial fishing. 16 U.S.C. § 1387(f)(7)(B)(i). The plans' goals are to reduce incidental take levels to below the potential biological removal level for these stocks within six months and to insignificant levels approaching zero within five years. The teams must recommend regulatory or voluntary measures to meet these reductions. 16 U.S.C. § 1387(f)(2). The Secretary must then implement an approved plan and set, *inter alia,* fishery-specific limits on takes and time as well as area restrictions on fishing operations. If a plan fails to achieve these targets, the Secretary must revise it and set regulations to meet the goals.

The most controversial take reduction plan is the one developed for the large whales of the Northwest Atlantic that are entangled by fixed fishing gear such as lobster traps and gillnets. The Atlantic Large Whale Take Reduction Plan (ALWTRP) is intended to protect three whale species (fin, humpback, and North Atlantic right whales) from entanglement in fishing gear. The plan covers a large number of fixed-gear fisheries, the largest of which is the New England and Mid-Atlantic lobster trap fishery.

d. Deterring Marine Mammal Interference and Damage

Section 1371(a)(4) of the MMPA allows the use of deterrents to discourage marine mammals from damaging fish catch, gear or other private property and to deter a marine mammal from endangering personal safety, so long as the deterrents do not result in death or serious injury of marine mammal. A commonly used deterrent is called an acoustical harassment device (AHD). Like other noise in the environment, little is known about the broader or long-term ecological effects of the use of such devices. The burden of proof is currently on the government to establish whether particular deterrents have "significant adverse effects" that would justify prohibiting their use. In light of the insufficiency of scientific information, many groups have suggested that the law take a more precautionary approach and require manufacturers to demonstrate that specific deterrents have negligible effects before NMFS can authorize their use.

The 1994 amendments to the MMPA deleted a provision that allowed fishermen to kill certain pinnipeds as a last resort when deterrents did not work. Seals and sea lions can be very aggressive, and deterrents (and even removal) have not always proved effective. There are concerns that increasing populations of California sea lions and West Coast harbor seals may not only interfere directly with fishing operations, but adversely affect other marine resource populations (e.g., salmon), the development of aquaculture, and coastal land uses. Some commentators advocate the reinstatement of a limited lethal take provision for "nuisance animals," culling "over-populated" areas, and allowing local officials to deal with site-specific conflicts involving the above species. These proposals are strongly opposed by scientists and environmentalists who advocate development of better, non-lethal deterrents. See *Humane Soc'y of the United States v. Locke*, 626 F.3d 1040 (9th Cir. Or. 2010) (holding that because NMFS failed to adequately explain its finding that sea lions were having a "significant negative impact" on the decline or recovery of listed salmonid populations, NMFS violated the MMPA when it authorized Idaho, Oregon, and Washington to kill up to 85 California sea lions annually at the Bonneville Dam to protect salmon in the Columbia River).

e. Exceptions to the Moratorium for Certain Other Incidental Activities

The final exception authorizes the Secretary to permit, upon request, the unintentional taking of "small numbers of marine mammals" incidental to interactions with activities other than fishing, such as OCS oil and gas development. Id. § 1371(a)(5). Before the Secretary can issue a Letter of Authorization (LOA), he must make specific findings that the taking will have a "negligible impact" on the species or its habitat. Such "small number" permits are allowed even for depleted species. In 1994, the MMPA was amended to expedite short-term authorization to incidentally take small numbers of marine mammals by "harassment" through

Incidental Harassment Authorizations (IHAs). 16
U.S.C. § 1371(a)(5)(D). Most LOAs and IHAs are
issued for the incidental acoustic harassment of
marine mammals and involve noise created by
seismic airguns (for scientific research or for seabed
oil and gas exploration), ship and aircraft noise, high
energy sonar systems, and explosives.

The most controversial authorizations are for
acoustic harassment (and possibly killing) of marine
mammals by the U.S. Navy in its testing and
deployment of high-intensity active sonar systems.
NMFS originally issued rules in 2002 authorizing the
Navy's one-year use of the active sonar program for
"training, testing, and routine military operations" in
roughly 75% of the world's oceans. In *Natural
Resources Defense Council, Inc. v. Evans* (*Evans I*),
232 F. Supp.2d 1003 (N.D. Cal. 2002) and in *Natural
Resources Defense Council, Inc. v. Evans* (*Evans II*),
364 F. Supp.2d 1083 (N.D. Cal. 2003), environmental
groups succeeded in limiting the area of testing
(*Evans I*) and then in receiving a permanent
injunction on grounds that the authorization decision
violated NEPA, the ESA, and the MMPA. However,
the victories were incomplete and short-lived. The
injunction did not prohibit the Navy from testing and
training with the sonar outside a 12-mile buffer and
outside certain deep ocean areas with concentrations
of marine mammals and endangered species so long
as additional measures were taken to avoid harm to
marine life. *Evans II.*

In late 2003, Congress amended the MMPA to
create separate "harassment" provisions for the

military and federally-supported scientific research and removed the "small numbers" and limited geographic area provisions in regard to military operations. Department of Defense Authorization Act of 2004, Pub. L. No. 108–136, 319, 117 Stat. 1392 (2003). Harassment for "military readiness activities" is limited to (1) acts that actually injure or have a significant potential to injure, and (2) acts that actually disturb or are likely to disturb by disrupting natural behavioral patterns to the point where they are abandoned or significantly altered. Id. § 319(a) (amending 16 U.S.C. § 1362(18)). The Secretary of Commerce can impose restrictions to ensure the least practicable adverse impact on the marine mammals only after taking into account personnel safety, practicality, the impact on military readiness, and the views of the Department of Defense. In addition, the Secretary of Defense was given power to exempt *any action or category of actions* from the MMPA for up to two years if "necessary for the national defense." Id., § 319(b), 117 Stat. at 1434 (adding 16 U.S.C. § 1371(f)).

When the NRDC again challenged authorization of the Navy's use of "mid-frequency active" (MFA) sonar in training exercises off southern California (SOCAL), the U.S. Supreme Court further limited protections potentially available to environmental groups to protect marine mammals.[2] In *Winter v.*

---

[2]   In addition, the Council on Environmental Quality (CEQ) authorized the Navy to implement "alternative arrangements" to NEPA compliance in light of "emergency circumstances," see 40 C.F.R. § 1506.11, and the President, granted the Navy an exemption from the CZMA pursuant to 16 U.S.C. § 1456(c)(1)(B)

NRDC, 555 U.S. 7 (2008), the Supreme Court vacated a preliminary injunction limiting the SOCAL exercises. See *NRDC v. Winter*, 518 F.3d 658 (9th Cir. Cal. 2008). The Court first found that NRDC had not met the irreparable injury requirement necessary for issuance of an injunction. The Court then held that even if it were the case that NRDC had shown irreparable injury, the plaintiffs had not met the further requirements involved in balancing the equities and consideration of the public interest. Finding that the injunction jeopardized national security, the Court held:

> ... We do not discount the importance of plaintiffs' ecological, scientific, and recreational interests in marine mammals. Those interests, however, are plainly outweighed by the Navy's need to conduct realistic training exercises to ensure that it is able to neutralize the threat posed by enemy submarines.

Not to be deterred, NRDC has continued to contest the Navy's sonar operations, most recently through a challenge to NMFS' Final Rule providing a 5-year authorization of the Navy's use of LFA sonar in the world's oceans. See 77 Fed. Reg. 50,290 (Aug. 20, 2012). In *NRDC v. Pritzker*, 2014 U.S. Dist. LEXIS 35404 (N.D. Cal. Mar. 17, 2014), the court rejected most of NRDC's attacks on the rule, but found that

---

that permits such exemptions when the activity is "in the paramount interest of the United States." The President determined that the exercises were "essential to national security" and that an injunction would "undermine the Navy's ability to conduct realistic training exercises that are necessary to ensure the combat effectiveness of . . . strike groups."

NMFS had used outdated population information on bottlenose dolphins in making its required determination that the authorized taking will have a "negligible impact" on marine mammal species or stock. See 16 U.S.C. § 1371(a)(5)(A), (D). Because analysis of "negligible impact" must be "based on the best scientific evidence available," the court granted summary judgment on that issue. On July 1, 2014, the Department of Defense announced that it would prepare a supplemental environmental impact statement "for the limited purpose of addressing the single deficiency identified by the court"—the failure to use the most recent data on bottlenose dolphin in its analysis of the impact of the LFA sonar. See 79 Fed. Reg. 372959 (July 1, 2014).

In 2015, the District Court of Hawaii found flaws in NMFS "negligible impact" analysis under the MMPA because NMFS failed to analyze the impact of the Navy's activities on all affected species and stocks of marine mammals, use the best scientific evidence available, and ensure that mitigation measures effected the least practicable adverse impact on affected species and stocks. *Conservation Council for Haw. v. Nat'l Marine Fisheries Serv.*, 97 F. Supp. 3d 1210 (D. Haw. 2015) (Finding NMFS' no jeopardy finding for whales arbitrary and capricious). After this decision, the Navy agreed to a settlement placing habitat for whales and other marine mammal species off-limits to the use of midfrequency active sonar and explosives.

In 2016, the 9th Circuit agreed with NRDC that NMFS must not only demonstrate "negligible impact" on marine mammals but also must meet a strict standard to ensure the least practicable adverse impact on marine mammals and their habitat in deciding appropriate mitigation measures associated with sonar usage. *NRDC v. Pritzker* 828 F.3d 1125 (9th Cir. 2016) (Finding that even where populations are not threatened significantly, NMFS must protect marine mammals and their habitat "to the greatest extent practicable" in light of military readiness objectives).

f. Exemption from the Moratorium for Coastal Alaska Natives

The MMPA contains an exemption from the moratorium for takings by Native Alaskans (Indian, Aleut, or Eskimo) for subsistence uses or traditional "authentic" handicrafts unless the Secretary imposes regulations for a species determined to be depleted. Id. § 1371(b). Any take of a protected marine mammal must not be "accomplished in a wasteful manner." Id.

In *Didrickson v. United States Dep't of the Interior*, 982 F.2d 1332 (9th Cir. 1992), the Ninth Circuit Court of Appeals struck down a regulation that limited "authentic" articles to those "commonly produced" prior to enactment of the MMPA and excluded all articles made from sea otter products. The court held that the MMPA sufficiently identified authentic native articles of handicrafts and clothing as being "made at least in part from 'natural materials,' and ... [produced] ... in traditional native ways, such as weaving, carving, and stitching." The agency had no discretion to impose additional requirements as to the type of articles or to exclude sea otter products.

Subsistence whaling by the Makah Tribe in the Pacific Northwest has been much more controversial than the whaling by Native Alaskans that is authorized both by IWC quotas and the MMPA. The MMPA had been amended in 1994 to clarify that it was not intended to alter Indian treaty rights (16 U.S.C.A. § 1361 note), such as the Makah 1855 treaty right to continue whaling for gray whales. In 1995, the Makah notified the government of their interest in resuming their right to cultural and subsistence whaling under the 1855 Treaty of Neah Bay. The Makah were allocated a quota by NOAA in 1998, and the tribe struck and landed one gray whale in 1999. This hunt generated a flurry of litigation. First, the Ninth Circuit Court of Appeals found that NOAA's environmental assessment (EA) and the issuance of a quota to the Makah violated NEPA. *Metcalf v. Daley,* 214 F.3d 1135 (9th Cir. 2000). Then in 2002, the Ninth Circuit ruled further that an EIS (rather than an EA) should have been prepared to comply with NEPA and that the Makah must comply with MMPA processes to pursue its treaty rights. *Anderson v. Evans,* 371 F.3d 475 (9th Cir. 2002).

In February 2005, the Makah Tribe submitted a request for a waiver of the MMPA's take moratorium, and NOAA began the NEPA process of reviewing the effects of Makah whaling in 2005. In 2006, the review was expanded to cover the effects of issuing quotas to the Makah under the Whaling Convention Act

(WCA), 16 U.S.C. § 916 et seq., because the Makah whaling cannot continue without receiving authorization under both the MMPA and WCA. In 2007, five Makah tribe members conducted a rogue whale hunt, killing a gray whale with a high-powered rifle. The Makah tribe denounced the illegal hunt.

The EIS process is still on-going. NMFS terminated the 2008 draft EIS in 2012 after the agency determined it did not reflect substantial new scientific information on the gray whales targeted by the hunt. In 2012, the IWC also extended a gray whale catch limit for the Makah for 6 years. A draft EIS was issued in March 2015. In 2019, NMFS announced a proposal to authorize the Makah Tribe to hunt three gray whales in even years and one gray whale in odd years as long as they protect Pacific Coast Feeding Group whales.

2. MMPA PRE-EMPTION

The MMPA specifically preempts state laws. The Act provides that "[n]o State may enforce . . . any State law or regulation relating to the taking of any species . . . of marine mammal within the State." 16 U.S.C.A. § 1379(a). But see *UFO Chuting of Hawaii v. Smith*, 508 F.3d 1189 (9th Cir. 2007) (Coast Guard license did not preempt a state statute banning thrillcraft and parasailing seasonally in the Maui Humpback Whale Protected Waters).[3]

---

[3]   K.L. Kaulukukui, *The Brief and Unexpected Preemption of Hawaii's Humpback Whale Laws: The Authority of the States to Protect Endangered Marine Mammals Under the ESA and the MMPA*, 36 ELR 10712 (2006).

Although the state preemption provision refers expressly only to the taking of marine mammals, one federal district court opinion holds that the MMPA also preempts state laws regarding importation of marine mammals. See *Fouke Co. v. Mandel*, 386 F.Supp. 1341 (D.Md. 1974). Authority to manage the taking of a species of marine mammal must be transferred to a state if the Secretary finds that a state conservation and management program meets the stringent standards and procedures of MMPA § 1379 to ensure that the state program is consistent with the MMPA and international obligations. This authority has yet to be transferred to any state.

3.   PENALTIES

Penalties for violation of the MMPA are substantial. The entire cargo of any vessel involved in the unlawful taking of a marine mammal is subject to seizure and forfeiture. The vessel will also be liable for a civil penalty up to $25,000. 16 U.S.C.A. § 1376(b). In addition, individuals are subject to fines of up to $10,000 for each violation of the Act or a permit, and fines of up to $20,000 per violation and one year of imprisonment can be imposed for knowingly violating the Act. Id. § 1375.

4.   THE DOLPHINS' TALE

Dolphins are protected under the MMPA. Early trade-focused protections of dolphins triggered decades of litigation described below. The U.S. continues to rely on the MMPA to protect dolphins both domestically and internationally.

a. WTO Case *Mexico v. United States* (GATT I Tuna/Dolphin Under the MMPA)

The MMPA prohibits importation of yellowfin tuna products associated with high dolphin mortality rates unless the Secretary of Commerce finds that fishing practices are in compliance with the MMPA. In 1990, Earth Island Institute obtained an injunction halting importation of tuna from Mexico pending NMFS' issuance of "comparability findings." See *Earth Island Inst. v. Mosbacher*, 929 F.2d 1449 (9th Cir. 1991). The U.S. imposed an embargo on Mexican yellowfin tuna on August 28, 1990. Mexico's response to the injunction was to request consultations with the United States as provided for in the General Agreement on Tariffs and Trade (GATT), opened for signature Oct. 30, 1947, 61 Stat. A3, 55 U.N.T.S. 14.

When the consultations requested by Mexico failed to resolve the dispute, Mexico requested that a GATT panel be established to consider whether the United States' restrictions on Mexican tuna—both directly and through intermediary countries—violated obligations under GATT which:

1) prohibit quantitative restrictions or prohibitions under GATT Article XI;[4]

---

[4]   Article XI of GATT provides, in relevant part, that:

"No prohibitions or restrictions ... whether made effective through quotas, import or export licenses or other measures, shall be instituted or maintained by any contracting party on the importation of any product of the territory of any other contracting party...."

2) prohibit discriminatory quantitative restrictions for a geographic area under Article XIII; and

3) mandate national treatment for imported goods under Article III.[5]

See GATT, United States Restrictions on the Import of Tuna, Adopted Sept. 3, 1991, Panel Report No. DS21/R, reprinted in 30 I.L.M. 1594.

The GATT panel rejected the argument by the United States that the ban was an internal regulation applied at the point of importation and that the foreign tuna was treated no less favorably than tuna caught by domestic vessels. The panel stated that Article III did allow imposition of internal regulations that were nondiscriminatory, not disguised protectionism, and provided national treatment. However, the panel found Article III inapplicable to the tuna embargo because the regulations related not to the product itself, but to its method of production. Article III applies solely to laws . . . affecting the internal sale . . . of products." Having found Article III inapplicable, the panel determined that the embargo violated Article XI's quantitative prohibitions.

---

5   Article III of GATT provides, in relevant part:

"The products of the territory of any contracting party imported into the territory of any contracting party shall be accorded treatment no less favourable than that accorded to like products of national origin in respect of all laws, regulations and requirements affecting their internal sale, offering for sale, purchase, transportation, distribution, or use."

THE MARINE MAMMAL

The United States also argued that the embargo was justified by exceptions under Article XX(b) and XX(g) which allow trade measures "necessary to protect human, animal or plant life or health" and "relating to the conservation of exhaustible natural resources if such measures are made effective in conjunction with restrictions on domestic production or consumption." The panel found that neither provision had been intended to apply extraterritorially. Application of such measures beyond a nation's jurisdiction would undermine the free trade regime, allowing nations to unilaterally dictate environmental policies to other countries and derogate from GATT on the basis of nonuniform protection of persons, animals, or resources. Even if the provisions of Article XX(b) and XX(g) could apply to animals or resources beyond U.S. jurisdiction, the panel found that they were inapplicable to the tuna embargo. The United States did not demonstrate that the embargo was "necessary," because there was no showing that less restrictive means, such as international agreements, could not have accomplished the protection. There was also insufficient showing under Article XX(g) that the measure was "primarily aimed at conservation" and was not simply a protection of the U.S. fishing industry.

Mexico's challenge to the Dolphin Protection Consumer Information Act (16 U.S.C.A. § 1385) "dolphin safe" labeling requirements was not successful, however. The GATT panel found that the labeling did not discriminate against a geographic area because the requirements applied to tuna harvested by any vessel in the eastern tropical Pacific regardless of the vessel's origin. The labeling standards did not restrict trade because they were not mandatory, and tuna with and without the labels could be sold; any disadvantage arose from the free choice of the consumer. The panel's decision stressed that "[t]he labeling provisions therefore did not make the right to sell tuna or tuna products . . . conditional upon the use of tuna harvesting methods."

The GATT panel decision was advisory and could not become effective unless adopted unanimously by the Council of Representatives.[6] Rather than voting to block adoption of the decision by the Council, the United States entered into further negotiations with Mexico, with the countries agreeing that the decision should not be brought to the Council.

b. WTO Case European Economic Community and Netherlands v. United States (GATT Tuna-Dolphin II Under the MMPA)

The MMPA prohibits the import of fish not just from primary nations but also intermediary nations whose industries pack and ship tuna products caught by fishing vessels from countries with high dolphin incidental mortality rates. The MMPA requires governments to "certify and provide reasonable proof to the Secretary of Commerce that it has not imported, within the previous six months, any yellowfin tuna or yellowfin tuna products that are

---

[6]   Under the current WTO/GATT regime, WTO Appellate Body recommendations are adopted unless affirmatively rejected by the Council.

subject to a direct ban on importation to the United States." 16 U.S.C.A § 1371(2)(D).

In 1992, the European Economic Community and The Netherlands brought a case against the United States arguing that the secondary embargo was prohibited under trade law. In 1994, the panel ruled against the secondary embargo provisions of the MMPA finding that it was a restriction on trade products. The panel rejected the U.S. arguments on Article XX (b) and (g) finding that U.S. law was not indispensable to protect dolphins.

c. International Dolphin Conservation Act

The International Dolphin Conservation Act of 1992, Pub. L. No. 102–523, amended the MMPA by imposing a five-year moratorium upon the harvesting of tuna with purse seine nets and lifting tuna embargos upon those nations making a commitment to implement the moratorium and take further steps to reduce dolphin mortality.

The same year, the U.S. entered into the La Jolla Agreement, a non-binding international agreement to protect dolphins from harm in the Eastern Tropical Pacific (ETP) and to allow purse seine fishing with dolphin mortality caps.

d. The Panama Declaration

The La Jolla Agreement led to the United States and eleven other nations signing the Declaration of Panama to strengthen the protection of dolphins by (a) reducing dolphin mortality to levels approaching zero, with the goal of eliminating dolphin mortality in the ETP; (b) establishing annual dolphin mortality limits (DMLs); (c) avoiding bycatch of immature yellowfin tuna and other non-target species such as sea turtles; (d) strengthening national scientific advisory committees; (e) creating incentives for vessel captains; and (f) enhancing the compliance of participating nations to these commitments. The Panama Declaration of 1995 served as the basis for an agreement to establish the International Dolphin Conservation Program (IDCP), contingent upon the U.S. amending its laws to lift the MMPA embargoes imposed, to permit the sale of both dolphin-safe and non-dolphin safe tuna in the U.S., and to change the definition of dolphin-safe tuna from tuna harvested without dolphin purse seine encirclement to tuna harvested without dolphin mortality.

e. International Dolphin Conservation Program Act

In 1997, Congress enacted the International Dolphin Conservation Program Act (IDCPA), Pub. L. No. 105–42, to implement the Panama Declaration. This amendment represented a major change in U.S. policy to pursue dolphin and ecosystem protection primarily through international cooperation. The IDCPA revised the criteria for banning imports to permit export of tuna to the U.S. if the exporter provides evidence of participation in certain international agreements to manage tuna and protect dolphins and that dolphin take does not exceed DMLs. The Secretary has made "affirmative findings" for the tuna fisheries of Ecuador, Mexico,

Spain, Guatemala, Peru and El Salvador, allowing tuna from those countries to be imported into the U.S. See 50 CFR 216.24(f)(requirements for an affirmative finding). The tuna embargo remains in place for Belize, Bolivia, Colombia, Honduras, Nicaragua, Panama, Vanuatu, and Venezuela. No intermediary nations are currently subject to import bans. See NOAA Fisheries, *Tuna/Dolphin Embargo Status Update*, available at https://www.fisheries. noaa.gov/national/marine-mammal-protection/tuna-dolphin-embargo-status-update.

The IDCPA also changed standards concerning dolphin-safe labeling. The 1990 Dolphin Protection Consumer Information Act (DPCIA), 16 U.S.C. § 1385, prohibited any producer, importer, exporter, distributor, or seller of any tuna product sold in or exported from the United States to label that product as "dolphin safe" if the product contained tuna harvested on the high seas by a vessel engaging in driftnet fishing or in the ETP by a vessel using the purse seine method, unless the tuna was accompanied by various statements that no dolphin was intentionally encircled during the trip in which the tuna was caught. The Secretary of Commerce was directed to conduct a study of the effects of chase and encirclement on dolphins in purse seine fisheries for yellowfin tuna in the eastern tropical Pacific. The study was intended to determine whether chase and encirclement are having a "significant adverse impact on any depleted dolphin stock in the eastern tropical Pacific Ocean." 16 U.S.C. § 1385(d)(2). In December 2002 the Secretary made a final finding of "no significant effect" which authorized him under the IDCPA to broaden the definition of dolphin-safe tuna to include all tuna harvested in sets in which no dolphin mortality or serious injury was observed.

The finding was immediately attacked by environmental organizations. The U.S. 9th District Court of Appeal issued an injunction in 2003 and in 2004 held the final finding of the Secretary arbitrary and capricious and contrary to the applicable law under the Administrative Procedure Act, because the finding had been motivated by policy considerations, rather than based solely on the best scientific evidence. See *Earth Island Institute v. Evans*, 2004 WL 1774221 (N.D.Cal. 2004).

f. WTO Case *Mexico v. United States* (Dolphin-Safe Labeling Under the Dolphin Protection Consumer Information Act)

Following the affirmation of the 2004 district court's holding in *Earth Island Institute v. Hogarth,* 494 F.3d 757 (9th Cir. 2007), the definition for dolphin-safe labeling reverted to section 1385(h)(2) of the DPCIA, which provides that tuna is deemed dolphin-safe only if "no tuna were caught in the trip in which such tuna were harvested using a purse seine net intentionally deployed on or to encircle dolphins, and no dolphins were killed or seriously injured during the sets in which the tuna were caught."

In response to this case, Mexico (with the EU and 11 other countries) requested that the World Trade Organization (WTO), the successor to GATT, set up a dispute settlement panel, The Panel found that U.S.

law did not discriminate against Mexican tuna products but that the labeling measures were more trade restrictive than necessary to achieve legal objectives. The dispute panel's decision was appealed to the WTO Appellate Body by both the U.S. and Mexico, which found that the U.S. dolphin-safe labeling scheme accords "less favorable treatment" to Mexican tuna products in violation of its obligations under GATT and the Agreement on Technical Barriers to Trade, because the U.S. measures did not set conditions for using the label in a way that reflects the risks faced by dolphins in different oceans.

In 2013, NOAA issued new final rules that attempted to conform to the WTO holding, U.S. legislation, and concerns of environmental organizations. See 78 Fed. Reg. 40997 (July 9, 2013). The discrimination against Mexico was addressed primarily by broadening the scope of the rule to cover oceans other than the Eastern Tropical Pacific (ETP) and requiring uniform verification from all tuna fishermen that dolphin-safe standards are met. Following the issuance of the rule, Mexico requested the WTO to establish a compliance panel—a mechanism for determining whether the losing party in a trade dispute has conformed to the rulings of the WTO. The U.S. issued an Interim Final Rule on March 22, 2016. On October 26, 2017, the compliance panel found that the U.S. labeling requirements conform to WTO rules. Mexico appealed and on December 14, 2018, the Appellate Body circulated its compliance report finding the U.S. regulatory tuna measures consistent with international trade law including Article XX. *United States—Measures Concerning the Importation, Marketing and Sale of Tuna and Tuna Products—Second Recourse to Article 21.5 of the DSU by Mexico* (DS381)

g. Class Action on "Dolphin-Safe" Tuna

In May 2019, the saga continued as consumers filed a proposed class action in federal court in California against the three largest canned tuna companies for claiming that their products are "dolphin safe." The law suit claimed federal racketeering charges and violations of state consumer laws. The law suit claims that the companies purchased tuna caught using methods that do not protect against dolphin mortalities. See "The 3 biggest US tuna companies use fishing techniques that hurt and kill dolphins, new lawsuits claim," at https://www.vox.com/the-goods/2019/5/15/18624941/dolphin-safe-tuna-lawsuit-bumble-bee-starkist-chicken-of-the-sea.

h. MMPA and Dolphins/Porpoises

Recent enforcement actions by NOAA's Office of Legal Enforcement include fining Hawaiian tour operators and snorkelers who have encircled and actively pursued spinner dolphins in violation of MMPA's prohibition on harassment. As of 2019, NOAA has proposed regulations to protect spinner dolphins during human interactions that have not yet been finalized.

Conservation groups have brought legal cases against the U.S. government for failure to protect the vaquita, the world's smallest porpoise, by implementing the "import provision" of the MMPA requiring NOAA to take action to ban certain seafood. Today there are 10 known vaquita, down from a population of 567, due in part to gill-netting in Mexican waters for shrimp and other species. In 2018, U.S. Court of International Trade (CIT) granted an injunction to ban the importation of fish or seafood products from Mexico caught by gillnets within the vaquita's range. *NRDC v. Ross*, 331 F. Supp.3d 1338 (C.I.T. 2018). The Federal Circuit upheld the injunction in 2019, pending remand to the CIT to determine whether change of circumstances justified lifting the injunction. NRDC v. Ross, 2019 WL 2173792, at *1 (Fed. Cir. May 20, 2019).

B.   WHALES AND WHALING

1.   BACKGROUND

Whales exist in every ocean of the world, and the whaling industry began as early as the eleventh or twelfth century. By the twentieth century, the excesses and waste of an unregulated whaling industry had decimated whale populations. Although the market for whale oil and products decreased with the increased availability of petroleum products, whaling continued to increase. At the turn of the twentieth century, fewer than 5,000 whales per year were taken; in 1931, over 40,000 whales were harvested.

The first efforts to control whaling in the 1920s culminated in the 1931 Convention for the

Regulation of Whaling, opened for signature Sept. 24, 1931, 49 Stat. 3079, 155 L.N.T.S. 349. The Convention prohibited the taking of right whales and bowhead whales. The primary provisions of the treaty were directed at controlling waste by prohibiting the taking of calves, immature whales, and females with suckling calves and by requiring that parties make the "fullest possible use" of all whales that were harvested. Negotiations in 1937 and 1938 resulted in further agreements to prohibit the taking of gray whales and established minimum lengths for species, limits for geographic areas, and whaling seasons for humpback whales. Nearly fifty countries, including the United States, were parties to the 1931 Convention, but the major whaling nations—Argentina, Chile, Germany, Japan, and the Soviet Union—were not parties.

These early efforts did not improve the status of whale populations. The interruption of commercial whaling during World War II and the failure of the 1931 Convention provided the impetus for negotiation of a new treaty following the war. The current regime for regulation of whaling is based on the 1946 International Convention for the Regulation of Whaling (Whaling Convention), done Dec. 2, 1946, 62 Stat. 1716, 161 U.N.T.S. 72. Although the 1946 Convention originally had fewer parties than the earlier treaty, all the major whaling nations were among the signatories. The preamble of the 1946 Whaling Convention sets out the dual purposes of the agreement which include both "safeguarding for future generations the great natural resources represented by the whale stocks" and "the orderly development of the whaling industry." The original intent of the Convention was clearly not preservation, but conservation and recovery of whale stocks to an "optimum level" as a basis for long-term exploitation.[7]

2.   THE 1946 INTERNATIONAL WHALING CONVENTION

Unlike most international fishing agreements which are generally limited to activities on the high seas, the Whaling Convention extends to "all waters in which whaling is prosecuted." Whaling Convention, art. I(2). This means that the Convention applies not only within 200-mile fishery and exclusive economic zones, but also within territorial seas and inland waters. The Convention does not define "whale," but the treaty's jurisdiction has been extended primarily to larger cetaceans. In fact, in the first two decades of treaty implementation, whales were not regulated by species, but in terms of "blue whale units," a methodology that treated some species of large baleen whales as fungible depending on the amount of oil they contained.

The Whaling Convention established the International Whaling Commission (IWC), which is composed of one voting representative of each party to the treaty. The IWC is authorized to recommend and carry out research, to collect statistics on stocks

---

[7]   See William Burke, *Legal Aspects of the IWC Decision on the Southern Ocean Sanctuary*, 28 Ocean Devel. & Int'l L. 3113 (1997).

and whaling operations, and to disseminate information on means of maintaining and increasing whale stocks. Id. art. IV(1).

a. Governance Under the Whaling Convention

The IWC governs the exploitation and protection of whales through a detailed set of regulations called the Schedule. Article V of the Whaling Convention gives the IWC the power to amend the Schedule by a three-fourths majority of the members voting. Measures that may be taken include designation of: "(a) protected and unprotected species; (b) open and closed seasons; (c) open and closed waters, including the designation of sanctuary areas; (d) size limits for each species; (e) time, methods, and intensity of whaling . . .; (f) types and specifications of gear . . .; (g) methods of measurement; and (h) . . . records." Id. art. V(1).

The Whaling Convention puts a number of limitations on amendments to the Schedule that are not in the direct interest of preserving whaling. Amendments to the Schedule must be based on scientific findings and must provide for "development, and optimum utilization of the whale resources". Id. art. V(2) . Because information on stocks and conservation methods is extremely deficient in spite of over fifty years of research, this requirement impliedly rejects the "precautionary principle."

The IWC is also authorized to "make recommendations . . . which relate to whales or whaling and to the objectives and purposes of th[e]

Convention" by a majority vote. An example is the 1979 recommendation by the IWC directed at "pirate" whaling. The IWC recommended that parties suspend imports of whale meat and products and suspend exports of whaling vessels and technology to non-party countries. Such recommendations do not have the force of law but have been widely effective.

b. Moratoria and Sanctuaries

Parties can object to amendments and a given amendment will not become effective for a party that objects within ninety days. Id. art. V(3). The most controversial amendment to the Schedule was the adoption in 1982 of a temporary moratorium—which is still in effect—on all commercial whaling that took effect in 1986. The Soviet Union, Japan, and Norway registered objections to the moratorium. Japan charged that the moratorium was a significant departure from the original objectives of the Convention, and that it was motivated by emotion and politics, rather than by science.[8] Norway legally resumed whaling operations in the spring of 1993 and continues whaling today. Iceland, which did not register an objection to the moratorium, withdrew from the Convention in 1992. Although Iceland rejoined in 2004, it included an objection to the moratorium as part of its reentry. In 2006, Iceland resumed commercial whaling. Greenland and the Faroe Islands both continue to take whales but are

---

[8]   Kazuo Sumi, *The "Whale War" Between Japan and the United States: Problems and Prospects*, 17 Denv. J. Int'l L. & Pol'y 317 (1989)

represented at the IWC by Denmark who supports the moratorium.

The IWC has designated two sanctuaries that prohibit all commercial whaling. The Indian Ocean Sanctuary was created in 1979 and comprises all of the Indian Ocean south of 55 degrees south latitude. The Southern Ocean Sanctuary surrounding Antarctica was created in 1994. Other proposals for sanctuaries have repeatedly failed to achieve the three-fourths vote necessary.

c. Taking Whales for Scientific Research

The only exemption provided for in the Whaling Convention is for special permits to be issued by nations for scientific research. Whaling Convention, art. VIII. To prevent waste, the Convention provides that whales taken for scientific purposes should be processed so far as practicable. Id. Critics have asserted that the ability to take whales when non-lethal research alternatives exist has led to abuse of the exemption, particularly by Japan. In 2014, the International Court of Justice (ICJ), who had compulsory jurisdiction for the dispute, ordered Japan to revoke existing scientific permits and to refrain from issuing additional permits under its scientific program. The ICJ found that the design and implementation of Japan's scientific program was not reasonable in relation to achieving its stated objectives and, consequently, the special permits granted by Japan for the killing, taking and treating of whales were not "for purposes of scientific research" as required by the Convention. *Whaling in the Antarctic (Australia v. Japan: New Zealand intervening)*, Judgment of 31 March 2014. In 2015, Japan withdrew recognition of ICJ compulsory jurisdiction for disputes related to living marine resources. In 2018, a majority of IWC states approved a non-binding resolution that commercial whaling was no longer a necessary economic activity. In 2019, Japan announced its withdrawal from the IWC to be effective in 2020 and its plan to resume commercial whaling in its territorial waters and EEZ.

d. Subsistence Whaling

There is no exemption in the Convention for whaling for subsistence and cultural needs, which arguably had not threatened the survival of whales before excessive commercial whaling operations depleted stocks. The IWC does not treat such whaling the same as commercial whaling, however, and the moratorium does not apply to subsistence whaling. Governments must provide the IWC with a "Needs Statement" that details the cultural and nutritional basis for the hunt. The IWC's Scientific Committee assesses the sustainability of the hunt and advises on catch limits. The Schedule provides catch limits for aboriginal subsistence whaling for certain natives of Alaska, Chukotka and Washington State, Greenland, and St. Vincent and the Grenadines. Japan has unsuccessfully argued to the IWC that the reliance of many of its small coastal communities upon subsistence whaling is virtually identical to aboriginal subsistence whaling.

It has been argued that the Whaling Convention was not intended to cover subsistence whaling. In *Hopson v. Kreps*, 622 F.2d 1375 (9th Cir. 1980), the Ninth Circuit held that justiciable questions had been presented as to whether the IWC had exceeded its jurisdiction in eliminating certain native subsistence whaling. The decision reversed the district court holding that interpretation of the treaty was a nonjusticiable political question. The question is still unresolved, because it was never addressed on remand, presumably because the IWC continued to authorize subsistence hunting of bowhead whales by Native Alaskans. See also *Adams v. Vance*, 187 U.S.App.D.C. 41 (D.C.Cir. 1978).

e. Implementation and Enforcement

The Whaling Convention places responsibility on each government to "take appropriate measures" to enforce the treaty and to punish "infractions . . . by persons or by vessels under its jurisdiction." Whaling Convention, art. IX(1). Infractions and punitive and remedial measures taken must be reported to the IWC. Id. art. IX(4). The Convention gives a party broad discretion in implementing the provisions and in defining the scope of the nation's jurisdiction. Some countries, like the United States, have taken extensive measures to implement the Convention provisions and to promote further conservation of whales and other marine mammals.

3.   UNITED STATES ENFORCEMENT OF THE INTERNATIONAL WHALING CONVENTION

The combination of the Whaling Convention's dual purposes, the objection procedure, and a weak enforcement mechanism has resulted in continued depletion of many species of whales and has frustrated attempts by the non-whaling majority of the IWC to incorporate reforms for further preservation of whales. United States' domestic policy on whaling, however, has had a significant influence on the implementation of IWC policies. United States policy on whaling is implemented through four statutes: (1) the Endangered Species Act, 16 U.S.C.A. §§ 1531–1544; (2) the Marine Mammal Protection Act (MMPA), 16 U.S.C.A. §§ 1361–1421h; (3) the Pelly Amendment to the Fisherman's Protective Act of 1967, 22 U.S.C.A. § 1978; and (4) the Packwood Amendment to the Magnuson-Stevens Fishery Conservation and Management Act (MSA), 16 U.S.C.A. § 1821(e)(2).

The MMPA is described in Section X.A. infra and the ESA is described in Section X.C. Under the MMPA, Congress specifically directs United States' agencies to initiate negotiations to amend existing international treaties, e.g., the Whaling Convention, to make the treaties "consistent with the purposes and policies" of the MMPA. 16 U.S.C.A. § 1378(a)(4).

a. Pelly Amendment

The Pelly Amendment, passed in 1967 due to concern over the implementation of international salmon treaties, directs the Secretary of Commerce to certify to the President findings that foreign nationals, "directly or indirectly, are conducting fishing operations in a manner or under circumstances which *diminish the effectiveness* of an international fishery conservation program." 22 U.S.C.A. § 1978(a)(i). (Note that application of the act does not require that a nation is in violation of a treaty obligation or international law.) The term "international fishery conservation program" is defined broadly to apply to programs pertaining to any "living resources of the sea" and was intended to include the Whaling Convention. Id. § 1978(h)(3). Upon certification, the President may direct the Secretary of Treasury to prohibit importation of fish products from the certified country. Id. § 1978(a)(4). The President's imposition of the sanction is, however, discretionary. Following enactment of the Pelly Amendment, the President imposed no sanctions in five cases of nations certified by the Secretary of Commerce as engaging in fishing that diminished the effectiveness of whaling quotas established by the IWC. The threat of sanctions did, however, result in negotiations that substantially changed the whaling practices of the nations involved.

b. Packwood Amendment

Congress' impatience with delays in certification and the President's failure to impose sanctions under the Pelly Amendment[9] was reflected in the 1979

---

[9]   Japan, for example, was certified three times—in 1988, 1995, and 2000, but no president had issued trade sanctions against Japan under the Pelly Amendment. In December 2000,

Packwood Amendment to the MSA. The Secretary of Commerce is directed to monitor activities of foreign nationals and "promptly" investigate and "promptly" make certification decisions. See id. § 1978(a)(3)(A)–(C). The Packwood Amendment also attempted to eliminate discretion in the imposition of sanctions. If the Secretary of Commerce certifies that foreign nationals, "directly or indirectly, are conducting fishing operations or engaging in trade or taking [of whales] which diminishes the effectiveness of the International Convention on the Regulation of Whaling," the Secretary of State was required to reduce, by at least fifty percent, the certified nation's fishery allocation within the United States EEZ. 16 U.S.C.A. § 1821(e)(2)(A)–(B). Certification under the Packwood Amendment is also deemed a certification for purposes of the Pelly Amendment.

In January 2014, the Secretary of Commerce certified Iceland under the Pelly and Packwood amendments for the third time. Iceland was certified in 2004 for its scientific whaling program; the certification was extended in 2006 when it resumed commercial whaling; and Iceland was again certified for diminishing the effectiveness of the IWC in 2011. Recently, Iceland has drastically increased its take of finwhales for export to Japan. Iceland's 2014–2019 quota of 154 finwhales per year is more than three times the number that the IWC deems biologically sustainable. The Obama administration decided,

---

President Clinton declared Japan ineligible to conduct fishing operations within the United States EEZ, but since Japan had no fisheries allocation, this was a purely ritualistic action.

however, to continue diplomatic approaches to deal
with Iceland's whaling.

c. Japan Whaling Ass'n v. American Cetacean Society

In *Japan Whaling Ass'n v. American Cetacean
Society*, 478 U.S. 221, 106 S.Ct. 2860, 92 L.Ed.2d 166
(1986), the U.S. Supreme Court addressed the issue
of whether the Secretary of Commerce was required
to certify that Japan's practices had "diminished the
effectiveness" of the Whaling Convention by
exceeding quotas established by the IWC. In 1981,
the IWC set a zero quota for certain sperm whales
and in 1982, the IWC adopted the commercial
whaling moratorium to be effective in 1986. Japan
had filed timely objections to both actions and was
not bound to comply with these IWC regulations.
Japan's actions could, however, be interpreted as
diminishing the effectiveness of the Whaling
Convention and be subject to sanctions under the
Pelly and Packwood Amendments. Rather than
"certifying" Japan, the Secretary of Commerce
entered into negotiations that resulted in an
agreement in 1984 that Japan would withdraw its
objections to the sperm whale quota and the
commercial whaling moratorium effective in 1988. In
return, the United States would agree that Japan
could harvest additional whales in the interim
without triggering certification. Before formal
adoption of the agreement, several environmental
groups filed suit to compel the Secretary of
Commerce to certify Japan. The district court
granted summary judgment and ordered the

Secretary to certify Japan immediately for violating the sperm whale quota. A divided court of appeals affirmed. *American Cetacean Society*, at 221–229.

On appeal, the Supreme Court, in a five-four opinion, first rejected the government's argument that the case involved foreign relations and was unsuitable for judicial review. The Court cast the issue as merely involving interpretation of United States legislation, i.e., the Pelly and Packwood Amendments. Id. at 233–234. The Court noted first that Japan had filed timely objections and was not in violation of any obligation under the Whaling Convention. The Court then considered whether Congress intended that the Secretary must automatically certify any nation that violates IWC quotas. Finding that Congress had not directly addressed the issue of whether quota violations per se "diminish effectiveness" of the treaty, the Court applied the test set out in *Chevron, U.S.A., Inc. v. Natural Resources Defense Council, Inc.,* 467 U.S. 837, 104 S.Ct. 2778, 81 L.Ed.2d 694 (1984). That is, reviewing courts should defer to the "executive department's construction of a statutory scheme it is entrusted to administer," unless the legislative history clearly reveals that the construction is contrary to the will of Congress. Id. at 240–241.

The Supreme Court found that the legislative history supported the Secretary's view that the phrase "diminish the effectiveness" in the amendments was intended to provide a range of discretion. Because Congress' "goal was to protect and conserve whales," Congress intended the

Secretary to have the flexibility to consider what course "would contribute more to the effectiveness of the IWC." The Court concluded, therefore:

that the Secretary's decision to secure the certainty of Japan's future compliance with the IWC's program through the 1984 executive agreement, rather than rely on the possibility that certification and imposition of economic sanctions would produce the same or better result, is a reasonable construction of the Pelly and Packwood Amendments.

Id. at 241. The dissenting justices read the legislative history as clearly demonstrating Congress' intent to impose a nondiscretionary duty on the Secretary to certify nations that violate IWC quotas. The Secretary's interpretation of the certification power, the dissenters stated, was merely a new "means for [the Executive Branch to] evad[e] the constraints of the Packwood Amendment." Id. at 249.

The availability of sanctions considerably bolsters the U.S. negotiating position and has led to significant changes in the actions of whaling countries.

d. Other United States Actions to Protect Whales

The United States has designated two national marine sanctuaries for the protection of whales. The Stellwagon Bank National Marine Sanctuary, an ocean area about 35 miles long and 25 miles wide, is located off the coast of Massachusetts between Cape

Cod and Cape Ann. The submerged sand bank is a feeding area and the summer habitat of humpback and other whale species, as well as the critical habitat of right whales. Atlantic right whales are among the world's most endangered marine species. In addition, NOAA has also taken measure to minimize vessel strikes and entanglement with fixed and other fishing gear.

The Hawaiian Islands Humpback Whale National Marine Sanctuary is intended to protect the whales and one of their primary breeding grounds. Regulations strictly prohibit approaching humpback whales (by any means) within 100 yards. The purposes of that sanctuary designation also include management of human activities consistent with protection of the whales and their habitat and creation of public education and interpretation programs.

Ship strikes are a major source of mortality for whales with 1,200 collisions recorded by the IWC between 2007 and 2016. In 2008, NMFS adopted a "Ship Strike" rule to protect right whales by relocating shipping lanes and requiring ships to reduce speed in certain "seasonal management areas" where right whales are likely to be found. NOAA, *Final rule to implement speed restrictions to reduce the threat of ship collisions with North Atlantic right whales.* 73 Fed.Reg. 60173–60191.

C. THE ENDANGERED SPECIES ACT

Legislation to preserve endangered wildlife was first enacted in 1966, but the Endangered Species Act of 1973 (ESA), 16 U.S.C.A. §§ 1531–1544, created the current regulatory regime for endangered species. The ESA provides an additional level of protection to more than 25 species of marine mammals. In all, NOAA lists 165 marine species as endangered or threatened.

The ESA is the primary means of protecting endangered marine species such as sea turtles (*State of Louisiana, ex rel. Guste v. Verity*, 853 F.2d 322 (5th Cir. 1988)); salmon (*United States v. Glenn-Colusa*, 788 F.Supp. 1126 (E.D.Cal. 1992)); seabirds (*Marbled Murrelet v. Babbitt*, 83 F.3d 1060 (9th Cir. 1996)); and sea turtles. It plays an important role in protecting other marine species, such as right whales (*Strahan v. Coxe*, 127 F.3d 155 (1st Cir. 1997)) that are also protected under the MMPA.

1.   ENDANGERED AND THREATENED

The ESA creates two groups of protected species: endangered and threatened. Like the MMPA, the ESA defines species to include distinct geographic populations. An endangered species is one that is "in danger of extinction throughout all or a significant portion of its range." 16 U.S.C.A. § 1532(6). See also *Center for Biological Diversity v. Lohn*, 296 F.Supp.2d 1223 (W.D.Wash. 2003).

A threatened species is one that is likely to become endangered in the foreseeable future. Id. § 1532(20). The Act defines a threatened species as "any species which is likely to become an endangered species within the *foreseeable* future." 16 U.S.C. § 1532(20). See *Safari Club Int'l v. Salazar (In re Polar Bear*

Endangered Species Act Listing & Section 4(d) Rule Litig.), 709 F.3d 1 (D.C. Cir. 2013) ("[T]the agency's reliance on climate projections was sufficient to support their definition of foreseeability.") The ESA category of threatened species was created not only to provide protection before a species becomes endangered, but also to phase down the level of protection for endangered species whose numbers are restored to survival levels. The Eastern North Pacific stock of gray whales was declared by the NMFS to be "fully recovered" and was removed from the endangered list and threatened status, but remains subject to the Whaling Convention and the MMPA. See also *Trout Unlimited v. Lohn*, 559 F.3d 946 (9th Cir. Wash. 2009) (ruling that NMFS may consider natural and hatchery-spawned salmon and steelhead together in one evolutionary significant unit when listing species under the ESA, and affirming the agency's decision to downlist the Upper Columbia River steelhead from endangered to threatened under the ESA).

All endangered or threatened species listed under the ESA are also categorized as "depleted" under the MMPA, although depleted marine mammal species may also include species that are below their OSP and thus likely to become threatened. See *Cook Inlet Beluga Whale v. Daley*, 156 F.Supp.2d 16 (D.D.C. 2001)(finding that the decision not to list the Cook Inlet Beluga whale as endangered was not arbitrary and capricious, when designation as depleted and moratorium legislation served to protect the species) and *Alaska v. Lubchenco*, 825 F. Supp. 2d 209 (D.D.C. 2011)(upholding subsequent listing of the species in

2008 as endangered because MMPA protections had been inadequate to halt further depletion of the species).

2.   PROHIBITION ON TAKE

Similar to the MMPA, ESA § 9 prohibits any person subject to U.S. jurisdiction from taking any endangered species within territorial waters or on the high seas and from importing or exporting such species. 16 U.S.C.A. § 1538(a)(1). The term "take" includes "to harass, harm, pursue, hunt, shoot, wound, kill, trap, capture, or collect." Id. § 1532(19). Prohibited takings include significant habitat modifications that actually injure listed species by altering their essential behavior patterns. See *Babbitt v. Sweet Home Chapter of Communities for a Great Oregon*, 515 U.S. 687, 115 S.Ct. 2407, 132 L.Ed.2d 597 (1995). See also *U.S. v. Town of Plymouth, Mass.*, 6 F.Supp.2d 81 (D.Mass. 1998) (issuing preliminary injunction prohibiting the Town of Plymouth from allowing off-road vehicles to drive on Plymouth Long Beach unless precautions are taken to protect threatened piping plovers). While the term "take" is a general term, it has not been applied to protect endangered marine animals held in less than optimal conditions in captivity. *People for the Ethical Treatment of Animals, Inc. v. Miami Seaquarium*, 189 F. Supp. 3d 1327 (S.D. Fla. 2016) (Court finds that a licensed exhibitor would only "take" an animal when its conduct gravely threatens or has the potential to gravely threaten an animal's survival.)

The ESA does not preempt more restrictive provisions of the MMPA where they are applicable. Id. § 1543.

3.   PENALTIES

Civil penalties for knowing violations of the ESA may be up to $25,000 per violation; other violations may receive up to a $500 penalty. Id. § 1540(a)(1). See *Block v. Josephson*, 156 F.3d 1235 (9th Cir. 1998). Criminal penalties of up to $50,000 and one year imprisonment may also be imposed. Id. § 1540(b). Perhaps the farthest-reaching penalty, however, is the provision that not only protected species involved in an unlawful act, but also guns, traps, boats, aircraft, and vehicles involved, are subject to forfeiture. Id. § 1540(e)(4)(B).

4.   DESIGNATION OF CRITICAL HABITAT

In drafting the ESA, Congress also recognized that protection of critical habitat may be as important as direct prohibitions on taking in ensuring the survival of a species or population. "Critical habitats" for endangered or threatened species are specific areas that are "essential to the conservation of the species," or areas that require "special management considerations or protection." Id. § 1532(5)(A). In general, critical habitat does not include the entire range of the species. Id. § 1532(5)(C). To the "maximum extent prudent and determinable," the Secretary must make critical habitat designations concurrently with the listing of a species. Id. § 1533(a)(3). See also *Center for Biological Diversity v. Evans*, 2005 WL 1514102 (N.D.Cal. 2005)(NMFS had a statutory duty to make the hard decision, i.e., to designate or not, unless it reasonably found the habitat was not determinable). More extensive habitat may be found to be essential to the survivability of a species over the long term, but critical habitat must at least include the minimum area necessary to avoid short-term jeopardy to the species. See *Alaska Oil & Gas Ass'n v. Salazar*, 916 F. Supp. 2d 974 (2013)(overturning the FWS designation of 187,157 square miles of coastal lands, barrier islands, and ice-dotted marine waters as critical habitat for the polar bear, concluding that the area was too big to be justified). Designation of critical habitat must be based on "the best scientific data." See, e.g., *Conner v. Burford,* 848 F.2d 1441, 1444 (9th Cir. 1988)(finding the agency was required to consider the scientific information available at the time, giving the species the benefit of the doubt). The Secretary must consider the economic impact of the designation and may exclude areas from critical habitat where the benefits of exclusion outweigh the benefits of including the areas as critical habitat unless the failure to designate the critical habitat will result in extinction of the species. 16 U.S.C.A. § 1533(b)(2).

5. EXCEPTIONS TO TAKING PROHIBITION

a. Scientific   Purposes,   Enhancement   of Survival and Self-Defense

Like the MMPA, the ESA contains a number of exceptions to section 9 takings prohibition. The ESA provides for permitting for scientific purposes, to enhance survival and for establishment of experimental populations. Id. § 1539(a), (j). A self-defense provision effectively acts as an exemption if a person acted on a good faith belief that he or she was acting to prevent bodily harm from an endangered or threatened species. Id. § 1540(b)(3).

b. Exception for Taking of Endangered or Threatened Species by Native Alaskans

The ESA also contains an exemption similar to (but more limited than) the MMPA for the taking of endangered or threatened species by Native Alaskans, who may also sell the non-edible byproducts of the wildlife when incorporated into "authentic native articles of handicrafts and clothing." Id. § 1539(e). In *United States v. Nuesca*, 945 F.2d 254 (9th Cir. 1991), two native Hawaiians, Nuesca and Kaneholani, appealed their convictions for taking two endangered green sea turtles and an endangered monk seal on the basis of aboriginal rights. The Ninth Circuit Court of Appeals found no evidence that the taking of green sea turtles or monk seals was a "traditional aspect of native Hawaiian life" or that a treaty protected such rights. Nuesca and Kaneholani also argued that the ESA could not constitutionally exempt one aboriginal group without exempting similarly situated groups. They contended that the Equal Protection Clause requires that all persons in similar circumstances be treated alike. The court found that the Hawaiian natives were not similarly situated to Native Alaskans, because the exemption was not created merely for indigenous populations, but for a particular indigenous group with subsistence needs and dependence on endangered and threatened species. The court also refused to apply a "strict scrutiny" analysis because the ESA discriminated on the basis of culture and food supply, not race. The court held that Congress had a rational basis for excepting Native Alaskans from the ESA, while not establishing an exception for other aboriginal groups, and upheld the convictions.

c. Exception for Antique Articles and Pre-ESA Parts

Because "possession" of endangered species or parts of such species is generally prohibited by the Act, two ESA exceptions deal with possession and importation in limited circumstances of antique articles and "pre-Act parts," particularly scrimshaw, made from endangered species. Id. § 1539(f)–(h).

d. Exception for Incidental Take

A 1982 amendment to the ESA added an exception for the Secretary to permit taking of endangered species that is "incidental to, and not the purpose of, the carrying out of an otherwise lawful activity." Id. § 1539(a)(1)(B). This section allowed incidental takings that had previously been prohibited under the Act. Because the provisions had rarely been enforced and had not been taken seriously in such circumstances, it has been argued that the permitting provisions for incidental taking actually strengthened the Act significantly.[10]

Applicants for an incidental taking permit must submit a conservation plan which specifies: (1) the impact of the taking; (2) a mitigation scheme that specifies measures to be taken to minimize the impacts and that assures adequate funding is available; and (3) the alternative actions considered and why they were not adopted. 16 U.S.C. § 1539(a)(2)(A). After the opportunity for public comment, the Secretary must make specific findings that the taking is incidental to lawful activity and that the applicant has adequate funding to implement a plan that minimizes and mitigates impacts of the taking to the maximum extent practicable. Finally, the Secretary must determine that "the taking will not appreciably reduce the likelihood of the survival and recovery of the species in the wild." Id. § 1539(a)(2)(B). See, e.g., *Loggerhead Turtle v. County Council of Volusia County, Florida*, 148 F.3d 1231 (11th Cir. 1998); *Sierra Club v. Babbitt*, 15 F.Supp.2d 1274 (S.D.Ala. 1988). The ESA also contains an incidental taking exception for federal agency actions under similar circumstances, 16 U.S.C.A. § 1536(b)(4), and provisions for the Endangered Species Committee to exempt certain agency actions. Id. § 1536(e)–(o).

---

[10]   Michael J. Bean & Melanie J. Rowland, The Evolution of National Wildlife Law 234–235 (3d ed. 1997).

6.   FEDERAL CONSULTATIONS

Section 7 of the ESA sets out the primary responsibilities of federal agencies under the Act:

> Each Federal agency shall, in consultation with and with the assistance of the Secretary, insure that any action authorized, funded, or carried out by such agency . . . is not likely to jeopardize the continued existence of any endangered species or threatened species or result in the destruction or adverse modification of habitat of such species which is determined by the Secretary . . . to be critical. . . .

Id. § 1536(a)(2); and

> After initiation of consultation . . . the Federal agency and the permit or license applicant shall not make any irreversible or irretrievable commitment of resources . . . which has the effect of foreclosing the formulation or implementation of any reasonable and prudent alternative measures. . . .

Id. § 1536(d). See *Hawksbill Sea Turtle v. Federal Emergency Management Agency*, 939 F.Supp. 1195 (D.V.I. 1996); *Pacific Rivers Council v. Thomas*, 30 F.3d 1050 (9th Cir. 1994).

In summary, ESA section 7 requires an initial determination of whether endangered or threatened species may be present in the area of a proposed activity. If so, the agency must consult with NMFS or the FWS to prepare a Biological Opinion before irreversibly committing resources. This Biological

Opinion must be based on the best data available and not necessarily the best data possible. *Oceana v. Ross*, 321 F. Supp. 3d 128 (D.D.C. 2018) (Reviewing a biological opinion of the impact of the Atlantic Scallop fishery on the threatened loggerhead turtle). NMFS is expected to incorporate its best data available from its climate-based models into its jeopardy findings. See *Turtle Island Restoration Network v. U.S. Department of Commerce,* 878 F.3d 725 (9th Cir. 2017)(finding NMFS' no-jeopardy finding in a Biological Opinion on increasing fishing effort by a longline swordfish fishery to be arbitrary and capricious in relation to the recovery for threatened loggerhead turtles).

If NMFS or FWS makes a determination that the activity will jeopardize an endangered species or adversely modify its critical habitat, the relevant service will suggest "reasonable and prudent measures" the agency may take. See *Greenpeace Foundation v. Mineta*, 122 F.Supp.2d 1123 (D.Ha. 2000) ("NMFS cannot speculate that no jeopardy to monk seals or adverse modification of their critical habitat will occur because it lacks enough information regarding the impact of the fishery on seals. Such a determination is arbitrary and capricious."); see also *Rarnsey v. Kantor*, 96 F.3d 434 (9th Cir. 1996).

7.   SEA TURTLES

a. U.S. Protection of Sea Turtles

Court, state, and municipal regulators have been actively involved in protecting sea turtles and sea turtle habitat. Federal Courts have asserted that the ESA prevails over the construction of sea walls to protect against erosion. *Sierra Club v. Von Kolnitz,* No. 2:16-cv-03815-DCN, 2017 WL 3480777, at *7 (D.S.C. 2017)(Enjoining installation of sea walls violating the ESA by interfering with sea turtle nesting and stating that "[i]n the balance between sea walls—that are by their very design temporary— and the ESA, which was enacted 'not merely to forestall the extinction of species [ ] but to allow a species to recover to the point where it may be delisted,' . . . the ESA prevails").

As with marine mammals, the regulation of interactions between endangered or threatened marine species and the fishing industry has proved to be a most controversial area. Six species of sea turtles, all of which are either endangered or threatened, are found in the waters of the Atlantic Ocean and the Gulf of Mexico where shrimping operations occur.[11] Studies have established that drowning of turtles in nets during shrimp trawls is a major cause of sea turtle mortality. Section 1533(d) of the ESA gives the Secretary authority to issue "regulations as he deems necessary and advisable to

---

[11]   Green turtle, Hawksbill turtle, Kemp's Ridley turtle, Leatherback Turtle, Loggerhead turtle, and the Olive Ridley turtle.

provide for the conservation" of threatened species. 16 U.S.C.A. § 1533(d).

In 1987, NMFS promulgated regulations requiring that turtle excluder devices (TEDs) be used by boats over 25-feet long in shrimp trawls during certain seasons in designated areas. Challenges to the implementation of the regulations pending further study of the relation between shrimping and sea turtle deaths were unsuccessful. See *Louisiana ex rel. Guste v. Verity*, 853 F.2d 322 (5th Cir. 1988)(record need only demonstrate that the regulations do in fact prevent prohibited takings, not that the regulations will enhance the species' chance of survival); *Louisiana ex rel. Guste v. Mosbacher*, 1989 WL 87616 (E.D.La.1989) (refusing to enjoin enforcement of TED regulations pending a National Academy of Science study required by ESA amendments in 1988). Following publication in 1990 of a study by the National Academy of Science recommending more extensive use of TEDs, NMFS issued regulations extending the use of TEDs to the entire year and to all shrimp trawlers. 50 C.F.R. Pts. 217 & 227.

Noncompliance with TED regulations is reported to be widespread, and the government has sought civil penalties as well as stiff fines for violations. See *United States v. Menendez*, 48 F.3d 1401 (5th Cir. 1995). See also *Center for Marine Conservation v. Brown*, 917 F.Supp. 1128 (S.D.Tex. 1996). In *United States v. Tran*, 765 F.Supp. 356 (S.D.Tex. 1991), the federal district court affirmed the application of a federal sentencing guideline that allows a sentence to be increased four levels if "the offense involved a quantity of fish, wildlife, or plants that was substantial in relation either to the overall population of the species, or to a discrete subpopulation." In spite of the fact that only a single Kemp's Ridley sea turtle was taken, the court found that the species' highly endangered status, the low rate of survival of eggs, and the length of time to reach reproductive maturity justified the increased sentence for possession of an endangered species and failure to use a TED.

b. WTO Case: Import Prohibition of Certain Shrimp and Shrimp Products (Shrimp/Turtle)

In 1997, India, Malaysia, Pakistan and Thailand brought a case to a WTO dispute panel challenging U.S. legislation prohibiting imports of shrimp from countries whose harvesting techniques may result in a "take" of sea turtles, unless the countries have a comparable regulatory program and rate of take comparable to U.S. vessels (see 16 U.S.C.A. § 1537 note, Section 609 of P.L. 101–102). The dispute panel found that the U.S. law was inconsistent with GATT Article XI limiting the use of import restrictions and was not justified under GATT Article XX. The U.S. appealed the panel's adverse decision to the new WTO Appellate Body. The Appellate Body held that the U.S. shrimp import prohibition was provisionally justified under Article XX(g). Specifically, it held that: (1) along with non-living resources, living resources such as the five species of sea turtles protected by the U.S. import prohibition are "exhaustible natural resources" that countries can protect through trade measures; (2) the U.S. prohibition is a measure "relating to" the conservation of such resources (not just an economic protection measure); and (3) the prohibition is a measure made effective in conjunction with restrictions on domestic production. WTO, United States Import Prohibition of Certain Shrimp and Shrimp Products, adopted Oct. 12, 1998, Appellate Body Report No. AB-1998-4.

The Appellate Body ultimately invalidated the U.S. prohibition, however, under the Article XX introductory clauses (the "chapeau") requiring that conservation measures not be applied in a manner which would constitute a means of arbitrary or unjustifiable discrimination between countries where the same conditions prevail. U.S. courts and governments officials in interpreting U.S. law had forced WTO members desiring to export shrimp to the U.S. to adopt sea turtle protection rules and technologies that were not merely *comparable,* but rather *essentially the same,* as those applied to the United States shrimp trawl vessels. Furthermore, U.S. procedures for certifying WTO members for eligibility to export shrimp to the U.S. were defective for not providing a transparent, predictable certification process. The Appellate Body also criticized the U.S. for failing to engage in serious, across-the-board negotiations for bilateral and multilateral sea turtle protection agreements beyond the 1996 Inter-American Convention for the Protection and Conservation of Sea Turtles with Brazil, Costa Rica, Mexico, Nicaragua, and Venezuela, and for failing to ratify relevant environmental conventions such as the 1982 Law of the Sea Convention and 1992 Biodiversity Convention.

While it found the U.S. shrimp import prohibition in violation of the GATT provisions, the WTO Appellate Body report is noteworthy for its explicit attempts to restore a balance between GATT free trade principles and environmental protection through the report's several endorsements of sustainable development, the precautionary approach and other principles of international environmental law found in the 1994 WTO agreement itself, the 1982 Law of the Sea Convention, and other conventions. Like the previous tuna cases, however, the Appellate Body continually stressed the importance of international cooperation over unilateral action.

The Appellate Body opinion is also noteworthy for what it did not say: It did not exclude the possibility of giving effect to extraterritorial environmental legislation, and it did not preclude regulations that went to the means of production, rather than to the product itself.

The Shrimp/Turtle case is a clear example of "losing the battle, but winning the war." The U.S. did not prevail in the case, but the WTO Appellate Body did interpret the GATT in a way that unambiguously allows nations to use economic and trade measures to protect marine species beyond their own borders. In a subsequent case in which Malaysia attacked the U.S. shrimp embargo, the Appellate Body found that by revising its procedures to comply with the recommendations and rulings of the earlier case, the U.S. import prohibition was justified under Article XX as a trade restriction "relating to the conservation of exhaustible natural resources." WTO, United States Import Prohibition of Certain Shrimp and Shrimp Products, adopted 15 June 2001, Appellate Body Report No. AB-2001-4.

c. U.S. Involvement in International Migratory Turtle Protection

In 1996, the U.S., Caribbean, Latin American and South American States adopted the Inter-American Convention for the Protection and Conservation of Sea Turtles. See http://www.iacseaturtle.org/ (entered into force 2001). The treaty requires parties to take measures, on the basis of the best available scientific evidence, for the protection, conservation, and recovery of sea turtle populations and their habitat. Among the measures that States are expected to take are prohibitions on domestic trade in sea turtles; restrictions on human activities impacting reproduction, nesting, and migration; scientific research, environmental education, and reduction of sea turtles as bycatch during fishing activities.

The U.S. has also entered into the 2001 South-East Asia Memorandum of Understanding on the Conservation and Management of Marine Turtles and their Habitats that was amended in 2009. See http://www.cms.int/iosea-turtles. This MOU which is deposited with the Convention on Migratory Species provides for multilateral cooperation to protect the same six species of turtles covered by the Inter-American Convention. Each party to the MOU is expected to implement the conservation and management plan in its land territory, in marine waters under its jurisdiction, and over vessels operating under its flag. Key objectives of the conservation and management plan include reducing direct and indirect causes of turtle mortality and conserving and rehabilitating marine turtle habitat.

d. U.S. Courts Cases Supporting Additional Sea Turtle Protection

In 1998, the federal court found that loggerhead turtles needed protection and that a county government could be held responsible for failing to regulate private persons and municipalities on lighting that interfered with turtle nesting. *Loggerhead Turtle v. County Council of Volusia County, Fla.*, 148 F.3d 1231 (11th Cir. 1998)(holding that Volusia County's "incidental take permit did not authorize it to take protected sea turtles through purely mitigatory measures associated with artificial beachfront lighting"); *Loggerhead Turtle v. County Council of Volusia County, Fla.,* 92 F. Supp. 2d 1296 (M.D. Fla. 2000) (finding the county's ordinance was sufficient to prohibit, restrict, and limit artificial beach lighting causing harm to turtles, but county could not be liable for residents not turning off lights).

The Volusia County beach lighting litigation was part of an almost decade long controversy over beach driving on the county's beaches—a practice going back a hundred years. In *Loggerhead Turtle v. Cty. Council of Volusia Cty., Fla.*, 896 F. Supp. 1170 (M.D. Fla. 1995), the court issued a preliminary injunction enjoining county from permitting private vehicles upon its beaches at night and from permitting vehicles to drive and park within the conservation zone on beaches. The litigation culminated with the development by the county of a Sea Turtle Habitat Conservation Plan, that was accepted by FWS which allowed it to issue an updated incidental take permit in 2005.

Beach driving is prohibited in most areas of the southeast United States, including all but five Florida counties. But just as in northeast Florida, beach driving has had a long tradition in other areas of the U.S., including Texas, the Outer Banks, areas of California, Oregon and Washington, and several national seashores. Development of plans and regulations to attempt to continue beach driving while protecting sea turtles and endangered nesting seabirds has been extremely controversial. Hatteras National Seashore has been particularly contentious. See, e.g., *Cape Hatteras Access Pres. All. v. Jewell*, 28 F.Supp.3d 537 (E.D.N.C. 2014)(rejecting declaratory and injunctive relief for group advocating for free access, and holding that National Park Service final rule limiting off-road vehicle use within national seashore did not violate national seashore enabling legislation or NEPA); *Cape Hatteras Access Pres. All. v. U.S. Dep't of Interior*, 731 F. Supp.2d 15 (D.D.C. 2010)(designation of critical habitat can take account of the economic impact of restricting ORV use).

CHAPTER XI

THE UNITED NATIONS CONVENTION ON THE LAW OF THE SEA (UNCLOS) AND THE UNITED STATES

A. THE HISTORICAL CONTEXT OF UNCLOS

Nations have long recognized the basic principle of the freedom of the high seas and of coastal State rights.[1] Between the 16th and 18th century, the extent of coastal State jurisdiction expanded from the distance of a cannon-shot to one-league to eventually three nautical miles. (A nautical mile is 1.15 miles or 1.85 kilometers). With each jurisdictional expansion, the existence of a land claim continued to dominate state interests at sea. Historically, any waters beyond three nautical miles were the high seas.

In the 20th century, the jurisdictional reach of nations into the oceans began to expand. In 1945, President Truman declared U.S. sovereign rights over the continental shelf. The 1945 Truman Proclamation on the Continental Shelf, 10 Fed. Reg. 12, 303 (1945), stated:

Having concern for the urgency of conserving and prudently utilizing its natural resources, the Government of the United States regards the natural resources of the subsoil and sea bed of the continental shelf beneath the high seas

---

[1] In this chapter the term "State" refers to an international nation and not to a U.S. State.

but contiguous to the coasts of the United States as appertaining to the United States, subject to its jurisdiction and control. . . . The character as high seas of the waters above the continental shelf and the right to their free and unimpeded navigation are in no way thus affected.

Although the U.S. claim to the continental shelf had no basis in international law, there was little international objection to the claim, and the Proclamation became the starting point of the international law of the continental shelf. The U.S. continental shelf claim initiated a flood of offshore claims that has been called the "ocean enclosure movement." See e.g., *North Sea Continental Shelf Cases* (F.R.G./Den; F.R.G./Neth.), 1969 WL 1 (1969).

International offshore claims proliferated during the 1950s. These claims ranged from extensions of 12-mile territorial seas to assertions by the President of Chile on June 23, 1947 and by the Government of Peru on August 1, 1947, of national maritime zones of 200 miles. The Chilean declaration proclaimed national "sovereignty over submarine areas, regardless of their size or depth, as well as over the adjacent seas extending as far as necessary to preserve, protect, maintain, and utilize natural resources and wealth" and the identification of "protection zones for whaling and deep sea fishery".[2] The 200-mile limit came into being five years later on 18 August 1952. The Santiago Declaration was signed by three Latin American countries that border

---

[2]   Presidential Declaration Concerning Continental Shelf of 23 June 1947, El Mercurio, Santiago de Chile, 29 June 1947.

the South Pacific: Chile, Ecuador and Peru. To harmonize international jurisdictional claims and lessen potential for conflict, codification of the law of sea became a shared goal of nations.

The First United Nations Conference on the Law of the Sea (UNCLOS I) in 1958 produced four treaties on the territorial sea and contiguous zone, the continental shelf, the high seas, and high seas fisheries. The U.S. acceded to all four treaties. The Convention on the Continental Shelf was a clear international sign that coastal States intended to control the oil and gas resources on their continental margins. Although these treaties were widely accepted as codifying international law, major issues, such as the allowable breadth of territorial sea and continental shelf claims, were not precisely addressed leading to concerns by parties, such as the U.S., over the protection of navigational freedoms. The treaties were also vague in how to address the growing stresses on fishery stocks and the environment. A second conference in 1960 failed to resolve these critical issues.

During the 1960s, marine fishery resources began to decline dramatically. Although part of the decline was probably due to degradation of the marine environment, the decline was primarily attributable to the intense fishing efforts of large, distant water fishing fleets. To attempt to deal with both the environmental impact on marine ecosystems and the economic impact on coastal fishermen, nations began to regulate high seas fisheries, at that point beyond 3–12 mile territorial seas, first through largely ineffective multilateral negotiations and then through controversial extensions of exclusive fishery zones.

Also during the 1960s, a number of private consortia were formed to develop technology to mine manganese nodules from the deep seabed. Manganese nodules are potato-sized masses of high-grade metal ores that are found on the deep ocean floor virtually all over the world. The nodules are composed primarily of manganese, but also contain iron, nickel, cobalt, and copper. Changing markets for metals, particularly copper and cobalt, and new technologies made mining of the manganese nodules commercially attractive for the first time.

Developing countries viewed the exploitation of the deep seabed as another example of hegemony and neocolonialism by developed countries. If developed countries were free to mine the seabed, developing countries would lose twice, because they lacked the technology to exploit the seabed and because developing countries are the major land-based producers of the ores with which seabed minerals would compete. Arvid Pardo, the ambassador from Malta, brought the issue to the United Nations in 1967. He proposed that the seabed should be declared the "common heritage of mankind" and be governed by an international regime. In a 108 to zero vote (including an affirmative U.S. vote), the General Assembly adopted these principles in the Declaration of Principles Governing the Seabed and the Ocean Floor, and the Subsoil Thereof, beyond the Limits of

National Jurisdiction. G.A. Res. 2749 (XXV), U.N. GAOR Supp. No. 28, at 28, U.N. Doc. A/8028 (1970).

The developments of the 1960s and the gaps in the 1958 treaty regimes set the stage for negotiation of a treaty that would deal with all aspects of the law of the sea. The United States played a lead role in pushing for the Third United Nations Conference on the Law of the Sea (UNCLOS III), convened in 1973. Of particular concern to the U.S. was freedom of navigation and jurisdictional delineation of maritime zones.

The U.S. and the Soviet Union pressed in negotiations for free passage through straits.[3] Coastal nations resisted this position and argued for the right to remain secure against potential foreign military vessels operating in close proximity to the shore. The eventual compromise was a regime of innocent passage and navigational freedoms that did not treat straits as equivalent to the high seas but did create a new right of "transit passage." How this regime is implemented is of crucial importance to U.S. national security interests. For the U.S., the ability for military vessels including submarines to transit oceans has been a key aspect of maintaining peace and order. For example, during the Cold War between the U.S. and the Soviet Union, the ability of nuclear submarines to navigate freely while submerged served as an important deterrent to

---

[3]   For geographers, a strait is a narrow passage between two larger bodies of water. In the context of the law of the sea, a strait takes on a narrower definition as a narrow passage between two bodies of water used for international navigation.

military engagement between the two superpowers. The Navy deployed its first nuclear submarine, the USS Nautilus, in 1954.

The work of the conference was divided among three main committees: The First Committee dealt with the international regime for exploitation of the deep seabed; the Second Committee was concerned with jurisdictional zones, maritime boundaries, and the rights and duties of nations; and the Third Committee dealt with marine scientific research and the marine environment. After a decade of draft texts, negotiations, and consensus building, the 1982 United Nations Convention on the Law of the Sea (UNCLOS) was adopted by a vote of 130 to 4, with 17 abstentions. The treaty coined the "constitution of the oceans" by Tommy Koh, the President of the Third Conference consists of 320 articles and nine annexes. UNCLOS, *opened for signature* Dee. 19, 1982, United Nations, Official Text of the United Nations Convention on the Law of the Sea with Annexes and Index, U.N. Doc. A/CONF.62/122, U.N. Sales No. E.83.V.5 (1983), *reprinted in* 21 I.L.M. 1261 One hundred and nineteen countries signed the Convention at Montego Bay, Jamaica, on December 10, 1982.

While the United States was an active participant in the negotiations, the United States did not sign the treaty because of disagreement with text in Part XI of the treaty governing the deep seabed beyond coastal nation jurisdiction called "the Area." Other industrialized states signed the treaty but did not ratify at that time.

In late 1993, the treaty received the requisite 60 ratifications to come into force on November 16, 1994. In anticipation of the treaty coming into force without the support from certain large coastal nations, the Secretary-General of the United Nations had begun negotiations in 1990 to address the "defects and shortcomings" of the seabed provisions and to establish the "universality" of the treaty. Intense negotiations through the summer of 1994, in which the U.S. was a leading participant, resulted in the Agreement Relating to the Implementation of Part XI of UNCLOS, which effectively amended the deep seabed mining provisions of UNCLOS. See U.N. Doc. A/Res/48/263 (1994), *reprinted in* 33 I.L.M. 1309 (1994).

The Agreement addressed many of the concerns voiced by countries who had yet to ratify and was adopted on July 28, 1994, by the General Assembly in a vote of 121 in favor, no opposition votes, and seven abstentions. Specifically, the Assembly of the International Seabed Authority (ISA), the international organization created in Part XI to regulate seabed mining in the Area, would no longer have one-nation one-vote system on most policy matters but would instead approve or reject recommendations forwarded by the ISA Council. The United States concerns that it might not be able to participate on the Council was addressed by amendments guaranteeing a seat to "the State on the date of entry into force of the Convention, having the largest economy in terms of gross domestic product," e.g., the United States. The United States also secured itself a seat on the Finance Committee.

Revisions of the treaty led to a removal of production limitations and other market restrictive measures on seabed minerals. Mandated transfers of technology from mining firms to the Enterprise, the operating arm of the ISA that would be able to participate in mining activities on behalf of the global community, were also eliminated. The new agreement on Part XI established that access to the seabed mineral resources would be based on a first come-first served basis while reducing financial obligations for States and private companies.

The United States signed the agreement on July 29, 1994 and agreed to be provisionally bound by the treaty on November 16, 1994, temporarily allowing for participation in the governance of the deep seabed mining regime. The agreement entered into force on July 28, 1996. Because the U.S. had yet to accede to UNCLOS and provisional arrangements terminated on November 16, 1998, the U.S. had to give up its seat on the ISA, the Finance Committee Council, and the Legal and Technical Commission. The U.S. has been since granted observer status at the ISA.

In late 1994, President Clinton transmitted the Convention to the Senate Foreign Relations Committee and, as required by the U.S. Constitution, requested the Senate to exercise its advice and consent powers and issue a "resolution of ratification" to accede to UNCLOS. It was not until February 2004 that the Senate Foreign Relations Committee recommended, by unanimous vote, that the Senate give its advice and consent, and transmitted the treaty to the Senate on October 7, 2004. Although

President Bush expressed unequivocal support for the treaty in December 2004 when he responded to a report and recommendations by the U.S. Commission on Ocean Policy that the U.S. should accede to the treaty "as a matter of national security, economic self-interest, and international leadership," political opposition in the Senate failed to produce a "resolution of ratification." When the Senate Committee on Foreign Relations favorably reported out the Convention again in 2012, the Senate again failed to vote and give its advice and consent.

At various times, over the last couple decades, the political reasons presented for opposition to accession include: a rejection of the concept of common heritage as applied to seabed mining, concerns over the comprehensive dispute settlement mechanism in UNCLOS, financial burdens associated with funding the treaty bodies, and a lack of strategic value in joining the treaty because the U.S. accepts most of the treaty as customary international law without exposing itself to potential dispute settlement. U.S. Courts have accepted UNCLOS as customary international law as articulated by one court's observation that "[a]lthough the treaty ... is currently pending ratification before the Senate, it nevertheless carries the weight of law from the date of its submission by the President to the Senate" and "expresses to the international community the United States' ultimate intention to be bound by the pact." *U.S. v. Royal Caribbean Cruises,* 24 F. Supp 2d

155, 159 (D.P.R. 1997).[4, 5] As of 2019, the United States is not a party to UNCLOS.

B. THE TERRITORIAL SEA, CONTIGUOUS ZONE, AND ARCHIPELAGIC WATERS

Negotiations leading to the 1958 Convention on the Territorial Sea and the Contiguous Zone (Territorial Sea Convention), *done* at Geneva, April 29, 1958, 15 U.S.T. 1606, 516 U.N.T.S. 205, provided no international consensus on the limit of territorial

---

[4]   This District Court correctly understood customary practices in international treaty law when they went on to observe "Pending a treaty's rejection or ratification by the Senate under Article 18 of the Vienna Convention, the United States is bound to uphold the purpose and principles of the agreement to which the executive branch has tentatively made the United States a party." Id. at 159.

[5]   Other cases citing UNCLOS as reflecting customary international law include: United States v. Alaska, 503 U.S. 569, 588 n.10 (1992) (reference to UNCLOS baseline provisions); *Barber v. Hawaii*, 42 F.3d 1185, 1195–96 (9th Cir. 1994) (reference to UNCLOS provisions on innocent passage); *United States v. Ramirez-Ferrer*, 82 F.3d 1131, 1136 n4 (1st Cir. 1996) (reference to UNCLOS on freedom of navigation); *Mayaguezanos por la Salud y el Ambiente v. United States*, 198 F.3d 297, 304–05 n.14 (1st Cir. 1999) (reference to UNCLOS jurisdictional provisions); *Martha's Vineyard Scuba Headquarters, Inc. v. Unidentified Wreck and Abandoned Steam Vessel*, 883 F.2d 1059, 1066. (1st Cir. 1987) (reference to high seas flag state jurisdiction); *Grupo Protexa, S.A. v. All American Marine Slip*, 20 F.3d 1224 (3d Cir. 1994) (reference to sovereign rights in Mexico's exclusive economic zone); *R.M.S. Titanic v. Haver*, 171 F.3d 943, 965 (4th Cir.1999) (high seas freedoms); *United States v. Hasan*, 747 F. Supp. 2d 599, 619 (E.D. Va., 2010) (Referencing UNCLOS to define the customary international law aspects of the crime of piracy). Not all U.S. Courts have viewed UNCLOS as customary international law see e.g., *United States v. Roberts,* 1 F. Supp. 2d 601, 606 (E.D. La. 1998) (Court refuses to apply UNCLOS provision on nationality of ships)

sea claims. By 1965, only 32 of 107 coastal nations continued to limit territorial sea claims to three miles. By the time UNCLOS III convened in 1973, only 25 countries continued to assert three-mile claims. Of the 86 coastal countries claiming more than three miles, 56 claimed a 12-mile territorial sea. At the conclusion of UNCLOS III negotiations in 1982, 77 of 135 nations claimed 12-mile territorial jurisdiction, and only 24 maintained a three-mile claim.

MARITIME JURISDICTIONAL ZONES

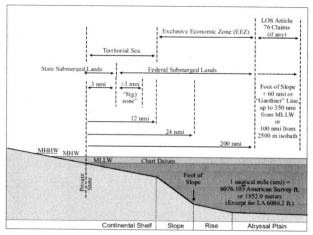

Source: NOAA, Office of Coast Survey

UNCLOS recognizes the right of coastal countries to claim a 12 nautical mile territorial sea and a 24 nautical mile contiguous zone. The U.S. courts have adopted UNCLOS jurisdictional zones as customary international law. In a case involving piracy off the coast of Somalia, the Fourth Circuit observed "UNCLOS explicitly restricts territorial seas from extending farther than twelve nautical miles. . . . With nearly 170 signatory nations today, UNCLOS enjoys widespread acceptance in the international community. . . . [A]lthough the United States is not a signatory to UNCLOS, this country recognizes the treaty's place as an accurate reflection of customary international law." *United States v. Beyle,* 782 F.3d 159, 167 (4th Cir. 2015) (Refusing to recognize that Somalia has a 200 nautical mile "territorial sea).

In order to protect freedom of navigation, UNCLOS provided for both a "right of innocent passage" through territorial seas (UNCLOS, art. 17) and "transit passage" through international straits, (UNCLOS, art. 38) and archipelagic waters.

1.   CREATING TERRITORIAL SEA BASELINES

The 12 nautical miles constituting the territorial sea are measured from baselines identified in the UNCLOS as the "low-water line along the coast as marked on large-scale charts officially recognized by the coastal State." (UNCLOS, art. 5) The baselines are the fundamental starting points for claiming maritime zones. Baselines are constructed from a series of basepoints.

The right of a coastal nation to a territorial sea is asserted unilaterally but conflicts can arise over the selection of basepoints and baselines. Measuring baselines is not straightforward because it depends on what basepoints a State chooses to rely upon. Certain basepoints are considered more important than other basepoints for determining the breadth of a maritime zone because baselines are generally drawn through an "envelope of arcs" methodology from basepoints that might be measured from a mainland location or from an island location.

ENVELOPE OF ARCS METHOD

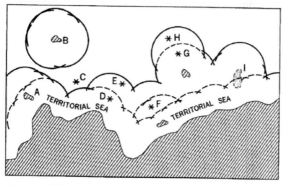

Source: NOAA, Office of Coast Survey, A. Shalowitz, Shore and Sea Boundaries.

It is important to note that U.S. states are not permitted to draw straight baselines in order to enlarge claims of internal waters. This is reserved for international States. *United States v. California*, 381 U.S. 139, 85 S.Ct. 1401, 14 L.Ed.2d 296 (1965); *United States v. Alaska*, 521 U.S. 1, 117 S.Ct. 1888, 138 L.Ed.2d 231 (1997).

In a pre-UNCLOS case, the U.S. Supreme Court relying on the 1958 Territorial Convention offered a definition for "low-water" line and measuring basepoints associated with certain features. In

United States v. California, 381 U.S. 139, 85 S.Ct. 1401, 14 L.Ed.2d 296 (1965), the Supreme Court held that the average of the lower low tides establishes the baseline from which the U.S. territorial sea is measured.

a. Straight Baselines

Straight baselines are more of an exception than a rule for drawing maritime zones. When a State draws a straight baseline, any waters on landward side of the baseline are deemed to be "internal waters" that are generally not governed by the UNCLOS regime. (art. 8)[6] When UNCLOS was being negotiated, States understood that unusual coastal geography might necessitate baselines that did not strictly follow the coast in order to avoid situations where enclaves (such as bays) might become non-territorial waters, i.e., internal waters.

Examples of where straight baselines might be drawn include:

- where there is a fringe of islands along the coast (art. 7(1));

- where there is a delta or other natural condition along the coast that makes the coast unstable (art. 7(2));

---

[6] Article 8 does provide that if a straight baseline is used in delineating a maritime zone that ends up creating "internal waters" in an area that did not previously have "internal waters", then the right of innocent passage persists through the newly created "internal waters".

- where the coastline is deeply indented and cut into, e.g., Norway (art. 7(1));

- where an archipelagic nation draws baselines joining the outermost points of its islands (art. 7(4); or

- where lighthouses that are permanently above sea level have been built on a low-tide elevation (art. 7(4)).

For purposes of measuring the territorial sea, low-water lines may in some cases be measured from low-tide elevations which are naturally formed areas of land "surrounded by and above water at low tide but submerged at high tide." (UNCLOS, art.13). In a limited number of cases, such low-tide elevations may be used to draw straight baselines but the straight baselines "must not depart to any appreciable extent from the general direction of the coast" and "the sea areas lying within the lines must be sufficiently closely linked to the land domain to be subject to the regime of internal waters." (UNCLOS, art. 7(4))

There have been a number of disputes over the legality of using straight baselines. In the *Fisheries Case* (U.K. v. Norway), 1951 WL 12 (1951), the International Court of Justice recognized the legality of straight baselines in certain limited instances. In *Maritime Delimitations and Territorial Questions Between Qatar and Bahrain* (Qatar v. Bahrain), Final Judgment (Mar. 16, 2001), the ICJ stated that "the method of straight baseline delineation codified in the 1982 LOS Convention must be applied restrictively and is an exception to the normal rules for the determination of baselines." More recently in the *South China Sea Arbitration (Philippines v. China),* PCA (12 July 2016), the arbitral panel rejected the use of straight baselines "in particular with respect to offshore archipelagos not meeting the criteria for archipelagic baselines [in UNCLOS]."

CANADIAN STRAIGHT BASELINES
PROTESTED BY THE US

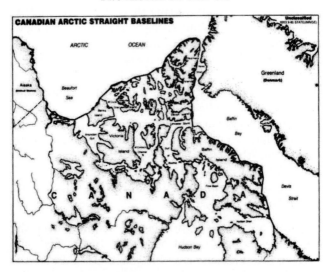

Source: US Dep't of State, United States Responses to Excessive National Maritime Claims, Limits in the Seas No. 112—March 9, 1992.

The United States policy has been not to draw straight baselines but to instead follow "normal baselines." The United States, as discussed infra, has actively protested "excessive straight baselines" as part of its freedom of navigation operations.

The United States follows the practice of drawing closing lines across the mouth of river flowing directly into the sea, at the low-water line of the river's banks (art. 9) and also across bays. But these lines are to be distinguished from straight baselines.

b. Bays

UNCLOS art. 10 adopts the so-called "twenty-four mile, semi-circle" rule to measure legal bays (sometimes called juridical bays) such as the Monterey Bay in California to distinguish between internal waters and territorial sea. The formula requires that the "bay area" be at least as large as the area of a semicircle whose diameter is equal to no more than 24 miles at the "bay mouth."

In order to determine whether a feature meets the criteria of Article 10, a State should measure between the "natural entrance points" of a bay and then draw a semi-circle from the line connecting the two entrance points. If the area of the semi-circle is less than the area of water, then the feature will qualify as a legal bay as long as the distance between the natural entrance points is less than 24 miles. The territorial sea will be measured from the closing line across the "bay mouth," an approach adopted by the Supreme Court in *United States v. California.*

JURIDICAL BAY

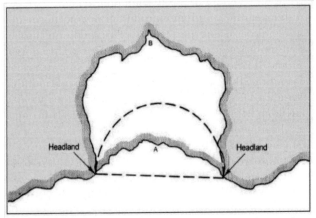

Figure 48. The semicircle test. Applying the semicircle test, indentation "B" qualifies as a bay, but indentation "A" does not. *(After I Shalowitz, Figure 4)*

Source: NOAA, Office of Coast Survey, A. Shalowitz, Shore and Sea Boundaries, volume 2.

In addition to a legal bay, there are also historic bays. A body of water may qualify as a historic bay if a State can demonstrates that it has openly, effectively, and over a long period of time continuously exercised authority over the waters with the acquiescence of foreign States.

The Chesapeake Bay and Delaware Bay have long been recognized as historic bays. The United States has often objected, however, to recognition of other historic bays both within the United States and on the shores of other countries. Domestically, the establishment of historic waters would change federal-state boundaries for purposes of oil

development and fisheries management. See, e.g.,
United States v. Alaska, 422 U.S. 184, 95 S.Ct. 2240,
45 L.Ed.2d 109 (1975). Internationally, the United
States' objections to assertions of historic bays by
other countries are usually related to preserving the
freedom of navigation. For example, the United
States has objected to Libya's historically-based
claim to the Gulf of Sidra, the former Soviet Union's
claim to the Peter the Great Bay, and Canada's claim
to waters in Hudson Bay.

c. Islands

An island can independently generate maritime
zones, but in some cases can also be a basepoint that
might be used in defining the maritime zones. An
island is a "naturally formed area of land,
surrounded by water, which is above water at high
tide." (UNCLOS, art. 121(1)). An island is
distinguished from a rock through its capacity to
sustain human habitation or economic life. (Id., art.
121(3).

In *The South China Sea Arbitration* (*The Republic
of the Philippines v. The People's Republic of China*),
PCA Case N° 2013–1912 (July 2016), the Permanent
Court of Arbitration (PCA) addressed the question of
when a "high tide feature" would be categorized
legally as an island. The PCA rejected the relevance
of geological and geomorphological characteristics,
and found that size alone was not determinative. Id.,
paras. 482. Characteristics of an "island" identified
as relevant by the PCA include the following:

1. The natural capacity of the feature does not take regard of modifications intended to increase its capacity. "As a matter of law, human modification cannot change the seabed into a low-tide elevation or a low-tide elevation into an island. A low-tide elevation will remain a low-tide elevation under the Convention, regardless of the scale of the island or installation built atop it. (Id., para. 305). Further, "a rock cannot be transformed into a fully entitled island through land reclamation. The status of a feature must be assessed on the basis of its natural condition." (Id., para. 508).

2. The "natural capacity" depends on such factors as the presence of enough water, food and shelter to sustain a long-term population. The PCA noted this must be assessed with the potential for a group of features to collectively sustain human habitation and economic life. (Id., paras. 490, 497).

3. "Habitation" refers to "inhabitants who can fairly be said to constitute the natural population of the feature, for whose benefit the resources of the exclusive economic zone were seen to merit protection. (Id,. paras. 490–492).

4. "Economic life" must be "oriented around the around the feature" and involve the local population. "Economic activity that is entirely dependent on external resources or devoted to using a feature as an object for extractive activities" falls short "with respect to this necessary link to the feature itself." (Para. 500).

5. If a high-tide feature has the *capacity* to sustain *either* human habitation or an economic life of its own, then the State can generate an EEZ and continental shelf from the feature. (Para. 497)(emphasis added). Capacity is not dependent on current use, but the PCA found historic use to be strong evidence. (Paras. 483–484).[7]

It should be noted that while the holdings of an international tribunal are binding only on the parties, they have been important in the development of the law of the sea in interpreting the major treaties of the last century and "crystallizing" customary international law.

d. The Question of Ambulatory Baselines

With expectations of sea level rise, there are questions about how such climate change driven phenomena will impact baselines identified under UNCLOS. Baselines can move because coastlines are dynamic. Two main legal approaches are possible to handle the physical movement. First, States can decide that baselines do move depending on changes to geography such as the submergence of an island that serves as a basepoint for drawing baselines. Second, States can decide that baselines may be legally fixed, and a State does not have to update its nautical charts for jurisdictional purposes though it may have to update charts for navigational purposes. The International Law Association discussed this issue at length and concluded that in order to

---

[7]   See also Bernard H. Oxman, The South China Sea Arbitration Award, 24 U. Miami Int'l & Comp. L. Rev. 235 (2017).

promote legal certainty any baselines and outer limits of maritime zones properly determined under UNCLOS "should not be required to be recalculated should sea level change affect the geographical reality of the coastline." International Law Association, Resolution 5/2018, Committee on International Law and Sea Level Rise. The topic of "sea level rise in relation to international law" which covers the question of the impact of sea level rise on baselines has been included as part of the long-term program of work for the International Law Commission.

2.   CONTIGUOUS ZONE

Beyond the territorial sea, a coastal nation may claim an additional zone to prevent infringement of sanitary, fiscal, customs, and immigration laws. UNCLOS art. 33 restricts the contiguous zone to no more than 24 nautical miles from the baselines that were used to measure the territorial sea.

3.   ARCHIPELAGIC STATES AND WATERS

"Archipelagic waters" refer to waters under the jurisdiction of an archipelagic State as defined in Part IV of UNCLOS located within its baselines. An "archipelagic State" is defined in UNCLOS Article 46(a) as "a State that is constituted wholly by one or more archipelagos and may include other islands." The regime of an archipelagic state is a new development under UNCLOS. Archipelagic straight baselines are subject to the same conditions as other baselines and, in addition, generally may not exceed 100 miles per segment. (UNCLOS, art. 47).

A country composed of both mainland and archipelagoes, e.g., Greece, Canada, or the United States, is not an archipelagic state for purposes of the law of the sea.

In terms of determining jurisdiction, archipelagic States have the right to enclose the main islands of the archipelago and may extend to the outermost points and drying reefs of the archipelago. To qualify as an "archipelagic State," a State must be able to prove that the "ratio of the area of the water to the area of the land, including atolls, is between 1:1 and 9:1." (UNCLOS, art. 47(1)). Waters within the "enclosure" are referred to as archipelagic waters. Territorial waters are measured from the archipelagic baselines. Under this formula, Trinidad and Tobago, Philippines, and Indonesia would qualify as an archipelagic States, but Cuba will not.

Reflecting concerns for freedom of navigation, the United States has narrowly interpreted the rights of nations to use straight baselines, particularly archipelagic baselines. A policy statement by President Reagan, infra, accepting most of the principles of UNCLOS, however, did not exclude archipelagic baselines and apparently means that the United States will acknowledge the right of archipelagic countries to use such baselines so long as navigation rights are recognized. But the United States has protested, and will continue to protest, excessive baseline claims by other nations by, for example, conducting Freedom of Navigation operations where U.S. vessels conduct innocent passage or transit passage through waters where another State asserts a particular "excessive" claim that impedes freedom of navigation, innocent passage or transit passage.

4.   UNITED STATES TERRITORIAL SEA AND CONTIGUOUS ZONE

Although the United States had not ratified UNCLOS, on December 27, 1988, President Reagan announced the extension of the United States territorial sea to 12 nautical miles by Presidential Proclamation No. 5928 "[i]n accordance with international law, as reflected in the . . . 1982 United Nations Convention on the Law of the Sea," and recognized a right of transit passage for foreign vessels in U.S. waters. 3 C.F.R. § 547 (1989).

The United States is a party to the 1958 Convention on the Territorial Sea and Contiguous Zone, *done* at Geneva, Apr. 29, 1958, 15 U.S.T. 1606, 516 U.N.T.S. 205, which allows a country to claim a contiguous zone beyond territorial waters to 12 miles from the shore. The United States claimed a nine-mile contiguous zone prior to the 1988 extension of the territorial sea from three miles to 12 miles. Apparently because the 1958 Convention limited the contiguous zone to no more than 12 miles, the Presidential declaration extending the territorial sea did not make a further claim to a 24-mile contiguous zone, which is recognized by UNCLOS. (UNCLOS, art. 33(2)). In 1999, however, President Clinton declared a contiguous zone extending 24 nautical

miles from U.S. baselines by Presidential
Proclamation. See Presidential Proclamation No.
7219. August 2, 1999, 64 Fed. Reg. 48701.

a. Innocent Passage

A coastal nation has the same sovereign rights
over the territorial sea as it has over its land territory
and inland waters except that the territorial sea is
subject to the right of innocent passage. The concept
of innocent passage is based on customary
international law and does not include overflight by
aircraft.

Innocent passage must be continuous, expeditious
navigation through the territorial waters for the
purpose of either traversing them or proceeding to or
from internal waters or a port. Ships may stop and
anchor when incidental to normal navigation, when
rendered necessary by *force majeure* or distress, and
when required to render assistance to persons, ships,
or aircraft in danger or distress. (Territorial Sea
Convention, art. 14; UNCLOS, art. 18).

Article 14(4) of the Territorial Sea Convention
adopted the following definition for "innocent
passage":

Passage is innocent so long as it is not
prejudicial to the peace, good order or security of
the coastal State. Such passage shall take place
in conformity with these articles and with other
rules of international law.

The article does not require a specific act or violation
of coastal country's law for passage to lose its

innocent character; however, it also does not provide that innocence is lost merely by the violation of a coastal country's law. The only circumstance in which the treaty provided that a breach of coastal country law *ipso facto* negates innocent passage is in the case of violation of laws to prevent vessels from fishing in the territorial sea. (Territorial Sea Convention, art. 14(5)).

UNCLOS adopted the definition of the Territorial Sea Convention, but also added a list of specific activities that will be considered "prejudicial" to peace, good order, and security. This list includes: fishing; scientific research or surveys; willful and serious pollution; interference with communications systems; acts of propaganda or spying; loading or unloading of goods, currency, or persons in violation of customs, fiscal, sanitary, or immigration laws; weapons exercises and the landing or launching of aircraft or military devices; "any threat or use of force against the sovereignty, territorial integrity or political independence of the coastal [nation]"; and "any other activity not having a direct bearing on passage." (UNCLOS, art. 19(2)).

Nations have a positive duty not to hamper vessels engaged in innocent passage by imposing requirements that effectively deny such passage or by discriminating against the vessels of any nation. Coastal countries must also assist navigation by giving appropriate notice of navigational dangers in the territorial sea.

The duty not to hamper innocent passage does not mean that foreign vessels are not subject to any regulation by coastal nations. In addition to regulations relating to fishing and living resources in territorial waters, a coastal nation may regulate foreign vessels with respect to: (1) navigation safety, maritime traffic, and protection of navigational aids; (2) protection of offshore facilities and installations, cables, and pipelines; (3) marine research; (4) environmental protection and pollution control; and (5) prevention of infringement of customs, fiscal, immigration, and sanitary laws. (UNCLOS, art. 21(1)). A coastal country may not impose regulations as to the design, construction, manning, or equipment of foreign ships engaged in innocent passage unless the laws are giving effect to "generally accepted international rules or standards," e.g., MARPOL 73/78 standards. (UNCLOS. art. 21(2)).

As a general proposition, coastal countries should not exert criminal jurisdiction on board foreign vessels exercising innocent passage in connection with crimes conducted onboard the vessel during its passage. However, the coastal country may investigate or make arrests on board the vessel:

(a)   if the consequences of the crime extend to the coastal State;

(b)   if the crime is of a kind to disturb the peace of the country or the good order of the territorial sea;

(c)   if the assistance of the local authorities has been requested . . .; or

(d) if such measures are necessary for the suppression of illicit traffic in narcotic drugs or psychotropic substances.

(UNCLOS, art. 27(1); see also Territorial Sea Convention, art. 19(1)).

U.S. courts have accepted as customary international law the UNCLOS definitions of "innocent passage."

b. Military Vessels and Innocent Passage

The right of military vessels, i.e., "warships," to innocent passage has been one of the most controversial issues in the law of the sea. Views have been so widely divergent that neither the Territorial Sea Convention nor UNCLOS address the issue directly.

After World War II, the United States and the United Kingdom led Western naval powers in asserting that warships as well as merchant vessels were entitled to innocent territorial sea passage. Countries, such as the U.S.S.R., China, and many developing countries, sought to require notification and even authorization for passage of warships.

In 1986 and 1988, the U.S. and the U.S.S.R. came dangerously close in the Black Sea to escalating a conflict over the parameters of innocent passage. In 1986, the U.S. sailed two naval vessels through Soviet territorial waters that had not been pre-authorized by the Soviet government for warship passage. The Soviet government responded by ordering its naval forces to be combat ready. The tensions de-escalated after U.S. vessels left Soviet waters. In 1988, the U.S. again sailed two vessels into the Black Sea. The Soviets responded by using one of its naval vessels to try and force one of the U.S. vessels into "international waters." The U.S. asserted that warships had a right of innocent passage that did not require pre-approval from a coastal state. In response to these two incidents, the leaders of the U.S. and U.S.S.R. issued in 1989 a Joint Statement on the Uniform Interpretation of Rules of International Law Governing Innocent Passage, which provided:

> All ships, including warships, regardless of cargo, armament, or means of propulsion enjoy the right of innocent passage through the territorial sea in accordance with international law, for which neither prior notification nor authorization is required.

28 I.L.M. 6 (November 1989).

It is clear under customary international law, as well as under Territorial Sea Convention article 14(6) and UNCLOS article 20, that "[i]n the territorial sea, submarines and other underwater vehicles are required to navigate on the surface and to show their flag." It is also unquestionable that neither military nor commercial aircraft have a right of passage through the airspace above territorial waters.

The issue of military vessel passage continues to be a sensitive issue for the United States. A number of States, including China, assert that they interpret UNCLOS to give a coastal state some discretion over the conditions for a foreign military vessel to be permitted to transit territorial waters.

c. International Straits and Transit Passage

An international strait is a maritime area consisting of the territorial sea of a State that bridges between territorial sea between one part of the high seas or an exclusive economic zone and another part of the high seas or an exclusive economic zone. The right of transit through international straits differs from other innocent passage through territorial waters in that the bordering nations may not suspend passage under any circumstances. See Territorial Sea Convention, art. 16(4). The higher level of protection of passage through international straits is based on the rationale that such passage is necessary for exercise of freedoms of the high sea.

In *The Corfu Channel Case* (U.K. v. Alb.), 1949 WL 1 (1949), the United Kingdom had sent warships through the channel to assert its right of passage without prior notification to Albania. The ICJ held that ships, including warships, of all nations have a right of innocent passage "through straits used for international navigation between two parts of the high seas without the previous authorization of a coastal [nation]."

UNCLOS took an additional step to mitigate the impact of the extension of 12-mile territorial seas on submerged passage of submarines and overflight in international straits by creating a new right of "transit passage." Transit passage is the "exercise . . . of the freedom of navigation and overflight solely for the purpose of continuous and expeditious transit of [an international] strait" subject to a number of conditions. (UNCLOS, art. 38(2)). Ships must proceed in normal modes of transit without delay, without threat or use of force, and in compliance with generally accepted international standards for safety and pollution control. (UNCLOS, arts. 39(1)–(2)). The reference to "normal modes" of transit includes submerged passage of submarines.

The UNCLOS regime of "transit passage shall not apply if there exists seaward of [an island bordering a strait and the mainland] a route through the high seas or through an [EEZ] of similar convenience with respect to navigational and hydrographical characteristics." (UNCLOS, art. 38(1)).

The United States proclamation extending a 12-mile territorial sea provides that "[i]n accordance with international law, as reflected in the . . . 1982 United Nations Convention on the Law of the Sea," the United States will recognize a right of transit passage by ships of all countries through international straits. 3 C.F.R. § 547 (1989).

d. Transit Through Archipelagic Waters

The regime created by UNCLOS for passage through "archipelagic waters," waters enclosed in archipelagic straight baselines, is similar to transit passage through international straits. For purposes of innocent passage, archipelagic waters are treated like territorial waters. (UNCLOS, art. 52(1)). In addition, the archipelagic nation may designate archipelagic sea lanes within which "rights of navigation and overflight in the normal mode" may be exercised. (Id. art. 53(1)–(3)). The Convention directs that sea lanes and air routes traversing archipelagic waters "shall include all normal passage routes used as routes for international navigation or overflight." (Id. art. 53(4)). If an archipelagic nation does not designate sea lanes or air routes, "the right of archipelagic sea lanes passage may be exercised through the routes normally used for international navigation." (Id. art. 53(12)).

e. The Right of Hot Pursuit

A right of hot pursuit exists when the coastal country has reason to believe a vessel has violated the law within the country's internal waters or territorial sea. Pursuit must begin while the vessel is within territorial waters after the vessel has been signaled; the pursuit must be hot and continuous. The right may only be exercised by a warship, military aircraft, or other ship or aircraft clearly marked as being on government service. The right of hot pursuit ceases when a vessel enters the territorial sea of another country. (UNCLOS, art. 111).

The right of hot pursuit also exists for violations within other offshore jurisdictional zones (e.g., EEZ). However, pursuit may be undertaken only for violations of rights related to the basis for which the zone was established, such as fishing violations. In 1995, the government of Canada claimed the right of hot pursuit when the government authorities arrested the Spanish fishing vessel, *The Estai,* on the high seas for violating Northwest Atlantic Fisheries Organization conservation measures inside Canadian jurisdictional waters. The impact of surveillance by drones or gliders on the "hot pursuit" doctrine is legally uncertain.

f. Freedom of Navigation Operations

The United States continues to protest excessive baseline claims by other nations by, for example, conducting Freedom of Navigation Operations (FONs).[8] During a FON, U.S. flagged vessels conduct innocent passage or transit passage through waters where another State asserts a particular "excessive" claim or participate in an overflight mission. The U.S. Department of Defense publishes a yearly summary of FON actions that provides a list of countries and a description of the "excessive" claim. Examples of past FON actions include U.S. vessels protesting Oman's limitation on passage through the Strait of Hormuz and the Maldives for requiring permission for nuclear-powered vessels to enter its territorial sea. Some countries remain on the Department of Defense list such as the Philippines for claiming archipelagic waters as internal waters.

The U.S. justifies these FONs as a global public good to keep sea lanes open for trade and as a national security measure to protect U.S. naval interests. By conducting these FONs since 1979 on an annual basis, the U.S. is acting as a persistent

---

[8] For a comprehensive review of the legal justification for these operations, see J.A. Roach, and R.W. Smith, *Excessive Maritime Claims* (Leiden, Brill Publishers, 2012).)

objector to prevent certain maritime practices from crystallizing into customary international law.

If the U.S. were to become a party to UNCLOS, there may be legal questions raised about whether the U.S. must obtain permission to conduct certain types of operations. It is probable that the U.S. on accession would seek to exclude FONs conducted for national security from the mandatory dispute settlement framework under UNCLOS Article 298(1)(b).

For a complete list of maritime claims and the U.S. position regarding specific claims, see U.S. Navy Judge Advocate General's Corps, *Maritime Claims Reference Manual*, at https://www.jag.navy.mil/organization/code_10_mcrm.htm.

C. THE CONTINENTAL SHELF

The continental shelf is the part of the seabed that gently slopes down from the low water line to a point, usually around a depth of around 200 meters, where it drops off more steeply in an area known as the continental slope. The breadth of the geologic feature of continental shelf varies around the world's coasts from less than the breadth of the territorial sea to over 300 miles. The 1945 Truman Proclamation based the United States' claim to control of the resources of the continental shelf on the fact that this geologic feature was "an extension of the land-mass of the [United States] and thus naturally appurtenant" and subject to its jurisdiction and control.

1.   LEGAL NATURE OF THE CONTINENTAL SHELF

The fact that rights exercised by the coastal nations arise from jurisdiction over its land territory made the development of the regime of the continental shelf unique. Unlike rights to territorial waters, contiguous zones, or exclusive economic zones, which must be exercised through positive acts or claims by the coastal nation, the exclusive right to the continental shelf arises through international law. In the *North Sea Continental Shelf Cases (F.R.G./Den.; F.R.G./Neth.)*, 1969 WL 1 (1969), the International Court of Justice stated that:

> the rights of the coastal State in respect of the area of continental shelf that constitutes a natural prolongation of its land territory into and under the sea exist *ipso facto* and *ab initio,* by virtue of its sovereignty over the land, and as an extension of it in an exercise of sovereign rights for the purpose of exploring the seabed and exploiting its natural resources. In short there is here an inherent right.

Both the 1958 Convention on the Continental Shelf (Continental Shelf Convention), *done* at Geneva, April 29, 1958, 15 U.S.T. 471, 499 U.N.T.S. 311, and UNCLOS recognize the inherent and exclusive nature of a coastal nation's rights over the continental shelf:

1.   The coastal State exercises over the continental shelf sovereign rights for the

purpose of exploring it and exploiting its natural resources.

2.   The rights are exclusive in the sense that if the coastal State does not explore the continental shelf or exploit its natural resources, no one may undertake these activities, or make a claim to the continental shelf, without the express consent of the coastal State.

3.   The rights of the coastal State . . . do not depend on occupation, effective or notional, or on any express proclamation.

Continental Shelf Convention, art. 2; see also UNCLOS, art. 77.

Although the continental shelf regime emerged primarily to control exploitation of mineral resources, it also extends coastal nation jurisdiction over living resources of the shelf. "[S]edentary species . . . which, at the harvestable stage, either are immobile on or under the seabed or are unable to move except in constant physical contact with the seabed or the subsoil" are considered continental shelf resources. (Continental Shelf Convention, art. 2(4); see also UNCLOS, art. 77(4)). For example, lobsters, crabs, and sponges are continental shelf resources, but scallops and finfish are not. See, e.g., 16 U.S.C. § 1802(4).

2.   GEOGRAPHIC SCOPE OF CONTINENTAL SHELF

The Truman Proclamation did not specifically define or describe the geographic scope of the United

States' claim, but a White House press release on September 28, 1945, offered the following commentary:

> The policy proclaimed by the President in regard to the jurisdiction over the continental shelf . . . is concerned solely with establishing the jurisdiction of the United States from an international standpoint. It will, however, make possible the orderly development of an underwater area 750,000 square miles in extent. Generally, submerged land which is contiguous to the continent and which is covered by no more than 100 fathoms (600 feet) of water is considered as the continental shelf. 13 Dep't St. Bull. 484 (1945).

The term "continental shelf" was intended to refer to a geologically or geographically identifiable area appurtenant to the coast, but has since become a term of art. By the time the 1958 Continental Shelf Convention was drafted, countries were skeptical about restricting claims to shelf resources. Rather than limit the continental shelf to a distance from shore or a depth, the 1958 Convention recognized a coastal nation's inherent exclusive rights out to the 200-meter isobath in depth *or to the limits of exploitability* of the seabed. (Continental Shelf Convention, art. 1.)

The 1982 UNCLOS contains a more certain, but extremely complicated, formula for calculating the extent of a continental shelf claim. A continental shelf may be claimed to 200 miles from shore, or to the extent of the continental margin (the actual submerged land prolongation including the continental shelf, slope, and rise), whichever is further. The legal fiction recognizing a 200-mile continental shelf, even in the absence of an offshore physical land prolongation, completes the evolution of the legal concept of the continental shelf. The maximum seaward extent of the continental shelf is 350 miles or within 100 miles of the 2500-meter isobath, whichever is further. See UNCLOS, art. 76(5). See the **Maritime Jurisdictional Zones** diagram, supra. UNCLOS provides that the proceeds of exploitation of the shelf beyond 200 miles must be shared with the International Seabed Authority. Id. art. 82(1).

For a coastal State, the continental shelf is an important jurisdictional zone, because the coastal State has control over exploration, exploitation, conservation, and management of both non-living resources (oil, gas, minerals) and sedentary living species (clams, crabs, corals, scallops, sponges, and mollusks). The coastal State also has authority over the construction, operation and use of artificial islands, installations, and structures located on the shelf as well as the course of pipelines across the shelf.

Because the delimitation of the extent of the continental shelf continues to be an indeterminate and complex process, UNCLOS provided for the establishment of a Commission on the Limits of the Continental Shelf (CLCS) to review continental shelf claims beyond 200 miles. Id. art. 76(8) and Annex II. The Commission provides technical assistance to countries, and when a country adopts a continental shelf limit based on the recommendations of the Commission, the limit of the shelf is "final and binding" (presumably in regard to the boundary between a coastal state's continental shelf and the deep seabed administered under U.N. Seabed Authority). Id. Commission recommendations are not binding on States, however. The United Nations will serve as a depository for charts and data "permanently describing" coastal states continental shelf claims beyond 200 miles. Id. art. 76(9).

The United States, a party to the 1958 Convention on the Continental Shelf, has placed no specific limit on its continental shelf claim by decree or statute. The Outer Continental Shelf Lands Act defines the continental shelf only as "all submerged lands lying seaward and outside of [lands granted to the states by the Submerged Lands Act] and of which the subsoil and seabed appertain to the United States and are subject to its jurisdiction and control." 43 U.S.C. § 1331(a).

The United States has embarked on an "Extended Continental Shelf Project," however, to document the extent of their continental shelf claims beyond the 200 miles currently recognized by UNCLOS and customary international law. Preliminary studies indicate that the U.S. Extended Continental Shelf is at least one million square kilometers—an area about twice the size of California. The melting of the Arctic Ocean ice cover due to global warming is a primary impetus for this project. Previously unrecoverable Arctic seabed resources may soon be exploitable due to the diminished ice cover, and nations surrounding the Arctic Ocean have been submitting claims to extended continental shelves to the CLCS for several years. If the United States ever joins the treaty, it will have ten years to submit a claim.

Some Arctic states may have competing continental shelf claims including Canada and Russia. The United States is eager to protect its national interests particularly in light of Russia permanently locating military personnel on Kotelny Island to protect both its extended shelf claims and the Northern Sea Route, which cuts commercial shipping time 40% between Europe and Asia and is likely to be a source of revenue.

D. EXCLUSIVE ECONOMIC ZONE

Before the conclusion of the UNCLOS III negotiations, ninety nations had established 200-mile offshore jurisdictional zones. The UNCLOS III negotiations led to an early consensus concerning coastal nation jurisdiction over economic and resource exploitation to 200 miles offshore. This 200-mile exclusive economic zone (EEZ) represented a compromise that incorporated the breadth of the most extensive offshore claims, the protection of navigation, the right of developing countries to control offshore economic development, and the need for better conservation of marine living resources. The extension of EEZs to 200 miles places approximately ninety percent of the ocean's fishery and oil resources within the jurisdiction of coastal countries.

On March 10, 1983, President Reagan proclaimed a U.S. 200-mile EEZ based on customary international law. Proclamation No. 5030, 3 C.F.R. § 22 (1984). The U.S. Magnuson-Stevens Act was subsequently amended to replace the fishery zone claim with the EEZ designation. The U.S. EEZ encompasses more ocean area than any other nation's EEZ covering 3.4 million square nautical miles of ocean[9]—larger than the combined land area of all fifty states.

U.S. Courts also recognize that the EEZ provisions in UNCLOS are customary international law. See *Mayaguezanos por la Salud y el Ambiente v. United States*, 198 F.3d 297, 304 n.14 (1st Cir. 1999).

---

[9]   A square nautical mile is the equivalent of 1.3 square miles.

UNITED STATES EXCLUSIVE ECONOMIC ZONE

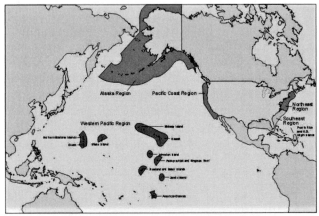

Source: U.S. Commission on Ocean Policy

1. EEZ RIGHTS

Within the EEZ, the 1982 UNCLOS recognizes sovereign rights of coastal nations "for the purpose of exploring and exploiting, conserving and managing the natural resources, whether living or non-living, of the waters superjacent to the sea-bed and of the sea-bed and its subsoil, and with regard to other activities for the economic exploitation and exploration of the zone, such as the production of energy from the water, currents and winds[.]" (UNCLOS, art. 56(1)(a)). In addition, coastal countries have jurisdiction with regard to artificial islands and offshore installations, marine scientific research, and marine environmental protection and preservation. (Id. art. 56(1)(b)). Within an EEZ, other nations enjoy freedom of navigation and overflight and the right to lay cables and pipelines. Id. art. 58(1).

2.   TRANSBOUNDARY FISHERIES AND THE UN FISH STOCK AGREEMENT

For discussion of U.S. fisheries management within the EEZ, see supra Chapter IX.B.

Because fisheries often migrate across or straddle international boundaries, cooperation is essential to maintain and conserve the susceptible species. In order to manage transboundary fisheries at a regional level, States responded to obligations recognized by UNCLOS to protect transboundary and high seas fisheries by forming regional fisheries management organizations (RFMOs) that often include jurisdiction over EEZ waters. For an interactive map viewer of areas of competence of all RFMOs and lists of member states, see Regional Fisheries Bodies Map Viewer, http://www.fao.org/figis/geoserver/factsheets/rfbs.html.

a.   The UN Fish Stocks Agreement

Article 63 of UNCLOS contemplated that future agreements would be necessary to deal with issues related to migratory and straddling fish stocks. States have sought to improve implementation of UNCLOS conservation measures for migratory and straddling stocks by negotiating the UN Fish Stocks Agreements in 1995. 34 ILM 1542 (1995); 2167 UNTS 88. The U.N. Fish Stocks Agreement provides an impetus for cooperation and compatibility in fisheries management beyond and within EEZs. Coastal nations are expected to adopt EEZ management strategies for migratory and straddling stock species that integrate the precautionary approach, protection of biodiversity, principles of sustainability, and ecosystem management.

The obligation for cooperation under the UN Fish Stocks Agreement can be implemented through existing treaties and international arrangements or by the creation of new RFMOs. Countries that fish for straddling or highly migratory species are obligated to cooperate through one of these arrangements. This obligation is intentionally inclusive in scope in that it purports to bind not only parties to the Agreement, but also non-parties. Article 8(3) and (4) provide that non-parties may not participate in managed high seas fisheries unless they are also members of the regional fisheries organization or accept the organization's management measures.

b. Expansion of Fishery Management Concepts

The Fish Stocks Agreement substantially expands upon conservation and management concepts fundamental to UNCLOS, such as the qualified maximum sustainable yield. The Agreement specifically incorporates more contemporary concepts recommended by the FAO on sustainability, ecosystem management, and integrated management, including requirements to:

(1) adopt measures to assure long-term sustainability of straddling and migratory fish stocks, art. 5(a);

(2) adopt measures to protect species within the same ecosystem, art. 5(e);

(3) take measures to prevent or eliminate overfishing and excess capacity to ensure fishing effort that will allow sustainable use of fishery resources, art. 5(h); (4) minimize pollution, waste, discards, and impact on associated or dependent species, art. 5(f); (5) protect biodiversity of the marine environment, art. 5(g); and (6) assess the impact of fishing, other human activities and environmental factors on target stocks, associate and dependent species, and other species in the ecosystem, art. 5(d). The Agreement also requires application of the precautionary approach. Agreement, articles 5(c), 6.

The Fish Stocks Agreement, which required only thirty ratifications to come into force in 2001, has 89 ratifications as of 2019. (Interestingly, although the United States is not a party to UNCLOS, it was among the first countries to ratify this implementing agreement in August 1996.)

Parties to the Agreement have held review conferences every five years. The last review conference was held in 2016. In the 2016, report States assessed the effectiveness of the agreement and concluded that while progress has been made, more work needed to be done. A/CONF.210/2016/5 (August 1, 2016). In terms of progress, the States highlighted the increase in number of parties to the Agreement as well as the creation of new regional fisheries management organizations and arrangements (RFMOs and RFMAs). Delegations to

the 2016 review conference raised a number of areas
for global improvement calling on States to:

- Reduce fishing capacity to sustainable levels

- Make fisheries subsidy information publicly
  available

- Develop a better understanding of the
  precautionary approach and ecosystem
  approach

- Move towards holistic management rather
  than single-species approaches

- Develop more data for fisheries management
  including information about bycatch and
  discards as well as information about social
  and economic components of fishing

- Improve efforts to standardize how data is
  collected and shared

- Cooperate better around management of
  shark species including on enforcement
  against shark finning

- Establish and implement long-term
  conservation and management measures for
  deep-sea fisheries

- Commit to address marine debris particularly
  abandoned or lost fishing gear

- Explore ways to understand impact of
  warming oceans and acidification on ocean
  fisheries

- Develop area-based management tools

- Establish rebuilding and recovery strategies

- Strengthen mandates in RFMOs and RFMAs

- Undertake regular performance reviews of RFMOs and RFMAs

- Provide incentives to non-members to join RFMOs and RFMAs

- Develop transparent criteria for allocating fishing opportunities within RFMOs and RFMAs

- Strengthen flag state control over vessels to ensure that flagged vessels do not undermine conservation and management measures

- Strengthen flag state responsibility to prevent IUU fishing and to ensure proper labor conditions for fishing crew

- Encourage States to become parties to the Port State Measures Agreement

The next review conference will be held in 2021.

c. Enforcement of the Fish Stocks Agreement

In terms of enforcement, the Fish Stocks Agreement offers the possibility of cooperative enforcement. Article 21 allows an inspector from a party to the Agreement to board and inspect fishing vessels flying the flag of other another party in order to ensure compliance with conservation and measurement measures. With the consent of the flag State, a party to the agreement can bring a violator to the nearest appropriate port as part of an enforcement action.

Article 17(2) directs non-complying and non-party states not to authorize fishing by their vessels in fisheries managed by RMFOs. Finally, the authority under Articles 17(4) and 33(2) allows parties to take "measures consistent with the Agreement and international law" to deter non-parties from undermining the effectiveness of regional management measures.

E.   THE HIGH SEAS

The waters beyond national jurisdiction that are open to all and in which no nation can assert sovereignty are generally referred to as the high seas.

1.   RIGHTS AND DUTIES ON THE HIGH SEAS

Both the 1958 Convention on the High Seas (High Seas Convention), done at Geneva, April 29, 1958, 13 U.S.T. 2312, 450 U.N.T.S. 82, and Part VII of the 1982 UNCLOS contain nonexclusive lists of the freedoms of the high seas. Both conventions identify the freedoms of navigation, overflight, fishing, and laying submerged lines and cable. (High Seas Convention, art. 2(1)–(4); UNCLOS, art. 87(1)). UNCLOS also specifically includes freedom of marine scientific research and construction of artificial islands and installations. UNCLOS, art. 87(1). High seas freedoms "shall be exercised . . . with reasonable regard to the interests of other States." (High Seas Convention, art. 2; see also UNCLOS, art. 87(2)).

As a general rule, only the flag country has jurisdiction over a vessel on the high seas. (High Seas Convention, art. 6; UNCLOS, art. 92). This exclusive jurisdiction is subject to a number of exceptions, including:

(1) vessels or aircraft involved in acts of piracy (High Seas Convention, art. 14, UNCLOS, arts. 100–107);

(2) vessels engaged in unauthorized broadcasting from the high seas (UNCLOS, art. 110);

(3) ships of uncertain nationality, no nationality, or sailing under two or more flags (High Seas Convention, arts. 6(2), 22; UNCLOS arts. 92, 110);

(4) vessels involved in maritime casualties threatening or causing major pollution and damage to a coastal country or its resources (UNCLOS, art. 221); and

(5) vessels that are the objects of hot pursuit for violation of laws within internal, territorial, or EEZ waters (High Seas Convention, art. 23; UNCLOS, art. 111).

The U.S. prosecutes piracy crimes and the Supreme Court has expressed its understanding that foreign citizens can use U.S. courts to make civil claims for damages caused by piracy. See Alien Tort Statute Act 28 U.S.C. § 1350; *Sosa v. Alvarez-Machain*, 542 U.S. 692 (2004). The U.S. prosecutes piracy crimes under 18 U.S.C. § 1651 and on the basis of customary international law as reflected in UNCLOS. See *United States v. Hasan*, 747 F. Supp. 2d 599, 606 (E.D. Va.) (2010)(finding that even though Somali pirates had not completed an act of robbery against the ship that was covered by the piracy statute, international customary law prohibiting violence towards vessels would qualify as general piracy); *United States v. Abdi Wali Dire*, 680 F.3d 446, 469 (4th Cir. 2012)(affirming findings on piracy in *United States v. Hasan*; *United States v. Shibin,* 722 F.3d 233, 240 (4th Cir. 2013); and *United States v. Ali*, 718 F.3d 929, 935 (DC Cir. 2013).

The law of the sea does not place slave trade or drug trafficking acts in the same category as piracy, i.e., universal crimes that may be enforced by any nation on the high seas. Prohibition of slave trade is considered a duty of the flag country. A vessel that is reasonably suspected of engaging in slave trade may be boarded on the high seas, but the only action a foreign nation may take is to report its findings to the flag country. (High Seas Convention, art. 13; UNCLOS, arts. 99, 110). In recent years, there are increasing claims that some members of foreign fishing crews are being held in conditions akin to slavery. U.S. Department of State, Trafficking in Persons Report (2016) at http://www.state.gov/j/tip/rls/tiprpt/2016/.

In the case of illicit drug trafficking, neither UNCLOS nor customary international law provides a basis for enforcement of laws on the high seas except with regard to a country's flagged vessels or if the vessel has no nationality (including when this is imputed by the vessel flying more than one flag). UNCLOS calls on nations to cooperate in the suppression of drug trade. (UNCLOS, art. 108).

United States intervention on the high seas of foreign flag vessels believed to be involved in drug trade is often carried out by obtaining permission of the flag country on a case-by-case basis, usually through radio or telephone communication with the country's officials. See, e.g., *United States v. Gonzalez*, 776 F.2d 931 (11th Cir. 1985) (holding that a formal treaty "arrangement" with a country is not necessary and that telephone communication with the flag country giving permission for the United States to act is sufficient). Modern communications have made this process workable for intercepting drug trade long before it enters territorial waters.

The Maritime Drug Law Enforcement Act (MDLEA) extends U.S. jurisdiction to any vessel with a connection to the United States plus "any foreign vessels on the high seas" and any vessels operating within waters characterized as territorial seas under the Law of the Sea Convention, as long as there is consent from the flag State. 46 U.S.C. § 70502(c)(1)(C). This act was deemed to be within the powers of Congress pursuant to Article I, Sec. 8 § 10 of the Constitution to "define and punish Piracies and Felonies committed on the high Seas, and Offences against the Law of Nations." U.S. Constitution, Article I, Sec 8, Cl. 10.

The constitutionality of the MDLEA has been recently challenged in the 11th Circuit case *U.S. v.*

Bellaizac-Hurtado, 700 F.3d 1245 (11th Cir. 2012), where Panamanian law enforcement arrested Colombian citizens in the territorial sea of Panama for drug trafficking and transported them to the U.S. for prosecution under the MDLEA. In their decision, the 11th Circuit decided that the act violated U.S. constitutional law because the arrest did not take place on the "high seas." Interestingly, a number of U.S. courts have used a definition of "high seas" that diverges from the meaning of "high seas" under UNCLOS. In *United States v. Portocarrero-Angulo*, Case No.: 3:16-cr-02555-BEN-01 (S.D.Cal. 2017), the court relied on a number of U.S. cases defining "high seas" for the purposes of enforcing the MDLEA as those waters that "begin after the territorial sea of 12 nautical miles."

The U.S. is also party to numerous interdiction agreements, mostly with nations in the wider Caribbean area, for cooperation in regard to maritime drug enforcement. See Department of State, United States Maritime Law Enforcement Agreements, available at http://www.state.gov/s/l/2005/87199.htm.

Article 88 of UNCLOS states that the "high seas shall be reserved for peaceful purposes." This does not mean that naval forces cannot navigate the high seas or conduct military exercises. The United States takes the position that military exercises are a traditional use of the high seas.

2.   UNITED STATES AND THE LEGAL MEANING OF THE "HIGH SEAS"

As noted above with the discussion of the MDLEA, the United States has a broader understanding of the "high seas" than the definition reflected in UNCLOS, international waters measured beyond 200 nautical miles. The United States for jurisdictional purposes has defined the "high seas" as waters beyond the bounds of the 12 nautical mile territorial sea. In *United States v. Beyle*, a case involving murders of Americans by Somalian citizens on a U.S. sailboat located 30–40 nautical miles from shore, the defendants were charged with felonies on the "high seas." 782 F.3d 159 (4th Cir. 2015)

The 4th Circuit indicated that while it understood that UNCLOS defined the "high seas" as areas beyond 200 nautical miles, the U.S. recognized that the UNCLOS' treaty provisions for the high seas are largely the same as its provisions for the EEZ. The Court stated that, "The EEZ bordering a particular nation's territorial sea is merely a part of the high seas where that nation has special economic rights and jurisdiction." Id. at 167. See also UNCLOS art. 58(2)(which preserves high seas rights in the EEZ not related to resource exploitation).

A number of other U.S. courts have adopted the same definition of "high seas." In *United States v. Matos-Luchi*, the Circuit court concluded that a vessel seized within the Dominican Republic's EEZ on the basis of a MDLEA violation was interdicted on the high seas. 627 F.3d 1, 2 n.1 (1st Cir. 2010). See also *United States v. Suarez*, No. 16-cr-453, 2017 WL

2417016, at *6–7 (S.D.N.Y. June 1, 2017); *United States v. Carvajal*, 924 F. Supp. 2d 219, 234 n.7 (D.D.C. 2013)(declining to adopt UNCLOS's definition of "high seas" and instead defining "high seas" as the waters beyond 12 nautical miles from the coast, explaining that such a definition "is the better reasoned understanding that has long been in use.")

Refined definition by Congress in statutes intended to reach activities in the EEZ as well as on the high seas could avoid confusion in application of U.S. law. The case *In The Matter Of The Arctic Sunrise Arbitration, Kingdom of the Netherlands v. Federation of Russia*, PCA Case N° 2014–02 (14 August 2015) involved a Greenpeace protest against a Russian oil production platform in the country's EEZ in the Barents Sea which led to the boarding and detention of the ship and crew of the *Arctic Sea*. The Permanent Court of Arbitration explained the relation of EEZ and high seas rights as follows:

225. The legal regime that applied to the *Arctic Sunrise*, under the flag of the Netherlands, in the EEZ of Russia, is governed by Part V of the Convention, which sets out the rights and duties of coastal and flag States in the EEZ.

226. According to Articles 58 and 87 of the Convention, within the EEZ all States enjoy the freedom of navigation and other internationally lawful uses of the sea related to that freedom.

227. Protest at sea is an internationally lawful use of the sea related to the freedom of

navigation. The right to protest at sea is necessarily exercised in conjunction with the freedom of navigation. Id.

3. NEGOTIATIONS FOR AN INSTRUMENT TO MANAGE "BIODIVERSITY BEYOND NATIONAL JURISDICTION"

On December 24, 2017, the UN General Assembly passed Resolution 72/749 calling for an intergovernmental negotiation to draft a text for an international, legally-binding instrument under the United Nations Convention on the Law of Sea on the conservation and sustainable use of marine biological diversity of areas beyond national jurisdiction.

The negotiations are scheduled over four sessions to be held between 2018–2020. As of the publication of this nutshell, negotiators have been meeting to debate four major topics as part of a "treaty package": 1) marine genetic resources; 2) area-based management tools, including marine protected areas; 3) environmental impact assessments, and 4) capacity-building and the transfer of marine technology. A negotiating draft was issued in June 2019.

States hold different opinions about whether the topic of fishing on the high seas should be discussed. Some non-governmental organizations hope that negotiators will consider the possibility of placing a moratorium on all fishing on the high seas. This outcome is unlikely because of vocal opposition from a number of the larger States who do not want the new instrument to interfere with RFMO management, which now incorporates virtually all areas of high seas.

F.   DEEP SEABED AND THE INTERNATIONAL SEABED AREA

The seabed beyond the continental shelf is the international seabed area or deep seabed. Prior to the 1960s, the legal status of the deep seabed was not a major issue and was presumed to be generally subject to the freedom of the high seas. This view allowed no country to claim sovereign rights over the seabed but, like high seas fishery resources, seabed resources could be exploited so long as due regard was given to the rights of other countries. This has been the United States' continuing position on the legal status of the deep seabed and its resources. See 2 Restatement (Third) Foreign Relations Law of the United States § 523(1)(a)–(b), cmts. a–c, reporter's notes 1–2 (1986). An alternative view that had been argued was that the seabed is *res nullius,* territory belonging to no one and subject to occupation and exploitation by the first country to make a claim.

The deep seabed gained attention as described in the introduction to this chapter because of the discovery of polymetallic nodules (found in concentrations off the west coast of Mexico in the Clarion-Clipperton fracture zone and the Central Indian Ocean Basis), polymetallic sulphides, and cobalt-rich crusts.

The 1982 UNCLOS declared the deep seabed to be the common heritage of mankind. (UNCLOS, Arts. 136–137.) The development of this concept of deep seabed resources required a different theoretical basis. As the common heritage, resources are considered *res communes*—belonging to everyone— and are not subject to appropriation by individual nations or persons.

1.   THE INTERNATIONAL SEABED REGIME OF UNCLOS

Part XI of UNCLOS implements the concept of the "common heritage of mankind" through creation of a regime to govern the exploitation of minerals of the deep seabed, called the Area. The regime purports to be exclusive, prohibiting any claim, acquisition, or rights over seabed mineral except in accordance with the Convention. (UNCLOS, art. 137).

The International Seabed Authority is the organization established to govern resource uses of the Area on behalf of "mankind." All parties to UNCLOS are members of the Authority. The organs of the Authority are the Assembly, the Council, and a Secretariat. Id. (UNCLOS, arts. 137, 156–158). The Assembly is composed of one representative of each party of the Authority and is the "supreme organ" of the Authority. The Assembly elects the Council and the Secretary General and is responsible for setting general policies of the Authority. (Id., arts. 158–160).

The Council is the executive organ of the Authority and is responsible for directly implementing the treaty through specific policies and approval of work plans for mining projects. (Id., art. 162). The Council has 36 members. The distribution of membership is intended to assure representation of nations involved in seabed mining and in terrestrial production of minerals, consumer nations, and developing countries. (Id., art. 161).

In addition to these governing and administrative organs of the Authority, the Enterprise is a separate organ created to engage in mining and marketing of seabed minerals. (Id., art. 170). Operation of the Enterprise is to be funded initially by the parties to the Convention and facilitated by an obligation of contractors to transfer mining technology to the Enterprise.

Part XI originally provided for a parallel system of development allowing mining by both the Enterprise and by national or private ventures that contract with the Authority. See id., Annex III. Applicants for mining contracts were required to identify two areas of equal potential and submit a work plan. The Authority would allocate one site to the applicant and reserve the other for exploitation by the Enterprise or a developing country. A contractor was required to pay a $500,000 fee for processing of the application, an annual $1,000,000 fee until production is started, and a production charge thereafter. Production would be subject to quotas to protect developing country producers of minerals.

2. THE UNITED STATES OBJECTIONS AND THE IMPLEMENTING AGREEMENT

The United States did not vote for the United Nations moratorium on seabed mining, but had anticipated that such mining would eventually be conducted under a regime established by UNCLOS.

The Deep Seabed Hard Mineral Resources Act, 30 U.S.C. §§ 1401–1473, was enacted as interim legislation, with licenses issued under the Act subject to termination if UNCLOS should come into force with United States participation. See Chapter V.C.2.

The United States' made the following objections to the original seabed mining provisions of UNCLOS:

1.   Technology Transfer. The United States objected to transfer of technology provisions as forced sales and unfair to private contractors who lose their technological advantage.

2.   Production Controls. The investment in technology development and production costs for seabed mining is extraordinarily high. Production controls would have been imposed by a three-fourths vote of the Council and subject to dispute settlement procedures. The United States labeled the decision making process, however, as discretionary and discriminatory.

3.   Decision-making Procedures. The United States did not receive adequate assurances that nations with major economic interests involved would have an affirmative influence on decision-making and the ability to prevent decisions adverse to their interests. The treaty also provided for amendments that could enter into force without ratification by the United States.

4.   Assured   Access.   Private   consortia wanted guarantees that mining rights would be automatically granted under the provisions of the treaty. The United States objected to the

degree of discretion in the contract approval process that did not protect the great initial investment by investors.

5.   Competitive Balance. The United States took the position that the regime did not protect the economic viability of U.S. mining operations and may create a competitive advantage for the Enterprise or land-based producers.

Statement by President Reagan on July 9, 1982, 18 Weekly Comp. Pres. Doc. 887 (1982).

The 1994 Agreement Relating to the Implementation of Part XI of UNCLOS addressed these issues by:

1.   Removing mandatory transfers of technology, substituting a duty of cooperation "consistent with the effective protection of property rights."

2.   Eliminating production ceilings and limitations.

3.   Changing decision-making procedures by requiring the Authority to follow the recommendations of the Council.

4.   Guaranteeing the United States a seat on the Council, which was redesigned to have four-member chambers that were more likely to be controlled by developed countries.

5.   Authorizing the Council to take actions with a two-thirds vote, unless opposed by the

majority of a chamber, thereby, allowing three members of the Council to block votes.

6.   Requiring the Authority to approve on a first-come, first-served basis, applicants meeting qualification standards.

7.   Setting payment rates comparable to land-based mining in order to avoid any artificial competitive advantage for land-based producers.

Even though the United States never signed the UN Convention on the Law of the Sea, it did sign the Part XI Implementing Agreement on July 29, 1994 with the intent of participating provisionally in the International Seabed Authority. The United States participated in the council from 1996–1998.

3.   WORK OF THE INTERNATIONAL SEABED AUTHORITY

Since the adoption of the Part XI Implementing Agreement, the ISA has entered into agreements with 29 contractors for the exploration of polymetallic nodules (primarily in the Clarion-Clipperton Fracture Zone), polymetallic sulphides (primarily in the Mid-Atlantic Ridge and Central Indian Ocean), and cobalt-rich ferromanganese crusts (primarily in the Western Pacific Ocean but also in the South Atlantic Ocean).

The ISA has issued three sets of regulations involving prospecting and exploration of seabed minerals as part of its Mining Code. *Regulations on Prospecting and Exploration for Polymetallic*

Nodules in the Area (revised July 25, 2013); *Regulation on Prospecting and Exploration for Polymetallic Sulphides in the Area* (May 7, 2010); and *Regulation on Prospecting and Exploration for Cobalt-Rich Crusts* (July 27, 2012). The Mining Code also includes recommendations from the ISA's Legal and Technical Commission on matters such as how to assess environmental impacts associated with deep seabed exploration.

G.   UNITED STATES AND THE ARCTIC

Article 234 of UNCLOS gives coastal States in ice-covered areas the power "to adopt and enforce non-discriminatory laws and regulations for the prevention, reduction and control of marine pollution from vessels in ice-covered areas within the limits of the exclusive economic zone, where particularly severe climate conditions and the presence of ice covering such areas for most of the year create obstructions or exceptional hazards to navigation, and pollution of the marine environment could cause major harm to or irreversible disturbance of the ecological balance."

As the last few decades have brought home to the public with images of stranded polar bears separated from the ice shelves, the Arctic is a region of high ecological vulnerability. The U.S. is an Arctic state and it has joined with other States in the development of a mandatory Polar Code for shipping which went into effect in 2017 amending MARPOL and the International Convention for the Safety of

Life at Sea.[10] With an expectation of a commercial shipping boom in the Arctic due to 40% decrease in shipping times between Asia and Europe, the Code harmonizes requirements for vessels operating within the region to ensure human and environmental safety. The Code contains not just mandatory pollution prevention measures but also vessel safety measures for operating in an unforgiving environment. United States vessels operating in polar regions are now required to carry a Polar Ship Certificate issued by the United States Coast Guard and to comply with heightened pollution requirements including on sewage discharge, even though the U.S. is not a party to MARPOL Annex IV. United States Coast Guard, Implementation of the International Code for Ships Operating in Polar Waters, CG-CVC Policy Letter 16–06 (December 12, 2016).

In addition to adhering to UNCLOS Article 234, the Arctic States including the United States have invested in creating cooperative governance responses for the region.[11] In 1991, the United States participated in the Arctic Environmental Protection Strategy which eventually evolved into the Arctic Council in 1996. The Council is an intergovernmental forum without legal personality that includes the

---

[10]   The full text of the Polar Code is available on the International Maritime Organization's website http://www.imo.org/en/MediaCentre/HotTopics/polar/Documents/POLAR%20COD E%20TEXT%20AS%20ADOPTED.pdf.

[11]   Other Arctic States include: Canada, the Kingdom of Denmark (including Greenland and the Faroe Islands), Finland, Iceland, Norway, Russia, and Sweden.

Arctic States, six Arctic indigenous community organizations, and several observer States. The Council cooperates by collecting scientific evidence and encouraging the adoption of national policies through its six working groups:

- Arctic Contaminants Action Program—US lead agency is Environmental Protection Agency

- Arctic Monitoring and Assessment Program— US lead agency is NOAA

- Conservation of Arctic Flora and Fauna Working Group—U.S. lead agency is U.S. Fish and Wildlife Service

- Emergency Prevention, Preparedness, and Response Working Group—U.S. lead agency is Department of Homeland Security

- Protection of Arctic Marine Environment— U.S. lead agency is NOAA

- Sustainable Development Working Group— U.S. lead agency is Department of State/ Bureau of Oceans and International Environment and Scientific Affairs

Different Arctic States take turns chairing the council for 2 years. The U.S. has chaired the council in 1998–2000 and 2015–2017. During their chairmanship, States may create new task forces or expert groups. During 2017–2019, for example, Finland created an expert group in support of the implementation of the Framework for Action on Black Carbon and Methane.

While the Arctic Council is not a legislative body, it has served as a forum for the negotiation of three binding agreements: the Agreement on Cooperation on Aeronautical and Maritime Search and Rescue in the Arctic (2011), adopted in Nuuk, Greenland; the Agreement on Cooperation on Marine Oil Pollution Preparedness and Response in the Arctic (2013) adopted at Kiruna, Sweden;, and the Agreement on Enhancing International Arctic Scientific Cooperation (2017), adopted in Fairbanks, Alaska.[12] The U.S. is a party to each of these agreements.

In 2018, the United States. became a party to the Agreement to Prevent Unregulated Fishing on the High Seas of the Central Arctic Ocean.[13] This agreement relying on the precautionary principle has placed an indefinite closure on high seas fishing until fisheries managers have collected sufficient ecosystem-based information to adequately protect fisheries resources. The United States in 2009 had already closed its EEZ regions north of Alaska to commercial fishing to provide fishery managers adequate time to do ecosystem-based management studies.

---

[12]   Full text versions of these agreements are available on the Arctic Council's website.

[13]   A copy of the text is available on the European Union website at https://eur-lex.europa.eu/resource.html?uri=cellar:2 554f475-6e25-11e8-9483-01aa75ed71a1.0001.02/DOC_2&format= PDF.

H. MARITIME BOUNDARY DELIMITATION

1. INTERNATIONAL PRACTICES

Neighboring States spend an increasing amount of negotiation and dispute settlement time on delimiting maritime boundaries.

a. Territorial Seas

In terms of overlapping territorial seas, States may not extend their territorial sea zones beyond an equidistance line unless there are "special" circumstances. (UNCLOS, art. 15) An unstable coastal area that makes it difficult to draw a provisional equidistance line might qualify as a "special" circumstance. *Territorial and Maritime Dispute between Nicaragua and Honduras in the Caribbean Sea*, (*Nicaragua v. Honduras*) Judgment, ICJ Report 2007, paras. 268–281. An arbitral panel convened under Annex VII of UNCLOS applied the same equidistance "special" circumstances test in *Guyana v. Suriname*, Arbitral Award (2007) to find that historical and navigational matters might create special circumstances.

b. Exclusive Economic Zone and Continental Shelf

With the proliferation of 200-mile EEZs and claims to extended continental shelves, overlapping maritime boundary claims have become common. A major part of the docket of the ICJ comprises maritime boundary disputes. UNCLOS article 74(1) on EEZ delimitation and article 83(1) on continental shelf delimitation both provide as follows:

The delimitation of the [exclusive economic zone and continental shelf] between States with opposite or adjacent coasts shall be effected by agreement on the basis of international law, as referred to in Article 38 of the Statute of the International Court of Justice, in order to achieve an equitable solution.

Historically, international courts and tribunals have taken a number of slightly different approaches to continental shelf and EEZ delimitations. In the *North Sea Continental Shelf Cases* (F.R.G./ Den.; F.R.G./Neth.), 1969 WL 1 (1969), the International Court of Justice (ICJ), decided that an equidistance method to designate delimitations did not rise to the status of customary international law. Rather, the court undertook delimitation on the basis of equitable principles, taking into account all relevant circumstances and maintaining each country's natural prolongation to the extent possible. In the *North Sea Cases*, relevant factors included the concave configuration of the coast, the physical and geologic structure of the shelf as evidence of natural prolongation of the land mass, the unity of natural resources of the shelf, and a reasonable degree of proportionality between the amount of coastline and the area of continental shelf.

In *Arbitration on the Delimitation of the Continental Shelf* (U.K. v. Fr.) (1977), reprinted in 18 LL.M. 397, the Tribunal followed an equidistance approach. The tribunal, however, in order to rectify the disproportionate effect created by the Scilly Islands on an equidistance line, only gave *"half-effect"* to the islands. The resulting line created an "equitable equidistance" line.

In the *Case Concerning the Continental Shelf* (Tunisia/Libyan Arab Jamahiriya), 1982 WL 247 (ICJ 1982), the Court concluded that equidistance had no privileged status among methods of delimitation, not even as a starting point that could be adjusted if the results are inequitable. The Court instead drew a line perpendicular to the coast to follow Tunisian and Libyan oil concessions. The line was adjusted offshore to reflect the change in direction of the Tunisian coast and to give offshore islands half-effect. The court verified that the delimitation created a roughly proportionate division when comparing length of coastline to area of continental shelf.

In the 2009 delimitation between the Ukraine and Romania, the ICJ set out a three-part methodology for delimitation that indicated:

First, the Court will establish a provisional delimitation line, using methods that are geometrically objective and also appropriate for the geography of the area in which the delimitation is to take place. So far as delimitation between adjacent coasts is concerned, an equidistance line will be drawn unless there are compelling reasons that make this unfeasible in the particular case. So far as opposite coasts are concerned, the provisional delimitation line will consist of a median line between the two coasts. . . .[T]he Court will at the next, second stage consider whether there are factors calling for the adjustment or shifting of the provisional equidistance line in order to achieve an equitable result. The Court has also made clear that . . . "the so-called equitable principles/relevant circumstances method may usefully be applied . . . 'to achiev[e]' an equitable result." Finally, and at a third stage, the Court will verify that the line (a provisional equidistance line which may or may not have been adjusted by taking into account the relevant circumstances) does not, as it stands, lead to an inequitable result by reason of any marked disproportion between the ratio of the respective coastal lengths and the ratio between the relevant maritime area of each State by reference to the delimitation line. A final check for an equitable outcome entails a confirmation that no great disproportionality of maritime areas is evident by comparison to the ratio of coastal lengths.

Maritime Delimitation in the Black Sea (*Romania v. Ukraine*), Judgment of February 2, 2009, para. 116. (Citations omitted).

The same approach was used again by the ICJ in the *Territorial and Maritime Dispute (Nicaragua v. Colombia)*, Judgment of November 19, 2012, paras. 190–194 and in the *Case Concerning Maritime Dispute (Peru v. Chile)*, Judgment of January 27, 2014, paras. 180–195.

The International Tribunal for the Law of the Sea has taken the same three-step approach in its first maritime delimitation case, the *Delimitation of the Maritime Boundary in the Bay of Bengal*, (Bangladesh v. Myanmar), Case No. 16, Judgment of March 14, 2012, ITLOS Reports 2012, para. 240.

In a decision that has generated some scholarly disagreement, a tribunal delimiting the boundary between Croatia and Slovenia applied the three-step approach used for EEZs and continental shelf delimitations to the territorial sea. *Croatia v. Slovenia,* Final Award, June 29, 2017, para. 998–999. In another recent case, a Special Tribunal of ITLOS applied the same delimitation methodology to the territorial sea, EEZ, and continental shelf for procedural economy reasons. *Ghana v. Cote D'Ivoire*, Case No. 23, Judgment of September 23, 2017, ITLOS Reports 2017, para. 360. By Special Agreement, Guatemala and Belize have submitted a maritime boundaries delimitation case to the ICJ that will likely involve the general application of the three-step approach.

2.   UNITED STATES MARITIME BOUNDARIES

When the United States asserted resource jurisdiction over approximately three million square miles of ocean space, more than 35 overlapping boundary claims resulted.

The U.S. has concluded a number of maritime boundaries including:

- <u>Canada</u>: Passamaquoddy Bay (1910) 36 Stat. 2477; Treaty Series 551; and

Delimitation of the Maritime Boundary in the Gulf of Maine: ICJ Judgment (1984):

A Special Chamber of the ICJ was requested to determine "in accordance with the principles and rules of international law applicable in the matter . . ., the course of the *single maritime boundary* that divides the continental shelf and fisheries zones of [the parties]." The case was the first to include fishery zone issues and to delimit a boundary for purposes of both the water column and continental shelf. On October 12, 1984, the ICJ Special Chamber announced a boundary line that, for the most part, equally divided the disputed area.

The boundary line was extended in three segments. Equal division of the "maritime projections" was found to be an equitable approach. The segments were not strictly median or equidistance lines, because the first segment was constructed to discount uninhabited islets, rocks, and low tide elevations; the second segment was adjusted from the median to reflect the relative lengths of coastlines and effect of islands; and the third segment, extending into the Atlantic Ocean, was a line perpendicular to a closing line drawn from Nantucket to Cape Sable, Nova Scotia.

- Cook Islands: Treaty between the United States of America and the Cook Islands (1980) TIAS 10774 (boundaries are based on the equidistance method giving full effect to all islands and fringing reefs).

- Cuba: Maritime Boundary Agreement between the United States of America and the Republic of Cuba (1977) Senate Treaty Doc. EX. H, 96–1.

- Mexico: 1) Treaty to Resolve Pending Boundary Differences and Maintain the Rio Grande and Colorado River as the International Boundary (1970) (established boundaries through the 12-mile territorial sea and contiguous zone); 2) Treaty on Maritime Boundaries between the United Mexican States and the United States of America (1978) Senate Treaty Document EX. F, 96–1; and 3) Treaty between the Government of the United Mexican States and the Government of the United States of America on the Delimitation of the Continental Shelf in the western Gulf of Mexico beyond 200 nautical miles (2000) UNTS Vol. 2143, I–37400 (dividing the continental shelf beyond the EEZs with an equidistance line and reserving a buffer zone on each side of the boundary to deal with possible transboundary oil and gas deposits).

- New Zealand: Treaty between the United States of America and New Zealand: Tokelau (1980) TIAS 10775.

- <u>Niue</u>: Treaty between the Government of the United States of America and the Government of Niue on the Delimitation of a Maritime Boundary (1997) (boundaries are based on the equidistance method giving full effect to all islands and fringing reefs).

- <u>Russian Federation</u>: The Agreement between the United States of America and the Union of Soviet Socialist Republics on the Maritime Boundary (1990) Senate Treaty Document 101–22 (World's longest maritime boundary).

- <u>United Kingdom</u>: Treaty on the Delimitation in the Caribbean of a Maritime Boundary relating to the U.S. Virgin Islands and Anguilla (1993) UNTS Vol. 1913, I–32636; and Treaty on the Delimitation in the Caribbean of a Maritime Boundary relating to Puerto Rico/U.S. Virgin Islands and the British Virgin Islands (1993) UNTS Vol. 1913, I–2637.

- <u>Venezuela</u>: Maritime Boundary Treaty between the United States of America and the Republic of Venezuela (1978) Senate Treaty Doc. EX. G, 96–1.

Overlapping claims remain between the U.S. and Canada seaward of the Strait of Juan de Fuca off Washington; from the Dixon Entrance in southeast Alaska; and in the Beaufort Sea in the Arctic.

I.   MARINE SCIENTIFIC RESEARCH

Traditionally, marine scientific research (MSR) was considered a freedom of the high seas, but could not be conducted in territorial waters without the coastal state's permission. Vessels could not engage in research while exercising the right of innocent passage through a territorial sea. The Continental Shelf Convention imposed the first restrictions on research outside territorial waters. Article 5(8) of the Convention provides:

> The consent of the coastal State shall be obtained in respect of any research concerning the continental shelf and undertaken there. Nevertheless, the coastal State shall not normally withhold its consent if the request is submitted by a qualified institution with a view to purely scientific research ... subject to the proviso that the coastal State shall have the right, if it so desires, to participate or to be represented in the research, and that in any event the results shall be published.

The term "concerning the continental shelf" left unclear whether the consent requirement applied to research that was not physically conducted on the shelf. The term "purely scientific research" was also vague because the line between pure and applied research is not always easily discernible. Since the 1970s, the extension of fishery zones has also had the effect of limiting marine research. Because fishery research necessarily involves the taking of fish, such research within extended fishery zones and EEZs is generally subject to coastal country regulation.

UNCLOS III negotiations had to attempt to resolve the conflict created by developing countries demanding more control over MSR and by scientists seeking to bring down the barriers that had already seriously limited marine research. Scientists had found that the emerging consent regimes for continental shelf and fisheries research were vague and subject to multiple interpretations and that requests for clearance often were bogged down by local bureaucracies. While UNCLOS developed a legal regime around MSR, the term "marine scientific research" was never defined in the convention even though numerous proposals were put forward.

While there is no specific definition of MSR, Article 240 provides a series of general principles to govern the conduct of marine scientific research including that MSR research be conducted:

- Exclusively for peaceful purposes;
- With appropriate scientific methods and means compatible with the Convention;
- In a manner that does not unjustifiably interfere with other legitimate uses of the sea compatible with the Convention; and
- In compliance with all relevant regulations adopted in conformity with the Convention including those for the protection and preservation of the marine environment.

States are expected to formulate international rules, standards, and recommended practices and procedures for the protection and preservation of the marine environment. UNCLOS, art. 197.

UNCLOS specifically codified MSR among the freedoms of the high seas, (UNCLOS, art. 87) and provided that all States have the right to conduct MSR in the Area as long as the research is peaceful and for the benefit of all humankind. (Id., art. 256). UNCLOS reaffirmed that research may be conducted in the territorial sea only with consent of the coastal country. (Id. art. 245). The Convention creates a new regime for marine science research conducted in the EEZ or on the continental shelf. While recognizing the right of all nations to participate in marine research and encouraging international cooperation, the Convention recognizes that MSR rights "are subject to the rights and duties of other States" and gives coastal countries authority to regulate and to authorize MSR in their EEZs and on their continental shelves. (Id., arts. 238 and 246(1)).

The UNCLOS consent regime for the EEZ and continental shelf distinguishes between applied and pure research. Applied research involves activities that are of "direct significance for the exploration and exploitation of natural resources," or that involve drilling, explosives, or construction of installations or artificial islands. (Id., art. 246(5)(a)–(c)). Pure research includes activities carried out "exclusively for peaceful purposes and in order to increase scientific knowledge of the marine environment for the benefit of all mankind." (Id., art. 246(3)). Consent for pure scientific research projects shall be granted "in normal circumstances." (Id.) The coastal nation has total discretion as to whether to consent to applied research, to research that pollutes the marine environment, and to research by countries that have provided inaccurate information or that have outstanding obligations from a previous project. (Id., art. 246(5)).

To address the concerns of developing countries, UNCLOS subjects researching countries to certain obligations. First, the coastal country must receive specific, detailed information about the project at least six months in advance. (UNCLOS, art. 248). Second, the Convention imposes a long list of detailed, and usually expensive, conditions on research projects, which include:

(1) ensuring that scientists of the coastal country are able to be represented or to participate in the research on board the vessel at no cost to the coastal country;

(2) providing preliminary and final reports on the research project and access by the coastal country to data and samples;

(3) if requested, providing the coastal country with assessment and interpretation of data and samples;

(4) ensuring that research results are appropriately published as soon as practicable; and

(5) unless otherwise agreed, removing any installations and equipment.

(Id., art. 249(1)). If the researchers fail to meet these conditions, the coastal country may suspend research or shut down the project. (Id., art. 253).

If States or international organizations cause harm while undertaking MSR, then they are responsible and liable for damage resulting from MSR. (Id., art. 263). Under Article 235, States and international organizations are responsible and liable for damage caused by pollution of the marine environment arising out of marine scientific research undertaken by them or on their behalf.

The treaty provisions attempt to address the concerns of marine scientists in a number of ways. First, to assure that consent is not unreasonably delayed or denied, countries must establish procedures and rules for processing clearance requests. (Id., art. 246(3)). Although the term "normal circumstances" for consent is not defined, the Convention does state that "normal circumstances may exist in spite of the absence of diplomatic relations between the coastal [country] and the researching [country]." (Id., art. 246(4)). Finally, the Convention provides for "implied consent" in certain circumstances. First, if research is to be carried out by or under the auspices of an international organization, such as the Intergovernmental Oceanographic Commission, in which the coastal country participates, consent is implied if the country does not object within four months of notification. (Id., art. 247). In other cases, if a researching nation has provided the coastal country with all necessary information concerning the research project, the project may proceed after six months unless within four months of notification, the coastal country gives notice that:

(a) it has withheld its consent . . .; or

(b) the information given ... regarding the nature or objectives of the project does not conform to the manifestly evident facts;

(c) it requires supplementary information . . .; or

(d) outstanding obligations exist with respect to a previous marine scientific research project. . . .

(Id., art. 252.) In addition, consent cannot be withheld for applied or pure research on the continental shelf beyond 200 miles unless the area is currently the focus of exploitation and development activity by the coastal country. (Id., art. 246(6)).

As far as researching nations are concerned, the consent regime has a major shortcoming in that it is not subject to effective dispute resolution procedures. In general, parties to UNCLOS may submit disputes concerning interpretation or implementation to compulsory third party settlement. However, the withholding of a coastal country's consent to MSR projects under Article 246 or the suspension of an MSR project under Article 253 is not subject to those procedures. (Id., art. 297(2)).

Limitations by coastal countries on publication of research are considered an unacceptable condition by most researchers. UNCLOS recognizes a coastal country's authority to require prior permission for publication only in the case of applied MSR that produces results "of direct significance for the exploration and exploitation of natural resources." (Id., art. 249(2)). As noted earlier, the line between applied and pure scientific research is not always readily discernible.

A consent regime for the EEZ and the continental shelf has become part of customary international law although the details may be vague. The U.S. does not generally require consent for MSR, but it does require permission if any portion of the research in the EEZ:

- is conducted within a national marine sanctuary, a marine national monument, or other marine protected areas;

- involves the study of marine mammals or endangered species;

- requires taking commercial quantities of marine resources;

- involves contact with the U.S. continental shelf; or

- involves ocean dumping research.

See Dep't of State, Marine Scientific Research Authorizations. The U.S. also reserves the right to participate in foreign research conducted in the EEZ. Id.

J.　DISPUTE RESOLUTION

UNCLOS includes comprehensive dispute resolution procedures. Disputes concerning interpretation or application of the treaty that cannot be settled by other peaceful means are subject to binding dispute resolution. Article 287 of UNCLOS provides:

When signing, ratifying or acceding to this Convention or at any time thereafter, a State shall be free to choose, by means of a written declaration, one or more of the following means for the settlement of disputes concerning the interpretation or application of this Convention:

(a)　the International Tribunal for the Law of the Sea constituted under Annex VI;

(b)　the International Court of Justice;

(c)　an arbitral tribunal constituted in accordance with Annex VII;

(d)　a special arbitral tribunal constituted in accordance with Annex VIII for or one or more of the categories of disputes specified therein.

If the parties to a dispute have not accepted the same settlement procedure, then the dispute will be submitted to arbitration in accordance with Annex VII, unless the parties agree to another forum.

1.   INTERNATIONAL TRIBUNAL FOR THE LAW OF THE SEA

The International Tribunal for the Law of the Sea (ITLOS) has jurisdiction over all disputes submitted in accordance with the Convention. Very few UNCLOS States have declared ITLOS to be its first choice for dispute resolution.[14] ITLOS has exclusive jurisdiction, through its Seabed Disputes Chamber, for disputes related to the international deep seabed area.

The 21-member tribunal was first elected in August 1996 and sits in Hamburg, Germany. The Seabed Disputes Chamber, first elected in 2005, is composed of eleven tribunal members selected by a majority of the Tribunal. To date, only 27 cases have been submitted to the Tribunal. The majority of the cases, like its first case *The M/V "SAIGA"* (1997), have invoked the Tribunal's special jurisdiction under article 292 to address the prompt release of vessels detained for violation of coastal country or international law, or similar situations involving the request for provisional measures.

ITLOS has issued two important advisory opinions: *Responsibilities and Obligations of States Sponsoring Persons and Entities with Respect to*

---

[14]   Algeria, Angola, Argentina, Austria, Bangladesh (for purposes of settling maritime boundary with Myanmar), Belarus (prompt release questions), Bulgaria, Cape Verde, Cuba, Estonia, Fiji, Finland, Greece, Madagascar, Montenegro, Oman, Panama (for purposes of settling dispute with Italy), Russian Federation (for prompt release questions), Trinidad and Tobago, Tunisia, Ukraine (for prompt release questions), Tanzania, and Uruguay.

Activities in the Area, Case No. 17 (February 1, 2011) and *Request for an Advisory Opinion Submitted by the Sub-Regional Fisheries Commission*, Case No. 21 (April 2, 2015). The first advisory opinion on sponsoring states found that states have due diligence obligation to seek compliance by contractors including through the requirement of environmental impact assessments. See Chapter 7.B.2. The second advisory opinion noted that flag states also have due diligence obligations to ensure that flagged vessels do not violates conservation and management measures within the EEZ of other states. A failure to meet due diligence standards such as having adequate administrative measures to control flagged vessels can result in liability for flag states.

ITLOS has decided two maritime boundary cases: *Bangladesh v. Myanmar*, Case No. 16 (March 14, 2012) and *Ghana v. Cote D'Ivoire*, Case No. 23 (September 23, 2017).

In April 2019, ITLOS decided a significant case on freedom of the high seas finding that Italy had violated Article 87 of UNCLOS by attempting to exercise domestic tax controls over bunkering activities of mega-yachts located on the high seas. *M/V "Norstar"* Case No. 25 (April 10, 2019) ("if a State applies its criminal and customs laws to the high seas and criminalizes activities carried out by foreign ships thereon, it would constitute a breach of article 87 of the Convention, unless justified by the Convention or other international treaties." para. 225). The court's finding may have implications for port state enforcement.

2. INTERNATIONAL COURT OF JUSTICE

The International Court of Justice (ICJ), also called "the World Court," is composed of 15 judges. According to the United Nations Charter, the ICJ has the responsibility to resolve legal disputes submitted to it by States and to give advisory opinions on legal questions referred to it by authorized United Nations organs and specialized agencies.

The Court has issued judgments in a number of matters related to Law of the Sea matters including the following decisions on maritime boundary disputes:

- Maritime Delimitation in the Caribbean Sea and the Pacific Ocean (Costa Rica v. Nicaragua) Case 157 (February 2, 2018).

- Maritime Dispute (Peru v. Chile) Case 137, (January 27, 2014).

- Territorial and Maritime Dispute (Nicaragua v. Colombia) Case 124 (November 19, 2012).

- Maritime Delimitation in the Black Sea (Romania v. Ukraine) Case 132 (February 3, 2009).

- Territorial and Maritime Dispute between Nicaragua and Honduras in the Caribbean Sea (Nicaragua v. Honduras) Case 120 (October 8. 2007).

- Land and Maritime Boundary between Cameroon and Nigeria (Cameroon v. Nigeria) Case 94 (October 10, 2012).

- Territorial and Maritime Dispute between Nicaragua and Honduras, Case 120 (October 8, 2007).

- Maritime Delimitation and Territorial Questions between Qatar and Bahrain Case 87 (March 16, 2001).

- Maritime Delimitation between Guinea-Bissau v. Senegal, Case 85 (November 12, 1991).

- Maritime Delimitation in the Area between Greenland and Jan Mayen (Denmark v Norway) Case 78 (June 14, 1993).

- Land, Island and Maritime Frontier Dispute (El Salvador/Honduras: Nicaragua intervening) (Three-member chamber and 2 ad hoc judges) Case 75 (September 11, 1992).

- Continental Shelf Case 68 (Libya v. Malta) (June 3, 1985).

- Delimitation of the Maritime Boundary in the Gulf of Maine Area (Canada v. United States) (Ad Hoc Chamber of the Court) Case 67 (October 12, 1984).

- Continental Shelf (Tunisia v. Libya) Case 63 (February 24, 1982).

- Aegean Continental Shelf (Greece v. Turkey) Case 62 (December 19, 1978).

The Court has also decided a series of North Sea fisheries jurisdiction cases on July 25, 1974 including *United Kingdom v. Iceland*, Case 55 and *Federal*

Republic of Germany v. Iceland, Case 56. Earlier it had decided a Fisheries case between United Kingdom and Norway, Case 5 (December 18, 1951).

The Court has also addressed two other Law of the Sea topics: the question of the rights of a landlocked State to ocean access. *Bolivia v. Chile*, Case 153 (October 1, 2018). and the sustainable use and conservation of marine mammals under the International Convention on the Regulation of Whaling, *Australia v. Japan*, Case No. 148 (March 31, 2014) discussed in Chapter 9.

3. ANNEX VII TRIBUNALS

Annex VII of the Convention provides for general jurisdiction, five-member arbitral tribunals set up on an ad hoc basis, often using the services of the Permanent Court of Arbitration. Annex VII tribunals are the default if another dispute settlement mechanism has not been selected. Examples of cases brought to Annex VII tribunals including the recent case of *Bangladesh v. India* involving delimitation of a maritime boundary. Final Award, (Permanent Court of Arbitration, July 7, 2014), Case No. 2010–16 and the *South China Sea Arbitration (Philippines v. China)*, Final Award, (Permanent Court of Arbitration, July 12, 2016), Case No. 2013–19.

Other Law of the Sea relevant cases include addressed by Annex VII tribunals include:

- Denmark (Faroe Islands) v. European Union, (September 23, 2014) Case No. 2013–30

(Dispute over Article 63 UNCLOS regarding a shared stock of herring).

- Guyana v. Suriname (September 17, 2007) Case No. 2004–04 (Maritime Boundary Dispute).

- Barbados v. Trinidad and Tobago Case (April 11, 2006) Case No. 2004–02 (Maritime Boundary Dispute).

- Eritrea v. Yemen (December 17, 1999) Case no. 1996–04 (Maritime Delimitation).

4. ANNEX VIII TRIBUNALS

Annex VIII arbitral tribunals have jurisdiction for disputes that require special scientific expertise and fact finding, such as fisheries, protection and preservation of the marine environment, marine scientific research, and navigation, including pollution or dumping from ships.

Countries may choose one or more of the dispute settlement fora when they ratify or accede to the Convention or by a written declaration after that. In submitting the Convention to the Senate for its advice and consent, the Senate Foreign Relations Committee recommended that the United States make the following declaration concerning choice of dispute resolution fora:

(A) a special arbitral tribunal constituted in accordance with Annex VIII for the settlement of disputes concerning the interpretation or application of the articles of the Convention relating to (1) fisheries, (2) protection and preservation of the marine environment, (3) marine scientific research, (4) navigation, including pollution from vessels and by dumping, and

(B) an arbitral tribunal constituted in accordance with Annex VII for the settlement of disputes not covered by the declaration in (A) above.

5.   EXCEPTIONS TO COMPULSORY DISPUTE SETTLEMENT

a. Exceptions Under UNCLOS Article 297–298

Certain disputes concerning consent to foreign marine scientific research in the EEZ as well as most disputes concerning EEZ living resources are exceptions to the mandatory dispute resolution procedures. (UNCLOS, art. 297(2)–(3)). Specifically, in the case of fisheries a country is not required to submit to dispute resolution "any dispute relating to its sovereign rights with respect to the living resources in the [EEZ], including its discretionary powers for determining the allowable catch, its harvesting capacity, the allocation of surpluses . . . and the terms and conditions established by its conservation and management laws and regulations." (Id., art. 297(3)).

Countries may also exercise certain optional exceptions to compulsory jurisdiction under article 298. Under these provisions a country may declare that it does not accept the dispute procedures with respect to disputes concerning maritime boundaries between neighboring States, disputes where the UN Security Council is exercising the functions assigned to it by the Charter of the United Nations, and disputes concerning military activities and certain law enforcement activities. Recently, in the *Case Concerning the Detention of Three Ukrainian Naval Vessels* (*Ukraine v. Russian Federation*) Case 26 (25 May 2019), the Ukraine sought ITLOS to impose provisional measures requiring Russia to release 3 military vessels and 24 servicemen. Russia argued that ITLOS had no jurisdiction because Russia had exercised the "military activities" exception to ITLOS's compulsory jurisdiction. Rejecting the application of the exception to the case as one that is not "military in nature," ITLOS ordered the immediate release of the naval vessels and servicemen pending the decision of an Annex VII tribunal.

The Senate Foreign Relations Committee recommended that the United States exercise all three exceptions available as optional exclusions from mandatory dispute settlement under UNCLOS article 298 when ratifying the treaty.

b. Compulsory Conciliation Option

In many cases that are excepted from the general dispute settlement procedures, the Convention provides for compulsory conciliation under Annex V procedures. For example, in the area of fisheries, disputes subject to compulsory conciliation include circumstances in which:

(i) a coastal State has manifestly failed to comply with its obligations to ensure through proper conservation and management measures that the maintenance of the living resources in the exclusive economic zone is not seriously endangered;

(ii) a coastal State has arbitrarily refused to determine, at the request of another State, the allowable catch and its capacity to harvest living resources . . .; or

(iii) a coastal State has arbitrarily refused to allocate to any State . . . the whole or part of the surplus it has declared to exist.

(UNCLOS, art. 297(b)). The report of a five-member conciliation commission must be deposited with the United Nations and detail any agreements reached by the parties, the commission's findings of fact and law and, failing agreement by the parties, its recommendations for an "amicable settlement." The report of the commission is not, however, binding on the parties. See Annex V.

The Annex V conciliation process was recently used for the first time in a dispute between Timor-Leste and Australia over location of the maritime boundary between the two States. The conciliation commission issued its report on May 9, 2018.[15]

---

[15]   PCA, Case No. 2016–10, In the Matter of the Maritime Boundary between Timor-Leste and Australia, https://pcacases. com/web/sendAttach/2327.

CHAPTER XII

THE FUTURE OF UNITED STATES OCEAN AND COASTAL POLICY IN A CHANGING CLIMATE

A. CLIMATE CHANGE AND THE OCEANS

As earlier chapters of this book have discussed, the decades following World War II were a time of great change for the United States' oceans and coasts. The promise of offshore oil and gas not only led to the Truman Proclamation and the creation of a new international doctrine concerning the continental shelf, but also to domestic federal conflicts over offshore resources. Development of oil and gas has also generated controversy due to its potential environmental and economic impacts. Large foreign fishing fleets and new technologies led to an overcapitalized and efficient world fishing industry capable of depleting the seemingly endless bounty of the seas. Largely uncontrolled land-based pollution led to numerous "dead zones" in coastal waters. Population in coastal areas grew at unprecedented rates.

All of these rapid changes have left an impact on the oceans. No change to the oceans is, however, more fundamental than the changes that are occurring now as a result of climate change. Three phenomena are of particular concern in the U.S.: rising sea level, warming oceans, and acidifying oceans. The 1990 Global Change Research Act requires the delivery of a National Climate Assessment to Congress and the

President every four years. Pub. L. No. 101–606. In 2018, the U.S. government published the Fourth National Climate Assessment with chapters on both coastal impacts and marine resources. U.S. Global Change Research Program, (2018) *Impacts, Risks, and Adaptation in the United States: Fourth National Climate Assessment, Volume II* [Reidmiller, D.R., C.W. Avery, D.R. Easterling, K.E. Kunkel, K.L.M. Lewis, T.K. Maycock, and B.C. Stewart (eds.)].

1.   GRADUAL SEA LEVEL RISE AND SEVERE STORM SURGE

As of 2013, coastal shore adjacent counties communities were home to 118.4 million people or approximately 37% of the U.S. population. These counties (which make up 18% of the U.S. land area) generate 43% of the U.S. GDP. Increases in storm surge and heavy precipitation will have impacts on coastal ecosystems and coastal economies. Coastal real estate alone accounts for $1 trillion USD of wealth.

Severe weather events such as tropical cyclones are likely to exacerbate already gradual sea level rise. In some areas such as Hawaii and the Pacific Islands, there will be increasing saltwater intrusion into coastal aquifers. At present, approximately, 60,000 miles of U.S. roads and bridges in coastal floodplains are at risk of damage because of direct and indirect climate change impacts. Rising sea levels will affect oil and gas infrastructure including refineries as well as coastal seaports that supply 99%

of overseas trade. Some cities such as Miami, Florida, have already installed additional pumping infrastructure to respond to increasing numbers of climate change driven coastal flooding events. Without climate change adaptation measures being implemented, researchers model between $92 billion USD and $3.6 trillion USD of damage to coastal properties from the combination of sea level rise and storm surge by 2100. The Atlantic and Gulf coasts face higher than average risks of flooding from rising sea levels. Some regions and cities have adopted climate adaptation plans to reduce vulnerability of coastal communities including The Texas Coastal Resiliency Master Plan, the Hawai'i Climate Adaptation Initiative Act, and the Charleston, South Carolina Sea Level Rise Strategy.

Rising sea levels and severe storms are impacting coastal ecosystems. In particular, wetlands and marsh degradation is expected to accelerate along the Atlantic Coast due to higher sea level rise than in other areas of the U.S. The shrinkage of these wetlands includes not just the loss of protection against storm surges but also loss of a natural carbon sink providing carbon storage. In addition to the loss of natural ecosystems, rising sea levels will fragment coastal-dependent communities, including subsistence fishing communities in Alaska and residents of sea islands off the coast of Georgia. Some of the community climate impacts raise questions of environmental justice, as communities are financially unable to relocate or are being expected to relocate from indigenous lands. The Fourth National Climate Assessment identified with "very high confidence" that "structural inequality in coastal communities will be exacerbated by climate change" including "questions about land ownership and home ownership." Id. at 342.

2.   WARMING OCEANS

Warming ocean temperatures are impacting both U.S. fisheries and ocean habitats. In addition to general warming trends, there have also been trigger events. In 2012, the northwestern Atlantic Ocean in the Gulf of Maine experienced a marine heat wave, and between 2014 and 2016 the northeastern Pacific Ocean (Pacific Northwest, California coast, and Alaska) weathered a series of warming events leading to increases in temperature of 3.6 degrees Fahrenheit over historical temperature ranges. These warming events led to species moving outside their historical ranges and harmful algal blooms.

Warming contributes to changes in fisheries behavior as increases in carbon dioxide contribute to a decline in oxygen in the water column with impacts on plankton. The stratification of the water column has changed patterns in fishing as fish have begun migrating. Warmer waters tend to reduce productivity of fishing stock. The 2016 warming events in the Gulf of Alaska led to an 80% reduction of the total allowable catch of Pacific cod in 2018. Fisheries managers have increasing concerns about how to manage stocks across transnational boundaries.

Warmer oceans are irrevocably changing habitats. Coral colonies particularly in the warmer tropical waters are unable to adapt to the warm ocean temperatures leading to a dieback of reefs. The U.S. has experienced major losses of coral in Florida, Hawai'i, and the Caribbean and Pacific territories; these regions are already expected to lose marine biomass as fish migrate towards cooler waters. The loss of coral habitat impacts coastal communities as they become more vulnerable to severe weather events and lose a reliable source of food security in the nearshore fisheries.

Sea ice is disappearing in the Arctic Ocean with impacts in the Alaskan ecosystem including declines in marine mammals. Indigenous communities will experience increasing challenges with accessing traditional food sources that have not just nutritional value but also cultural value.

3.   ACIDIFICATION

Models predict that 86% of U.S. marine ecosystems by 2050 will experience substantial changes in not just temperature but also pH. Ocean acidification will increase the vulnerability of a number of keystone species including corals, krill, shellfish, and sea grass. This acidification will interfere with the ability to adapt through ecological restoration. Particularly problematic in nearshore regions will be a combination of ocean acidification and low-oxygen levels. In order to avoid many of the projected ocean impacts, there will need to reductions in atmospheric carbon dioxide concentrations through either mitigation or other interventions.

B.   U.S. OCEAN POLICY AND CLIMATE CHANGE

1.   A NATIONAL OCEAN POLICY FOR THE U.S.

On July 19th, 2010, following the Deepwater Horizon disaster, President Obama issued Exec. Order 13547 establishing the first United States national ocean policy. 75 FR 43021. The Order described the purposes of the national ocean policy as:

> . . . to ensure the protection, maintenance, and restoration of the health of ocean, coastal, and Great Lakes ecosystems and resources, enhance the sustainability of ocean and coastal economies, preserve our maritime heritage, support sustainable uses and access, provide for adaptive management to enhance our understanding of and capacity to respond to climate change and ocean acidification, and coordinate with our national security and foreign policy interests.

The Executive Order establishes a National Ocean Council (NOC)[1] at the Executive level and directs executive agencies, under the guidance of the Council, to implement recommendations developed by an Interagency Ocean Policy Task Force and

---

[1]   The National Ocean Council (NOC), a body of twenty-seven federal agencies, departments and offices co-chaired by the chair of the Council on Environmental Quality and the Director of the Office of Science and Technology Policy, was established to advise the president and provide guidance to agencies on implementation of national ocean policy.

adopted by the Order. The Final Recommendations of the Interagency Task Force provided:

(1)   our Nation's first ever National Policy for the Stewardship of the Ocean, Our Coasts, and the Great Lakes (National Policy);

(2)   a strengthened governance structure to provide sustained, high-level, and coordinated attention to ocean, coastal, and Great Lakes issues;

(3)   a targeted implementation strategy that identifies and prioritizes nine categories for action that the United States should pursue; and

(4)   a framework for effective coastal and marine spatial planning (CMSP) that establishes a comprehensive, integrated, ecosystem-based approach to address conservation, economic activity, user conflict, and sustainable use of ocean, coastal, and Great Lakes resources.[1]

The Recommendations of the Task Force focused on five priority areas or "areas of special emphasis"— resiliency and adaptation to climate change and ocean acidification; regional ecosystem protection and restoration; water quality and sustainable practices on land; changing conditions in the Arctic; and ocean, coastal, and Great Lakes observations, mapping, and infrastructure. Focusing on these areas was intended to provide for better informed

---

[1]   Recommendations are archived at: https://www.nsf.gov/geo/opp/opp_advisory/briefings/nov2010/optf_finalrecs.pdf.

management decisions by Federal, State, tribal, local, and regional agencies responsible for oceans and coasts. See Recommendations at 28.

The national ocean policy divided United States marine waters into nine planning regions based on large marine ecosystems: Alaska/Arctic, Pacific Islands, Caribbean, West Coast, Gulf of Mexico, South Atlantic, Mid-Atlantic, Northeast and Great Lakes. The geographic scope of planning and coordination envisioned by the Task Force incorporated not only the federal EEZ and continental shelf, but also the territorial sea, including state waters landward to the mean high-water line, including inland bays and estuaries. Because implementation of a national ocean policy has no legislative mandate, ocean policy planning needed to be based on existing authorities at both the federal and state levels.

The Task Force Recommendations for stewardship of the oceans anticipated that the national ocean policy would be implemented through comprehensive, integrated, coordinated ocean management, utilizing the best science and coastal and marine spatial planning (CMSP) on an eco-regional basis. CMSP is described as follows:

> CMSP is a comprehensive, adaptive, integrated, ecosystem-based, and transparent spatial planning process, based on sound science, for analyzing current and anticipated uses of ocean, coastal, and Great Lakes areas. CMSP identifies areas most suitable for various types or classes of activities in order to reduce

conflicts among uses, reduce environmental impacts, facilitate compatible uses, and preserve critical ecosystem services to meet economic, environmental, security, and social objectives. In practical terms, CMSP provides a public policy process for society to better determine how the ocean, coasts, and Great Lakes are sustainably used and protected now and for future generations.

See Interagency Ocean Policy Task Force, *Interim Framework for Effective Coastal and Marine Spatial Planning* at 1 (2009). The Recommendations envisioned regional planning bodies (RPB) composed of federal, state, and tribal authorities being responsible for development of regional plans. State participation on regional planning bodies and in implementation of regional plans was necessarily voluntary.

In April 2013, the National Ocean Council released its *National Ocean Policy Implementation Plan* to "translate the goals of the National Ocean Policy into on-the-ground change" and provide "clear direction" for federal agencies, partners and stakeholders. Nat'l Ocean Council, *National Ocean Policy: Implementation Plan* (2013) During the two years that the NOC was developing the plan, however, significant opposition grew to the President's national ocean policy, in particular, to the coastal and marine spatial planning (CMSP) aspects. The *Implementation Plan* reflected this opposition by placing emphasis on ocean economies, security, and resilience of coastal communities and the oceans, with the terms "CMSP" and "spatial planning" conspicuously missing from the *Plan*. In 2016, regional management plans were adopted for the Northeast and Mid-Atlantic.

The *Implementation Plan* was clear that even if an RPB is not established to generate a regional ocean plan, federal agencies were still bound under Executive Order 13547 to proceed with implementation of the national ocean policy and the Task Force recommendations.

2.   END OF THE COMPREHENSIVE U.S. NATIONAL OCEAN POLICY FOR THE U.S.

In spite of the significance of having coordination across agencies to protect and conserve the ocean, the National Ocean Policy was revoked in 2018 when President Donald Trump issued Executive Order 13840 entitled "Ocean Policy to Advance the Economic, Security, and Environmental Interests in the U.S." 83 FR 29431 (June 22, 2018). President Trump's order revoked President Obama's Executive Order 13457. Even though the words "environmental interests" are in the title, the new Executive Order prioritizes ocean resource use and does not address climate change, ecosystem-based management or ocean acidification. President Trump's policy has shifted national attention from long-term resource stewardship to short-term resource use. "Climate change" is never mentioned directly or indirectly in President Trump's executive order.

Section 4 of the Executive Order created an interagency Ocean Policy Committee to be co-chaired by the Office of Science and Technology Policy and the Council on Environmental Quality. The Committee has two sub-committees: one on ocean science and technology and one on ocean resource management.

The subcommittee on ocean resource management, in 2019, is facilitating the release of unclassified ocean data held by NOAA, BOEM, and others on a platform called "Marine Cadastre." As of early 2019, the subcommittee on ocean science and technology had accomplished very little except to indicate that it would prioritize ocean technology and research needs.

With the declaration of Executive Order 13840, the National Ocean Council and its committees plus the Regional Planning Bodies ceased to operate. Agencies were ordered to cease implementing the National Ocean Policy Implementation Plan, the Northeast Regional Ocean Plan, and the Mid-Atlantic Regional Ocean Plan. In particular, federal agencies were required to stop designating special ecological areas under the two regional plans.

Even without the same level of federal engagement in the Regional Ocean Plans, implementation continues by regional partners. The Northeast Regional Ocean Partnership (formed in 2005) maintains on its website the Ocean Plan adopted in 2016 before Trump's order which "continues to be an important documentation of regional ocean management priorities and activities." See Northeast Regional Ocean Council, https://neoceanplanning.

org/about/; see also https://eelp.law.harvard.edu/2018/09/national-ocean-policy-executive-order/.

2. CLIMATE CHANGE AND FISHERIES

Climate information is being factored into fishery decision making. NMFS, Climate Science Strategy (2015) at https://www.st.nmfs.noaa.gov/Assets/eco systems/climate/documents/NCSS_Final.pdf. The strategy requires national agencies to:

- identify "climate-informed reference points;"

- identify robust management strategies;

- design adaptive decision-making;

- identify future states of ecosystems, living marine resources, and communities that depend on living marine resources;

- identify specific mechanisms of climate impacts;

- provide for early warnings by monitoring changes in ecosystems, living marine resources, and communities that depend on living marine resources; and

- build and maintain "science infrastructure" to ensure healthy fisheries under changing climate conditions.

Based on this strategy, regional fisheries councils developed regional fisheries plans. The following regional action plans have been completed:

1) Northeast Regional Action Plan (2016)— Includes plans to improve "spatial

management of living resources" and development of living marine resource forecasting products.

2) Pacific Islands Regional Action Plan (2016)—Includes plans to incorporate climate data into stock assessments.

3) Gulf of Mexico Regional Action Plan (2016)—Includes the construction of a specific model for the northern Gulf of Mexico to predict stock behavior and the development of new baseline data.

4) Western Regional Action Plan (2016)— Includes assessing relevance of existing recovery goals under climate change and impacts on a number of species including salmon across the full lifecycle.

5) Alaska-Bering Sea and Gulf of Alaska Regional Action Plans (2016)—Includes building multispecies interaction models and undertaking comprehensive climate assessments every 5 years.

Copies of the full regional action plans are available at: https://www.st.nmfs.noaa.gov/eco systems/climate/rap/northeast-regional-action-plan.

As ocean temperatures increase, fishermen are understandably concerned that failure to act on climate change will cost them their livelihood. In *Columbia Riverkeeper et al. v. Scott Pruitt et al.*, C17-289RSM (D. Wash. 2018), conservation groups and fishermen prevailed on their request for the EPA to take action to ensure that Columbia River salmon and steelhead are protected from increased river temperatures caused by the impact of climate change on dam water. Fishermen in California and Oregon filed a suit in November 2018 against private oil firms with a variety of claims based on nuisance, strict liability, and negligence related to domestic acid outbreaks caused by spikes in ocean temperature. See *Pacific Coast Federations of Fishermen's Associations v. Chevron et al.*, CGC-18-571285 (Superior Ct. Cal. 2018).

3. CLIMATE CHANGE AND ACIDIFICATION

In 2009, Congress passed the Federal Ocean Acidification Research and Monitoring Act of 2009. 33 U.S.C.A §§ 3701–3708 This law provided the catalyst for the formation of an interagency working group and plan to monitor acidification, develop a strategic plan to counter acidification, and to continue research on necessary adaptation. The interagency working group is a coordination group and has no authority as a group to direct agency-level policy. Some of the agencies contributing to the implementation of the Act include NOAA, National Science Foundation, NASA, EPA, Bureau of Indian Affairs, BOEM, U.S. Geological Survey, Department of Agriculture, Department of State, U.S. Navy, FWS, Smithsonian Institution, National Parks Service, and the U.S. Department of Energy Pacific Northwest National Laboratory.

In 2014, the interagency working group released the Strategic Plan for Federal Research and

Monitoring of Ocean Acidification. The plan recommended the creation of the National Ocean Acidification Program and associated Program Office to coordinate ocean acidification activities among interested Federal and non-Federal stakeholders. In December 2016, the National Science and Technology Council published an implementation plan for the strategic plan identifying programs by each of agencies in the interagency working group intended to be implemented within 2 years as well as opportunities to coordinate with other agencies.

In addition to the interagency network, there are regional networks monitoring acidification including the Alaska Ocean Acidification Network, the California Current Acidification Network, Gulf of Mexico Coastal Acidification Network, the Northeast Coastal Acidification Network, the Mid-Atlantic Coastal Acidification Network, and the Southeast Coastal Ocean Acidification Network. In 2019, bills to address coastal and ocean acidification impacts with strong bipartisan support in Congress included the Coastal Communities Ocean Acidification Act (providing better federal research and monitoring plans focused on the needs of coastal communities vulnerable to ocean acidification); the Ocean Acidification Innovation Act (providings funds to support adaptation to ocean acidification); the National Estuaries and Acidification Research (NEAR) Act, and the COAST Research Act of 2019 (ensurings continuing funding for existing monitoring on acidification and expand funding to focus on coastal zone impacts).

The Center for Biological Diversity brought a case in December 2018 against the EPA for a failure to identify Oregon waters as "impaired waters" under Clean Water Act Section 303(d) due to ongoing acidification caused by carbon dioxide and nutrient runoff. *Center for Biological Diversity v. EPA,* 6:18-cv-02049 (D. Or. 2018).

C. FUTURE OF OCEAN AND COASTAL LAW: ENFORCING RESPONSIBILITIES

Ocean and coastal law has been for centuries a matter of allocating rights among competing users—ranging from riparian rights to fishing allocations to rights to exploit oil and gas on the continental shelf. Collectively in seeking wealth, we have taken for granted the health of the oceans.

When laws have assigned responsibilities to public and private actors, such as, not to pollute, implementation has been limited or non-existent. The pursuit of rights at the expense of responsibilities has had visible and invisible consequences on ocean health ranging from depleted ecosystems to ubiquitous microplastics. This generation has a non-derogable duty to be accountable for harm to the oceans. While we may have made technological advances in the form of certain types of aquaculture or ocean energies, all states must take legal measures to ensure the conservation and restoration of coastal and ocean spaces. This is likely to require a different mentality. As States jockey for position in promoting sustainable "blue economy" and "blue growth" strategies, there are opportunities to change directions. Where States, however, in managing long-term relationships with the oceans remain fixed on measuring traditional financial outcomes, the rhetoric of legal rights to exploit will, at great peril, neglect our growing responsibilities to change our course.

INDEX

References are to Pages

ABORIGINAL AND NATIVE ALASKAN RIGHTS
See Endangered Species Act; Marine Mammal Protection Act; Oil
and Gas Development

ACCRETION
See Ambulatory Boundaries

ADMIRALTY JURISDICTION
See Oil Pollution; Salvage, Finds and Preservation of Historic
Shipwrecks

AIR POLLUTION FROM VESSELS
MARPOL, Annex VI, 342
North American Emission Control Area (ECA), 342–343

AMBULATORY BOUNDARIES
See also Coastal Boundaries
Generally, 13–22
Accretion, 13–15
Exceptions, 14
Reasons for rule, 13–14
Alluvion, 13
Artificial accretion, 14
California rule, 14–15
Avulsion, 15, 21–22
Texas rule, 15
Rebuttable presumption against, 15
Beach restoration and, 21–22
Choice of law, 18–20
Erosion, 15
Fixing coastal boundaries, 17–20, 21–22
Hawaii, 18
State or federal law, 18–20
Sea level rise and, 17